JULIA MARGARET CAMERON
A CRITICAL BIOGRAPHY

JULIA MARGARET CAMERON

A CRITICAL BIOGRAPHY

COLIN FORD

THE J. PAUL GETTY MUSEUM
LOS ANGELES

Published in Great Britain by National Portrait Gallery Publications,
London, 2003. Original hardback edition © 2003 National Portrait Gallery, London
Text © Colin Ford

First published in North America in 2003 by
Getty Publications
1200 Getty Center Drive, Suite 500
Los Angeles, California 90049-1682
www.getty.edu

At Getty Publications:
Christopher Hudson, *Publisher*
Mark Greenberg, *Editor in Chief*

At National Portrait Gallery Publications:
Celia Joicey, *Publishing Manager*
Susie Foster, *Senior Editor*
Ruth Müller-Wirth, *Production*
Pentagram, *Design*

Published to accompany the exhibition *Julia Margaret Cameron: 19th Century Photographer of Genius* held at the National Portrait Gallery, London, from February 6 to May 26, 2003, at the National Museum of Photography, Film & Television, Bradford, from June 27 to September 14, 2003, and at the J. Paul Getty Museum, Los Angeles, from October 21, 2003 to January 11, 2004.

The publisher would like to thank the copyright holders for granting permission to reproduce works illustrated in this book. Locations and lenders are given in the captions, and further acknowledgements are given in the picture credits at the back of the book. Every effort has been made to contact the holders of copyright material, and any omissions will be corrected in future editions if the publisher is notified in writing.

Library of Congress Control Number: 2002113570

ISBN: 0-89236-707-5

Printed and bound in Italy

Front cover: *Iago, Study from an Italian* (Angelo Colarossi), 1867
National Museum of Photography, Film & Television, Bradford
Back cover: *The Mountain Nymph Sweet Liberty* (Mrs Keene), June 1866
Royal Photographic Society

For Richard, Clare and Tom

9
Acknowledgements

11
Foreword

13
Preface

15
Prologue: the old world

25
A Victorian Bloomsbury

35
Photography: 'lisping and stammering'

45
Immortal heads

53
A dream of fair women

61
Solemn eyes and fair waving locks

69
Madonnas, May queens and virgins

77
Ceylon

83
Epilogue: genius and love

92
Plates

205
Bibliography

208
Index

212
Picture credits

Acknowledgements

My interest in Julia Margaret Cameron began over twenty-five years ago, when I was Keeper of Film and Photography at the National Portrait Gallery in London. At the time, I led a public campaign to purchase the supreme album of photographs presented by Julia Margaret to Sir John Herschel, and subsequently wrote *The Cameron Collection* (1975) for the Gallery, my first book on the subject. So it is highly appropriate – and very satisfying – that this book, and the exhibition that coincides with its publication, derives from an invitation from Charles Saumarez Smith, the Director of the National Portrait Gallery from 1994 to 2002. On hearing of my involvement in the creation of the first catalogue raisonné of a photographer's work, funded by the J. Paul Getty Museum, Los Angeles, he suggested that I curate an exhibition and publish a more accessible study of Julia Margaret Cameron's life. I am immensely grateful to him for the original invitation, and to his successor, Sandy Nairne, for continuing to support the project.

The list of those who have helped me find photographs and information while preparing this book is a very long one. In recording my grateful thanks to everyone named, I also offer my profound apologies to anyone I have missed. It has been a very long journey!

I am hugely indebted to Weston Naef, Curator of Photographs, and to my co-author on the catalogue raisonné Julian Cox, Assistant Curator of Photographs, both at the J. Paul Getty Museum. Julian and I have worked so closely together over the five years of the project that I know some ideas in this book will have come from him, or originated in discussions between us, and Weston's enthusiasm and encouragement were a great support.

At the National Portrait Gallery, I would particularly like to thank Peter Funnell, Curator of Nineteenth-century Portraits, and Beatrice Hosegood and Claire Everitt in the Exhibitions Department, who have created the exhibition. I am grateful to my ever patient and precise editor Susie Foster, and to Production Manager Ruth Müller-Wirth. I would also like to thank Kathleen Soriano, Head of Exhibitions and Collections Management; Jude Simmons, Head of Design; Robert Carr-Archer, Head of Trading; Celia Joicey, Publishing Manager; the staff of the PR and Development Department, especially Pim Baxter, John Haywood, Hazel Sutherland and Naomi Conway; and the staff in the Heinz Archive and Library. Terence Pepper and Clare Freestone, in the Gallery's Photographs Collection, were a constant source of advice and support.

The National Museum of Photography, Film & Television in Bradford merits a paragraph to itself. Amanda Nevill, my successor as Head of Museum, has been unstinting in her help and support, and Bob Cox, Head of Studios, has made many excellent transparencies of Julia Margaret's originals. I have received unfaltering assistance from Brian Liddy, Barbara Binder, Paul Goodman, Colin Harding, Greg Hobson, Russell Roberts and – most of all – the indefatigable Philippa Wright, who was properly speaking my research assistant solely on the catalogue raisonné, but who has cheerfully gone on helping me with this book without a murmur of complaint.

Among the most pleasurable and rewarding of my contacts have been the descendants of Julia Margaret Cameron and her sitters whom I have met – and pestered – over the years. Among them are Lucille van der Bogaerde, Ewen Cameron, Muriel Campion-Low, The Rt. Hon. the Earl of Crawford and Balcarres, Maurice Curtis, Julia Emsden, James Hervey-Bathurst, Sir Hew Hamilton-Dalrymple, Anne Hewat, The Rt. Hon. the Earl of Lichfield, Tom Luckock, Margaret McManus, Mr and Mrs Stephen Norman, Mary, Raymond and Tony Philpot, Sybil Pryor, Countess of Rosebery, John Vaughan, Lady Wallace, Lord and Lady Wemyss, and Mr and Mrs Michael Wilson. My profound thanks to them all.

I am immensely grateful to the lenders to the exhibition, without whom this book would not have been possible: the National Museum of Photography, Film & Television, Bradford; the Royal Photographic Society; the J. Paul Getty Museum, Los Angeles; Victoria and Albert Museum, London; Tennyson Research Centre, Lincoln; Metropolitan Museum of Art, New York; Art Institute of Chicago; Harry Ransom Humanities Research Center, University of Texas at Austin; George Eastman House, International Museum of Photography and Film, Rochester, New York; Howard Stein; Julia Margaret Cameron Trust, Isle of Wight; Liverpool City Libraries; Michael and Jane Wilson Collection; and various private collections. There are other owners of Cameron prints and related material to whom I owe a considerable debt, especially those who have kindly allowed their pictures to be reproduced in this book. They include Meir Berk, Sven Gahlin, Mr and Mrs Ken Jacobson, Mr and Mrs Kevin Molony, Marion Shaw, and Mr and Mrs Stephen White.

Julia Margaret's work has been collected by many institutions, in this country and elsewhere. It is a pleasure to acknowledge these institutions and the help I have received from their curators and other staff: Colin Harrison at the Ashmolean Museum, Oxford; Peter James at Birmingham Public Library; Colin Harris at the Bodleian Library, University of Oxford; Dr Brian Hinton, Ron Smith and all the staff and volunteers at the Julia Margaret Cameron Trust; Lindsay Stewart at Christie's; Melanie Blake and Dr Jane Cunningham at the Courtauld Institute of Art, University of London; Roy Flukinger at the Harry Ransom Humanities Research Center, University of Texas at Austin; Dr Elizabeth Adey and John Paul Carr at the Borough of Luton's Museums Division; Richard Mangan at Mander & Mitchenson Theatre Collection; Kevin Thomas at the National Museums & Galleries of Wales; Philippe Garner at Phillips, de Pury & Luxembourg; Victor Gray and Melanie Aspey at the Rothschild Archive, London; Marilyn Ward at the Royal Botanic Gardens, Kew; Pam Roberts at the Royal Photographic Society; Juliet Hacking at Sotheby's, London; Mark Haworth-Booth, Charlotte Cotton and Martin Barnes at the Victoria and Albert Museum, London; and Richard Jefferies, Emma Duncan and Hilary Underwood at the Watts Gallery, Compton. I am grateful to Graham Chapman of Olympus Optical (UK) for the loan of a digital camera; it was a boon and a timesaver.

There are many others who have answered my endless questions and volunteered their knowledge about Julia Margaret. I am extremely happy to thank them – both for their help and for their patience: Vicki Balfour, John Beaumont, Nicky Bird, Jane Corkin, the late John Feakins, Veronica Franklin Gould, Violet Hamilton, Anne Hammond, John and Judy Hillelson, Roy and Jean Hooper, Erika Ingham, Ken and Jenny Jacobson, Sigrun Lyne, Professor Joanne Lukitsh, Professor Joss Marsh, Victoria Olsen, Richard and Leonee Ormond, Larry J. Schaaf, Marion Shaw, Mike Shaw, Douglas Silvanus-Davies, Professor Graham Smith, Roger Taylor, Lynne Truss, Sue Underwood, Edward Wakeling, and Dr Mike Weaver.

To all of these, and to those others whose names I have inadvertently omitted, and to my ever-tolerant wife Sue and son Tom, who are themselves very busy people, my profound thanks. This book could not have happened without your help and support.

COLIN FORD

Foreword

Julia Margaret Cameron was resolutely her own woman. Her photographs speak to us with an instantly recognisable voice, which is as distinct and contemporary now as it was over a century ago. An individual to the core, she was more influenced by the writers and painters who made up her vibrant social and cultural network than by contemporaries in her field.

Cameron's pursuit of beauty, regardless of the conventions of full-length portrait studio work, or the painstaking, forensic multi-negative compositions that contrived to emulate painting, involved the creation of fantastic scenarios using family, friends and servants as her performers. Flights of romantic fancy recreated Arthurian, biblical tableaux, complete with cherubs, angels, knights, muses and sirens. As a portraitist, she created some of the most memorable images of the key figures of her age. Her eccentric reputation might suggest a lack of concern for public opinion, but her self-awareness and her obsession for photography belied her ambitious drive for artistic recognition and financial success.

The test of any great art is surely its durability. This book, and the exhibition it accompanies, pay tribute to the creativity and genius of one of the world's greatest artists – as such they provide a significant milestone in our understanding of just how important, influential, and completely enchanting, Julia Margaret Cameron's legacy is.

The still quiet of the gallery, or the pristine pages of this book, conceal the cast of many who have contributed to the final result. Having completed the catalogue raisonné with Julian Cox at the J. Paul Getty Museum, Los Angeles, of Julia Margaret Cameron, the project's creator and curator, Colin Ford, a past colleague at the National Portrait Gallery, London, and the first Head of the National Museum of Photography, Film & Television in Bradford, was perfectly placed to bring about this logical succession. We will be always grateful for his generosity in bringing to us the idea of an exhibition with the simple but direct thesis of gathering together the finest prints of the most important photographs by Julia Margaret Cameron – an exhibition that would demonstrably re-position her contribution to the photographic canon.

In 1975 Colin Ford led the campaign at the National Portrait Gallery for the acquisition of the Julia Margaret Cameron album created for Sir John Herschel. That was an important milestone in the recognition both of the importance of photography within the national collections and of the quality and beauty of Cameron's work. Such a definitive survey of Cameron's photography would not have been possible without the work on the catalogue raisonné and it is appropriate that the exhibition will end its tour at the J. Paul Getty Museum.

Colin Ford's dedication and tenacity in bringing the current project to fruition over almost five years is to be applauded. It is important, too, to pay tribute to Philippa Wright, a curator of photographs at the NMPFT, who has been not only his research assistant, but also his constant ally and supporter. Bring to this creative cauldron the dynamism of colleagues from both institutions, the generosity and magnificent support of the exhibition lenders and contributors, plus supporters including Reuters who are sponsors of the London exhibition, and you have an exhibition designed from the start to cast a spell, to bewitch and charm, and from which, we warn, it will be hard to return to any mundane reality.

SANDY NAIRNE
Director
National Portrait Gallery

AMANDA NEVILL
Head of Museum
The National Museum of Photography, Film & Television

DEBORAH GRIBBON
Director
The J. Paul Getty Museum, Los Angeles

Preface

It has been part of my purpose in writing this book to demonstrate that Julia Margaret Cameron, so long regarded as an 'English eccentric' – more or less lovable depending on one's point of view – was in fact an artist of considerable sophistication and skill. In reaching this conclusion, I was much influenced by working on the first ever catalogue of all her known works. Research for the catalogue raisonné conclusively demonstrates how Cameron worked deliberately and consciously towards her final results, with only a small percentage of which she was totally satisfied. Many of these supreme achievements are illustrated in these pages.

The book often uses many of Julia Margaret's own words. We know that she wrote thousands of letters: surprisingly few survive, and these are currently being collated and edited for publication. In quoting from her unpublished autobiographical fragment, 'Annals of my Glass House', I have gone back to the original manuscript rather than the various edited and printed editions in circulation for over a century. Here, and wherever I quote Julia Margaret herself, I have retained her spellings, her distinctive punctuation (or lack of it), her frequent capitalisations, and even her crossings out. Doing this will, I hope, bring readers closer to the character and thought processes of this nineteenth-century photographer of genius.

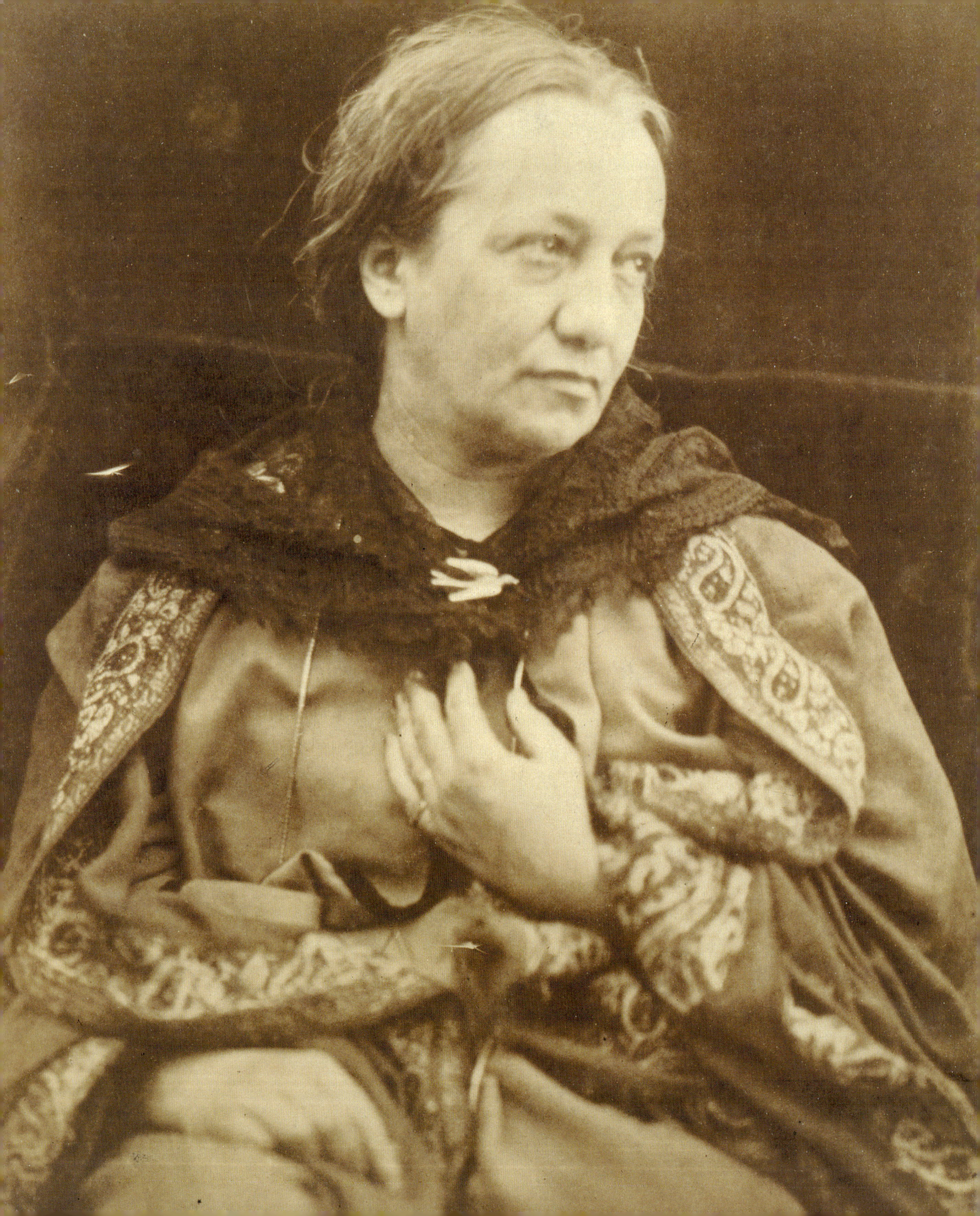

Prologue: the old world On 7 January 1839, François Arago (1786–1853), Director of the Paris Observatory, made a remarkable announcement to the members of the Académie des Sciences. Reminding his audience of the accuracy and beauty of the images seen in a 'camera obscura',[1] a device which had been known and used since the sixteenth century, he told them that they need no longer regret the fact that these images could not be made permanent.

Arago was both patron and publicist for Louis Jacques Mandé Daguerre (1789–1851), a painter and co-owner of the Paris Diorama,[2] who had, as Arago told the Académie, 'discovered special screens on which the complete image was reproduced in minutest detail, with exactness and incredible delicacy'.[3] Arago was describing in public, for the first time ever, the process of photography. Three weeks later, the eminent scientist Michael Faraday (1791–1867) told the Royal Institution, England's equivalent of the Académie des Sciences, that the landowner and scientific experimenter William Henry Fox Talbot (1800–77) had developed his own method of photography four years earlier. Fox Talbot's negative and positive photogenic drawings were very different from daguerreotypes, which were direct positives on silvered metal, but they too would later be called 'photographs'. A vital new nineteenth-century technology and art form had been born – in both Britain and France.

The year 1839 was also important for two young, short, plump Englishwomen, living thousands of miles apart. In London, the 20-year-old Queen Victoria (1819–1901), who had been on the throne for less than two years, renounced her earlier intention to be a spinster queen like Elizabeth I, and found herself a husband, Prince Albert of Saxe-Coburg-Gotha (1819–61). Given the spirit of the age, it was rare and difficult for even a royal woman to go through life unmarried. In Calcutta, then the capital of India, the 24-year-old Julia Margaret Cameron (1815–79), who a year earlier had made the sort of 'good marriage' all parents wished for their daughters, gave birth to her first child and only daughter, Julia Hay Cameron (1839–73).

The England of 1839 would have been almost unrecognisable to those born in the later years of Victoria's reign. As the novelist William Makepeace Thackeray (1811–63) put it in 1860, looking back on his youth:

> *It was only yesterday, but what a gulf between now and then.* Then *was the old world. Stage-coaches, more or less swift riding-horses, pack-horses, highwaymen, Druids, Ancient Britons … all these belong to the old period … We who lived before railways and survive out of the ancient world, are like Father Noah and his family out of the Ark.*[4]

The prestige of the royal family was at an all-time low, and the young queen was even booed at Epsom Races. There was no such thing as universal suffrage – even for men – and the People's Charter (proposing reforms of the electoral and parliamentary system) was rejected by parliament, for the first but not the last time, in 1839. The first train had only reached London in the previous year, and railways were only just beginning to replace the horse-drawn and water-borne modes of transport for passengers and freight. There were no postage stamps. A series of bad harvests was to lead to the 'Hungry 40s'. The Church of England, though in the midst of the biggest boom in new church building it had known, was being threatened on the one hand by a growth in nonconformism and, on the other,

Julia Margaret Cameron
Henry Herschel Hay Cameron, 1870
Albumen print, 244 x 203mm (9⅝ x 8")
National Portrait Gallery, London (NPG P696)

by a High Church 'Tractarian' movement. The population of England and Wales was barely 20 million. Huge numbers of Britons lived abroad in the still-growing Empire, where they were administrators, teachers, lawyers, doctors and soldiers. Many families had been doing such jobs in the Empire for generations.

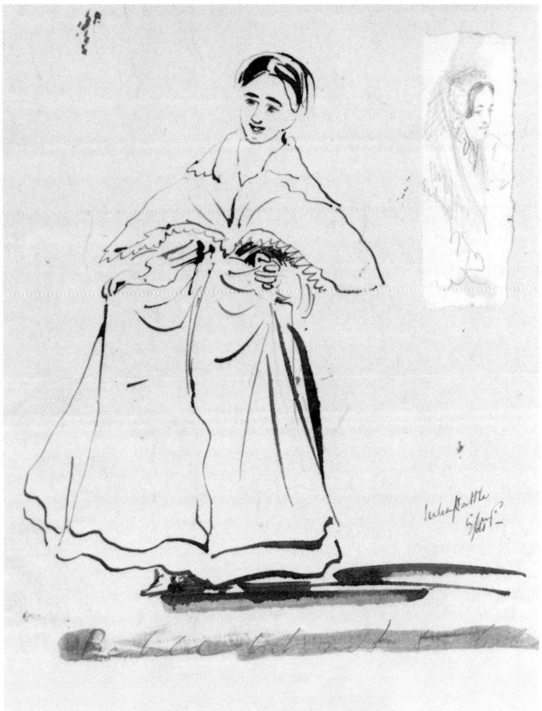

Julia Margaret Cameron (1815–79)
James Prinsep, n.d.
Drawing (detail)
Collection Sven Gahlin, London

Julia Margaret Cameron came from just such a family. She was the fourth of ten children born to James and Adéline Pattle (née de l'Étang). Her mother, Adéline (1793–1845), was French and her father, James Pattle (1775–1845), could trace his ancestry back to seventeenth-century London, but the Pattles had been involved for over a hundred years with India and the East India Company – a monopoly which had virtually ruled India since the 1750s. There was some Indian blood in the family, and the similarity of the name 'Pattle' to the well-known Hindu name 'Patel' seems to have been a frequent subject of gossip. Lady Emily Bayley, related to Julia Margaret by marriage, wrote about the 'daughters of Mr Pattle, of whom in olden days there were many facetious stories in Calcutta, although all *that* is ancient history and of no interest to the present generation'.[5] Even today, descendants of the Pattles still talk of the 'Pondicherry eyes' inherited by some members of the family, and it appears that, throughout their lives, 'Amongst themselves the sisters talked in Hindustani … that seemed to an outsider the language best suited to express their super-abundant vitality.'[6]

James joined the Indian Civil Service at the age of fourteen and, by the age of forty, had attained the very senior position of Second Judge. Three of the Pattle children (including the only boy) died in infancy and the seven surviving girls, like the children of many Europeans in India, were sent back to Europe for the sake of their health and their education. At the age of three, Julia Margaret went with her sisters Adeline Maria (aged six) and Sarah (aged two) to be brought up by their maternal grandmother in Paris and Versailles. Although Adeline Maria returned to India four years later, Julia Margaret and Sarah stayed with their grandmother until their late teens, and were educated privately. Julia Margaret particularly excelled at music and literature, playing the piano well and later publishing poetry. She left Versailles for India in late 1833, arriving in 1834, and Sarah followed her at the end of the year.

Back in India, Sara (1816–87), as she now preferred to spell her name, married a very senior East India Company official, Henry Thoby Prinsep (1792–1878; he was twenty-four years older than his wife) on 4 May 1835 and, with her unmarried sisters, became very much part of the Calcutta social scene. In February 1836, Isabella Fane – daughter of the English Commander-in-Chief – went to a performance of *Macbeth* with them:

Nasty Mrs Thoby (Sara) was of our party and did not behave with what I would call propriety. She had a sister, Miss Pattle (Julia), a little ugly, under-bred looking thing; but she has the reputation of being very clever, which is better than beauty … These two doves sat behind me at the play, and the tiresome creatures did nothing but coo the whole time … they kept up such an incessant jabber that they disturbed me much.[7]

Isabella rarely mentions Sara in her journals of life in India without appending the adjective 'nasty', though she once grudgingly admits to admiring 'her good nature, or rather her obliging qualities'.[8]

Many British in India went to the South African Cape to escape the worst extremes of Indian weather and ill health, and the Pattles were no exception. They first took their three eldest children on a trip there at the end of 1815, when Julia Margaret was only four months old. On that occasion their ship, the SS *Mornington,* was burned out off the Madras coast, and they had to be rescued by an East India Company schooner. In 1828, during another trip to the Cape, their daughter Harriet was born; she died in infancy. In 1830, their eldest daughter, Adeline Maria (1812–36) met her future husband, Colin Mackenzie, there. During an 1836 visit, Julia Margaret, who had been nursing her sister Sara and her newborn eldest son Henry in Calcutta, joined her parents at the Cape, and soon met two men who were to be of enormous importance in her life – the astronomer Sir John Herschel and the lawyer and colonial administrator Charles Hay Cameron.

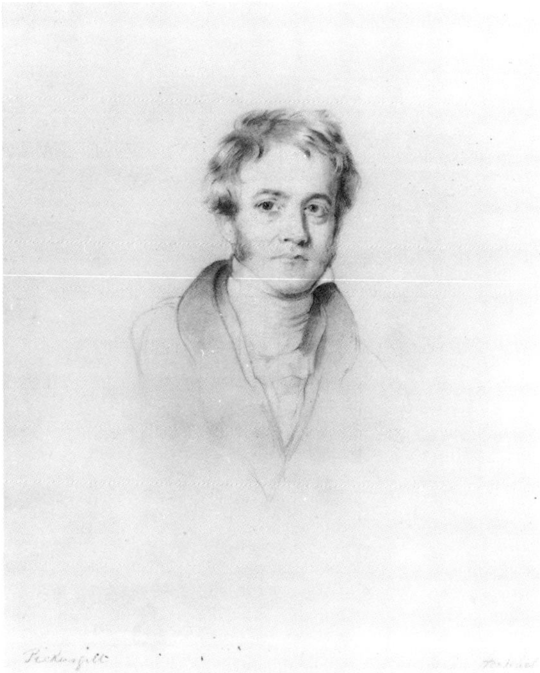

Sir John Herschel (1792–1871)
Henry William Pickersgill, *c.*1835
Pencil, 330 x 254mm (13 x 10")
National Portrait Gallery, London (NPG 1386)

Sir John Herschel (1792–1871) had been elected a Fellow of the Royal Society while still a student. After the death of his father Sir William (King George III's court astronomer and discoverer of the planet Uranus) in 1822, John continued his father's work and was knighted in 1831, aged only thirty-nine. Having completed and published Sir William's astronomical survey of the northern hemisphere,[9] Sir John went to South Africa to implement his father's unfulfilled plan to make an astronomical map of the skies of the southern hemisphere. In 1833 he built an observatory at Feldhausen, Claremont, close to Table Mountain, near Cape Town. Here, over the next four years, he discovered no less than 1,202 pairs of nebulae in Orion, observed the return of Halley's Comet, and made measurements of solar activity and radiation.[10]

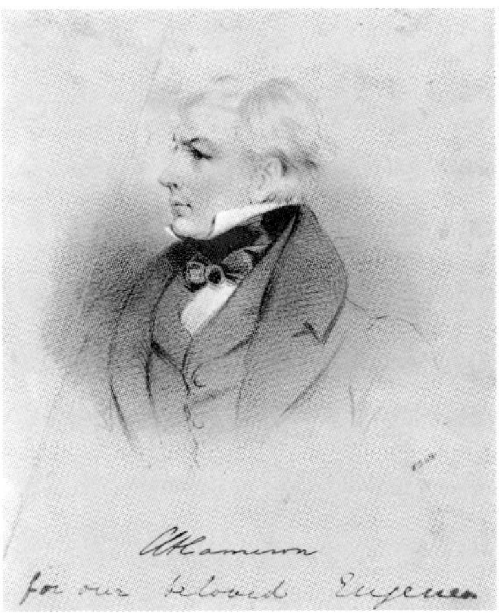

Charles Hay Cameron (1795–1881)
Eden Upton Eddis, 1836
Chalk drawing
Private Collection

Early in 1837, after Sunday church, the wife of the Colonial Secretary at the Cape, Lady Catherine Bell, introduced Julia Margaret to Herschel. We do not know how often they met thereafter, though Julia Margaret and her parents certainly dined with the Herschels at their temporary home in Feldhausen in October. Ten years later, she reminded Sir John how much they had helped and supported her in South Africa:

> *There is not a sweeter feeling in the soul I think than that of gratitude and I never can tell you how I cherish the remembrance of those friends who brightened my solitary life and cheered my time of trial when I was sick & desolate at the Cape & amongst them your dear wife.*[11]

After her marriage, the two families remained close friends, and the Herschels called their second daughter, born in 1843, Julia (Julia Margaret was a godparent, but did not attend the christening). Herschel was also godfather to Julia Margaret's first child.

In Cape Town, the Pattles and Herschels met another convalescent from India, Charles Hay Cameron (1795–1881). Cameron's highly successful official career had mostly been in India. Soon after having been called to the Bar in 1820, he had served on Royal Commissions on reform of the poor laws and of charities. In 1829, he and Colonel (later Sir) William Colebrooke were commissioned to write a report on the 'judicial establishment and procedure' of Ceylon (now called Sri Lanka). His 11-month stay on the island (25 March 1830 to 21 February 1831) was Cameron's introduction to the 'wild woods & favorite forests & seductive Estates'[12] of a country that was to play a central role in his life, and to which he would return in old age. The report was published in 1832, and two years later Cameron successfully applied to become the first English member of the Indian Law Commission, helping its President Thomas Babington Macaulay (1800–59; later Baron Macaulay), who had come to India to make his fortune and reform the legal system, by writing a new Indian Penal Code.

Cameron, twenty years Julia Margaret's senior, was unmarried, though he had fathered two illegitimate children, Charles Henry and Ellen (later Mrs Langlois). In January 1838, he and Julia Margaret sailed back to Calcutta together, and were married in the cathedral there on 1 February. After her marriage, Julia Margaret would presumably have been outraged if anyone but a relative or very close friend had called her anything but the formal 'Mrs Cameron' but, for the sake of consistency, I shall continue to refer to her as 'Julia Margaret'.

Herschel was by then back in London, and surely found the announcement of the invention of photography in January 1839 of

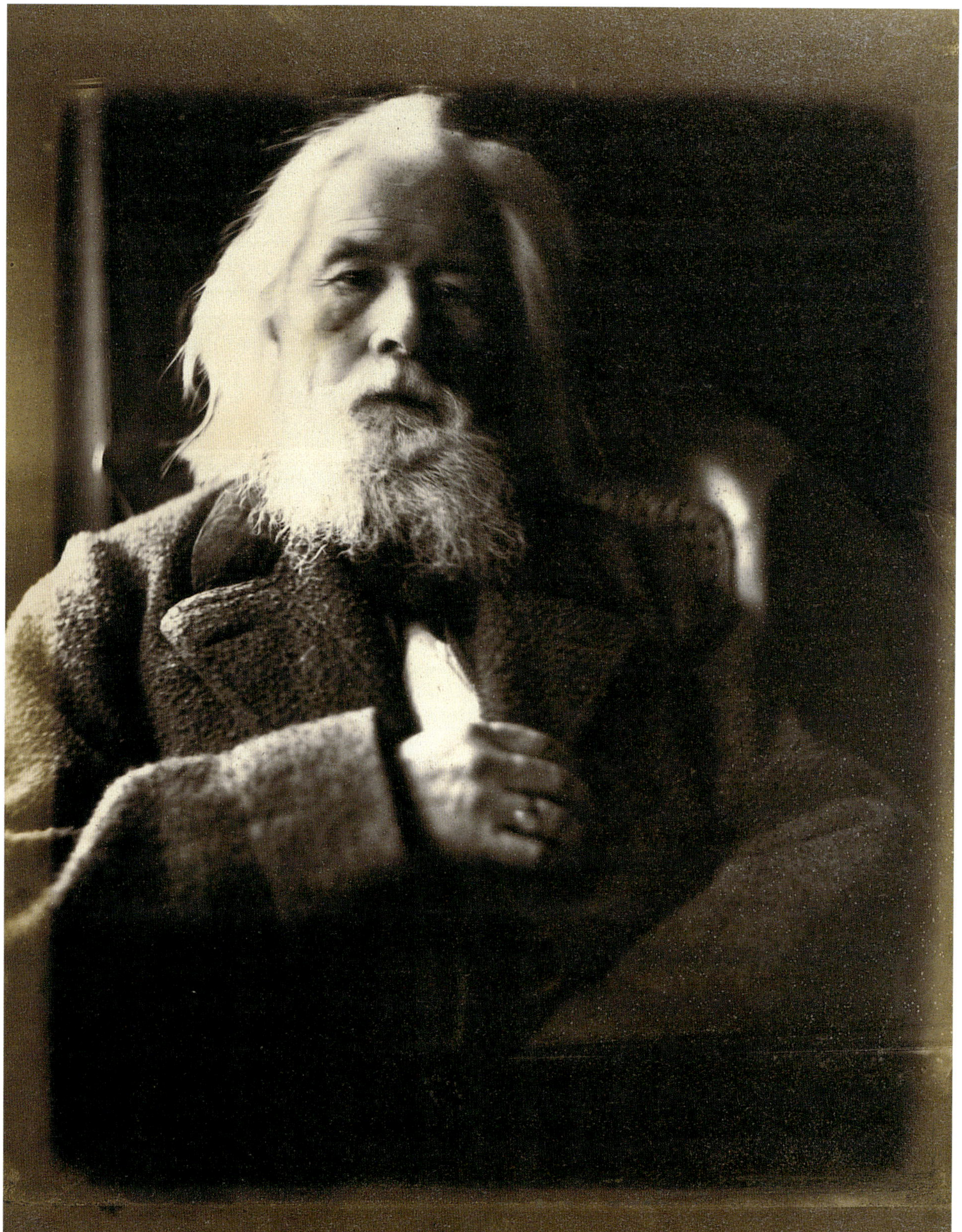

Charles Hay Cameron, 1864
Albumen print, 291 x 223mm (11½ x 8¾")
The J. Paul Getty Museum, Los Angeles

particular interest. Although he did not know how Daguerre's or Fox Talbot's processes worked, he at once gave the matter some thought, and began to experiment for himself, recording the results in notebooks: 'Jan 29 Expts. tried within the last few days since hearing of Daguerre's secret and that Fox Talbot has also got something of the same kind ... Three requisites: (1) Very susceptible paper; (2) Very perfect camera; (3) Means of arresting the further action.' Herschel already knew how to achieve the third of these – the fixing agent that had eluded the earliest pioneers. He had discovered hyposulphite of soda – known to photographers ever since as 'hypo' – twenty years earlier. Within a week he had invented his own, totally original, process of photography, borrowed a camera obscura and

Formed image of telescope with the aplanatic lens of Dolland's [sic] make on my construction and placed in focus paper with Carb. Silver. An image was formed in white on a sepia-col[d]. ground after about 2 hours exposure which bore washing with the hypos. Soda & was then no longer alterable by light. Thus Daguerre's probl is so far solved – for granting a perfect picture, the picture of this may be taken.[13]

Herschel is describing a photographic negative, and has already grasped the idea of making a positive from it.

He had taken a day or so to reach the point that Daguerre and his partner Joseph Nicéphore Niépce (1765–33) had needed more than a decade to achieve and Fox Talbot about six years. The subject of Herschel's first attempt was his father's 40-foot telescope at Slough. A glass negative of the same telescope, taken in September 1839 – the world's oldest surviving photograph on glass – is now in the collection of the National Museum of Photography, Film & Television, Bradford.

Herschel soon sent samples of the new wonder to his friends the Camerons and, later, when he learned of the discovery that gun-cotton, an explosive prepared by soaking cotton in acid, could, when dissolved in ether, be spread to produce a smooth, even and impenetrable membrane (its first use was in hospitals, to seal wounds), sent them samples of that too. The compound, known as 'collodion', enabled photographic chemicals to be spread evenly and thinly over glass, creating much smoother and far more translucent negatives than ever before. Its discovery changed the whole practice of photography, enabling amateurs like Julia Margaret to take it up. Herschel's own contributions to photography seem to have included not only the discovery of 'hypo', but the coining of the words 'snapshot', 'negative' and 'positive' in their photographic senses, and perhaps even of 'photography' itself.

By 1838, the year of the Camerons' marriage, Macaulay had completed his legal work in India and returned to England. In 1839, Charles Hay Cameron succeeded him as President of the Law Commission and in 1843 took over his place on the ruling Supreme Council, of which he was the only member not an employee of the East India Company. It was a time of Utilitarianism, the hugely influential notion of 'the greatest good for the greatest number', first propounded by the philosopher Jeremy Bentham (1748–1832), but most succinctly described by his disciple John Stuart Mill (1806–73): 'Utility or the Greatest Happiness Principle, holds that actions are right in proportion as they tend to promote happiness, wrong as they tend to produce the reverse of happiness. By happiness is intended pleasure ... by unhappiness, pain.'[14] Utilitarianism was supported by many in the administration of India, including – after early opposition – Macaulay. Cameron, a confirmed Benthamite, believed that governments should pursue 'useful' policies, disseminate useful knowledge and ensure the happiness (not to be confused with freedom, of course) of their subjects. His position as a member of the Supreme Council and his beliefs, then favoured by the government in London, put him for a time near the pinnacle of Anglo-Indian society and, when the new Governor-General, Sir Henry Hardinge (1785–1856; later Lord Hardinge), took up his duties in Calcutta a year later, leaving his wife in England, Julia Margaret became virtually the official hostess at Government House.

After five years in this exalted position, however, Charles retired from it and returned to London with Julia Margaret and their two younger sons, Ewen and Hardinge. It is not altogether clear why. Though Charles was held in great respect, neither the East India Company nor the Colonial Office seem to have entirely approved of his wish to provide proper education for all Indians, enunciated in his *Address to Parliament on the Duties of Great Britain in India in Respect of the Education of the Natives, and their Official Employment* (1853). He may perhaps have been asked to step down. Aged only fifty-three, he did not quite give up the idea of public life, however, and later made a bid to become Governor of Ceylon. But he may also have left because of ill health: he was a semi-invalid for most of the rest of his life and the Indian climate, particularly during the rainy season, had always been hard on him. Between 1840 and 1844 he had purchased coffee plantations in Ceylon, and he seems to have hoped that these would earn him enough income to live off (he bought considerably more land in 1852). Years later, the Camerons' friend, the author Anne Thackeray Ritchie (1837–1919), daughter of William Makepeace Thackeray, certainly believed that 'Mr Cameron had amassed a considerable fortune while in India, which he had invested in coffee estates in Ceylon.'[15]

The Camerons also presumably missed their two eldest children, Julia Hay and Eugene, who were at the time living in England with three of Charles Cameron's sisters (two widowed and one unmarried) in Worthing, Sussex. Julia Margaret's parents had both died in 1845 and some of her sisters were already back home: the family focus was shifting back from India to England. Coincidentally, Charles's illegitimate son was posted to India in February 1848, and Charles may have seen this as a potential source of embarrassment. For some or all of these reasons, the Camerons returned to England that year. After staying two months in Lord Lennox's house in Chesham Place, Belgrave Square, in London's Mayfair, where their fifth child, Charles Hay, was born, they moved to Ephraim Common in Tunbridge Wells, Kent, forty miles south-east of London.

In Tunbridge Wells, the Camerons found themselves living next to the summer home of a now-forgotten Victorian celebrity Sir Henry Taylor (1800–86) and his wife Alice. Taylor was not only a respected senior civil servant at the Colonial Office, but also a successful author. He found Julia Margaret 'a simple, ardent, and honest enthusiast, and her husband a simple, manly, kind, agreeable, and very able man'.[16] The two families became lifelong friends and, when the Taylors returned to their main residence in Mortlake, Surrey, the Camerons moved to Upper East Sheen Lodge, East Sheen, to be near them.

It was in East Sheen that Anne Thackeray first met the Camerons. She probably wrote more about Julia Margaret and her world than any other contemporary witness and, taking after her more famous father, had a way with words (according to her memorial stone in St Agnes Church, Freshwater, 'Her writing reveals the inheritance of genius'). Her 'charming impressionist writing'[17] brings to life the cultural world of the time, and the extraordinary role played in it by Julia Margaret, whose character, friends, family and sitters are all vividly described:

> *My own first meeting with Mrs Cameron was one summer's day when my father took my sister and myself to Sheen to see an old friend lately returned from India. I remember a strange apparition in a flowing red velvet dress, although it was summer time, cordially welcoming us to a fine house and some belated meal when the attendant butler was addressed by her as 'man' and was ordered to do many things for our benefit; to bring back the luncheon dishes and curries for which Mrs Cameron and her family had a speciality. When we left she came with us bareheaded, with trailing draperies, part of the way to the station as her kind habit was. A friend of mine told me how on one occasion she accompanied him the same way carrying a cup of tea which she stirred as she walked along.*[18]

In 1854 the Camerons moved again, to Ashburton Cottage, Putney Heath, where there were even more famous residents. Alfred Tennyson (1809–92; later Lord Tennyson), Queen Victoria's Poet Laureate since 1850, and his wife Emily (1813–96) had, on advice from Taylor, rented Chapel House in Twickenham. Taylor had introduced the Tennysons to the Camerons on 16 June 1851, and Emily soon wrote in her journal that Julia Margaret was 'a delightful picture in her dark green silk with wide open sleeves, the dress fastened by a silk cord round the waist and having the courtly charm of manner which was one of her many phases & one which became her right well'.[19] Thus, within three years of their return from India, the Camerons had become intimate with two of Britain's most celebrated writers of the age. For Tennyson, Julia Margaret became 'almost the only woman outside his relations whom he called by her Christian name, and who called him in turn by his'.[20]

Putney was not only close to the Taylors and Tennysons. Julia Margaret's married sister Sara Prinsep had returned to England with her husband Thoby, as he preferred to be known, in 1843, five years before the Camerons, and set up house in London's fashionable Mayfair. Two sisters, Sophia (1829–1911) and Virginia (1826–1910), lived with them until they married. Sophia married John Warrender Dalrymple (1824–88) of the Bengal Civil Service in 1847 – thereby apparently disappointing her admirer, the Pre-Raphaelite painter Edward Burne-Jones (1833–98) – and went to live with him in India. Four years later, she returned to the more congenial climate of England, staying with the Prinseps until her

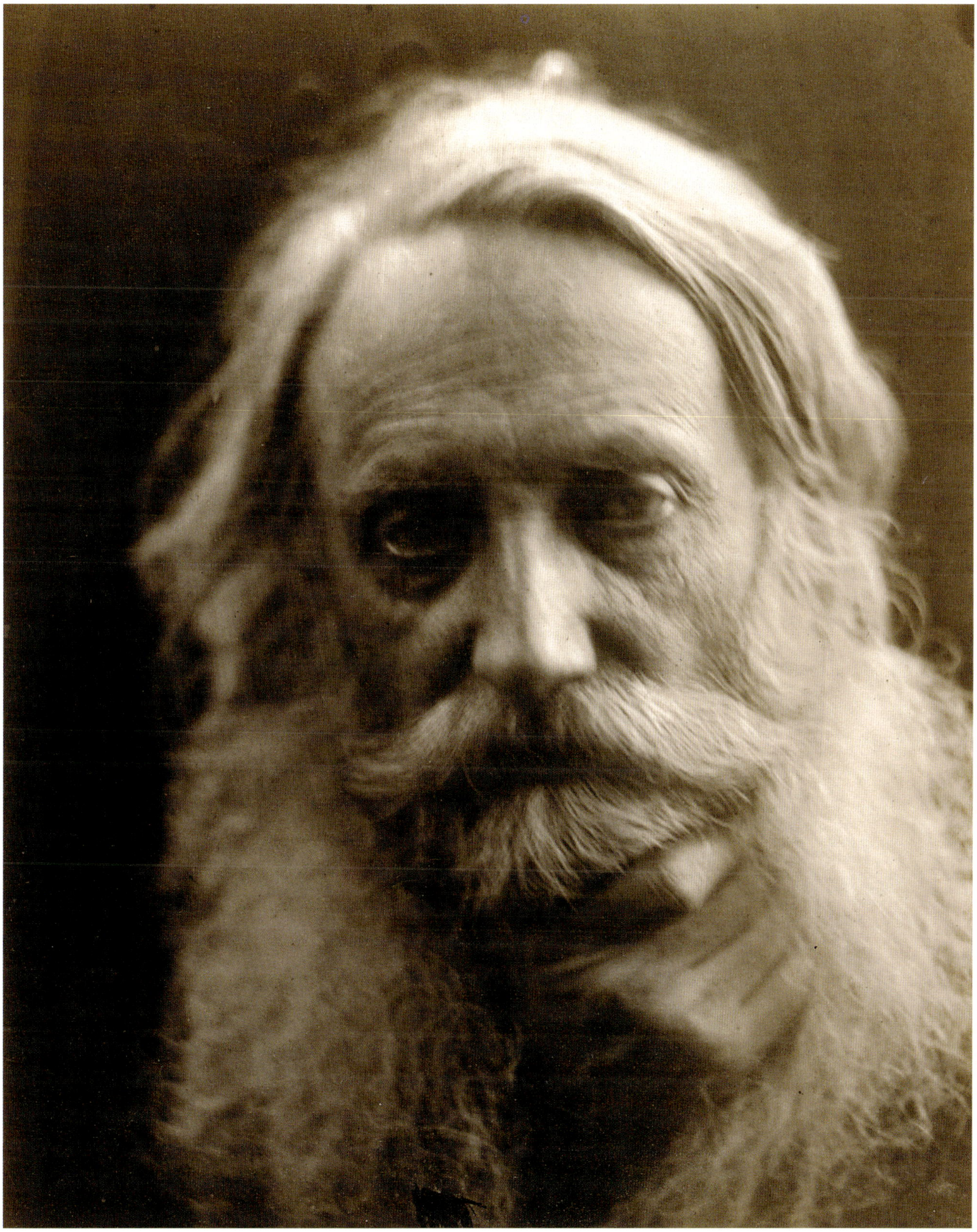

Sir Henry Taylor, 10 October 1867
Albumen print, 344 x 269mm (13½ x 10⅝")
The J. Paul Getty Museum, Los Angeles

husband came back to England in 1873. On his elder brother's death in 1877, Dalrymple became the 7th Baronet Dalrymple of North Berwick. Virginia Pattle married Viscount Eastnor (1819–83; later 3rd Earl Somers) in 1850, which apparently disappointed a number of admirers, including the painters William Holman Hunt (1827–1910) and George Frederic Watts (1817–1904), and – probably most of all – Thackeray. Thackeray had first been infatuated with her in Paris and had just published an article in *Punch* 'On a Good-looking Young Lady' (June 1850). This was apparently based on some rather embarrassing and saccharine verses by Henry Taylor, yet another of Virginia's admirers. After her wedding, Thackeray wrote that 'She looked beautiful and has taken possession of Eastnor Castle and her rank as Princess, and reigns to the delight of everybody.'[21]

The Prinseps' home soon became a meeting place for the most famous politicians, artists and writers of the day; one assumes it was Sara who was the driving force, as Thoby had been described in India as 'the greatest bore Providence ever created, and so contradictory that he will not let anybody agree or differ with him'.[22] Sara's first, and most important, regular visitor was Watts, whose studio was in nearby Charles Street. 'England's Michelangelo', as Watts thought of himself, repaid her support and encouragement by forwarding the career of her son Val (1838–1904), a painter who was the original of Taffy in George du Maurier's 1894 novel *Trilby*, and making portraits of the Pattle sisters – including Julia Margaret – who were naturally flattered and delighted. 'I was never dazzled by any other painter's brush,' Virginia told Mary Seton Watts (the painter's widow) many years later, '... all other brushes were like boot-brushes to me.'[23] It is said that Somers first fell in love with Virginia's portrait by Watts.

It was presumably Watts who told the Prinseps that his patron, Lord Holland, who spent most of the year in Italy, owned an empty farmhouse in the grounds of his Jacobean home, Holland House. Though only three miles from Chesterfield Street, it was reckoned to be too far out of the centre of town for smart people. But Sara fell in love with its rambling layout and 'decided to snap her fingers at fashion in this matter as she had done over dress. She would make it fashionable to live outside London.'[24] It delighted her to think that the distinguished guests she meant to entertain would have to duck their heads beneath a porch of untidy thatch. And Thoby assuredly would find it very refreshing to retire to a land of meadows and haystacks after his work at the India Office. The Prinseps moved into Little Holland House in January 1851. Here, the salon that Sara had started in Mayfair was to reach its apogee, to become a sort of 'Victorian Bloomsbury'.

NOTES

1. Camera obscura (from the Latin for 'dark chamber'): a dark room or box into which rays of light enter through a tiny aperture – sometimes with a lens in it – to project an image onto the opposite wall. This is the fundamental recording device of photography.
2. Diorama: an early nineteenth-century device in which light is thrown upon a giant painting from different directions, allowing effects of night and day to be reproduced. Dioramas were popular attractions in many cities.
3. *Comptes Rendus Hebdomadaires des Séances de l'Académie des Sciences*, VIII, January–June 1839.
4. Quoted in Newsome, 1997, p.8.
5. Quoted in Kaye, 1980, p.114.
6. Fitzpatrick, 1923, p.15.
7. Pemble, 1985, p.61.
8. Pemble, 1985, p.86.
9. 'Observations of nebulae and clusters, made at Slough, with a 20-feet reflector, between the years 1825–1833' (*Philosophical Transactions*, 1833) and 'Descriptions and approximate places of a total of 4528 double, triple and multiple stars' (*Memoirs of the Astronomical Society*, 1826–36).
10. Evans and others, 1969.
11. Letter from Julia Margaret to Herschel, 24 May 1847, Herschel Correspondence Books, Library of the Royal Society of London.
12. Letter from Julia Margaret to Herschel, 26 February 1859, Herschel Correspondence Books, Library of the Royal Society of London.
13. Herschel's notebook containing these experiments is in the Science Museum Library, London.
14. Mason, 1994, p.61.
15. Thackeray Ritchie and Cameron, 1893, p.10.
16. Taylor, 1885, p.42.
17. The words are those of Virginia Woolf, who wrote an affectionate portrait of her Aunt Anne in the character of 'Katherine Hilbery' in her novel *Night and Day*. This was published in 1919, the year Anne Thackeray Ritchie died (see Bell, 1972, p.42).
18. Thackeray Fuller and Hammersley, 1951, p.110.
19. Hoge, 1981, p.21.
20. Weld, 1902, p.64.
21. Ray, II, 1945, p.704.
22. According to the Hon. Emily Eden, quoted in Hill, 1973, p.42.
23. Watts, I, 1912, p.122.
24. Chapman, 1945, p.50.

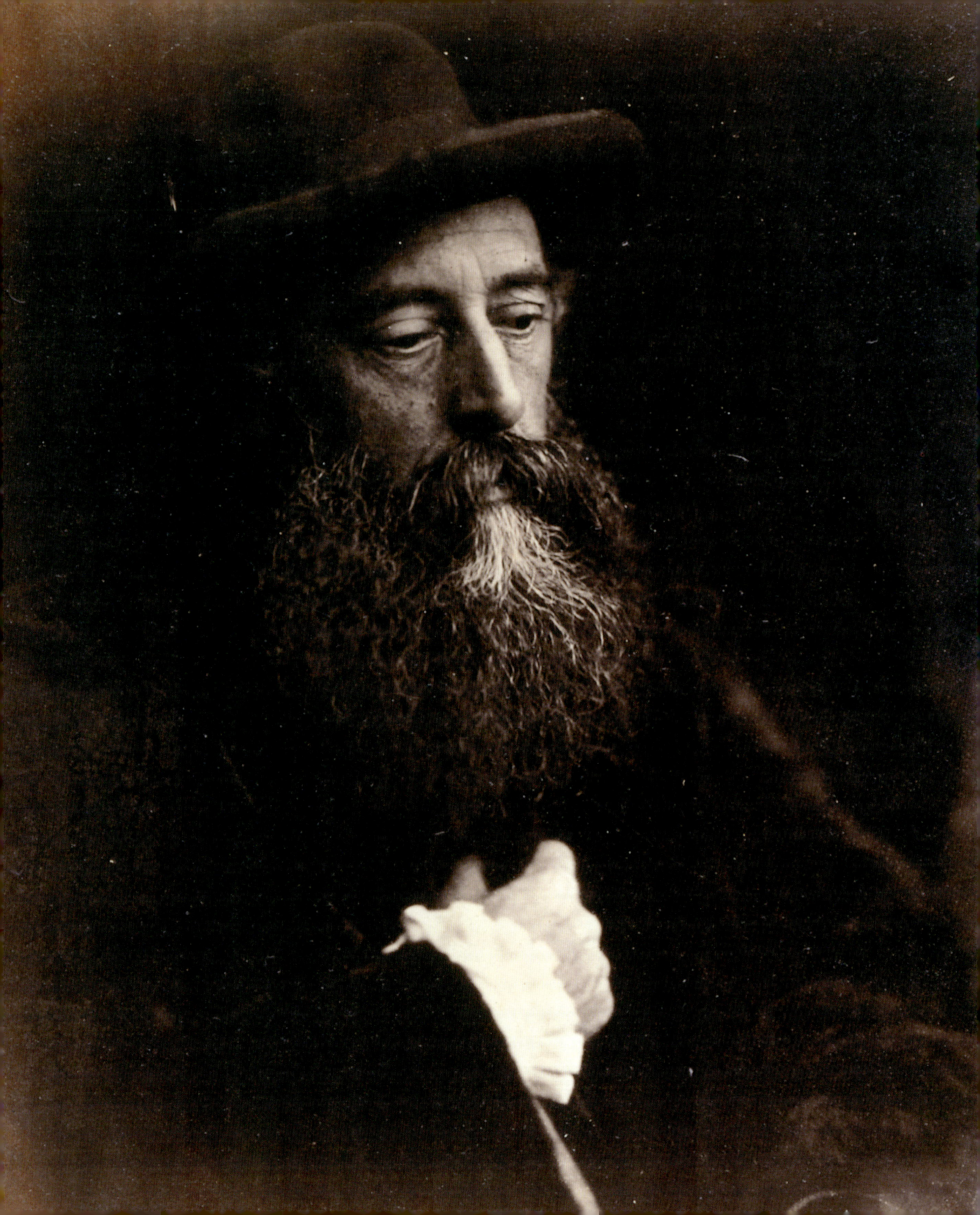

G.F. Watts with hat, 1864 (detail from p.101)
National Museum of Photography,
Film & Television, Bradford

A Victorian Bloomsbury Sara Prinsep's salon in Mayfair had evolved from a group of men drawn to Watts. In his studio in Charles Street, he had surrounded himself with friends, one of whom, the miniature painter and copyist Charles Couzens (*fl.*1838–75), whose studio was downstairs, soon became an assistant as well as a friend. A frequent visitor was the literary jack of all trades Tom Taylor (1817–80), about to become one of London's best-known playwrights. At Charles Street, according to Holman Hunt, Watts's 'artistic and other numerous friends had taken steps to keep together and extend the circle of remarkable men of differing intellectual activity';[1] the group even gave themselves a name, the 'Cosmopolitan Club'.

If the Prinseps were to make Little Holland House an even more successful centre of cultural life than their former home in Chesterfield Street, they needed to persuade Watts to shift his focus too. There had apparently once been a plan for him to live with Lord and Lady Holland, which had fallen through, so it was probably not all that difficult to get him to come and live with the Prinseps – though there is some doubt about whether he was invited to move into Little Holland House, or whether he invited himself:

How Mr Watts came to live there was once picturesquely described to me by Mrs Prinsep: 'he came to stay three days, he stayed thirty years' she said, with a little descriptive action of her hand, and it seems a pity to destroy such dramatic summing up by mere fact. But Mr Watts's recollection was different, and he felt certain that the arrangement was made from the first. Perhaps neither memory was quite at fault, the arrangement most likely being proposed at first, but not carried out, and some months later initiated somewhat accidentally.[2]

Whatever the truth of the matter, Little Holland House soon provided Watts with both a home and a studio; indeed, by 1856 'he had two painting-rooms, and a third in the course of building'.[3] He began to cover the walls of the house with frescoes, assisted (as he had been in Chesterfield Street) by his pupil John Roddam Spencer-Stanhope (1829–1908), and to paint the Pattle sisters Sara, Virginia and Julia – sometimes dubbed 'Dash', 'Beauty' and 'Talent'. They were a powerful and constant presence:

Mrs Cameron and other members of her family … realised for themselves the artistic fitness of things, the natural affinity between use and beauty, and being a very beautiful and interesting family of sisters, they were able to live out their own theories and to illustrate them … Many will remember that, among other gifts, some of these ladies had that of uniting Paris art and the draperies of Raphael into a happy combination for their own daily wear and use. To see one of the sisterhood float into a room with sweeping robes and falling folds, was almost an

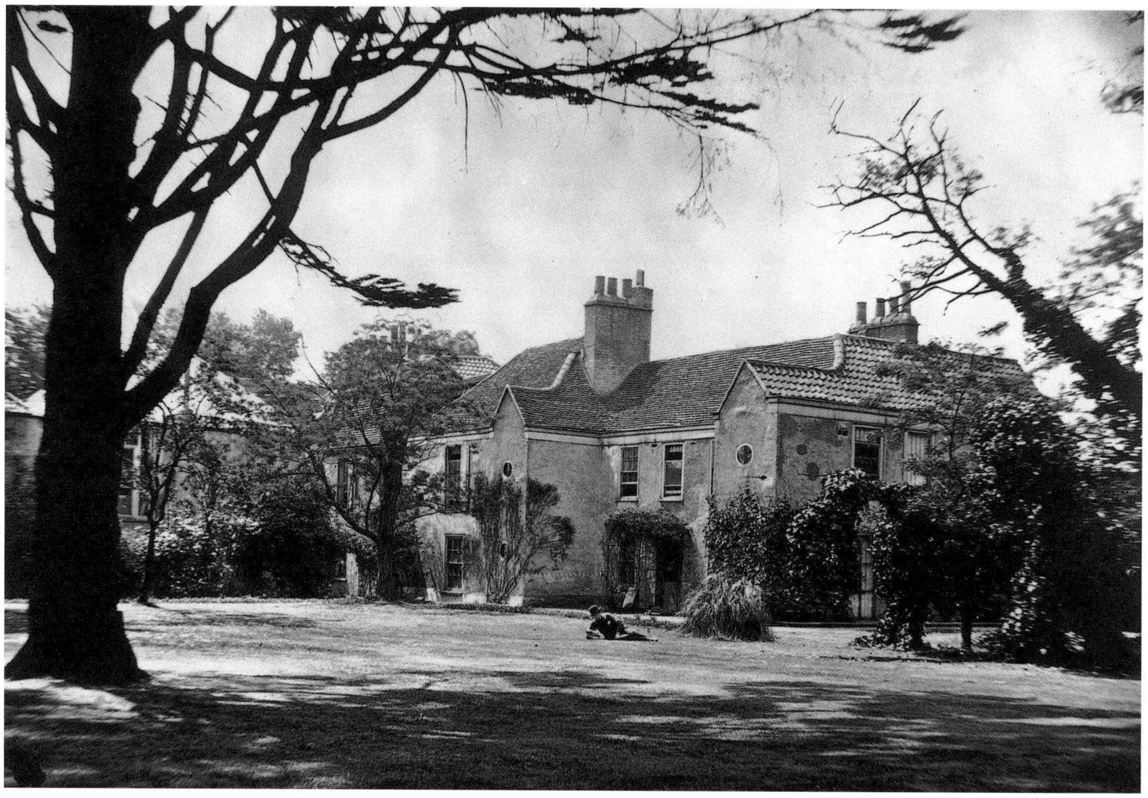

Little Holland House
Unknown photographer, before 1875
(when it was demolished)
The Royal Borough of Kensington & Chelsea
Libraries and Arts Service

event in itself, and not to be forgotten. They did not in the least trouble themselves about public opinion (their own family was large enough to contain all the elements of interest and criticism). They had unconventional rules for life, which excellently suited themselves, and which also interested and stimulated other people. They were unconscious artists, divining beauty and living with it.[4]

The words are those of Anne Thackeray Ritchie, who was once again on hand to be 'the un-acknowledged source of much that remains in men's minds about the Victorian age ... the transparent medium through which we behold the dead. We shall see them lit up by her tender and radiant glow,'[5] as the writer Virginia Woolf (1882–1941), Julia Margaret's great-niece, later put it.

Ritchie's description certainly gives a vivid impression of the three sisters and her repetition of the word 'beauty' is significant. All the Pattle sisters dedicated much of their lives to Beauty – a word they used all the time, and usually with a capital 'B'. In the pursuit of this, Watts was central ('he taught us values, the beauty of beauty, the joy of joy, the marvel of heroic deeds' reminisced one of Prinsep's daughters many years later).[6] His presence also ensured the success of Sara's salons. The members of the Cosmopolitan Club and others were soon coming to Little Holland House on Sunday afternoons, when the house and gardens were peopled by painters (Burne-Jones, Holman Hunt, Frederic Leighton and Sir Coutts Lindsay), writers (Robert Browning, Thomas Carlyle, George Eliot, James Spedding, Tennyson, Thackeray and Tom Taylor), musicians (Charles Hallé, the Czech violinist Joseph Joachim and Adelina Patti), scientists (Sir John Herschel) and politicians (Benjamin Disraeli, W.E. Gladstone). Here was a sort of Victorian predecessor of twentieth-century Bloomsbury (indeed, the Bloomsbury Group itself, which included Virginia Woolf, started life in respectable Kensington before moving to the more middle-class Bloomsbury).

If all these celebrities came to Little Holland House because of Watts – 'Watts ... is worshipped till his manliness hath almost departed,' observed the author and illustrator George du Maurier (1834–96)[7] – it was also to meet each other, and to enjoy a rural atmosphere only three miles from Marble Arch. Anne Thackeray Ritchie's novel *Old Kensington,* a fictional account of life in what is recognisably Little Holland House, described it as looking

like a farm-house, with its many tiles and chimneys, standing in the sweet old garden fringed with rose bushes. There were poplar-trees and snowball-trees, and may-flowers in their season, and lilies of the valley growing in the shade. The lawn was dappled with many shadows of sweet things. From the thatched porch you could hear the rural clucking of poultry and the lowing of cattle, and see the sloping roof of a farmhouse beyond the elms.[8]

It was through Little Holland House that Watts contracted his first, disastrous marriage.

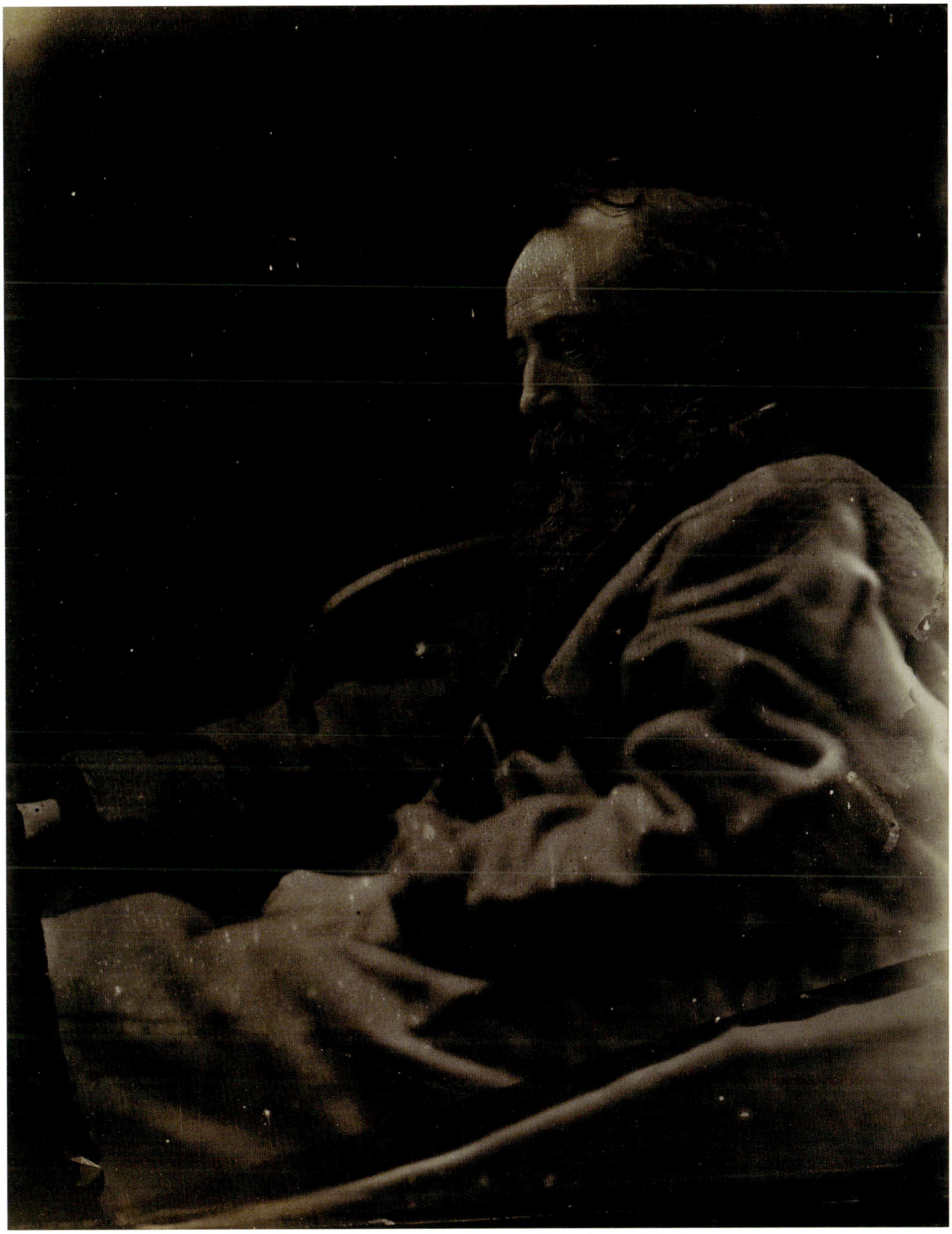

G.F. Watts profile, 1864
Albumen print, 273 x 210mm (10¾ x 8¼")
National Museum of Photography,
Film & Television, Bradford

In 1862, he was introduced to the two attractive teenaged daughters of a well-known theatrical family, Kate (1844–1924) and Ellen Terry (1847–1928), by Tom Taylor, who wanted Watts to paint a double portrait of them.[9] The two girls can hardly fail to have been impressed. Watts soon began to think of adopting Ellen, or even, as he wrote to a friend

> *to remove the youngest from the temptations and abominations of the stage, give her an education and if she continues to have the affection she now feels for me, marry her. There is a great difference between her age and mine and I shall not think of putting any pressure upon her inclinations, but I think whatever the future brings, I can hardly regret taking the poor child out of her present life and fitting her for a better.*[10]

And marry her he did – he was forty-seven years old, and his bride a week short of her seventeenth birthday.

Such disparities in age between husband and wife were not so uncommon in Victorian England as they are today: Sara and Julia Margaret were themselves married to men twenty years and more their seniors, and until 1875 the legal age of consent for girls was only twelve. Henry Taylor believed 'that the bridegroom should be thirty-seven years of age and the bride eighteen'.[11] But the only thing that Watts and Ellen seemed to have in common was a love of 'Beauty' (that word again). To Ellen, Little Holland House 'seemed to me a paradise, where only beautiful things were allowed to come. All the women were graceful, and all the men were gifted.'[12] But beauty was not enough to sustain them in the hothouse atmosphere of Sara Prinsep's household, with its constant parade of cultural heroes and high-flown conversation.

Ellen Terry felt more at home with the children than with these very serious adults. So Sara 'never ceased to treat Ellen as a naughty child who must be scolded and made obedient, and a high-spirited, unconventional girl naturally resented this treatment, while Watts, absorbed in his art, was little aware of the mischief which was preparing.'[13] Less than a year later, the marriage was over, the cause quoted in the legal deed of separation summing it all up – 'incompatibility of temper'. Ellen herself thought it more 'incompatibility of *occupation*, and the interference of well-meaning friends'.[14] George du Maurier surely based the poor put-upon artist's model heroine of his novel *Trilby* on her, a victim of artists and the hypnotist Svengali (who must have owed something of his inspiration to both Sara Prinsep and Watts). By the time Terry had become the most celebrated British actress of her generation, and Sir Henry Irving's leading lady at the Royal Lyceum Theatre, London, from 1878 to 1904 (in which year Watts died), the whole episode was probably little more than a bad memory. The handful of Watts's portraits of her as a beautiful young woman that he did not destroy – notably *Choosing* (*c.*1864), in which she is, poignantly, wearing her silk wedding dress[15] – are surely the best memorials of her short marriage.

Life at Little Holland House was never quite the same after the Terry episode. Many of its regular visitors drifted to a rival salon established a few streets away by the rich silk merchant Arthur Lewis (himself an amateur artist), who coincidentally was to marry Kate Terry in 1867, when she retired from the stage. George du Maurier noted the shift when he wrote to his mother in 1863: 'Half the peerage will be there tonight and very likely the Prince of Wales.'[16] In any case, many of the regulars were beginning to have had enough of the atmosphere at Little Holland House. Holman Hunt, for instance, rather resented the fact that Julia Margaret was 'perhaps the most perseveringly demonstrative in the disposition to cultivate the society of men of letters and of art';[17] the poet Christina Rossetti (1830–94) and the artist and writer Edward Lear (1812–88) had always hated everything about it. It was time for the centre of attention to shift – and it did, to another cultured, and genuinely rural, world almost exactly a hundred miles away. This time, it would be the Tennysons and the Camerons who were the focus of attention.

The Isle of Wight, only a few miles off the south coast of England, is just over twenty miles long and half as wide. Even today, it seems cut off from the real world, a haven of peace and gentle scenery. This remoteness, and its picturesque landscape, appealed to Alfred and Emily Tennyson and in 1853 they rented 'Farringford', a Georgian house in Freshwater, at the quieter western end of the island. Tennyson had been Queen Victoria's Poet Laureate for just three years and, apparently coincidentally, Prince Albert had just designed Osborne House, an Italianate holiday residence for the Queen and himself at the eastern end of the island, sixteen miles away. The Queen wrote to her uncle Prince Leopold, King of the Belgians, that 'It is impossible to imagine a prettier spot – we have a charming beach quite to ourselves – we can walk anywhere without

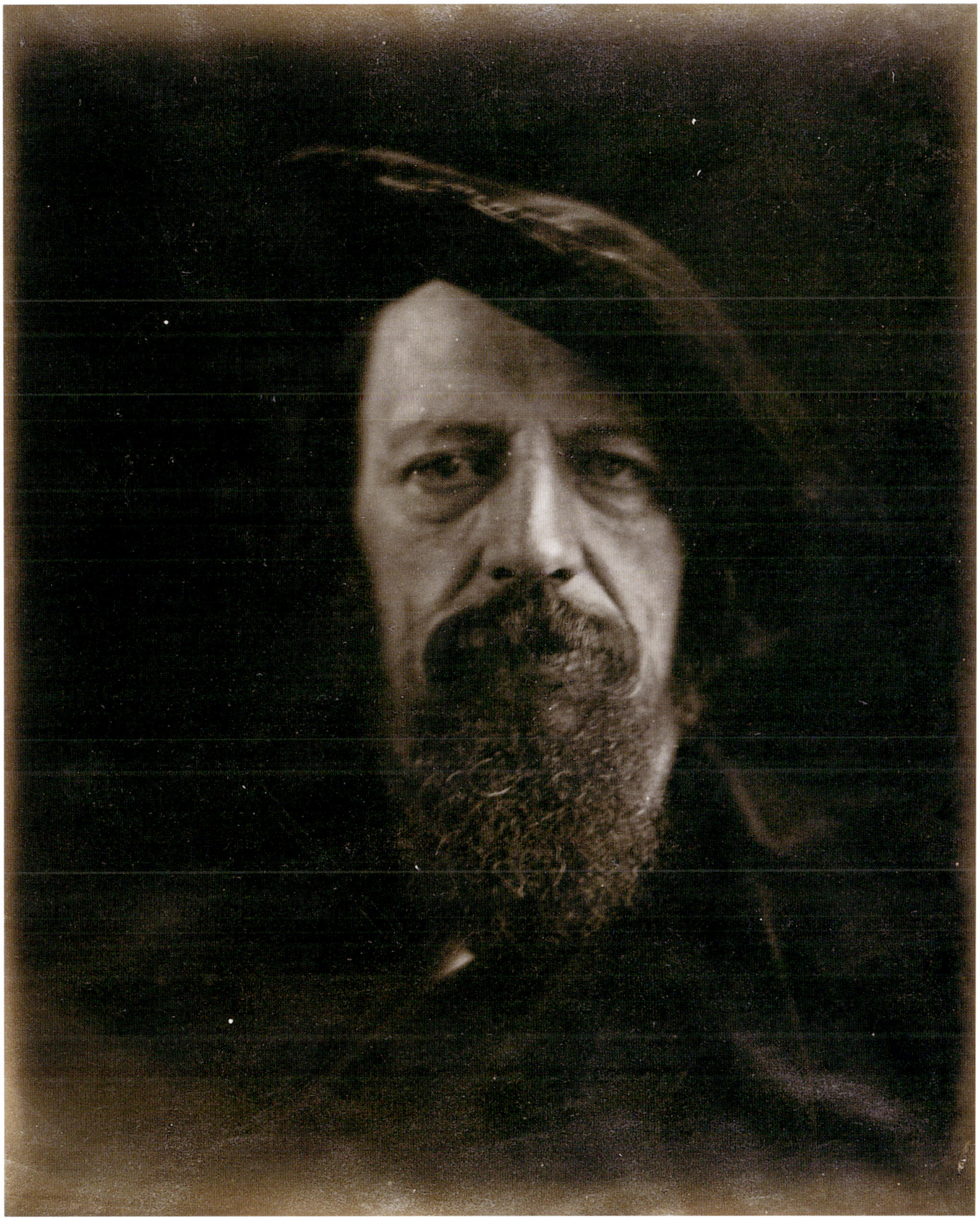

Alfred Tennyson, 1866
Albumen print, 328 x 260mm (13 x 10¼")
National Museum of Photography,
Film & Television, Bradford

being followed or mobbed.'[18] Prince Albert called at Farringford before the Tennysons had even unpacked. Tennyson and his family visited the Queen at Osborne House after Albert's death.

In 1856, enriched by the profits from the success of his long narrative poem *Maud*, Tennyson purchased Farringford, to which – three years later – Julia Margaret brought her three younger sons for a holiday while her husband and two elder sons were away in Ceylon (where Charles had spent a good deal of time in the previous few years). The Cameron children had first holidayed on the Isle of Wight in the 1840s, while living with their aunts in Worthing, and Julia Margaret liked what she saw so much that she wrote to Charles:

> *This island might equal your island now for richness of effects – The downs are covered with golden gorse & beneath them the blue hyacinth is so thickly opened that the valleys look as if the 'sky were upbreaking thro' the Earth' ... The trees too are luxuriant here – far more flourishing than they usually are by the sea – and Alfred Tennyson's wood may satisfy any forester.*[19]

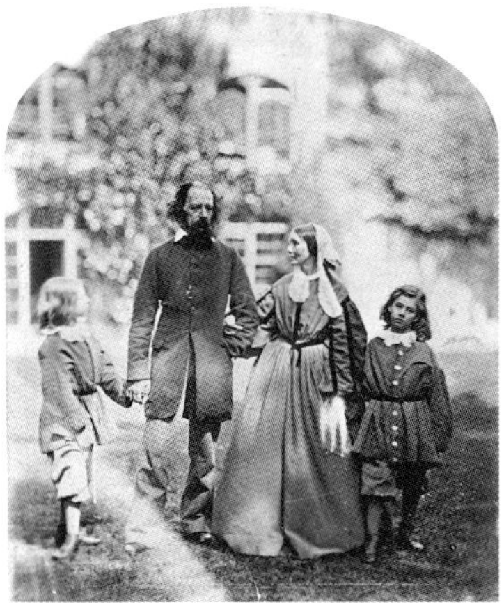

Alfred and Emily Tennyson with their sons at Farringford
Oscar Gustave Rejlander, *c.*1862
Albumen print, 180 x 148mm (7⅛ x 5⅞")
The Museum of Reading

In October 1860 the Camerons bought two cottages (modest-sized houses by today's standards) from a local sailor and lodging-house keeper, Jacob Long. They named one 'Dimbola', after one of their coffee estates in Ceylon, and the other 'Sunnyside' (ten years later, they were to join the two together with a new castellated tower, naming the rather grand single house 'Dimbola Lodge'). The Camerons' new home adjoined the Tennysons' estate and, in November 1860, Tennyson had some trees cleared out of the way in order to drive a road down to the sea and open a private gate into the grounds of Dimbola. The main players were in place.

> *Let us walk on past the great cedar to the little green door which opens into the lane near the bridge. Tennyson passed this way very often to Dimbola, the house of his restless friend and neighbor, Mrs Cameron, which stands by the roadside some half the way from Farringford to the sea. In the days between 1860 and 1878 [*sic*], when the Camerons left for Ceylon, Mrs Cameron was almost as famous and well-known a figure in Freshwater as Tennyson himself.*[20]

Soon Freshwater could be 'compared to Athens in the time of Pericles, as being the place to which all the famous men of the reign of Queen Victoria gravitated'.[21]

One Isle of Wight resident claimed that Freshwater drew even more of the great men and women of the age than Little Holland House:

> *The Freshwater society of those days approached nearer to realizing the purpose and ideal of a French salon than any social group I have myself known in England. It is, of course, startling to compare people who met in the most informal way in the green lanes of the Isle of Wight, and at the houses of friends who were for the most part in no sense people of fashion, with such Parisian a coterie as was grouped around Madame Récamier and Chateaubriand. Nevertheless, it appears to me that the ideal of the salon, which has proved so impossible to realize in London, was largely realized in Freshwater. We had our Chateaubriand in Tennyson and, surprising as the comparison may be, we had our Madame Récamier in Mrs Cameron. The essential work of gathering together the interesting people who were to form the Tennyson society, the enthusiasm for the hero and for genius in general, was Mrs Cameron's part, as it was Madame Récamier's.*[22]

Tennyson had come to the Isle of Wight because he thought the narrow strip of water between it and the mainland, crossed only by infrequent ferries, would keep him safe from the sightseers who had begun to dog his footsteps like modern fans pursuing a pop star. It was a false hope: the sightseers were relentless. Tennyson and Emily never fully adjusted to the strains of being public figures and devised all sorts of strategies to keep themselves from prying eyes. They built, for instance, a bridge over the main road to take Tennyson unseen onto his favourite walk on the downs above Freshwater. Even in his own grounds he was not safe, though a photograph by the Swedish photographer Oscar Gustave Rejlander (1813–75), who visited Freshwater several times, makes it look idyllic:

> *There is a photograph I have always liked, in which it seems to me the history of this home is written, as such histories should be written, in sunlight, in the flashing of a beam, in an instant, and for ever. It was taken in the green glade at Farringford. Hallam and Lionel Tennyson stand on either side of their parents. The father and mother come advancing towards us.*[23]

Although he was trying to avoid gawpers, Tennyson must nevertheless have welcomed the many cultured intellectuals who came to call, judging by the roll-call of famous names and Victorian worthies who visited Freshwater – William Allingham, George Granville Bradley, W.H. Brookfield, Lewis Carroll, Charles Darwin, George du Maurier, Charles Kingsley, Edward Lear, Henry W.

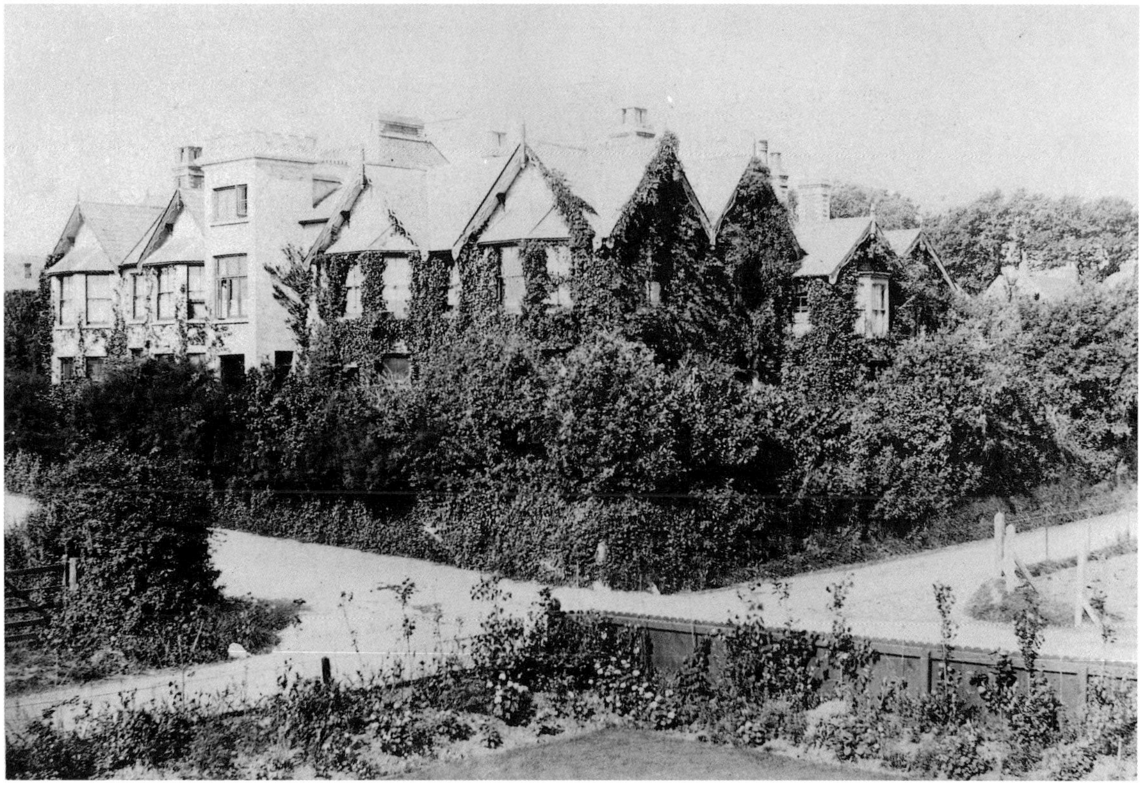

The Camerons' house, Dimbola Lodge, at Fresh Water Bay, Isle of Wight
Unknown photographer, *c.*1871
Private Collection

Longfellow, Sir Henry Taylor, Henry Halford Vaughan, Anne Thackeray Ritchie, Anthony Trollope, G.F. Watts himself (who later was to build his own house at Freshwater), and many other Little Holland House regulars. A number of the names on this incomplete list published reminiscences that include chapters about Farringford, and these often mention Tennyson's unusual neighbour – 'a remarkable woman. Visitors were attracted to her hospitable home in Freshwater no less by her own talents than by the reputation of her venerable husband,' wrote Henry Cotton (1845–1917), who was in due course to marry Julia Margaret's long-serving maid and photographic model, Mary Ryan.[24]

It is scarcely surprising that all this activity inspired so many writers, not just of reminiscences, but also of fiction. Longfellow even wrote an Isle of Wight poem, which can still be read on a drinking fountain near the Crab Inn, Shanklin:

O traveller, stay thy weary feet;
Drink of this fountain, pure and sweet;
It flows for rich and poor the same.
Then go thy way, remembering still
The wayside well beneath the hill,
The cup of water in His name.

Anne Thackeray Ritchie got to know Dimbola and Farringford particularly well after her father died, when Julia Margaret invited her and her sister Minnie to stay. Thackeray Ritchie wrote her novel *From an Island* (1877) making use of the setting, just as she had done with *Old Kensington*. This time, the identities of residents and visitors were only thinly disguised. Years later, in 1935, Virginia Woolf wrote a one-act farce, *Freshwater*, in which Julia Margaret and Charles Cameron, Tennyson, Watts, Ellen Terry, a maid called 'Mary' and even Queen Victoria were all characters – given their own names.[25]

In real life, the ever-energetic Julia Margaret seems to have assumed most of the responsibility for organising the daily lives of everybody – family, residents and visitors. The Camerons and the Tennysons shared many aspects of their lives, and usually 'dined at 7 and only got up from dinner at 11. All this while the most brilliant conversation,' according to Julia Margaret.[26] Describing one such occasion, when Anne Thackeray Ritchie, Henry Taylor and Tennyson were among the dinner guests, she wrote: 'The whole range of poetry comprised, every immortal poet brought to life, and living again in the glowing and wise breath of Alfred Tennyson, in the quotations from Henry Taylor's rich and faithful memory. Each one recited favourite passages from Beaumont and Fletcher, favourite sonnets of Shakespeare's, all that was finest in my adored Wordsworth, and the god of poetic fire, Milton. They were like two brilliant fencers crossing their rapiers, or flashing their foils, giving and evading clean thrusts.'[27] Visitors to Freshwater frequently commented on this wide-ranging conversation. The Catholic writer and biographer Wilfrid Ward (1856–1916) remembered it as being 'stamped by the simplicity, directness and wide range of interests which marked Tennyson himself. He gave the tone to his company. We all felt, moreover, in those days that we were in the making of history.'[28] Charles Kingsley recalled an occasion when Tennyson 'talked on all sorts of topics and walked up and down for hours smoking furiously, and affirming that tobacco was the only thing which kept his nerves quiet'.[29] Spiritualism, a subject of fascinated speculation to many at the time, was another constant topic and Tennyson's friend James Mangles noted how curious Tennyson was about it.[30] After the poet died, Hallam Tennyson told Henry Sidgwick that his father 'was in uncertainty as to what to think of it; altho' he was anxious to believe in it',[31] because he wanted to have faith in the idea of life after death.

One name missing from the Freshwater roll-call is that of John Ruskin (1819–1900), artist, art critic and theorist. He often criticised Tennyson's work and, when the poet invited him to Freshwater, replied: 'Thank you, you've got nothing there but chalk and sand.'

'I beg to assure you my own house stands on clay,' Tennyson told him.

Ruskin: 'Thank you, when I want bricks, I'll apply.'[32]

As we have seen, the Camerons' life in Freshwater began when Charles and his two elder sons were in Ceylon. That, it seems, is where his heart always was. Julia Margaret, perhaps, preferring to be in England and as close as possible to the heart of its cultural life, led her family to the Isle of Wight not just to be near the Tennysons, but to tempt Charles to settle in the nearest equivalent to the subtropical pleasures of Ceylon she could find. Her strategy worked for nearly two decades, and ensured that Dimbola Lodge and Farringford were the stage for an island manifestation of the 'Victorian Bloomsbury' first created in Mayfair. In the end, Charles won the battle – mostly, one suspects, because Julia Margaret's attempts to make enough money to continue living in England came to nought. But until then Farringford, its grounds, and the neighbouring Dimbola were the places to be.

Four years after her impulsive decision to buy two seaside cottages, the already middle-aged Julia Margaret found another way of dealing with loneliness and isolation when her husband and sons were away in Ceylon. Her new obsession would lead to her becoming one of the most extraordinary artists in the history of photography.

NOTES

1. Holman Hunt, I, 1905, p.345.
2. Watts, I, 1912, pp.128–9.
3. Holman Hunt, II, 1905, p.122.
4. Thackeray Ritchie and Cameron, 1893, p.13.
5. Virginia Woolf's obituary of Lady Ritchie, *Times Literary Supplement*, 6 March 1919. Quoted in Gérin, 1981, p.284.
6. Troubridge, 1925, p.23.
7. Quoted in Blunt, 1975, p.80.
8. Thackeray Ritchie, 1873, pp.132–8; in reprint, 1995.
9. The resulting painting *The Sisters* hangs in the Octagon Room at Eastnor Castle, home of Virginia Pattle after she married the 3rd Earl Somers. Kate Terry looks unfinished, but Watts seems to have lavished a great deal more care on his portrait of Ellen.
10. Letter from Watts to his neighbour Lady Constance Leslie, quoted in Dakers, 1999, p.68.
11. Taylor, 1847, p.67.
12. Ellen Terry's *The Story of My Life*, quoted in Auerbach, 1987, p.92.
13. John Roddam Spencer-Stanhope, quoted in Blunt, 1975, p.114.
14. Craig and St John, 1933, p.46.
15. This, and another fine portrait of Ellen Terry by Watts, are now in the National Portrait Gallery, London (NPG 2274 and NPG 5048).
16. Taylor, II, 1885, p.42.
17. Holman Hunt, II, 1905, p.123. Cameron's photographs of Holman Hunt were taken at her sister Maria's house in Hendon.
18. Letter from Queen Victoria to Prince Leopold, King of the Belgians, quoted in Charlton, 1972, pp.3–4.
19. Watts papers, letter from Julia Margaret to Charles Hay Cameron, 25 May 1860, Watts Gallery, Compton, Surrey.
20. V.C. Scott O'Connor, 'Mrs Cameron, Her Friends, and Her Photographs', *The Century Magazine*, LV, 1, November 1897, p.3.
21. Thackeray Fuller, 1955, p.9.
22. Wilfrid Ward, 'Tennyson at Freshwater', *Dublin Review*, 150, January 1912, p.68.
23. Thackeray Ritchie, 1892, pp.40–1.
24. Cotton, 1911, p.52.
25. A more modern comedy set in the Freshwater of Julia Margaret's time is by Lynne Truss, *Tennyson's Gift* (Hamish Hamilton, London, 1996). Less humorous works of fiction based on the story include Helen Humphries, *After Image* (Bloomsbury Publishing, London, 2000).
26. Letter from Julia Margaret to 'Mr Digby' (Hallam and Lionel Tennyson's tutor in 1868–9), quoted in Tennyson, II, 1898, p.84.
27. Tennyson, II, 1898, p.84.
28. Ward, op. cit., p.70.
29. Kingsley was writing about a visit to Farringford on 8/9 November 1859, Kingsley, II, 1877, p.72. He and Tennyson were both heavy smokers.
30. Thwaite, 1996, p.460.
31. Manuscript in the Philpot family collection.
32. Thwaite, 1996, p.264.

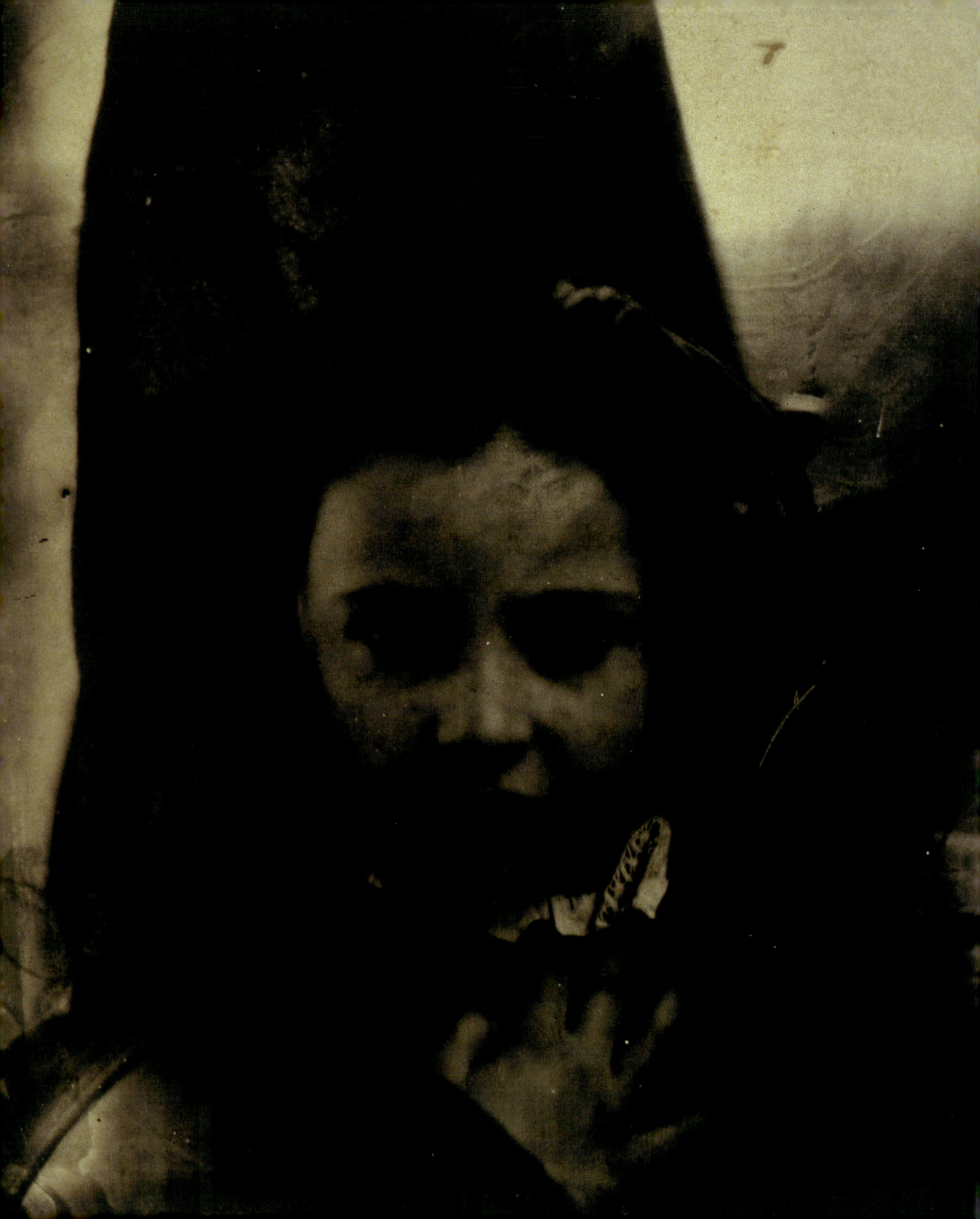

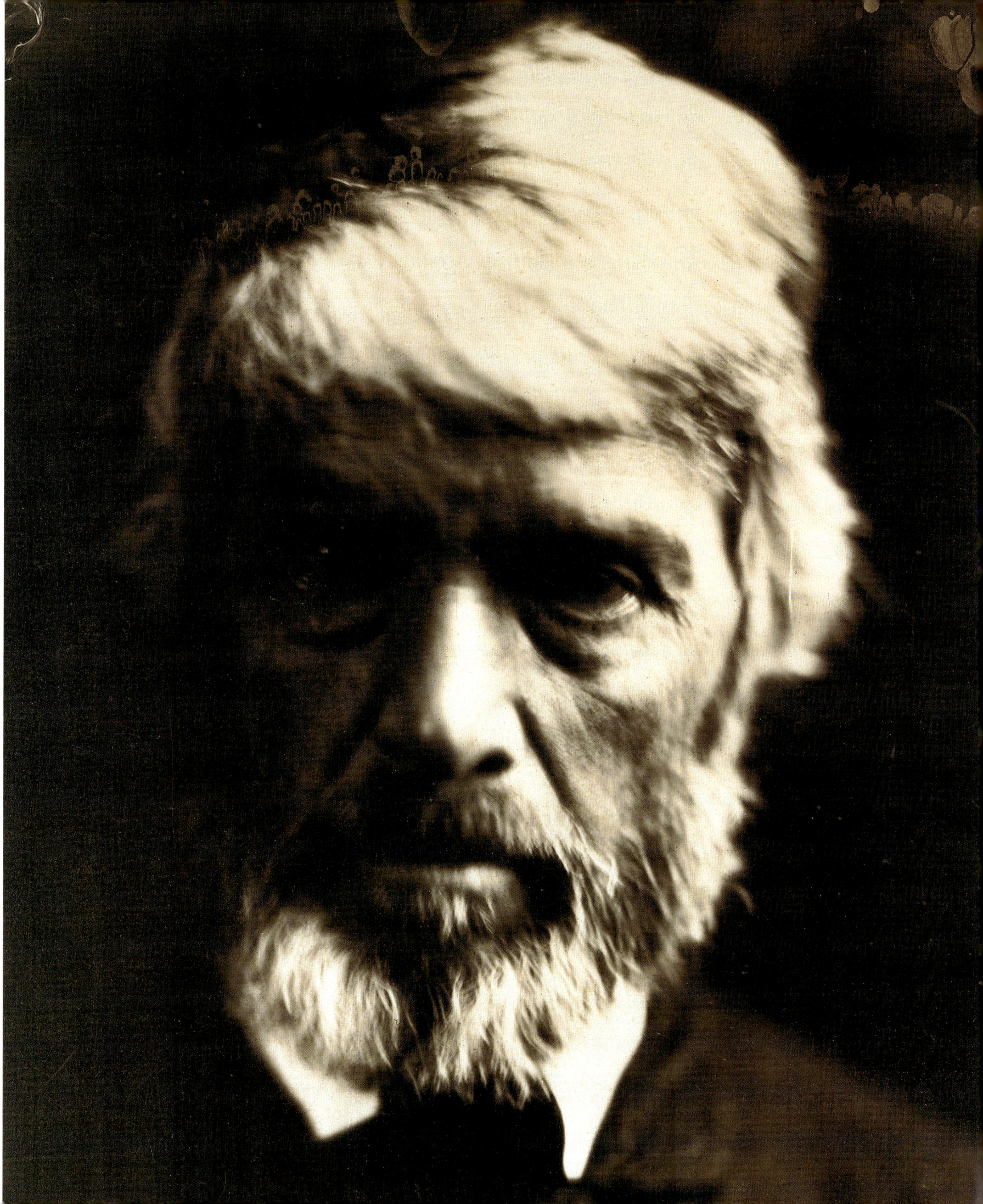

Photography: 'lisping and stammering' Julia Margaret Cameron had first heard about the new invention of photography in 1839, when she was newly married and still living in India. Her great friend Sir John Herschel had sent the Camerons some very early examples, as Julia Margaret reminded him in 1866: 'I remember gratefully the very first information I ever had of Photography in its Infant Life of Talbotype and Daguerreotype was from you in a letter I received from you in Calcutta.'[1] Curiously, however, it is not at all clear when she actually began to practise photography herself and the evidence she has left is conflicting. In a letter to Herschel on 26 February 1864, she wrote:

> *At the beginning of this year I first took up Photography ie my kind and loving son Charles Norman gave me a Camera & I set to work alone & unassisted to see what I could do.*
>
> *All thro' the severe month of January I felt my way literally in the dark thro' endless failures, at last came endless successes! May I not call them so?*[2]

This date is confirmed by her unpublished autobiographical note 'Annals of my Glass House', written in 1874, which opens with the words '"Mrs Cameron's Photography" now ten years old has passed the age of lisping and stammering and may speak for itself having travelled over Europe ~~and~~ America and Australia & met with a welcome which has given it confidence and power.'[3]

There is, on the other hand, a considerable body of evidence to show that Julia Margaret had done some photographic work before acquiring her own camera, which could explain why her daughter Julia and son-in-law Charles Norman gave her one, with the words 'It may amuse you Mother to try to Photograph during your solitude at FreshWater.'[4] At the time she was feeling lonely because her husband and two eldest sons had gone to their coffee plantations in Ceylon, and her only daughter had just got married. Using such equipment, and the chemistry needed to make negatives and prints, when photography was only just over twenty-five years old, would not have seemed in the slightest bit amusing to many women of the time, especially if they were already in their late forties – which would then have been considered rather late middle age. But to someone who had already shown some interest in photography, practised it, and understood how it worked, such a present would not have seemed so unusual or unwelcome.

The likelihood that Julia Margaret had been involved with photography before 1864 derives mainly from the half-dozen or so albums of prints she assembled and presented to various members of her family and friends before that year. The earliest was given to Watts, the most important mentor of her artistic ambitions, in 1857 (in which year a writer in the *Quarterly Review* called photography 'a household word and a household want'). The

Daisy, January 1864
Margaret Louisa Bradley (detail from p.93)
National Museum of Photography,
Film & Television, Bradford

album cover is inscribed with the name by which he was known at Little Holland House – 'Signor'. Two years later, she presented a more elaborate album to Lord Holland's cousin, Henry Petty-Fitzmaurice, 3rd Marquess of Lansdowne. As the historian Joanne Lukitsh has pointed out,[5] many of the pictures in these two albums seem to be related to paintings by Watts. In the Lansdowne album, and in another assembled by Julia Margaret's sister Sophia, for instance, there are photographs of Sara Prinsep and Sophia, separately and together, posed much as they are in *Britomart and her Nurse* by Watts (1878–1900; now in Birmingham Museum and Art Gallery).[6] Watts certainly regarded photographs as useful aids, quickly made equivalents of preliminary sketches, as did other portrait painters of the time.

Another of Julia Margaret's early albums was given to her niece Adeline MacTier in 1860 (I have been unable to trace this album)[7] and a second assemblage for Watts was inscribed 'JMC to GFW'. Though undated, this seems to have been made at about the same time as the two albums she gave in the second half of 1863 to her sisters Maria ('Mia') Jackson (on 7 July) and Virginia Somers (on 24 December). There are a number of duplications between all these assemblages, and those given to Julia Margaret's two sisters are particularly close.[8] Though Maria's album contains a number of Julia Margaret's early prints, including one she acknowledged as 'my first success', taken on 29 January 1864, these can only have been added to the album after its first donation. Indeed, this album reads in two ways. Start from one end and you see only Cameron prints. Start at the other, and there are pictures by a number of mainly unknown and unidentifiable photographers. The only one who can be named with absolute confidence is Oscar Gustave Rejlander, a Swedish artist who trained as a painter but settled in Britain, where he made a name for himself as a practitioner of, and theorist about, art photography, and – as we have seen – visited Freshwater more than once.

In October 1890, just over a decade after Julia Margaret's death, the eminent amateur and pungent critic of conventional photography Peter H. Emerson (1856–1936) wrote about Cameron's early enthusiasm for photography:

That this passion was strong is well known in the family circle, for long before that memorable day in 1864, on which little Miss Philpot was conjured as with a magician's wand upon a glass plate covered with chemical film, and in her new and beauteous form re-named 'My first Success', Mrs Cameron had spent hundreds of pounds paying the degraders of the art to fix the faces of her friends. Her generous nature did not consider money, photographers were ordered with lavishness to work for her, often under her immediate supervision. The best of this vicarious photography was Rejlander's portrait of Tennyson, taken at Freshwater, but truth to tell it is a sorry product: what were the feelings of that operator when he saw his patroness produce the masterly Tennyson, it were better to leave to the imagination.[9]

Apart from Oscar Rejlander, we really have no idea who took the pictures in these early albums. Identifying the photographer, or photographers, of these anonymous prints is of no mere academic interest. 'My first success', after all, could signify 'the first time I ever made a picture with which I was totally satisfied', rather than 'my first ever picture'. Could some of these unacknowledged prints be early essays by Julia Margaret herself, or could the person – or persons – who showed her how to use a camera have taken them? There are three principal candidates.

Julia Margaret herself acknowledges only one master: 'I have had one lesson from the great Amateur Photographer Mr Wynfield and I consult him (in correspondence) whenever I am in a difficulty.'[10] It was Watts who suggested that she look at Wynfield's work, because there was 'perhaps no better in this field'.[11] Later, she wrote to the critic and writer William Michael Rossetti (1829–1919) about Wynfield: 'To my feelings about his beautiful photography I owed *all* my attempts and indeed consequently all my success.'[12]

David Wilkie Wynfield (1837–87), a founder member of the 'St John's Wood Clique' of painters, took a number of fancy-dress pictures of his fellow members and other painters of the time. But this was not until the early 1860s (he registered ten photographs for copyright in December 1863). When Julia Margaret first exhibited her work, at the Photographic Society of London exhibition in the summer of 1864, one reviewer noted that they were made by 'Mr Wynfield's method'. This is described by M.H. Stephen Smith, nephew of the man who donated the collection of Wynfield's photographs now in the library of the Royal Academy of Arts, London: 'His method was to adjust the camera slightly out of focus, which softened and did away with the stereotyped hard look of the professional photographs of the day. He also gave his plates a special preparation.' One certainly sees some

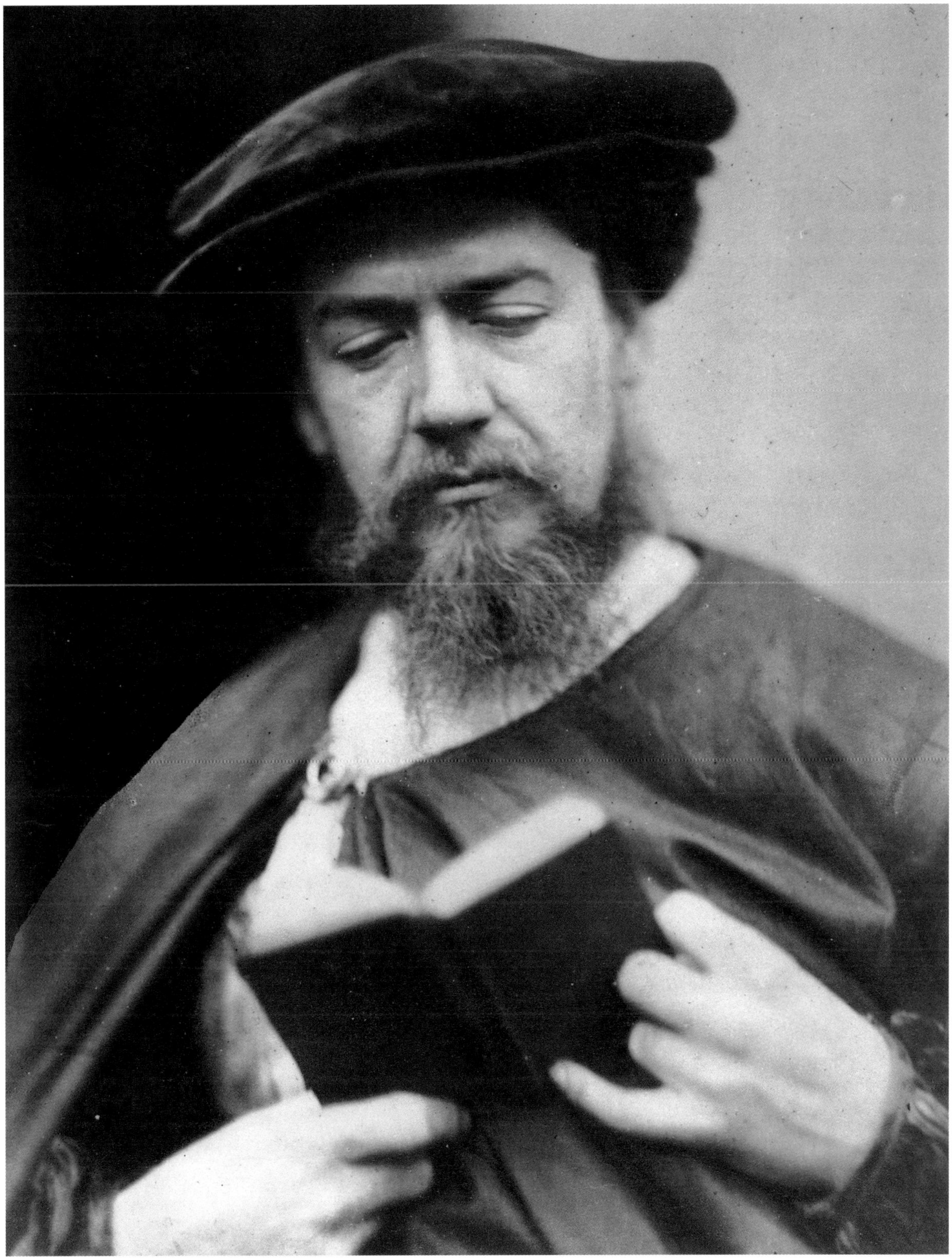

David Wilkie Wynfield (1837–87)
Self-portrait, 1860s
Albumen print, 212 x 161mm (8⅜ x 6⅜")
National Portrait Gallery, London (NPG P87)

basic elements of Julia Margaret's style here, though I have no idea what that 'special preparation' was. But one has only to look at Wynfield's photographs of the same sitters (such as Thoby Prinsep and Watts himself) and others to be convinced that Wynfield did not take any of the pictures in the early albums assembled by Cameron.[13]

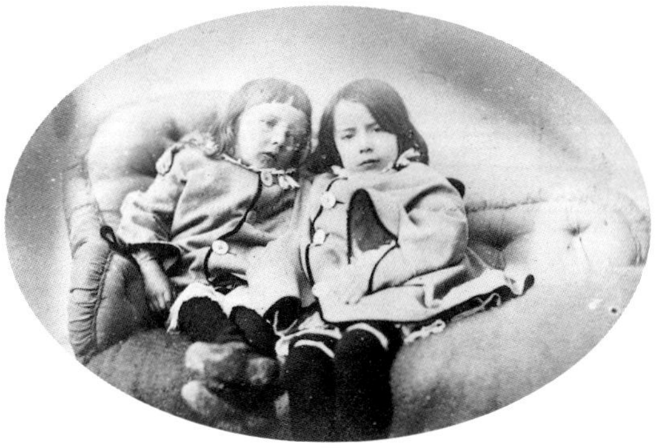

Charles (1848–?) *and Harry (Henry)* (1852–1911) *Cameron*
Freshwater, Isle of Wight
Reginald Southey, 1857
Albumen print, 84 x 137mm (3⅜ x 5⅜")
Cotsen Children's Library
at Princeton University Library

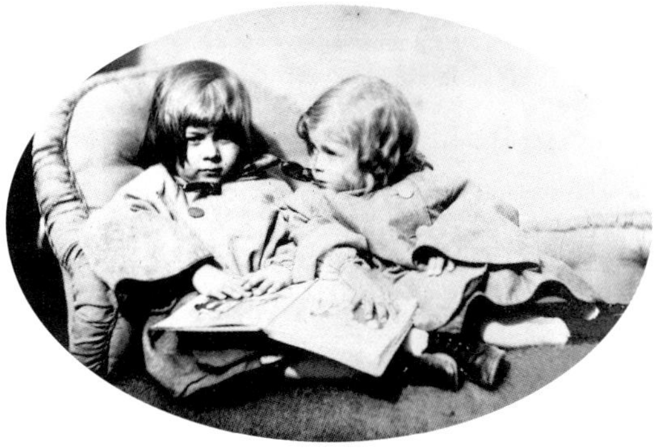

Hallam (1852–1928) *and Lionel* (1854–86) *Tennyson*
Freshwater, Isle of Wight
Reginald Southey, 1857
Albumen print, 84 x 137mm (3⅜ x 5⅜")
Cotsen Children's Library
at Princeton University Library

The detection process then takes us back to Julia Margaret's brother-in-law the 3rd Earl Somers (as Viscount Eastnor became on the death of his father in 1852), to whom several of the photographs in his wife Virginia's album and elsewhere have sometimes been attributed. One can see why. Lord Somers would like to have been a professional artist and knew most of the Pre-Raphaelites, being especially close to the artist and patron Coutts Lindsay (with whom he and Virginia once spent two months 'in a tent on Mount Athos'[14]). In 1853, he was one of the three founding vice-presidents of the Photographic Society of London. But the Society's minute books reveal that he probably never attended a meeting, and he was replaced as vice-president in just over a year. There is no trace of his photographic equipment, nor of any photographs signed by him, or acknowledged to be his, in his family home (Eastnor Castle, Herefordshire) or in either of the stately homes into which his two daughters married (Badminton House, Gloucestershire, and Woburn Abbey, Bedfordshire). But, in 1855, Lord Lansdowne (later to be a recipient of one of Julia Margaret's mature albums) wrote to Fox Talbot, the English inventor of photography, to tell him that Lord Somers – 'one of the best of Photographers as perhaps you know'[15] – was staying with him at his home Bowood House, in Wiltshire. Talbot wrote back to regret losing 'the opportunity of making the acquaintance of so distinguished a photographer and such a well informed traveller as L[d] Somers'.[16] It is obviously possible that some of our mystery photographs were indeed by Somers.

Perhaps the most intriguing candidate for the unidentified photographer is Reginald Southey (1835–99), who took up photography as an amateur while a medical student at Christ Church, Oxford, in the 1850s. Here he introduced photography to his friend Charles Lutwidge Dodgson (1832–98), who became better known as the children's author Lewis Carroll but was also an obsessive photographer for twenty-five years. Carroll first mentions Southey's interest and skill as a photographer in his diary on 1 March 1855: '… I went to look at Southey's photographs: he has done a very successful one of the Broad Walk from his window – about the best amateur attempt that I have seen.'[17] In March 1856, Southey accompanied Carroll to London where the latter bought a camera for £15.

At least one scholar has credited Reginald Southey with introducing Julia Margaret to photography. In his biography of Tennyson, Michael Thorn says that, in April 1857, while the Camerons were visiting Freshwater partly to attend Horatio Tennyson's wedding (it would be two years before they bought their own house there) 'Julia Cameron supervised her first Tennyson photograph session. The camera was not her own … Staying with the Camerons was a 22-year-old medical student named Southey, who was also an enthusiastic amateur photographer. It was from this young man that Julia Cameron caught the photography bug.'[18] Emily Tennyson refers to Southey's portrait sessions in a journal entry for 24 April 1857: 'Mr Reginald Southey's photograph of the boys arrives. One can trace some likeness to Hallam in that of Hallam little ruffian tho' he be. Lionel comes out still less distinctly but one is grateful.'[19] Tennyson himself wrote to Southey to thank him for the prints, suggesting that he might like to visit Farringford if he were to return to Freshwater.

Southey's photographs of the Tennyson boys, and of the Camerons' sons Charles and

Henry, were apparently posed in the house where the Camerons were staying. Although very small, and lacking the scale and impact of Julia Margaret's own photographs, Southey's portraits are close-ups, with background and extraneous detail carefully omitted. There is no evidence to suggest Julia Margaret's involvement in them. Nevertheless, there is an intriguing possibility that this medical student – who went on to become a Commissioner in Lunacy, a successful author of medical books and inventor of medical equipment – introduced not one, but two, of the greatest photographic portraitists of the nineteenth century to the medium.

If manipulating a bulky camera, with its tripod and heavy lens, was difficult enough for a woman, the chemistry of photography in the later 1850s and early 1860s was also very complicated. For most of the quarter century or so since photography had been invented, its pioneers had struggled with chemicals spread on metal (the French daguerreotype) or paper (the British calotype). Both materials had major disadvantages as bases for photographic negatives or prints. Metal is opaque, unsuitable for making copies and only viewable in the right light conditions. Paper has a coarse grain, which does not permit the sharp reproduction of details. Herschel had experimented with glass, much better than either, as early as 1839, but it was the Englishman Frederick Scott Archer (1813–57) who, in 1851, had the idea of suspending photochemicals in the newly discovered collodion and spreading them on glass. The resulting photosensitive plate had to be exposed while it was still wet.

The wet collodion process was complex, messy, and even dangerous. When Lewis Carroll purchased his first camera, he noted in his diary the chemicals he bought at the same time: 'Got some chemicals from London: 4oz iodised collodium; 2oz Glacial Acetic Acid; ½oz Pyro Gallic [*sic*] acid'.[20] Once a photographer had acquired the right chemicals, she or he had to mix a fresh new syrupy mixture for each session. When it was spread evenly over a sheet of clean, dry glass (not easy when the plates were as large as those used by Julia Margaret), the prepared plate was put in a holder while still wet, to be exposed before it could dry out and lose its photosensitivity. Then it was back to the darkroom to pour a previously prepared developing solution of pyrogallic acid and water over the plate. Water was liberally used at every stage (Julia Margaret claimed each photograph required 'nine cans of water fresh from the well') and potassium cyanide was used to remove any excess developer.

All these difficulties I have still to master & the Cyanide of Potassium is the most nervous part of the whole process to me – Is it such a deadly poison – need I be so very afraid of the Cyanide in case of a scratch on my hand? – And when my hands are as black as an Ethiopian Queen's, can I find no other means of recovering and restoring them but this dangerous Cyanide of Potassium?

Are any of the Chemicals prejudicial to health if inhaled too much?[21]

Herschel later warned her 'about your free use of the dreadful poison the Cyanide of Potassium, letting it run over your hands so profusely. – Pray! Pray! Be more cautious,' and sent his own recipe for cleaning silver salts off her hands.[22]

Despite all these difficulties and fears, it seems that Julia Margaret became interested in making prints well before she even owned a camera , or took the picture she acknowledged as 'my first success' in 1864. She inscribed Adeline MacTier's album with the words 'From Life year 60 printed by me J.M.C.'[23] and her sister Virginia Somers' album with 'Photographs of my own printing', so we know that she did more than merely assemble them. Comparing the prints in Virginia's album with those duplicated in the earlier one she gave to her sister Mia Jackson six months previously, it is clear that Virginia's are much darker and stronger, suggesting that Julia Margaret was dissatisfied with those she gave Mia. It is hard to believe, too, that she did not at least have a hand in posing and arranging some of the photographs which she then went on to print. If she looked at the scene on the ground-glass focusing screen, helped to place the sitters and furniture, sometimes sat herself, and then developed (perhaps) and printed (certainly) the resulting print, was she not in fact the photographer, whether she owned the camera or not?

There is no room for doubt about which photograph marked the true beginning of Julia Margaret's artistic photography. In her own eyes at least, it was the one she called 'my first success'. When her daughter and her husband had given her a camera, she 'did not know where to place my dark box how to focus my sitter,'[24] but she nevertheless took her first picture on 29 January 1864. The sitter was Annie Wilhelmina Philpot (1854–1930), daughter of a poetry-writing vicar, William Benjamin Philpot (1823–89), who was holidaying on the island at the time and having long talks with

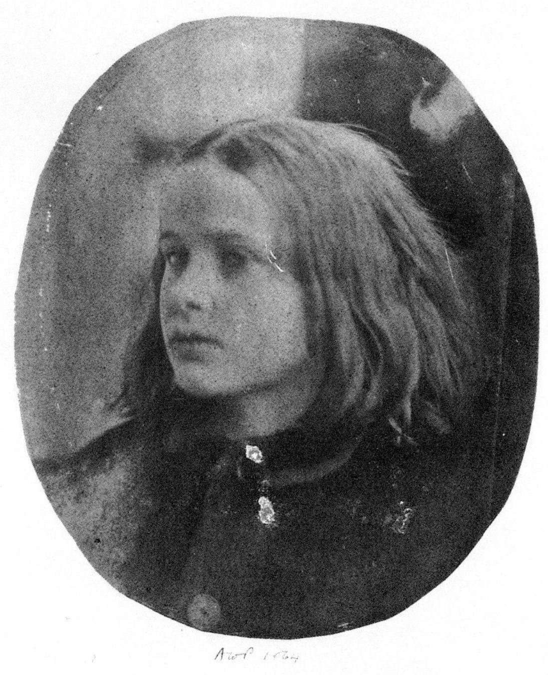

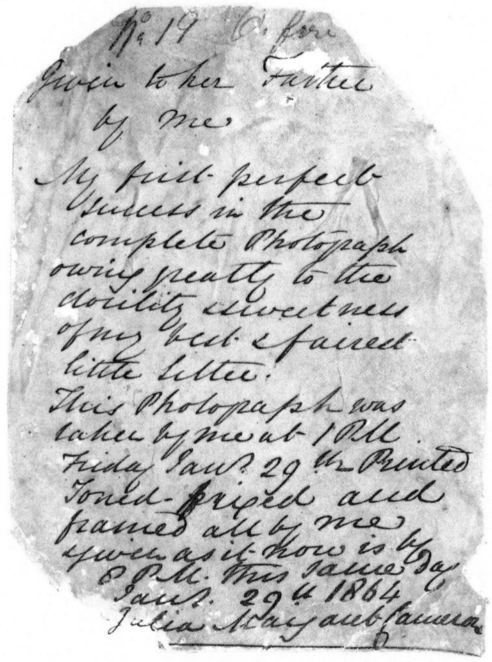

Given to her Father
by me
My first perfect
success in the
complete Photograph
owing greatly to the
docility & sweetness
of my best & fairest
little sitter.
This Photograph was
taken by me at 1 PM.
Friday Janr 29th Printed
Toned-fixed and
framed all by me
& given as it now is by
8 PM. this same day
Janr. 29th 1864
Julia Margaret Cameron

Annie Wilhelmina Philpot (1854–1930)
Julia Margaret Cameron's first print and accompanying letter to the sitter's father, 29 January 1864
Private Collection

Tennyson at neighbouring Farringford about spiritualism and other subjects. Actually, Julia Margaret first tried to photograph a local farmer whom she paid half a crown (12½ pence) an hour: 'after many half crowns & many hours spent in experiments, I got my first picture'.[25] Unfortunately, she rubbed the chemicals off the negative before she had a chance to print it, so she moved on to two children, whom she thought might be more pliant – and, presumably, cheaper. These were the 9-year-old Annie Philpot and her slightly younger cousin Margaret Louisa (Daisy) Bradley (see p.93), but:

I was half-way thro' a beautiful picture when a sputter of laughter from one of the Children lost me that picture & less ambitious now I took one child alone appealing to her feelings & telling her of the waste of poor Mrs Cameron's Chemicals and strength if she moved. The appeal had its effect & I now produced a picture which I called My first success.[26]

The girl who responded to Julia Margaret's appeal was Annie (see p.92), and the photographer 'was in a transport of delight. I ran all over the house to search for gifts for the child.'[27] More importantly for history's sake, Julia Margaret sent the print to Annie's father with a covering note – which is still preserved in the family album:

Given to her Father by me My first perfect success in the complete Photograph owing greatly to the docility & sweetness of my best & fairest little sitter. This Photograph was taken by me at 1 pm Friday Janr. 29th Printed – Toned – fixed and framed all by me & given as it now is by 8 pm this same day Janr. 29th 1864 Julia Margaret Cameron.[28]

A mere seven hours from start to finish!

This reference to success with 'the complete Photograph' presumably refers to the fact that, as we have seen in some of the early albums she gave to her two sisters and other close friends, she had apparently experimented with printing other people's negatives. But she still encountered lots of difficulties, and once again turned to Herschel for help less than two months after her first success:

– a White Bar sometimes repeats itself on an otherwise perfect picture. After searching for the causes I suppose it is light getting into the Camera

– the film comes off my plate in certain weathers

– the plate is not equally covered in film – a streak repeats itself on the side of each Glass as I take it out of the bath – tho' I know of no cause in the bath to scratch it, it seems scratched.

– a print beautifully printed often turns green. I suppose it is the Hypo Sulphite fixing that causes this tho' I wash it in endless Waters

– the Nitrate of Silver used for exciting my paper turns red – tho' never exposed to the light. I conclude it is the Albumen in the paper that reddens the Nitrate.[29]

In her own time, and more recently, critics have sometimes dismissed Julia Margaret as a mere amateur. She certainly loved what she did, but she also hoped to make money from it. As early as November 1865, she had a selling exhibition at the French Gallery in London, owned by the successful print dealer Ernest

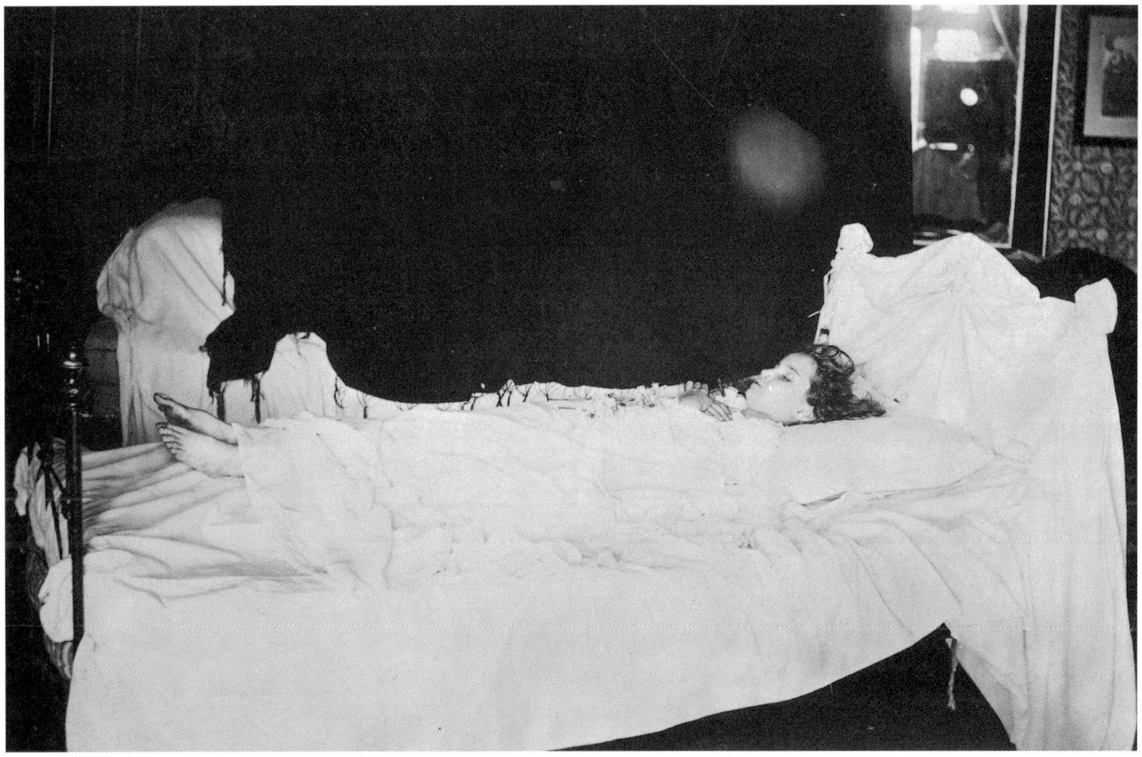

Deathbed Study
Adeline Grace Clogstoun
Julia Margaret Cameron, June 1872
Albumen print, 136 x 203mm (5⅜ x 8")
National Gallery of Art, Washington, DC

Gambart (1814–1902). On show were 146 prints (151 were listed, but numbers 91 to 95 were omitted). Curiously, half-a-dozen of these are described as being on glass, which suggests that they were original negatives with a black backing. This technique, which has the effect of reversing dark and light tones and giving negatives the look of positives, was commonly used in portrait studios. But these commercial products – conscious attempts to ape painted miniatures – were tiny by comparison with Julia Margaret's prints, usually less than 10 x 8cm (4 x 3"). Today, they are usually known by their American name, ambrotypes. Julia Margaret's is the only use I know of the technique applied to large negatives.

The French Gallery put prices of between five and ten shillings (25 to 50 pence) on the prints, with a few marked 'Not for sale'. Artists could buy them for even less – the watercolour painter George Price Boyce (1826–97) recorded in his diary 'I bought 5 (for which, being an artist, I paid half prices)'.[30] This was presumably part of Julia Margaret's bid to be accepted by the art world. By June, when she had put her pictures on sale at the leading printsellers P. & D. Colnaghi of Bond Street (who had opened a photography department in 1857), she told her friend Jane Senior, 'I have a long time ago no a short time ago told Colnaghi that all artists were to have my prints at half price.' Julia Margaret told Senior that she had received 'one cheque for six months sale of photos fm. Colnaghi amounting to £42–2,' and one assumes that her willingness to sell prints to artists cheaply, and to give them away to anyone she thought might be influential in making her work better known, kept the figure down. In the 1860s even many professional photographers were struggling for profits.

In her letter to Senior, Julia Margaret reveals that she was already worried about making money from photography:

The bad Photos I never like to sell at all at any price – and as to reducing the price of the good ones if I were to do that I simply must literally shut up shop – or go to jail – So many have written to me to propose the reduced price as being likely to cause a greater sale – but of course the greater sale would have to be met by greater outlay as to materials & greater labor & you know it is all the labor of my own hand – When I am set up eno' to have a Printer of my own I could print more cheaply – as it is I can't sell more cheaply because you see I have to start with a difference between my work & a professional work of full £800 ~~Sixteen~~ (?) Eight Hundred Pounds loss to me! I will have four hundred glasses (Negatives) upon which every Professional wd. have his first two guineas & I have nothing! Therefore if my prints did not in some measure bring in more than the mere expense of printing – what would or could cover the expenses of my Photography in all its branches.[31]

The equipment Julia Margaret used for her photography further demonstrates how serious she was about it. Her camera and tripod were so heavy that it apparently needed two men to even move them (the camera appears reflected in a mirror in the photograph on p.41). Her lens, made by the French lens-maker Jamin, survives.[32] Made in Paris, it is about 8cm (3") in diameter, and has a fixed stop of 5cm (1⅞"), or about f6 or f7. According to the lens-maker Thomas Dallmeyer,[33] it had 'positive chromatic aberration' and a focal length of about 30cm (12"). The point about all this technical description is that it tells us it would have been virtually impossible with such a lens to get a close-up portrait in focus on the 28 x 23cm (11 x 9") plates used in Julia Margaret's camera. Even in her first portrait session: 'My son Hardinge being on his Oxford vacation helped me in the difficulty of focussing.'[34] Early in 1866, she changed her original camera for one that took even bigger negatives, 38 x 30cm (15 x 12"), which made the problem even worse. So at least some of Cameron's trademark lack of focus was caused by the camera and lens.

There may – just possibly – have been another physical reason for Julia Margaret's highly original approach to focus. The Camerons' eldest son, Eugene, never saw properly out of his left eye, and their third son, Hardinge, had a squint (as one can detect from some of his portraits). The youngest boy, Henry Herschel Hay Cameron (the 'Herschel' was in honour of Sir John, one of his god-parents), was actually blind in one eye. There was clearly a congenital sight problem in the family, as Julia Margaret told Herschel: 'very unaccountably it has happened that with every other child I have had there has been some infirmity of vision.'[35] There is no evidence that she suffered from any such infirmity herself, and most of us will prefer to believe her view of the matter, as recorded in 'Annals of my Glass House':

I believe that what my youngest Boy Henry Herschel who is now himself a very remarkable Photographer told me, is quite true, that my first successes viz my out of focus pictures were 'a fluke' = That is to say that when focussing & coming to something which to my eye was very beautiful I stopped there, instead of screwing on the Lens to the more definite focus which all other Photographers insist upon.[36]

It is remarkable how quickly Julia Margaret established both her subject matter and her visual style. The photographs taken in the few months after her first success include close-up portraits of her hero Watts, the writers Sir Henry Taylor, James Spedding (editor of the works of Francis Bacon) and Aubrey de Vere (Irish poet and dramatist), Tennyson's friend, the Reverend W.H. Brookfield, and her brother-in-law Dr John Jackson. A number of her studies of Madonnas and children, literary illustrations and photographs of friends and family also date from this time. If her style would in later years become more assured, and her prints stronger, she had by the end of 1864 set out her stall for the next decade of intensive photography. She had also, one assumes, created permanent photographic facilities at Dimbola: 'I turned my coal-house into my dark room, and a glazed fowl house I had given to my children became my glass-house!'[37] As early as 1865, she was sufficiently confident of her achievement that she had her first public exhibition.

Julia Margaret received tremendous support from her husband. Although he was frequently confined to his bedroom by ill health, or to sitting indoors and reading, he shared his wife's excitement:

Personal sympathy has helped me on very much. My Husband from first to last has watched every picture with delight & it is my daily habit to run to him with every glass upon which a fresh glory is ~~indelibly~~ newly stamped & to listen to his enthusiastic applause. This habit of running into the dining room with my wet pictures has stained such an immense quantity of Table linen with Nitrate of Silver indelible Stains that I should have been banished from any less indulgent household.[38]

With such encouragement, Julia Margaret was ready to embark on a series of portraits unrivalled in the history of photography – before or since.

NOTES

1. Letter from Julia Margaret to Herschel, 28 January 1866, Library of the Royal Society of London.
2. Letter from Julia Margaret to Herschel, 26 February 1864, Library of the Royal Society of London.
3. 'Annals of my Glass House', p.1. The manuscript is in the Royal Photographic Society Collection at the National Museum of Photography, Film & Television, Bradford.
4. 'Annals of my Glass House', p.3.
5. In her essay 'Before 1864: Julia Margaret Cameron's Early Work in Photography', Cox and Ford, 2003, pp.95–105.
6. The relationship between Cameron's photography and the paintings of Watts and the Pre-Raphaelites is explored in Bartram, 1985.
7. It is described by the historian Mike Weaver in his essay on Julia Margaret in *British Photography in the Nineteenth Century* (Cambridge University Press, Cambridge, 1989).
8. The contents of Maria's album have been published twice in: Ovenden, 1975, and Parry Janis and others, 1994.
9. P.H. Emerson in *Sun Artists*, 5, October 1890 (Kegan Paul, Trench, Trübner & Co., London), p.35.
10. Letter from Julia Margaret to Herschel, 26 February 1864, Library of the Royal Society of London.
11. Letter from Watts to Julia Margaret, National Portrait Gallery, London.
12. Letter from Julia Margaret to Rossetti, 23 January 1866, Gernsheim Collection, Humanities Research Center, University of Texas at Austin.
13. The main source for information about Wynfield and his photographs is Hacking, 2000.
14. Dalrymple, 1998, p.5.
15. Letter from Lord Lansdowne to Fox Talbot, undated, the Fox Talbot Museum, Lacock, Wiltshire.
16. Letter from Fox Talbot to Lord Lansdowne, 5 January 1855, Collection of Camellia plc, Maidstone, Kent.
17. Wakeling, I, 1993, p.66.
18. Thorn, 1992, p.301.
19. Hoge, 1981, p.91.
20. Wakeling, II, 1995, p.68.
21. Letter from Julia Margaret to Herschel, 20 March 1864, Library of the Royal Society of London.
22. Letter from Herschel to Julia Margaret, 1 January 1867, Smithsonian Institution, Washington, DC.
23. Weaver, 1989, p.154.
24. 'Annals of my Glass House', p.4.
25. 'Annals of my Glass House', p.5.
26. 'Annals of my Glass House', pp.6–7.
27. 'Annals of my Glass House', p.7.
28. The photograph, still owned by the Philpot family, was first reproduced in Colin Ford, 'Rediscovering Mrs Cameron – and Her First Photograph', *Camera*, 58, May 1979 (C.J. Bucher, Lucerne).
29. Letter from Julia Margaret to Herschel, 20 March 1864, Library of the Royal Society of London.
30. Surtees, 1980, p.43.
31. Letter from Julia Margaret to Jane Senior, 29 June 1865, National Museum of Photography, Film & Television, Bradford.
32. In the Royal Photographic Society Collection at the National Museum of Photography, Film & Television, Bradford.
33. Quoted by Emerson, op. cit., p.36.
34. 'Annals of my Glass House', p.6.
35. Letter from Julia Margaret to Herschel, 25 October 1858, Library of the Royal Society of London.
36. 'Annals of my Glass House', p.8.
37. 'Annals of my Glass House', p.5.
38. 'Annals of my Glass House', p.11.

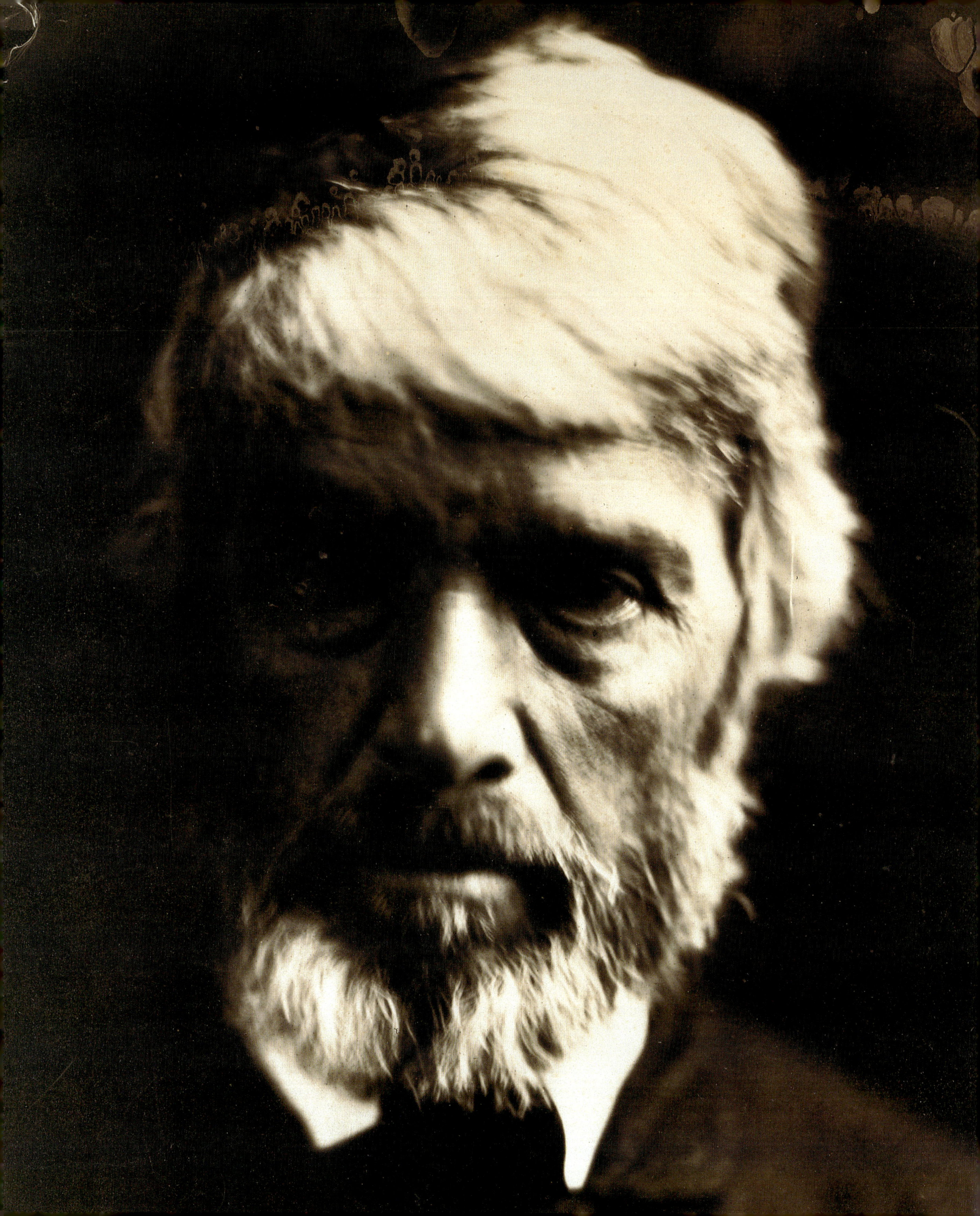

Immortal heads 'No great man lives in vain,' wrote the historian Thomas Carlyle (1795–1881) in 1840, soon after Queen Victoria came to the throne, in his series of lectures *On Heroes, Hero-Worship & the Heroic in History:* 'The history of what man has accomplished in this world, is at bottom the History of the Great Men who have worked there.'[1] This agenda for nineteenth-century Britain's worship of heroes started the process that led to the establishment of the National Portrait Gallery in London in 1856. When the Prime Minister, Henry Temple, 3rd Viscount Palmerston (1784–1865), proposed its creation in Parliament, he argued that the features of great men were an 'incentive to mental exertion, to noble actions, to good conduct'.[2]

It is surprising that the first director, Sir George Scharf (1820–95), and Trustees of the Gallery (of whom Carlyle became one in 1857), responsible for collecting 'the Portraits of the most eminent Persons in British history', did not at first even consider photographs suitable for the Gallery's main, or 'primary', collection. After all, photographic portrait studios had been flourishing, at first in London and then all over Britain, for a decade and a half before the Gallery was founded. To understand their reluctance, however, it is perhaps only necessary to read the following description while looking at the photographic portrait of Prince Albert (see p.46) that was taken on 1 December 1861 by J.J.E. Mayall (1810–1901), an American who enjoyed considerable success in London, especially after he photographed several members of the royal family: 'An intellectual head has the forehead and chin projecting, the high facial angle presenting nearly at a straight line; bottom lip projecting a little.'

The irony of this rather accurate description is that it was not written about Prince Albert at all. It is an extract from an article in the *Photographic News* published two years before Mayall's portrait,[3] containing detailed hints to professional portraitists on how to take the ideal image of a man. Following such advice, of course, could only lead to stereotyped portraits. So did the long exposure needed for the slow wet collodion process then in use. The need to reduce the length of time sitters were required to remain motionless led to professional photographers building glasshouse studios to let in daylight from all directions. This even lighting flattened the sitters' features and in effect 'smoothed out' their characters. This stereotyped blandness makes it perhaps not so surprising that the decision-makers at the National Portrait Gallery thought paintings, drawings and

Carlyle like a rough block of Michael Angelo's sculpture, 1867
Thomas Carlyle (detail from p.97)
The J. Paul Getty Museum, Los Angeles

sculptures of the great men and women of their age likely to make better memorials to show to visitors of the time and to preserve for posterity.

To make portraits that were neither mass-produced nor production-line stereotypes called for a photographer more interested in aesthetics than money, and with the time to take infinite pains over every picture; in other words, an amateur. Julia Margaret Cameron was one of a tiny group of British nineteenth-century amateurs who lifted portrait photography out of its conventional, studio-based and professionally dominated rut (others were Lewis Carroll, Lady Hawarden and David Wilkie Wynfield).

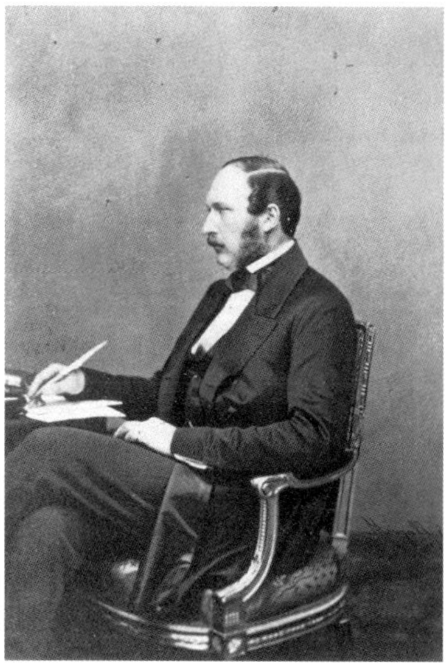

Prince Albert of Saxe-Coburg-Gotha (1819–61)
J.J.E. Mayall, 1 December 1861
Albumen carte-de-visite, 85 x 58mm (3⅜ x 2¼")
National Portrait Gallery, London (NPG x24128)

Julia Margaret's methods, apparently simple and unpretentious, demanded serious and even painful commitment from her sitters. In March 1867, when preparing to visit Herschel, her 'Teacher and High Priest', she wrote to his wife in order to choose a room in which to photograph him: 'The room cannot be too humble, if it is capable of having all light excluded except that of one window or one aperture which I will myself cover with a yellow calico that is all I desire.'[4] All four portraits Julia Margaret took on this occasion (see, for instance, pp.98, 99 and 100) demonstrate that, only three years after taking up photography seriously, she had thoroughly mastered its elements. In particular, the soft quality of her chosen yellow light playing on Herschel's shock of white hair (which – as with many of her subjects – she insisted on being tousled before taking the picture) and unshaven chin makes a significant contribution. As in so many of her head-and-shoulder portraits, one senses that she has somehow got beneath her subject's skin rather than merely charted the surface contours.

Both sitter and photographer immediately recognised the success of their collaboration. Herschel wrote to Julia Margaret: 'The picture of the old paterfamilias with the black cap on is, I think, the climax of photographic art, and beats hollow anything I ever beheld in photography before.'[5] He made 'a promise to her not to sit for one to any other artist-photographer ... the lady in question has done *her* part so admirably and with such an amount of personal pains and made so strong a point of the promise.'[6] This encouraged Julia Margaret – who, despite her amateur status, never lost hope that she might make money out of her photography – to put the ambitiously high price of £1 on prints of the portrait offered by her dealers, Colnaghi's. By the time of her exhibition at the German Gallery in early 1868, only the prints signed by Browning, Herschel and Tennyson – and one of Julia Jackson – commanded such a high price. The other 200 or so photographs at the German Gallery were priced between three and sixteen shillings (15 to 80 pence). In September 1867, she took back from Herschel the fine album of her work she had given him three years earlier 'with a grateful memory of 27 years of friendship', and added to it examples of her later work, putting the portrait of *Sir John Herschel with Cap* on the first page of the album before returning it to him.

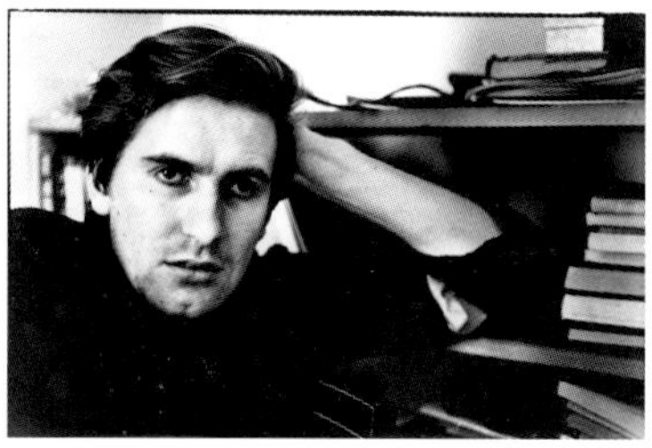

Keith Johnstone
Roger Mayne, *c.*1960
Bromide print, 188 x 283mm (7⅜ x 11⅛")
Private Collection

It is impossible to know how long an exposure Julia Margaret had to give Herschel's portrait in the limited light conditions she imposed, but it may well have been several minutes. She claimed that the profile of her niece Julia Jackson (see p.119) was 'done under ... circumstances of experiment – our dining room no adjustment of light – every door & every window closed, fire lit inside the room – Ice & snow outside – 4 min[ute] sittings'.[7] Such uncomfortably long exposures meant that the sitters could hardly avoid moving. Furthermore, the lens of Julia Margaret's camera, her propensity for placing it as close to a sitter's head as possible to make it fill the frame, and her consistent aesthetic preference made it inevitable that her photographs would always be at least partly out of focus and blurred. Curiously, this gives her subjects' eyes a particular intensity, an 'abstracted look'. The poet Edward Fitzgerald (1809–83) described this, and Tennyson's appreciation of it:

> *I remember A.T. admiring the abstracted look of a Murillo Madonna at Dulwich; the eyes of which are on you, but seem 'looking at something beyond, beyond the Actual into Abstraction'. This has been noticed of some great men; it is the Trance of the Seer: I do not remember seeing it in A.T. himself; great as he was from top to toe, and his eyes dark, powerful and serene.*[8]

When Julia Margaret makes Tennyson look straight at the camera, however, he has just that faraway look (see p.104), as Fitzgerald later admitted; so do many of her sitters. Almost a century later, the British street photographer Roger Mayne (b.1929) demonstrated how to achieve the effect in an experimental long exposure portrait.

Julia Margaret may well have considered people's eyes the 'windows on the soul' – as many are still inclined to do. But they were not the only prominent features on the surface of the distinguished heads she photographed. There was at the time an intense interest in human physiognomy as an indicator of character and mental ability. The Irish poet and diarist William Allingham (1824–89) discussed with Carlyle the 'size of heads. C. said (I think) that his own head was 23½" round, one inch more than Burns's. Goethe's head was large, Byron's small. Browning's is small ... The brain of ordinary persons begins to shrink at sixty, of superior men not till seventy ... Greatest weight of the brain 62oz.'[9]

It was not just the size of the head that was understood to indicate the size, and therefore the intellectual capacity, of the brain beneath. The so-called 'science' of phrenology – deducing the power and range of a person's mental abilities from the actual shape of the head – was a widely practised branch of physiognomy. Physiognomy was developed in Switzerland in the late eighteenth century by Johann Kaspar Lavater (1742–1801) and in Germany by Franz Joseph Gall (1758–1828) at the very beginning of the nineteenth century, its principal British proponent was the Scotsman George Combe (1788–1858), who founded the Phrenological Society in 1820 and the *Phrenological Journal* in 1823.[10] His book on the subject, *Essay on the Constitution of Man* (1828), sold 17,000 copies in the year it appeared, outdoing every other publication of the time except the Bible, *Pilgrim's Progress* and *Robinson Crusoe*; even Darwin's *Origin of Species* (1859) only sold 15,000 in five years. Combe lectured on the subject in America and Germany. 'Phrenology has done good service by showing us, with more emphasis than had ever been done before, that human beings are widely different in their mental tastes and aptitudes,' wrote one learned professor.

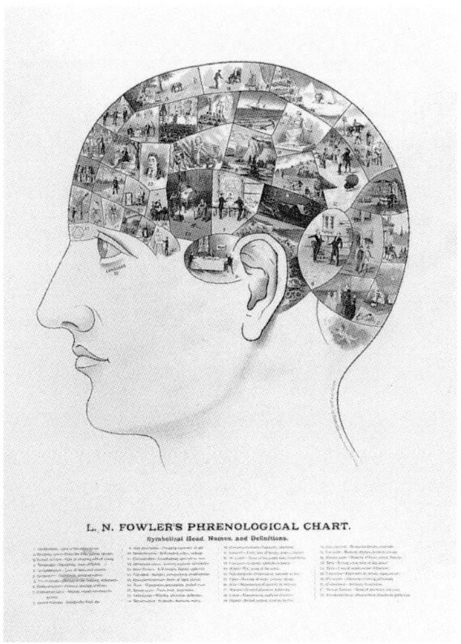

L.N. Fowler's Phrenological chart
Private Collection

Phrenologists analysed people's characters by measuring and assessing twenty-seven bumps on their subjects' heads. Honoré de Balzac, Charles Baudelaire, George Eliot and Karl Marx, among others, submitted to having their characters read in this way. Queen Victoria had her children's heads analysed. Lewis Carroll visited a phrenologist in Edinburgh who identified his 'Emulousness' (which I take to mean hero worship), mathematical ability, and love of children.[11] Combe, who lived in Edinburgh and had been photographed there in the 1840s by Julia Margaret's great precursors David Octavius Hill (1802–70) and Robert Adamson (1821–48), believed that phrenology could help choose careers, arrange ideal marriages and even rehabilitate criminals. Much of the appeal of phrenology was that its principles could be grasped by anybody, whether they had any scientific or medical knowledge or not, and it captured the imagination of people in all walks of life.

There are no references to phrenology in Julia Margaret's writings, and her attitude to it cannot be divined. Photographers certainly knew about it (the anonymous author of the advice in the *Photographic News* quoted earlier on how portrait photographers should make their sitters look refers his readers to 'Lavater, or some such author, on "Physiognomy"'). And Julia Margaret certainly could not have been ignorant of it – she gave her eldest son Eugene boys' story books by Captain F.S. Marryat, with phrenological scenes in them. Phrenology may well have been a subject of conversation just as much as spiritualism, which we know interested Tennyson. We do know something of Tennyson's own views of phrenology, and those of his elder brother, the poet Charles Tennyson Turner (1808–79). While still in his teens, the latter wrote a dismissive poem: '... 'tis at best / An awkward system, and not over-wise, / And badly built on incoherencies'.[12] Thirteen years later, a more mature Alfred wrote: 'visited [William] Brookfield at Southampton ... and met Charles Elton: "You must have done many a foolish thing in your time with that great big bump of benevolence of yours".'[13]

Whatever Julia Margaret's views, it is fair to ask whether phrenology may at least partly have informed her approach to the portraiture of men in particular. Did it, for instance, explain why she refused to take a portrait of the Dorset poet the Reverend William Barnes (1801–86), because 'she objected to the top of his head',[14] or even why she so often photographed men in particular in profile? Profile silhouettes were popular before photography was even invented; what to modern eyes seems a slightly unnatural way of looking at people was seen at the time to give the subjects a sort of Classical and Renaissance grandeur. But it also had the advantage of bringing out clearly the precise shape of heads for those who believed, like the inventor of phrenology, that the profile was 'the truest representation that can be given to a man'.[15] Julia Margaret's profile of Tennyson (see p.102), for instance, lit from the front so as to emphasise his high forehead (where 'reverence' was said to be located immediately behind 'benevolence') and domed skull (which hinted at a large brain), gives considerable prominence to the bags under his eyes. These, as can be seen by looking at any phrenological head, or at the American phrenologist Lorenzo Fowler's widely circulated phrenological chart, were supposed to indicate mastery of language. Even today, after the nineteenth-century's faith in phrenology has been long abandoned (it stayed in vogue well into the twentieth century), we might agree that Tennyson was a 'highbrow', as was Prince Albert, at least in the portrait illustrated on page 46. Phrenology could turn anyone into a stereotype, like the commercial studio portraiture which Julia Margaret dismissed as 'mere topographic photography'.[16] She herself may, nevertheless, have hoped to distil something fundamental about her intellectual subjects by defining the very contours of their skulls.

By determined application over roughly a decade, Julia Margaret assembled a considerable portfolio of fine close-ups of – mostly male – heads, virtually life-sized because of the large negatives she used. The increased size of her negatives and prints when she acquired a second, larger camera in 1866 added to her difficulties – from preparing the negative, through the length of exposure, to making and finishing the final print. But from then on her portraits had an extra intensity, living up to the exhortation from Watts to make 'photographs that are not only *From* the Life, but *To* the Life, and startle the eye with wonder and delight'.[17] The results are Julia Margaret's own photographic equivalents of Watts's later 'Hall of Fame' series of his great contemporaries, donated or bequeathed to the National Portrait Gallery by the artist from 1895; sometimes they show the same people.

These extraordinarily powerful portraits are virtually the first 'close-ups' in photographic history. Each of them is taken against a totally dark background and shows only the sitter's head and shoulders, with the torso often draped in dark velvet or other cloth. The effect is much enhanced by Julia Margaret's virtuoso handling of light, which became increasingly accomplished over the years. Illuminating these heroic heads from one side only highlights every detail, every valley and every bump.

Julia Margaret first used the term 'immortal head'[18] for the man she considered perhaps even more important in her gallery of eminent Victorians than Carlyle and Herschel – Alfred Tennyson. Although Tennyson was far from enthusiastic about being photographed (his was, after all, already one of the most painted, drawn and photographed faces of the age), he was often persuaded to move from the Camerons' dining room at Dimbola to Julia Margaret's 'little dark room – half-reluctant, half-willing to take part in this shadowy presentment, but wholly interested in his old friend's success'.[19] No less than seventeen of Cameron's solo portraits of him survive, in addition to two with his sons, Lionel and Hallam. Because they never flatter him, nor attempt to make him appear urbane or sophisticated, nor disguise the effects of age, illness, introspection, gloom and even despair, they tell us more about the real Tennyson than all the other painted and photographed portraits of him put together.

Tennyson himself may well have realised that Julia Margaret did not make him look his handsome best. When he came to select a frontispiece for the 1884 edition of his collected works, he chose a formal studio portrait by Mayall, who had ensured that Tennyson was tidily dressed, his collar neatly turned down, his hair properly coiffed, his deeply lined, swarthy complexion pale and smooth. Julia Margaret was appalled, writing of her own profile portrait (dubbed by Tennyson 'The Dirty Monk'; see p.102):

> *It is a fit representation of Isaiah or of Jeremiah & Henry Taylor said the Picture was as fine as Alfred Tennyson's finest Poem. The Laureate has since said of it that he likes it better than any ~~thing~~ photograph that has been taken of him* except *one by Mayall that* 'except' *speaks for itself. The comparison seems too comical. It is rather like comparing one of Madame Tussaud's Wax work Heads to one of Woolner's Ideal heroic Busts.*[20]

There is, of course, nothing unusual about a sitter preferring a flattering image to one that is revealing. But it is hard not to side with Julia Margaret. Her raffish unwashed monk is an intellectual and an artist. Even if one knew nothing about him, one might guess he was a writer from the book clasped in his left hand (which looms unnaturally large, because of the short focal length of her lens). Mayall's Tennyson is a dull and respectable Victorian gentleman – a banker perhaps.

Julia Margaret's son, Henry Herschel Hay Cameron, who was for a time himself a portrait studio photographer in London, believed that 'Thought, learning – intellectual power of any kind – leaves its stamp on a face and, indeed, on the whole individuality of a man. Tennyson, for instance, had a magnificent presence; he looked like a latter-day Homer.'[21] In much the same vein, the philosopher Frederick Denison Maurice (1805–72) responded to

Julia Margaret's gift of some portraits of the poet: 'Had we such portraits of Shakespeare and Milton, we should know more of their own selves. We should have better commentaries on *Hamlet* and *Comus* than we now possess, even as you have secured for us a better commentary on *Maud* and *In Memoriam* than all our critics have given us or ever will.'[22]

Among the other great names who had their portraits taken in Julia Margaret's 'glazed fowl house' studio – most of whom had come to Freshwater to visit Tennyson – were Charles Darwin, Joseph Joachim, Benjamin Jowett, Henry W. Longfellow (Tennyson left him in the studio with the words: 'You will have to do whatever she tells you. I'll come back soon and see what is left of you'),[23] George du Maurier, Anthony Trollope and Watts. Others, including the writers Robert Browning, Thomas Carlyle, James Spedding and Aubrey de Vere, had their portraits taken at Little Holland House, to which Julia Margaret occasionally brought her equipment from the Isle of Wight. Nor far away was the Victoria and Albert Museum, where Julia Margaret photographed Louise de Fonblanque among others, and the house at 7 Cromwell Place, Kensington, which belonged to the wealthy Norman family, into which her daughter had married and where she took one of her portraits of Watts, as well as the 1864 study of his teenage wife Ellen Terry as 'The South West Wind'. Herschel was one of the few for whom Julia Margaret was willing to transport her cumbersome equipment to his own house, Collingwood, near Hawkhurst, in Kent.

Modern eyes cannot fail to be struck by the fact that the majority of the men in these pictures have beards. The fashion for the 'toga virilis', as it was dubbed in reference to the Roman toga worn to symbolise manhood, was perhaps a reaction to the dull and sombre men's fashions of the time and seems to have begun with artists: 'It was not by any means accidental that the beard movement should have originated with artists, who, however artificial their pursuit may be in itself, are brought into more contact with real nature, and are more observant of its beauties, than any other class of persons.'[24] Julia Margaret's portraits have the ability to penetrate even such a mask. Her husband Charles (see p.105) possessed perhaps the most spectacular example ('a philosopher with his beard dipt in moonlight'[25]), closely rivalled by the civil servant and author Sir Henry Taylor:

There is a feature of my life, conspicuous in these photographs, which dates from this period, and the importance of which be it far from me to underrate. This is my beard. In 1859 my hand was so liable to be shaken by asthmatic spasms that the razor was not safe in it, and was laid by. In the last days of that year, I notified to one of my girl friends the small beginnings of what was soon to be developed into the phenomenon presented by Mrs Cameron's art ...[26]

Writing about Julia Margaret ten years after her death, Peter H. Emerson described a portrait of Taylor 'whose only fault is an unpleasant wiriness of beard',[27] but it was this beard above all which surely prompted Millais to try to persuade Taylor to pose as Moses for him – in vain.

Taylor was, however, a regular sitter for Julia Margaret: 'Our chief friend, Sir Henry Taylor, lent himself greatly to my early efforts.'[28] She thought him 'as great & grand as Alfred Tennyson aye grander & greater too, I wd. say,' as she wrote to Watts when persuading him to paint Taylor for his 'Hall of Fame' series.[29] But, though Taylor was so respected in mid-nineteenth-century Britain that he was thought of as a possible alternative to Tennyson as Poet Laureate in 1850,[30] he is now only remembered, if at all, as the subject of no less than thirty of Julia Margaret's portraits, to say nothing of the many pictures in which he appears as biblical or fictional characters (see pp.106 and 185), an indignity Tennyson managed to avoid. Nothing could be a better proof of Julia Margaret's ability to make someone immortal. Nor could anything more convincingly demonstrate that the widely held view that she was some kind of 'hit or miss' amateur, whose best images were as much a result of fluke as of skill, is simply wrong. Look at the dozens of portraits of Taylor and Tennyson, and a clear process of careful trial, patient development and growing confidence emerges. Cameron was in no sense a 'Sunday photographer', and Taylor was right to say that she had transformed photography from 'a lifeless transcript to a miracle of portraiture'.[31]

Until such portraits existed, Carlyle and his fellow Trustees of the National Portrait Gallery might well have rejected photographs because it was only too obvious that they cut down to size the famous men and women shown as heroes in paintings, revealing that in real life they looked exactly like ordinary people. John Ruskin, whose early interest in photography turned into lifelong opposition, would certainly have supported their view.

Of the general belief that 'The camera never lies'[32] he wrote:

*Photographs ... are popularly supposed to be 'true', and, at the worst, they are so, in the sense in which an echo is true to a conversation of which it omits the most important syllables and reduplicates the rest. But this truth of mere transcript has nothing to do with Art properly so called; and will never supercede [*sic*] it.*[33]

Perhaps these views explain why Ruskin is one of the few eminent Victorians known to Julia Margaret whom she never photographed:

During the time that Mr Ruskin was with us Mrs Cameron, a very well-known artistic portrait photographer of those days was also with us on a visit and the two had frequent skirmishes about photography. I was lying on my couch in the drawing room one day when Mrs Cameron insisted on showing Mr Ruskin some of the wonderful heads of well-known people which she had taken. He got more and more impatient until they came to one of Sir John Herschel in which his hair all but stood up like a halo of fireworks. Mr Ruskin banged to the portfolio upon which Mrs Cameron thumped his poor frail back exclaiming 'John Ruskin you are not worthy of photographs!' ... Mrs Cameron wore a red bonnet with strings & when she got very excited she pushed it back & it hung down her back by the strings. Apparently they went out but arrived back to luncheon arm in arm with bonnet on & peace signed.[34]

Had Julia Margaret not hit Ruskin on his back, she might perhaps have made him, too, look like a hero. It was her ability to do this which made it inevitable that one day the National Portrait Gallery would have to take her photographs seriously. In fact, it was only in 1932 that a photograph – of the celebrated cookery writer and journalist Isabella Beeton (1836–65), by Maull & Polyblank – entered the collection. Six years earlier, the critic and painter Roger Fry (1866–1934) had written 'One day we may hope that the National Portrait Gallery will be deprived of so large a part of its grant that it will turn to fostering the art of photography and will rely on its results for its records instead of buying acres of canvas at great expense by fashionable practitioners in paint.'[35]

It is curiously apt that one of Julia Margaret's very greatest portraits – perhaps the greatest – is of the hero-worshipper Carlyle himself, not in profile, but staring balefully at the camera 'like a rough block of Michael Angelo's [*sic*] sculpture', as Cameron subtitled it (see p.97). According to Julia Margaret, Carlyle found the session with her 'a kind of *Inferno*',[36] but one hopes that he also found it worthwhile. It was he, after all, who thought that 'Portraits are the candle by which we read history.'[37] Cameron's fiercely angled lighting leaves one side of his craggy face completely in the dark and one eye invisible. Carlyle might not have approved – he once complained to the American poet and philosopher Ralph Waldo Emerson (1803–82) that the daguerreotype Emerson had sent him was 'a bad photograph: no eyes discernible, at least one of the eyes ...'[38] – but his strength and intellect emerge from the shadows. So does his pain – his wife of forty years had died a few months before the portrait was taken and he never again wrote anything of consequence. This is a hero no longer as heroic as he was, but one nevertheless still capable of confronting a dominant woman, and of refusing to be cowed by her enormous wooden camera with its mammoth brass lens. Cameron might well have written on the result the comment with which she once inscribed a portrait of Tennyson: 'A column of immortal grandeur – done by my will against his will'.[39]

Carlyle was undoubtedly a tremendous subject. Even his portrait by Watts is less bland than most of those in his 'Hall of Fame' series – indeed, Carlyle complained that it made him look 'like a mad labourer'.[40] Julia Margaret knew exactly what she wanted to do. 'When I have had such men before my camera,' she wrote, 'my whole soul has endeavored to do its duty towards them in recording faithfully the greatness of the inner as well as the features of the outer man'[41] (just what the phrenologists thought was achieved by paintings that took account of phrenological principles). Julia Margaret's ambition brought out not only the strength and stubbornness of Carlyle's character, but also his vulnerability and bitterness. For the photographer, such a photograph was 'almost the embodiment of a prayer'.[42] It is difficult to imagine ever being closer to the very soul of a woman or man in a portrait, and the photograph is a triumphant vindication of Carlyle's dictum – 'A portrait is worth a dozen biographies'.

NOTES

1. Thomas Carlyle, *On Heroes, Hero-Worship & the Heroic in History*, 1840. The lectures, written in 1840, were published in 1841 (James Fraser, London, p.1). Carlyle gave his first lecture, 'The Hero as Divinity', on Tuesday 5 May 1840.
2. Quoted in Piper, 1957; second edition 1978, p.264.
3. *Photographic News*, II, 37, 20 May 1859, p.125. The article 'Lessons in Colouring Photographs' is spread over several issues.
4. Letter from Julia Margaret to Lady Herschel written from Little Holland House, 17 March 1867, Library of the Royal Society of London.
5. Inscribed by Julia Margaret on the back of a print of her portrait of Herschel (see p.100), Royal Photographic Society Collection (now at the National Museum of Photography, Film & Television, Bradford.
6. Letter from Herschel to Mr J. Samuelson, May 1868, Library of the Royal Society of London.
7. Letter from Julia Margaret to Herschel, 26 February 1864, Library of the Royal Society of London.
8. Fitzgerald took Tennyson to the Dulwich Art Gallery on 26 March 1842, as a relief from the task of correcting the proofs of an edition of his poetry (Pinion, 1990, p.35). Fitzgerald was so struck by Tennyson's eyes that in 1844 he urged Samuel Laurence to paint Tennyson's portrait 'looking full at you'.
9. Allingham and Radford, 1907; second edition 1985, p.233.
10. George Combe's other claim to fame in photographic history is that the pioneer Scottish photographers David Octavius Hill and Robert Adamson (see pp.85–8) made a fine portrait of him in the 1840s.
11. Hudson, 1995, pp.68–9.
12. *Poems by Two Brothers* (Macmillan & Co., London and New York, 1893), pp.200–3.
13. Pinion, 1990. Tennyson's lifelong friend William Brookfield was a curate at Southampton at the time (26 August 1840) and was engaged to Charles Elton's daughter Jane, whom he later married.
14. Tennyson, I, 1898, p.514.
15. John Casper Lavater's *Essays on the Physiognomy, for the Promotion and the Love of Mankind.* Quoted in Mozley, 1974, p.39.
16. Letter from Julia Margaret to Herschel, 31 December 1864, National Museum of Photography, Film & Television, Bradford.
17. Letter from Julia Margaret to Herschel, 18 February 1866, Herschel Correspondence Books, Library of the Royal Society of London.
18. 'Annals of my Glass House', p.20.
19. Among Julia Margaret's male heroes, only Henry Taylor was photographed more frequently than Tennyson. The complete catalogue of her works includes sixteen portraits of Tennyson, taken between 1846 and 1869, as well as two with his sons Hallam and Lionel (1865).
20. 'Annals of my Glass House', p.21.
21. Interview on 'The Art of Photography' with Marie A. Belloc, published in *The Woman at Home*, IV, London, 1897.
22. Quoted in Thackeray Ritchie and Cameron, 1893, p.7.
23. V.C. Scott O'Connor, 'Mrs Cameron, Her Friends, and Her Photographs', *The Century Magazine*, LV, 1, November 1897, p.4.
24. P.G. Hamerton, Portfolio Paper 1889, pp.189–90, quoted in Hacking, 2000, p.88.
25. Tennyson, II, 1898, p.84.
26. Taylor, II, 1885, p.163.
27. P.H. Emerson in *Sun Artists*, 5, October 1890 (Kegan Paul, Trench, Trübner & Co., London), p.38.
28. 'Annals of my Glass House', p.11.
29. Letter from Julia Margaret to Watts, 30 December 1860, National Portrait Gallery, London.
30. Among the other names canvassed were Robert and Elizabeth Barrett Browning, Leigh Hunt and Samuel Rogers.
31. Taylor, 1924, p.217.
32. The credit for coining this phrase is usually given to the Liberal politician and Prime Minister, William Ewart Gladstone, to whom Cameron was introduced by Tennyson.
33. John Ruskin, *Cestus of Agalia*, XIX, 1865.
34. Sarah Angelina Acland, 'Memories in my 81st Year', quoted in Hilton, 2000, p.462.
35. Fry, 1926, p.28.
36. Allingham and Radford, 1907; second edition 1985, p.153.
37. Allingham and Radford, 1907; second edition 1985, p.233.
38. Slater, 1964, p.405.
39. Hill, 1973, p.111.
40. Chesterton, 1904; reprinted 1975, p.68.
41. 'Annals of my Glass House', pp.17–18.
42. 'Annals of my Glass House', p.18.

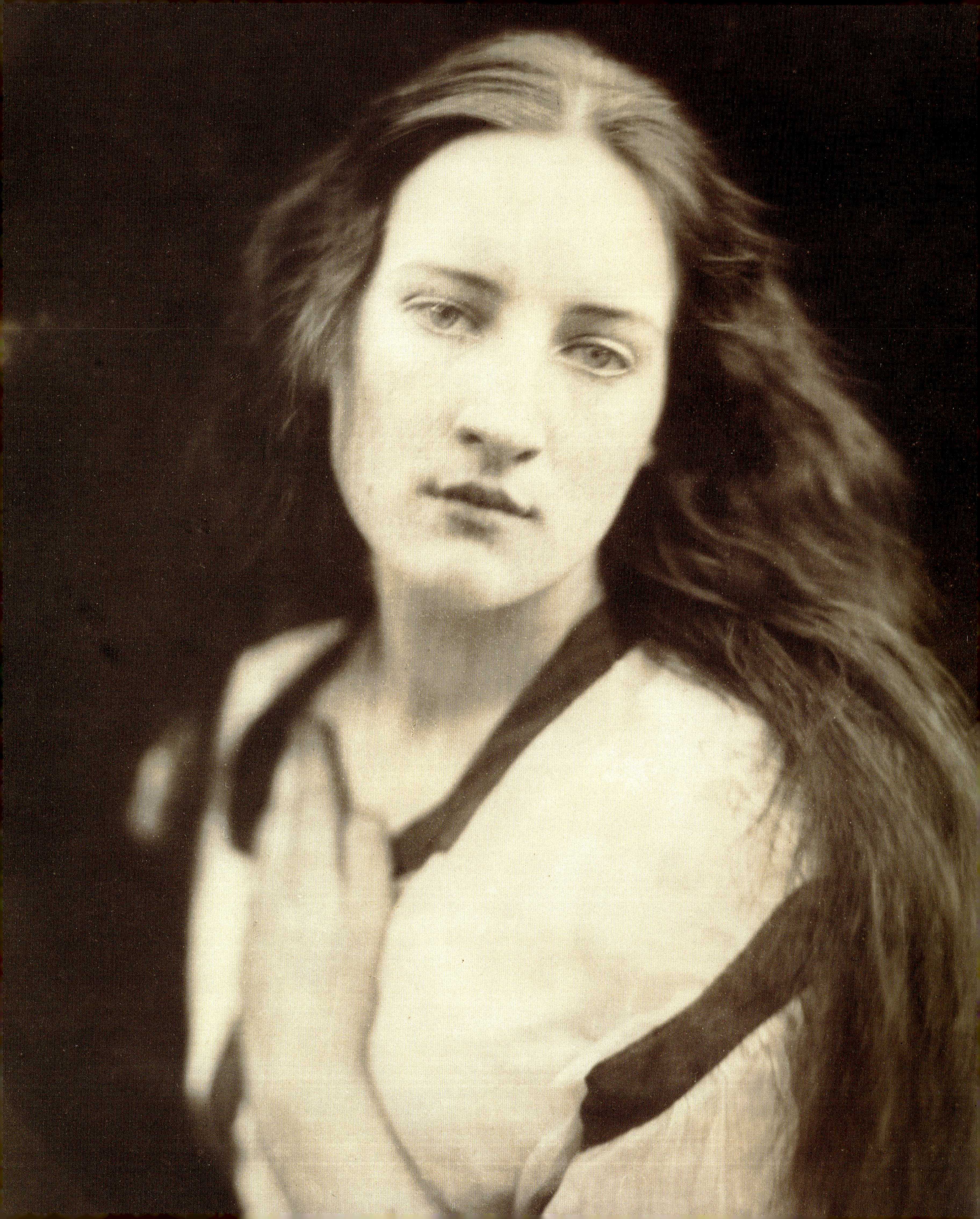

A dream of fair women In the late twentieth and early twenty-first century, our ideas of history have become considerably less hero-oriented than Carlyle's. Historians, and others, have shown increased interest in the women who achieved success in previous centuries – when the odds were so heavily stacked against them – as well as in the wives of famous men, and women of all classes whom history has overlooked. Naturally, Julia Margaret Cameron scholarship and criticism has moved in the same direction. The last major exhibition of her work in the twentieth century, in 1998, was called simply *Julia Margaret Cameron's Women*. Its curator, Sylvia Wolf, began her work by 'wondering if there truly was a unique quality to Cameron's portraits of women'. Her answer was an unequivocal yes.

Julia Margaret photographed a handful of well-known women of the day, such as the botanical painter Marianne North (1830–90; see p.194) and the model and painter Marie Spartali (1843–1927; see p.137), daughter of the Greek consul in London and later wife of the American landscape painter and journalist W.J. Stillman. No print of Julia Margaret's portrait of Christina Rossetti has so far been identified – how different would it have been, one wonders, from the female stereotype so painstakingly outlined by the anonymous writer in the *Photographic News* of May 1859:

A handsome face is of an oval shape ... The nose slightly prominent in the centre, with small, well-rounded end, fine nostrils; small, full, projecting lips, the upper one slightly hanging down in the centre, both turned up a little at the corners, and receding inside; chin round and small; very small, low cheekbones, not perceptibly rising above the general rotundity. Eyes large, inclined upwards at the inner angles, downwards at outer angles; upper eyelids long, sloping beyond the white of the eye towards the temples. Eyebrows arched, forehead round, smooth and small; hair rather profuse.[1]

Just as we saw in the previous chapter how precisely the recommended look for men in professional photographers' portraits fitted Prince Albert, so too the female version closely matches the first portrait photograph ever accepted into the National Portrait Gallery's primary collection. Maull & Polyblank's photograph of Mrs Beeton was taken in the late 1860s, but the offer of it to the Gallery by her son Sir Mayson Beeton was only accepted in 1932 – three-quarters of a century after it was taken, and this was only because no painting or

The Echo, 1868
Hatty Campbell (detail from p.135)
The J. Paul Getty Museum, Los Angeles

drawing of her was known to exist. Nor indeed does there seem to be any other print of this image, which was apparently hand-coloured by Sir Mayson's sister shortly after Mrs Beeton died.

It was extremely difficult for women in Victorian Britain to achieve public status in their own right. Most of Julia Margaret's female subjects were family and friends, and on the whole it was not their strength of character, nor their talent, which interested her, but their physical beauty – usually the sort of long-necked, long-haired, immature beauty familiar to us from Pre-Raphaelite paintings. A particularly favourite model, her niece Julia Jackson (1846–95), appears in no fewer than fifty portraits (in some of them she is named 'Julia Duckworth', after her first marriage to the barrister Herbert Duckworth in 1867). In most of these, unusually for a woman, she is portrayed with the same close-up scrutiny which Julia Margaret usually reserves for her male sitters who were successful professionals. In fact, though Julia Jackson did write a few children's stories and essays, these were never published and her only known published works were a book on nursing and the entry on Julia Margaret Cameron for the *Dictionary of National Biography*.[2] This was founded and edited by her second husband, Sir Leslie Stephen (1832–1904), and it is more as a wife (first of Duckworth, then of Stephen) and mother – of the publisher Gerald Duckworth and, following her marriage to Stephen, the Bloomsbury artists Vanessa Bell (1879–1961) and Virginia Woolf – that she is usually remembered. Woolf later vividly portrayed her mother in the complex character of Mrs Ramsay, heroine of her 1927 novel *To the Lighthouse*: 'Fifty pairs of eyes were not enough to get round that one woman with.'[3]

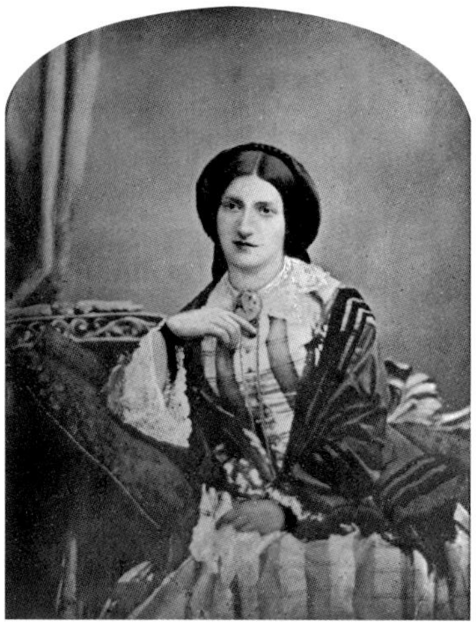

Isabella Beeton (1836–65)
Maull & Polyblank, *c.*1860–5
Hand-tinted albumen print, 184 x 149mm (7¼ x 5⅞")
National Portrait Gallery, London (NPG P3)

The fact that even Julia Jackson, for whom Julia Margaret clearly had admiration and respect as well as affection, should be remembered primarily as a wife and mother serves to reinforce our understanding of the position of women in Victorian society. Jackson's mother, Maria (who was Julia Margaret's sister), was a friend and admirer of Coventry Patmore (1823–96), whose best-known work, the long sequence of poems *The Angel in the House* (published in four parts from 1854 to 1862), celebrated the virtues of domestic life and the place in it of the innocent, devoted, spiritual and caring wife, always subservient to her husband. Woman's greatest attribute, says Patmore, is love, while man's is truth:

For love is substance, truth the form;
Truth without love were less than nought;
But blindest love is sweet and warm,
And full of truth not shaped by thought;
And therefore in herself she stands
Adorn'd with undeficient grace,
Her happy virtues taking hands,
Each smiling in each other's face.
So dancing round the Tree of Life,
They make an Eden in her breast,
While his, disjointed and at strife,
Proud-thoughted, do not bring him rest.[4]

Julia Margaret's photographic portrayal of *The Angel in the House* (see p.122) is a head-and-shoulders close-up, but one has only to compare it with her portraits of male heroes to see how much more softly lit and conventional it is. The model, Emily Peacock, is dressed in dark velvet, as are many of Julia Margaret's men, but the velvet is edged with white fur, giving a much gentler, prettifying effect. *Sisters* (see p.123) is so closely related that it was probably taken on the same day. Anne Thackeray Ritchie's novel *From an Island*, set in what is clearly a fictionalised Freshwater (a central character, Hexham the photographer, is surely at least partly modelled on Julia Margaret), describes a girl who comes to the dinner table 'dressed in a floating gauze dress ... one great white lily in her hair'.[5]

Julia Margaret usually photographed her female models when they were teenagers, though their dress makes them seem older to modern eyes. With such girls, she drew her camera back from its extreme close-up position, uncovered all the windows in her glasshouse studio (or even took her subjects out into the garden) and modelled their faces and figures in a softer and more flattering light than that she used for her heroic men. Her most frequent female models – apart from Julia Jackson – were May Prinsep (1853–1931), an orphan who was adopted by Thoby and Sara Prinsep (her uncle and aunt), and two of the Camerons' maidservants, Mary Ann Hillier (1847–1936) and Mary Ryan (1848–1914). All had somewhat the same, slightly unformed, teenage faces, with soft contours, full lips and dreamy eyes. This was presumably the look Cameron found most photogenic and perhaps that is why she employed the two Marys, though Ryan had joined the household well before Cameron took up photography. 'She chose her parlourmaids largely for their beauty,' wrote Wilfrid Ward,[6] and Julia Margaret's friend Adolphus Liddell (1846–1920), cousin of Lewis Carroll's muse Alice Liddell, said of the two Marys that 'One of them usually sat for the full face, the other for the profile.'[7] There are certainly more full-face pictures of Hillier than of Ryan, and more profiles of Ryan than Hillier. The two Marys and May Prinsep look so alike that one has often to look extremely carefully to be certain which is which; the Cameron literature has a considerable number of misidentifications.

Mary Ryan was in some ways treated more as a member of the family than a maid, as Sir Henry Taylor noticed during a visit to Dimbola in April 1861:

Went to the schoolhouse to pay my respects to the governess: and there I found at her studies besides the two small Cameronian boys, a very pretty little girl of thirteen, whom I supposed to be a visitor or the child of a neighbour taking a casual lesson. She proved to be a beggar who, with her mother, had begged of Mrs Cameron on Putney Heath some months ago. They were Irish, and Mrs Cameron had got a good account of them from a priest (in Glasgow, I think) and established them in her lodge in Putney Heath and gave them work: and when she came hither she put the mother in the way of getting a living, and brought the child with her. She is very quick, and excessively fond of reading and learning. What will become of her?[8]

Mary Ann Hillier, the daughter of an Isle of Wight shoemaker, was perhaps the less obviously beautiful of the two Marys: 'Her particular favorite for a long time was a servant girl, who to the ordinary eye was no beauty, but who became the artist's idol. She certainly posed beautifully, and … some of her finest photographs were pictures of this girl, of whom she made a pet.'[9] Watts used her as a model for a few paintings, among them *Fair Daffodils* (present whereabouts unknown), begun in the 1860s but not finished until the 1890s.

Whatever it was about Hillier ('one of the most beautiful & constant of my models'[10]) that appealed to Julia Margaret, it clearly made her think of religious subjects, and Hillier was frequently posed as the Madonna. When she became an angel, it was as a specifically Christian one – as in *The Angel at the Sepulchre* and *The Angel at the Tomb* (see pp.128 and 129), though the biblical originals were of course male. *Call, I Follow, I Follow, Let Me Die* (see p.134), another profile of Hillier, dressed in velvet and with her hair down (no respectable woman ever let her hair down in company), shows Julia Margaret's work in its most Pre-Raphaelite manner, demonstrating that although the Brotherhood had dissolved a decade before she took up photography, she was familiar with their paintings. This picture, in particular, is very like some of Dante Gabriel Rossetti's (1828–82) portraits of the great loves of his life, Jane Morris and Elizabeth Siddal (especially *Beata Beatrix*, painted in 1870, now in Tate Britain, in which the blurred background has a distinctly Cameronian feel). But it is actually more expressive than either.

The artist Walford Graham Robertson (1866–1948) commented on the similarity between Jane Morris and one of Julia Margaret's favourite models, Marie Spartali: 'The two marvels had many points in common: the same lofty stature, the same long sweep of limb, the "neck like a tower", the night-dark tresses and the eyes of mystery.' Robertson thought Spartali's 'loveliness conformed to the standard of ancient Greece and could at once be appreciated' and Julia Margaret, who photographed her a score of times, responded to these looks by frequently making Marie a character from Greek mythology.[11]

Mary Ryan, though she could also look very Pre-Raphaelite, appears more often to have inspired Cameron in a more secular way. Her youthful beauty and grace made her the obvious choice for Shakespeare's Miranda, Tennyson's 'May Queen' and, most romantically of all, his 'Gardener's Daughter' (see p.127). However, although Ryan is seen in solo religious poses less frequently, Julia Margaret obviously considered her to resemble the models of Renaissance painters closely enough for her to be posed in *After the manner of Perugino* (see p.124), a print clearly cropped from the full original image, and in *A Study after the manner of Francia* (see p.125). In deliberately alluding to the style of painters admired by the Pre-Raphaelites, Julia Margaret was once again influenced by Watts, who wrote of the supremacy of Angelico, Perugino, Francia and Raphael as painters of religious subjects, and of Michelangelo for 'the might of his imagination'.[12] Julia Margaret made pictures in homage to them all, as well as Giotto and Leonardo da Vinci. She, and her more sympathetic critics, called her Madonnas 'Raphaelesque'.

The Madonna and Child pictures demonstrate one of Julia Margaret's practical difficulties. Look carefully at a Renaissance original, and the Infant Jesus sometimes seems

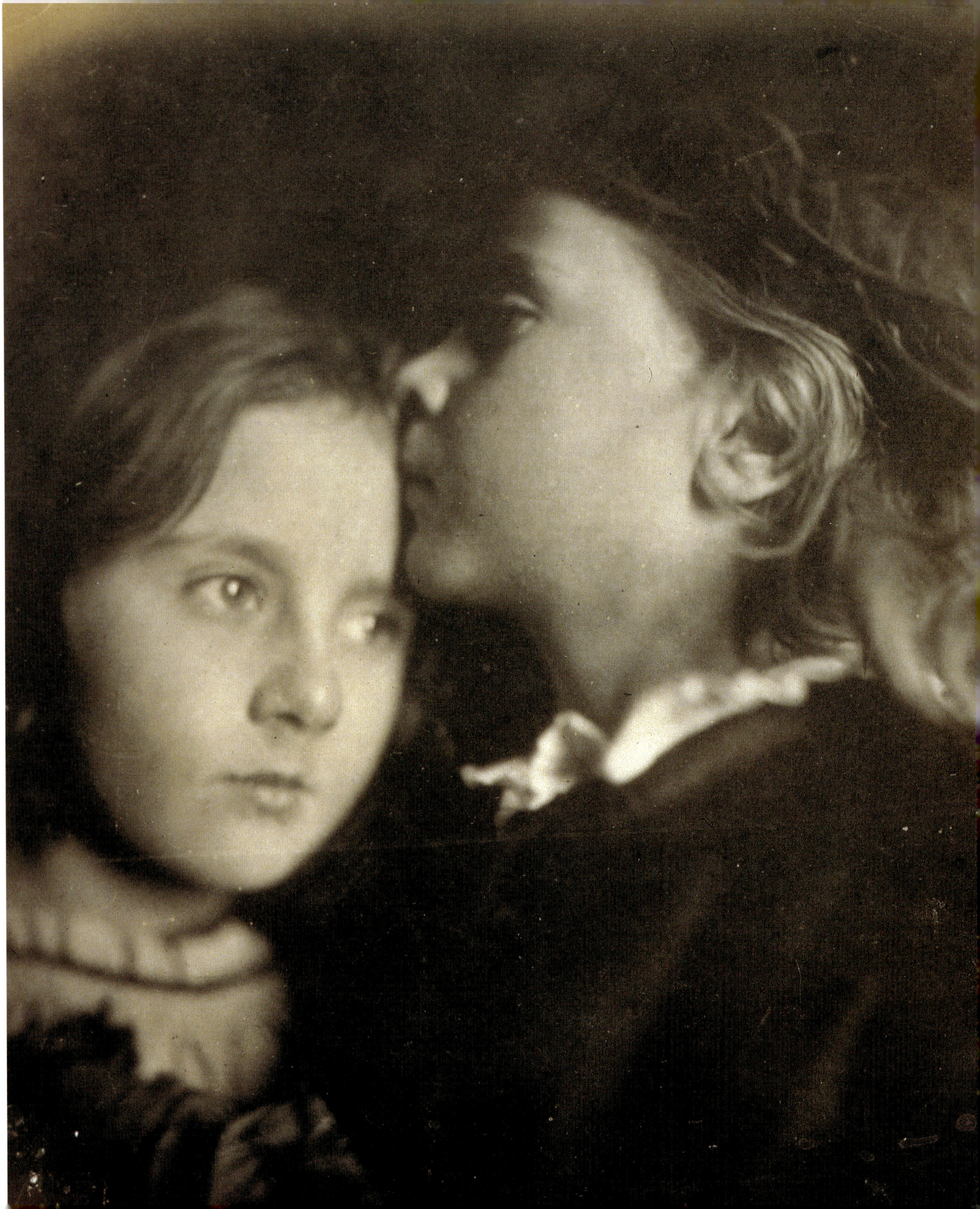

chose her parlourmaids largely for their beauty,' wrote Wilfrid Ward,[6] and Julia Margaret's friend Adolphus Liddell (1846–1920), cousin of Lewis Carroll's muse Alice Liddell, said of the two Marys that 'One of them usually sat for the full face, the other for the profile.'[7] There are certainly more full-face pictures of Hillier than of Ryan, and more profiles of Ryan than Hillier. The two Marys and May Prinsep look so alike that one has often to look extremely carefully to be certain which is which; the Cameron literature has a considerable number of misidentifications.

Mary Ryan was in some ways treated more as a member of the family than a maid, as Sir Henry Taylor noticed during a visit to Dimbola in April 1861:

Went to the schoolhouse to pay my respects to the governess: and there I found at her studies besides the two small Cameronian boys, a very pretty little girl of thirteen, whom I supposed to be a visitor or the child of a neighbour taking a casual lesson. She proved to be a beggar who, with her mother, had begged of Mrs Cameron on Putney Heath some months ago. They were Irish, and Mrs Cameron had got a good account of them from a priest (in Glasgow, I think) and established them in her lodge in Putney Heath and gave them work: and when she came hither she put the mother in the way of getting a living, and brought the child with her. She is very quick, and excessively fond of reading and learning. What will become of her?[8]

Mary Ann Hillier, the daughter of an Isle of Wight shoemaker, was perhaps the less obviously beautiful of the two Marys: 'Her particular favorite for a long time was a servant girl, who to the ordinary eye was no beauty, but who became the artist's idol. She certainly posed beautifully, and … some of her finest photographs were pictures of this girl, of whom she made a pet.'[9] Watts used her as a model for a few paintings, among them *Fair Daffodils* (present whereabouts unknown), begun in the 1860s but not finished until the 1890s.

Whatever it was about Hillier ('one of the most beautiful & constant of my models'[10]) that appealed to Julia Margaret, it clearly made her think of religious subjects, and Hillier was frequently posed as the Madonna. When she became an angel, it was as a specifically Christian one – as in *The Angel at the Sepulchre* and *The Angel at the Tomb* (see pp.128 and 129), though the biblical originals were of course male. *Call, I Follow, I Follow, Let Me Die* (see p.134), another profile of Hillier, dressed in velvet and with her hair down (no respectable woman ever let her hair down in company), shows Julia Margaret's work in its most Pre-Raphaelite manner, demonstrating that although the Brotherhood had dissolved a decade before she took up photography, she was familiar with their paintings. This picture, in particular, is very like some of Dante Gabriel Rossetti's (1828–82) portraits of the great loves of his life, Jane Morris and Elizabeth Siddal (especially *Beata Beatrix*, painted in 1870, now in Tate Britain, in which the blurred background has a distinctly Cameronian feel). But it is actually more expressive than either.

The artist Walford Graham Robertson (1866–1948) commented on the similarity between Jane Morris and one of Julia Margaret's favourite models, Marie Spartali: 'The two marvels had many points in common: the same lofty stature, the same long sweep of limb, the "neck like a tower", the night-dark tresses and the eyes of mystery.' Robertson thought Spartali's 'loveliness conformed to the standard of ancient Greece and could at once be appreciated' and Julia Margaret, who photographed her a score of times, responded to these looks by frequently making Marie a character from Greek mythology.[11]

Mary Ryan, though she could also look very Pre-Raphaelite, appears more often to have inspired Cameron in a more secular way. Her youthful beauty and grace made her the obvious choice for Shakespeare's Miranda, Tennyson's 'May Queen' and, most romantically of all, his 'Gardener's Daughter' (see p.127). However, although Ryan is seen in solo religious poses less frequently, Julia Margaret obviously considered her to resemble the models of Renaissance painters closely enough for her to be posed in *After the manner of Perugino* (see p.124), a print clearly cropped from the full original image, and in *A Study after the manner of Francia* (see p.125). In deliberately alluding to the style of painters admired by the Pre-Raphaelites, Julia Margaret was once again influenced by Watts, who wrote of the supremacy of Angelico, Perugino, Francia and Raphael as painters of religious subjects, and of Michelangelo for 'the might of his imagination'.[12] Julia Margaret made pictures in homage to them all, as well as Giotto and Leonardo da Vinci. She, and her more sympathetic critics, called her Madonnas 'Raphaelesque'.

The Madonna and Child pictures demonstrate one of Julia Margaret's practical difficulties. Look carefully at a Renaissance original, and the Infant Jesus sometimes seems capable of sitting up entirely unsupported, or is so unnaturally small that he can fit into the Madonna's hand. Living babies can do neither, of course, and their poses have to be adjusted accordingly. Real children would have found it difficult to keep absolutely still, especially for the length of time Julia Margaret required for an exposure. This is why she made so many experiments in photographing them asleep, even making montages of a sleeping baby with a watching Madonna.

It was, of course, a difficult business for models of all ages to sit for one of Julia Margaret's photographs, as Anne Thackeray Ritchie attested:

Mrs Cameron followed her art of photography with extraordinary trouble and devotion. Sitting was a serious affair not to be lightly entered upon. Her sitters came to her summons, they trembled, or would have trembled, could they have dared, when the round black eye of the Camera was turned upon them. They felt what consequences, what disastrous waste of time and money and effort might ensue from any passing quiver of emotion. For not only had Mrs Cameron to take her own negatives, but sitters in those days would have to sit without moving for not less than ten minutes while the cap was off the lens.[13]

The reporter who interviewed the 78-year-old Mary Ann Hillier for an Isle of Wight newspaper wrote that 'she really detested the sittings, but was always a willing sufferer as she felt, to use her own words, that if it gave pleasure to others to photograph her it was her duty to put up with the inconvenience.'[14] But she, like her brother and sister – who worked for the Tennysons at Farringford – spent most of her life as a domestic servant, and knew her place, even in a free-thinking and generous household like that of the Camerons. Mary Ryan, on the other hand, put all such things behind her before she was twenty years old, as Adolphus Liddell recorded:

Just before I made their acquaintance one of these beauties had become engaged, to the great delight of Mrs Cameron, to a young Indian Civil Servant. There had been an exhibition of her works in London, and the young man had seen some of the portraits of the maiden ... he wrote to Mrs Cameron, and asked leave to pay his addresses. Mrs Cameron at once asked him to stay, and after a time the affair was settled.[15]

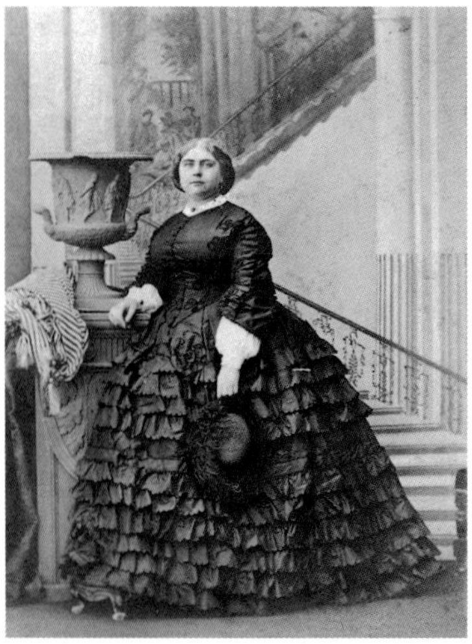

Augusta Wilhelmina Louisa, Duchess of Cambridge (1797–1889)
Camille Silvy, October 1860
Carte-de-visite, 90 x 68mm (3½ x 2¼")
National Portrait Gallery, London (NPG x50823)

More than one visitor noted Mary's presence at Julia Margaret's exhibition at the French Gallery in November 1865. The artist George Price Boyce, for instance, wrote in his diary: 'A very pretty fair girl with lovely tender eyes and light brown hair in attendance'.[16] But it was Henry Cotton – who later became Sir Henry – who married the one-time Irish beggar girl, and made her literally a Lady. This romantic story is told in almost all the eye-witness accounts of life in and around Dimbola, which suggests that Julia Margaret was properly proud of how she had changed Mary Ryan's life for the better, and told everybody about it. Cotton tells it in his own autobiography but, unlike everyone else, says it was at Little Holland House that he first got to know his wife-to-be, rather than Dimbola:

It was within those walls when she was staying there with Mrs Cameron, that I wooed and won the fairest of fair young girls who became my wife on the 1st of August, 1867, and who has since been my devoted companion and help-mate for better and for worse through many years of vicissitudes and successes, sorrows and aspirations, clouds and sunshine.[17]

Nowadays, we would find Julia Margaret rather patronising about her local models: 'The peasantry of our island is very handsome. From the men, the women, the maidens and the children I have had lovely subjects, as all the patrons of my photography know.'[18] Nevertheless, her photographs accord these men, women and children, if not heroic qualities, real dignity. Perhaps this is one of the ways in which the influence of her husband, so rarely acknowledged, played a part. He was, after all, a disciple of the Utilitarian Jeremy Bentham and believed in 'the greatest good for the greatest number'. Part of his difficulties with the establishment in India, as we have seen, derived from his wish to see that the children of Indians received the best possible education.

To gauge the full originality and impact of Julia Margaret's pictures of people, whether famous or unknown, one has only to study family albums of the time, full of the sort of portraits that were in vogue. Since the beginnings of the 1860s, these had been the tiny cartes-de-visite (so called all over the world as they had been invented in France), measuring about 10 x 6cm (4 x 2¼"). In an essay on Julia Margaret's photography for an exhibition of her work at Colnaghi's, Anne Thackeray Ritchie rightly pours scorn on these stereotyped and mass-produced portrayals of people surrounded by the 'dining room chairs, small tables, and plaster pedestals to which photography has accustomed us'. The skill of the man (and occasional woman) behind the camera was restricted to instructions to 'place one elbow upon the table ... to point the little finger if you are a lady, to put one hand into your pocket if you are a man'. Thackeray Ritchie goes on to describe very accurately the difference between such pictures and Julia Margaret's:

People like clear hard outlines, and have a fancy to see themselves and their friends as if through opera-glasses, all complete, with the buttons, &c. nicely defined. These things Mrs Cameron's public may not always find, but in their stead are very wonderful and charming sights and suggestions ... A well-known photographer said the other day that hers was the real and artistic manner of working the camera; that he, too, had tried to photograph 'out of focus' as it is called but the public would not accept it, and he had therefore been obliged to give it up.[19]

Curiously, there is a set of about twelve of Julia Margaret's photographs of May Prinsep which seem to embrace the conventional, overdressed, sharp aesthetic of the carte-de-visite. In these atypically domestic scenes, May, her hair neatly up rather than let down and tousled, writes letters, winds wool, and performs other lady-like tasks. Equally lady-like accoutrements – writing paper, pen, candle, a bible, birdcage, etc. – surround her, all clearly lit and sharply focused, as are her desk and chair. One can of course read these as symbols: a bible represents Christian virtue and a bird in a cage often symbolises the trapped status of women at the time (in one picture, the stuffed bird has left the cage and perches on the desk). But these pictures were also probably a manifestation of Julia Margaret's wish to make money from her photography. She told Herschel that: 'When I started photography I hoped it might help me in the education of one of my Boys: I soon found that its outlay doubled its returns so that it became a duty to me to recover my expenditure.'[20] As any such hopes were constantly disappointed, it is tempting to think that this group of pictures was a conscious attempt to create something that would be more acceptable to the general public. It was an experiment she did not repeat.

With the exception of the May Prinsep series, and a handful of more conventional portraits of mature women (including Anne Thackeray Ritchie herself), the dresses and poses Julia Margaret chose for her female models surely also owe something to her husband Charles, and his 1835 essay 'The Sublime & the Beautiful':

Everything ... which droops ... has a sorrowful and beautiful expression. Hence it is, that the painters when they would fill the mind with images of grief, not only dispose the heads and limbs of their figures as grief would dispose them, but take care that the hair and the drapery shall also droop.[21]

Julia Margaret frequently made her models let their hair down and wear the sort of flowing drapery that she and her sisters preferred. Watts was so much in favour of this kind of dress that he became the President of the Anti-Tight Lacing Society![22]

The fact that Julia Margaret's models never smile has a lot to do with the extreme length of exposure she used: 'I longed to arrest all beauty that came before me,'[23] she said. To understand how difficult it is to smile and keep still for a minute or more – without moving a muscle – stand in front of a mirror and try it! But it seems to me that the Cameronian ideal of beauty – like that of the Pre-Raphaelites – was in any case essentially an unsmiling, melancholy one. For Julia Margaret, life, love and the personification of beauty were a very serious business. Today, by contrast, the tendency is to smirk at any camera we notice pointing at us. As we shall see, Julia Margaret's taste for the melancholy tended to make her choose characters in tragic situations (*Suspense*; see p.140).

Of course, life for a Victorian woman was in truth serious and tough. In the 1860s, an ideal wife and mother was expected, as Mrs Beeton put it, to be 'a formidable leader with a responsibility to teach, nurse, and above all exemplify to her servants the proper morality, charity, cleanliness, frugality, and self-sacrifice'.[24] Julia Margaret, always short of money, with a houseful of children and a semi-invalid husband who virtually never left the house or its gardens, had to accept even more responsibility than most of her middle- and upper-class peers – and they were not usually attempting to fulfil an ambition to be major artists.

As I have already suggested, Julia Margaret photographed a number of more mature women, none of whom look remotely Pre-Raphaelite. I share Anne Thackeray Ritchie's regret that she never photographed Emily Tennyson: 'would that Mrs Cameron herself had also pictured the friend to whom all her life long she was so tenderly attached.'[25] But she did photograph a number of aristocratic women, such as Lady Elcho (who became the Countess of Wemyss when her husband succeeded to the title in 1883), Lady Hood (who married the 4th Viscount in 1865) and the Marchioness of Lothian (who married the

8th Marquess in 1857). Their images will not be found in this book because they seem to me to be the dullest of her works. Nevertheless, it would have been interesting to see the results of what was apparently her only royal photographic session. In the summer of 1867, according to Adolphus Liddell, who was staying with her at Dimbola: 'She had had another triumph. The Crown Prince and Princess of Prussia had come to Ventnor for a quiet time, and were living in the strictest retirement, seeing no one but their own family. Mrs Cameron, however, set to work, and somehow or other succeeded in time not only in being admitted to their house, but in photographing the Crown Prince himself.'[26]

The Crown Princess was Queen Victoria's eldest daughter, Victoria Adelaide Mary Louise (1840–1901), and the couple were staying at the royal holiday home, Osborne House, rather than Ventnor. Julia Margaret herself wrote that 'it has just fallen to my lot to have the privilege of photographing the Crown Prince and Crown Princess of Germany and Prussia,'[27] and later received the Princess's permission to dedicate her illustrated edition of Tennyson's *Idylls of the King* to her, so we can be sure the portrait session actually took place, probably in 1874. But, since no print of either the Crown Prince or Princess has so far been identified, it must surely have been a failure – or perhaps the negatives were broken. Otherwise, Julia Margaret would certainly have made numbers of prints for circulation, exhibition and sale.

It seems to me that Julia Margaret's heart was not in these 'straight' portraits of conventional women. The individuals who demanded her fullest attention, apart from heroic men, were immature young women and enchanting children – in whom she could see the 'Beauty' which was the ultimate target of all her work. And with them, she achieved the most remarkable, and enduring results: 'Woman herself, her soul withdrawn behind those heavy eyelids, the mystery, the challenge, the torment, the solace.'[28]

The woman so described was Ellen Terry, whose portrait appeared in Helmut Gernsheim's 1948 monograph *Julia Margaret Cameron*. The author who responded to it so strongly, and so convincingly, was J.B. Priestley (1894–1984). Nowadays, we might quibble at his distinction between a photograph and 'art', but it is nevertheless a well-deserved tribute to a photographer who certainly knew how to make women look beautiful, and who also preserved their characters and their individuality for posterity.

NOTES

1. *Photographic News*, II, 37, 20 May 1859, p.125.
2. Sir Leslie Stephen (ed.), *Dictionary of National Biography*, VIII (Smith, Elder & Co., London, 1882–1900), p.300.
3. Woolf, 1927; reprint 1932, p.303.
4. Patmore's 'domestic epic', inspired by – and dedicated to – his wife, Emily, remained popular throughout the nineteenth century. In the twentieth century, it naturally fell out of favour and Virginia Woolf thought that 'Killing the Angel in the House was part of the occupation of a woman writer' (in her 1931 essay 'Professions for Women').
5. Thackeray Ritchie, 1877; reprinted 1996, p.35.
6. Wilfrid Ward, 'Tennyson at Freshwater', *Dublin Review*, 1912.
7. Liddell, 1911, p.85.
8. Taylor, II, 1885, p.154.
9. Ellison, 1907, p.75.
10. 'Annals of my Glass House', p.13.
11. W. Graham Robertson, *Time Was*, p.95. Quoted in Maas, 1984, p.119.
12. Taylor, 1853, quoted in Ford, 1975, p.129.
13. Thackeray Fuller and Hammersley, 1951, p.110.
14. Interview published in the *Isle of Wight County Press*, 3 April 1926.
15. Liddell, 1911, pp.85–6.
16. G.P. Boyce, *Diary*. Quoted in Maas, 1975, p.186.
17. Cotton, 1911, p.54.
18. 'Annals of my Glass House', p.7.
19. This essay is published in Thackeray Ritchie, 1874, pp.224–9.
20. Letter from Julia Margaret to Herschel, 28 January 1866, Library of the Royal Society of London.
21. C.H. Cameron, 'The Sublime & the Beautiful', from *Two Essays* (privately printed, London, 1835), p.186.
22. He was asked to accept the post by the society's secretary, Gertie Tippla of Norwood, who did not want 'any old women or "strong-minded" (so-called) females in our committee' (Chapman, 1945, p.138).
23. 'Annals of my Glass House', p.4.
24. Isabella Mary Beeton's *Book of Household Management* (1861), quoted in Wolf, 1998, p.44.
25. Thackeray Ritchie and Cameron, 1893, p.11.
26. Liddell, 1911, p.85.
27. 'Annals of my Glass House', p.16.
28. Priestley's 1949 essay on an 'Old Photograph' is quoted in Hopkinson, 1986, p.30.

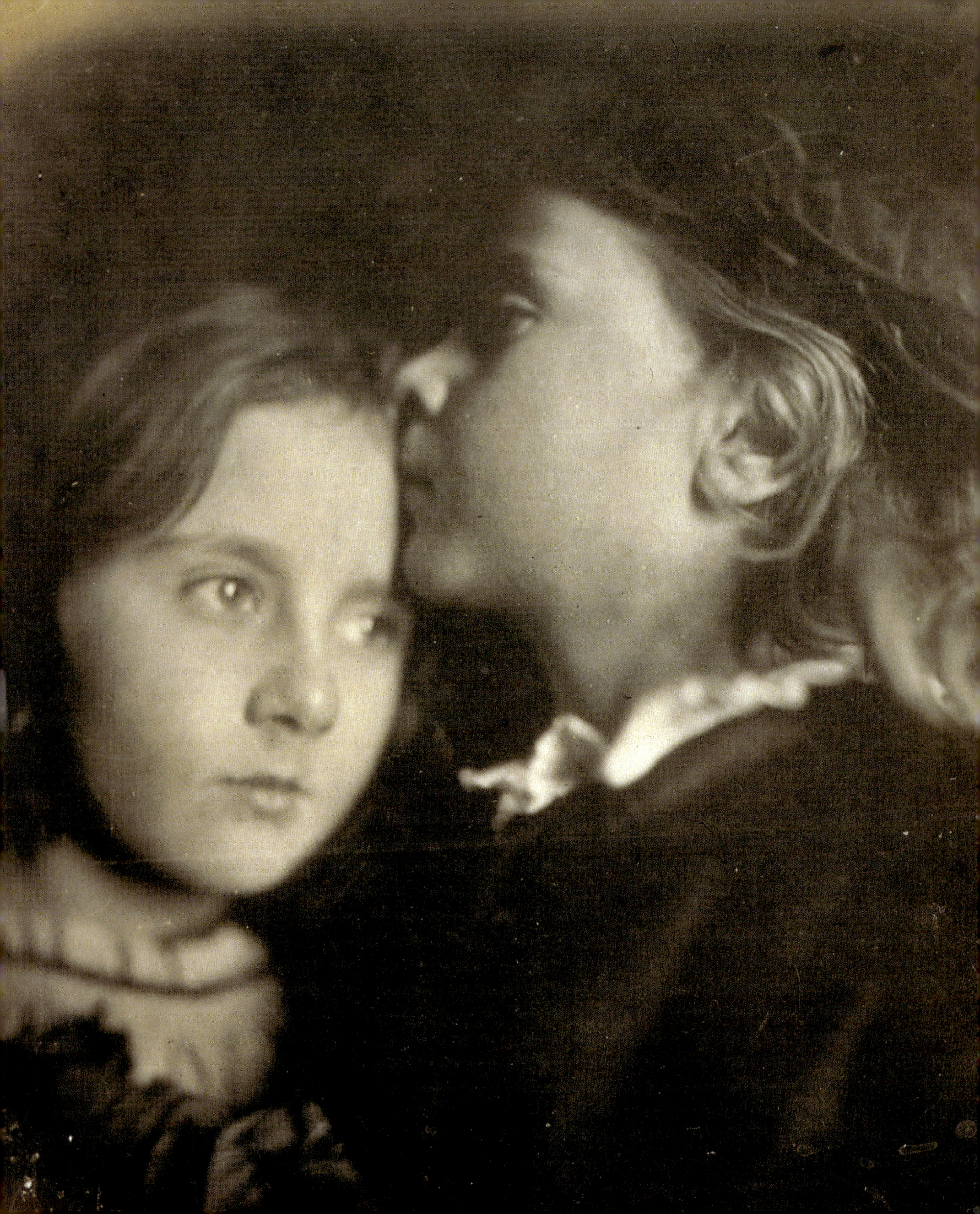

Solemn eyes and fair waving locks When Julia Margaret Cameron photographed Ellen Terry, the young actress was sixteen years old (though she told everyone she was fifteen, thinking all her life that she had been born a year later than she really was). The fact that Ellen had specialised in playing young boys on the stage perhaps made her even more child-like; she certainly looks more a child than a woman of marriageable age. If, as we have seen, Julia Margaret found a particular beauty in such teenage femininity, she loved children of all ages, boys as well as girls ('The eyes of the first grandchild should be more beautiful than any flower,' she told her husband),[1] and brought up no fewer than twelve of them.

In addition to her own five sons and a daughter (as well as a son who died in infancy), Julia Margaret adopted five other children. Two of these – Mary and Adeline Clogstoun – were the granddaughters of her eldest sister Adeline Maria and her husband Colin Mackenzie, a captain in the Madras Infantry. Mary and Adeline were taken into the Camerons' care after the deaths of both their own parents, Herbert Mackworth Clogstoun (who had won a Victoria Cross leading a charge during the Indian Mutiny in January 1859) and his wife Mary Julia (Herbert died in 1862, Mary in 1870). Their grandmother had died when she was only twenty-four years old. By tragic coincidence, Adeline Clogstoun herself died at an even younger age than her mother and grandmother. She was only ten years and eight months old when Julia Margaret photographed her on her deathbed on 8 June 1872.[2] Nowadays we might find such pictures distasteful, but they were frequent subjects for Victorian painters, illustrators and photographers, and were undoubtedly a great comfort in an age with such a high rate of infant mortality.

Ernest and Maggie, 1864–5
Unknown sitters (detail from p.170)
National Museum of Photography, Film & Television, Bradford

The other three Cameron adoptees – Cyllena, Melita and Sheridan Wilson – were the grandchildren of the Reverend Samuel Sheridan Wilson.[3] After their mother, Cyllena, died in 1863, and their father and grandfather in the early 1860s, the orphans were taken into the Cameron household. The teenaged Cyllena (1851–83) appears in a number of Julia Margaret's pictures but seems to have rather disliked the experience, which was perhaps partly why she ran away from Freshwater in 1870. The twelfth child in the Cameron household, brought up by Julia Margaret if not actually adopted by her, was Mary Ryan, the favourite model we met in the last chapter.

Having been used to her various homes being full of children for so long, Julia Margaret wrote to William Michael Rossetti at the beginning of 1866 that 'for the *first* time in 26 years I am left without a child under my roof – but they are all doing well and struggling to improve and I must not grudge the sacrifice of their sweet society.'[4] From now on, she would have to search beyond her immediate family for child models. We have already seen that her very first successful photograph was of a child, and her ideal of beauty found a particular manifestation in children's 'solemn eyes and fair waving locks'.[5] She shared this – and her view of the sanctity of childhood – with many of her contemporaries. Lewis Carroll – though he had some doubts about Julia Margaret's aesthetics and technique – surely agreed with her. The two photographers certainly knew each other, having apparently first met in April 1862, when they showed their photographs to each other, and mutually criticised them. On that occasion, Julia Margaret gave Carroll a photograph of Tennyson and he gave her a copy of his Index to Tennyson's *In Memoriam*.[6] The well-documented fact that Carroll was most at ease in the company of children is reflected in the considerable number of photographs he made of them. By coincidence, he saw Julia Margaret's first two child models on the beach during a summer holiday in Freshwater in 1864, and asked Julia Margaret 'if she would photograph for me (*in* focus) the prettiest two, one being a child of Mr Bradley's, the master of Marlborough'.[7] These were Margaret Louisa 'Daisy' Bradley (whom Carroll himself managed to photograph eight years later), and Annie Wilhelmina Philpot, Julia Margaret's 'first success'.

Like Carroll, Julia Margaret was always on the lookout for child models, as young visitors and residents alike soon learned:

Mrs Cameron was neither mysterious nor awe-inspiring, but just a kind, exacting, though benevolent, tyrant. Children loved but fled from her. I can see her now, clad in the never-failing wrapper, stained – as were her hands and eager face – with the chemicals she used in her work, her hair falling any way but the right way, lying in wait some fine morning at her garden-gate for the young ones passing down the road on their way to Farringford or to the sands of Freshwater bay.

'She's coming! She'll catch one of us!'

And sure enough an arm would intercept the passage of some luckless wight, and, bribed by jars of preserve or other toothsome dainty, the victim was led away to spend the sunny hours posing in the studio. Photography was then, at the best, a slow and tiresome process, and Mrs Cameron never hurried in her work. Endless were the poses, especially if, as was often the case, the chosen victim was to represent some character in poem and story.[8]

Julia Margaret's young victims were – like Daisy Bradley and Annie Philpot – often the children of visitors to Dimbola and Farringford. But they were also often local residents. Young Freddy Gould, who posed as several biblical characters, including Christ, was the son of a fisherman. With him often appear one or more of the four children of Thomas Keown, Master Gunner at Freshwater Redoubt, the Royal Artillery fort within sight of Dimbola. Julia Margaret photographed Gould and the two youngest Keowns – Alice Jessie and Percy Seymour – from the age of three. She posed one of her grandsons, Archibald Hay Cameron, at the age of two years and three months, as the infant Christ, asleep – presumably that was the only way to ensure that he kept still. Given this problem, one of the most striking of Julia Margaret's early child portraits is that of Georgina Anna Mary Pictet, a great-niece, aged not much more than a year old (see opposite). Little *Baby 'Pictet'* had apparently survived two shipwrecks off the Indian coast, which seems to have earned her the right to be warmly dressed and bonneted rather than in her underclothes, and to be given her own name rather than that of some character in fiction. Also taken in the summer of 1864, the 3½-year-old Alice du Cane (see p.94) is wrapped in a cloth or sheet, but she too looks unblinkingly at the camera during what can only have been a long exposure time. Even one of Julia Margaret's admirers at the time thought that 'The masses of white in the children's dresses ... are such as to destroy any balance of colour in composition,'[9] but this is more than counter-balanced by what the same writer calls 'the truth of physiognomic expression that may be recognised in these faces' and by the way the photographer fills the frame with these youngsters' heads and shoulders (just as she did with adults), bringing them dramatically close to her camera and to the viewer. For her models, it must have been an uncomfortable experience:

As I write, a respectable matron beside me exclaims at the remembrance of that solemn ordeal of the glass house and the prick of the angels' wings fastened upon her bare shoulders in infant days. What was it to her in those times whether or not an exquisite little picture of cherubim, or seraphim, was given to the world, a picture which is now a delight and possession to her own descendants in turn.[10]

For some of these children, Julia Margaret's fondness for photographing them in very few clothes must have been somewhat embarrassing. Some years ago, a descendant of Alice Keown wrote to tell me that the little girl had tears running down her cheeks in one photograph, because she was posing in only a vest; not only was she very cold, but the

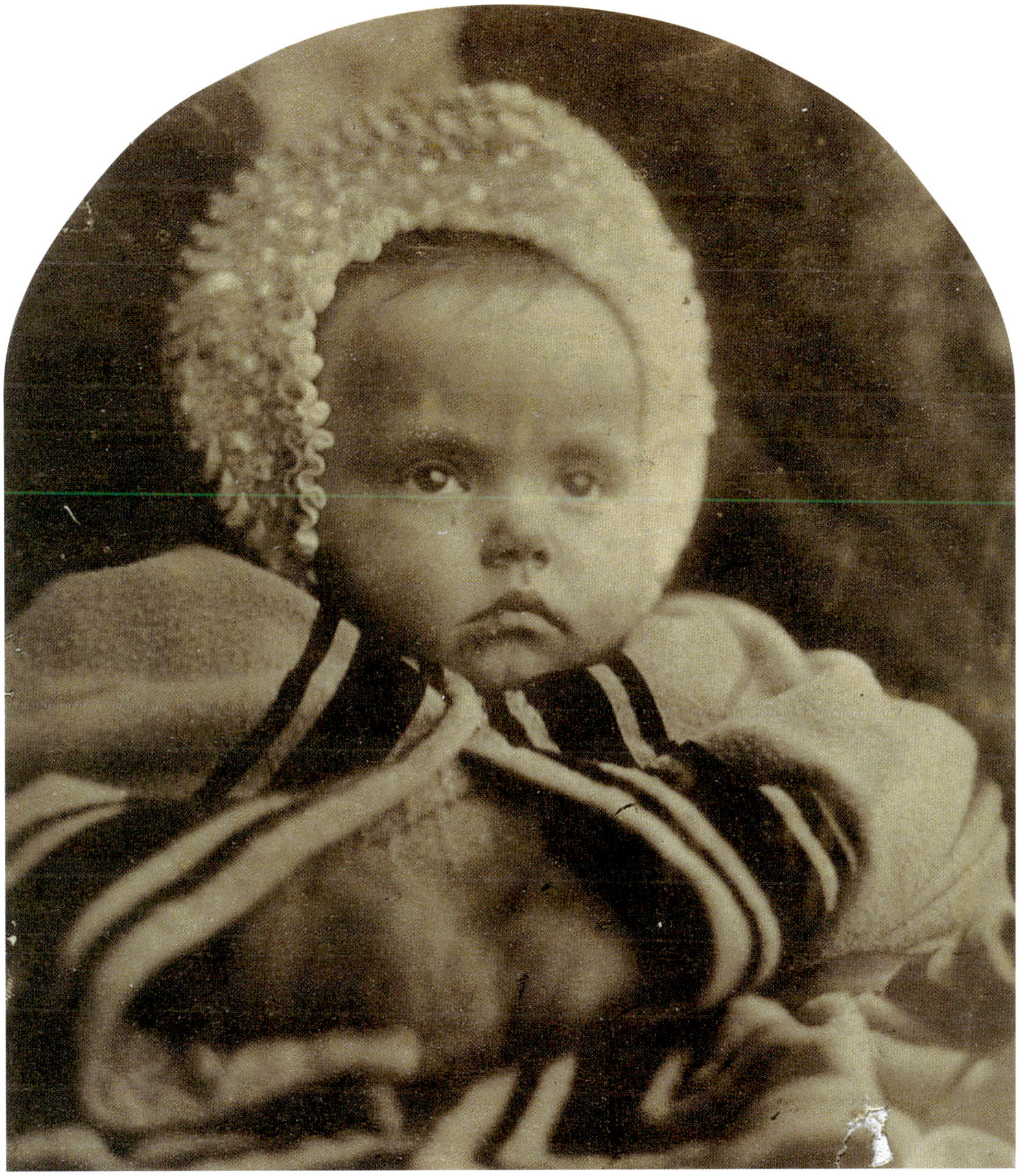

Baby 'Pictet', April 1864
'One year Old Infant shipwrecked once in the Madras Surf
& again in the wreck of the Colombo Steamer'
Georgina Anna Mary Pictet
Albumen print, 172 x 148mm (6¾ x 5⅞")
National Museum of Photography, Film & Television, Bradford

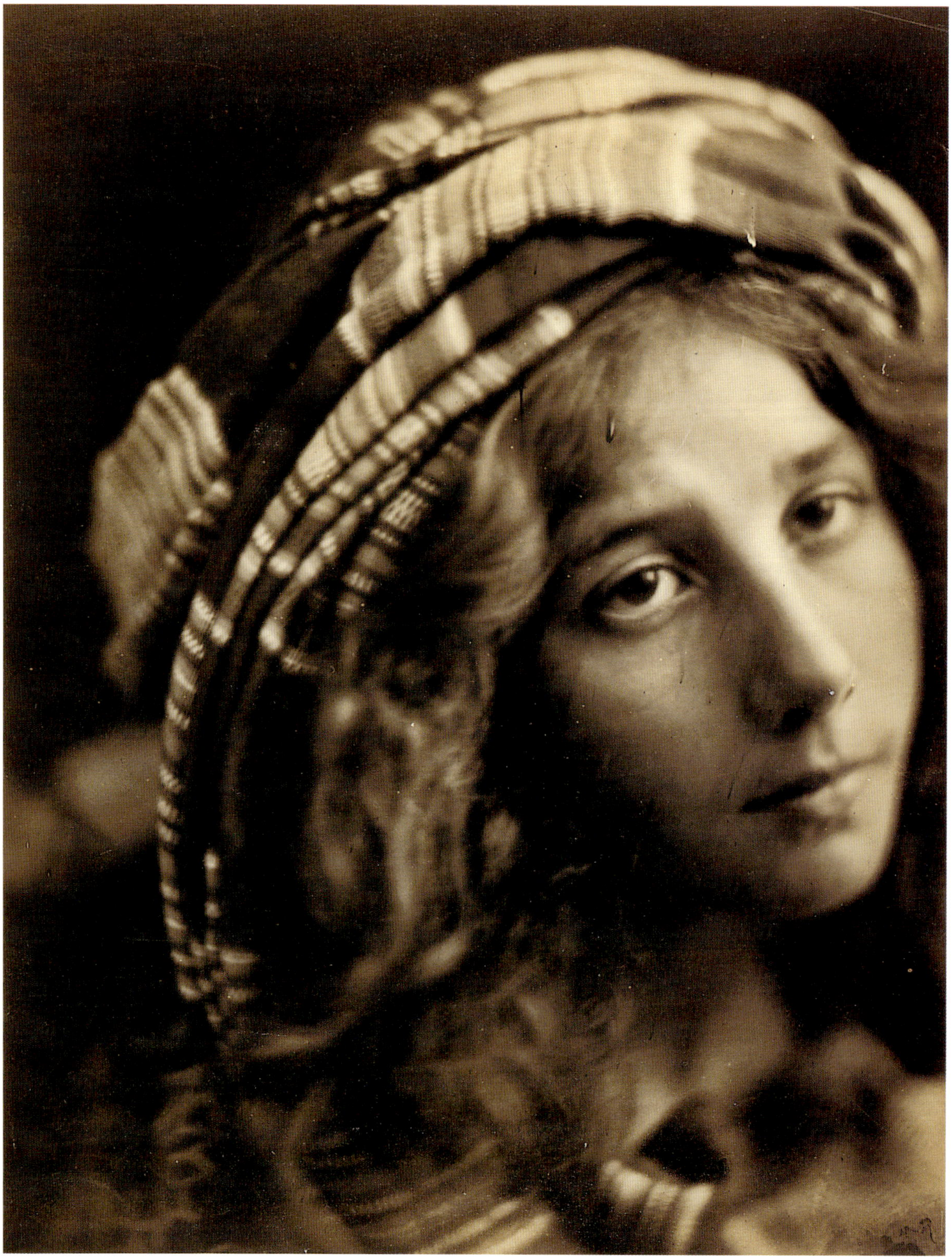

Beatrice Cenci, May 1868
Kate Keown
Albumen print, 327 x 246mm (12⅞ x 9⅝")
The J. Paul Getty Museum, Los Angeles

curate at Freshwater church came in! On another occasion, I was informed, Elizabeth Keown refused to pose with Tennyson because he had a runny nose. This must surely be a family legend, since Tennyson never seems to have consented to pose in any of Julia Margaret's photographic illustrations; I rather doubt if she ever dared ask him.

Julia Margaret undoubtedly found it easier to scare children into participating, as her great-niece Laura Gurney later recalled:

Aunt Julia appeared as a terrifying elderly woman, short and squat, with none of the Pattle grace and beauty about her. Dressed in dark clothes, stained with chemicals from her photography (and smelling of them, too) with a plump eager face and piercing eyes, and a voice husky and a little harsh, yet in some way compelling and even charming. We were at once pressed into the service of the camera ... No wonder those old photographs of us, leaning over imaginary ramparts of heaven, look anxious and wistful. This was how we felt ... 'Stand there,' she shouted, and we stood for hours, gazing at the model of the heavenly babe (in reality a sleeping child deposited in a property manger). The parents, anxious and uneasy, were outside, no more able to rescue their infant until Aunt Julia had finished with it than we would have been.[11]

Reviewing an exhibition ten years after Julia Margaret's death, George Bernard Shaw (1856–1950), while an art critic for the *Star*, wrote about the results of that and similar photo sessions:

While the portraits of Herschel, Tennyson and Carlyle beat hollow anything I have ever seen, right on the same wall, and virtually in the same frame, there are photographs of children with no clothes on, or else the underclothes by way of propriety, with palpably paper wings, most inartistically grouped and artlessly labelled as angels, saints or fairies. No one would imagine that the artist who produced the marvellous Carlyle would have produced such childish trivialities.[12]

Many commentators have shared Shaw's view that these photographs are inartistic and trivial, and it is true that the young children chosen by Julia Margaret often find it difficult to take on with any conviction the personae which she thrusts upon them. The younger the child, the more difficult it is to be anything but herself or himself. The problem is exacerbated by the fact that Julia Margaret frequently opts for rather younger children than the narrative she is illustrating calls for. The 4½-year-old Freddy Gould represents the 12-year-old Christ on his return from the Temple after the annual Passover celebration (see p.155); Kate Keown (1857–1922) plays the 16-year-old Beatrice Cenci (see opposite). Julia Margaret also seems indifferent to the gender of her child models (which rather belies the modern tendency to find sexuality in them). She poses one great-niece, Florence Fisher, as St John the Baptist as a child, and two others, Rachel and Laura Gurney, as angels and archangels. Sixty years later, the latter recalled the experience:

We, Rachel and I, were pressed into the service of the camera. Our roles were no less than those of two Angels of the Nativity, and to sustain them we were scantily clad, and each had a pair of heavy swan wings fastened to her narrow shoulders, while Aunt Julia, with ungentle hand, tousled our hair to get rid of its prim nursery look.[13]

Julia Margaret surely dressed these young children in their white underclothes to underline their purity. Carroll wrote to the illustrator of his *Sylvie and Bruno* (1889): 'I am charmed with your idea of dressing her [Sylvie] in *white*: it exactly fits my own idea of her: I want her to be the embodiment of a sort of Purity.'[14] But the soft texture of underwear, and the sort of loose drapes that Julia Margaret often used for her younger women models, also helped her to give a sculptural, three-dimensional quality to her subjects. It is a softer, more feminine, equivalent to the raking lighting she used for her heroic male subjects. Add to this her mastery over lighting ('a well-arranged light is of paramount importance ... as without it all softness of feature is hopeless,'[15] wrote Carroll in a review of the 1860 Photographic Society of London exhibition) and soft focus, and Julia Margaret was able to round out and model the three-dimensional human face and form in a way which other photographers simply could not match. As she told Herschel at the end of her first year of photography: 'I believe in other than mere conventional topographic photography – map making and skeleton rendering of feature and form without that roundness and fullness of face and feature, that modelling of flesh and limb which the focus I use only can give.'[16] Even the occasional photography critic of the time admitted that he had never seen 'more life-like heads'.[17]

A number of modern commentators on Julia Margaret's pictures – and those of Lewis Carroll and Lady Hawarden, both of whom frequently dressed their young women and children in underclothes or nightdresses – see a sexual element in these pictures, finding the skimpy clothing, or the way it is draped when it is worn, suggestive. Such views are surely a product of our own age, with its frequent revelations about paedophiles and child abuse, than of the nineteenth century. Compare our attitude towards them with our view of those Victorian erotic photographs of adult women which really were intended to be pornographic. Today, these seem harmless enough: exploitative of their models perhaps, but almost charming – and totally unarousing. Once-shocking images have become safe, while Carroll's innocent nudes of children (taken at a time when child prostitution was rife), have become dangerous and threatening. Now regularly attacked as some kind of secret paedophile, he would have been horrified at the mere suggestion.

The most exotic and unexpected of Julia Margaret's child pictures is the series she took in 1868 of the 7-year-old Prince Déjatch Alámayou of Abyssinia (now Ethiopia). Earlier that year, his father Emperor Theodore II had committed suicide in order to avoid capture by a military expedition led by General Robert Napier, 1st Baron Napier of Magdala (1810–90). Déjatch came to Britain as the protégé of Queen Victoria, and visited the Isle of Wight with his guardian and tutor, Captain Tristram Speedy. Since living in England, Déjatch had worn Western dress but, as Emma Darwin, wife of Charles, wrote to her son George in 1868: 'Yesterday the little Abyssinian Prince & his Capt. Speedy came to be phoed [*sic*] – they dressed up in Abyssinian dress & we went over to see them.'[18] The costume in the photograph (see p.177) was described by William Allingham: 'They dress to be photographed by Mrs C. The Prince in a little purple shirt and a necklace, Captain Speedy in a lion tippet, with a huge Abyssinian sword of reaping-hook shape ("point goes into your skull").'[19]

One of Julia Margaret's most successful photographs of children is the double portrait of *Ernest and Maggie* (see p.170). I have never been able to identify the subjects. As there seem to be no documented boys and girls with these names in the family circles of the Camerons or their friends and relatives, it might be thought that they were the children of villagers. But Julia Margaret rarely photographed such children 'in their own right', as it were, or gave them their own names. They were usually made to stand in for characters in illustrations of narrative stories, and I do not know any work of prose or poetry with leading characters called Ernest and Maggie (which sounds rather like a nickname). So this remains one of the many unanswered questions of Cameron scholarship. On the whole, I think it more likely that the answer will be found in an unremembered work of fiction. Certainly, as we shall see in the next chapter, Julia Margaret devoted a great deal of artistic effort and energy to subjects such as these.

NOTES

1. Quoted in Gernsheim, 1948; second edition 1975, p.23.
2. A third orphaned sister, Blanche Margaret Standish Clogstoun (1862–95), was brought up first by Sara Prinsep, then by Lady Henry Somerset. Finally, she was adopted by Watts, inherited his house in Freshwater, and later married Herbert Haldane Somers-Cocks, of Eastnor Castle. Their son Arthur became the 6th Baron Somers.
3. The Reverend Samuel Sheridan Wilson (1797–1866) was a missionary in Malta (where he perhaps met Charles Hay Cameron) and the Ionian Islands. He published a virulently anti-Catholic novel *Agnes Moreville* (1845) and *The Bath Fables on Morals, Manners and Faith, with Illustrative Prose from Many Writers of Celebrity* (1850).
4. Letter from Julia Margaret to Rossetti, 23 January 1866, Humanities Research Center, University of Texas at Austin.
5. 'A Book of Photographs', in Thackeray Ritchie, 1874, pp. 224–9.
6. Taylor and Wakeling, 2002, p.192.
7. Letter from Carroll to his sister Louisa, quoted in Cohen, I, 1979, p.66.
8. Ellison, 1907, pp.72–3.
9. *Art Pictorial & Industrial* (Sampson Low, Marston, and Low & Searle, London, January–June 1872), p.26.
10. Thackeray Ritchie and Cameron, 1893, p.13.
11. Troubridge, 1925, p.38.
12. As quoted in Gernsheim, 1948; second edition 1975, p.67.
13. Troubridge, 1925, p.38.
14. Quoted in Cohen, 1995, p.229.
15. Carroll's unsigned review, 'Photographic Exhibition', was published in *The Illustrated Times* of January 1860.
16. Letter from Julia Margaret to Herschel, 31 March 1864, National Museum of Photography, Film & Television, Bradford.
17. Andrew Wynter, writing in the *British Journal of Photography*, 25 March 1869, p.150.
18. Healey, 2001, p.278.
19. Allingham and Radford, 1907; second edition 1985, p.185.

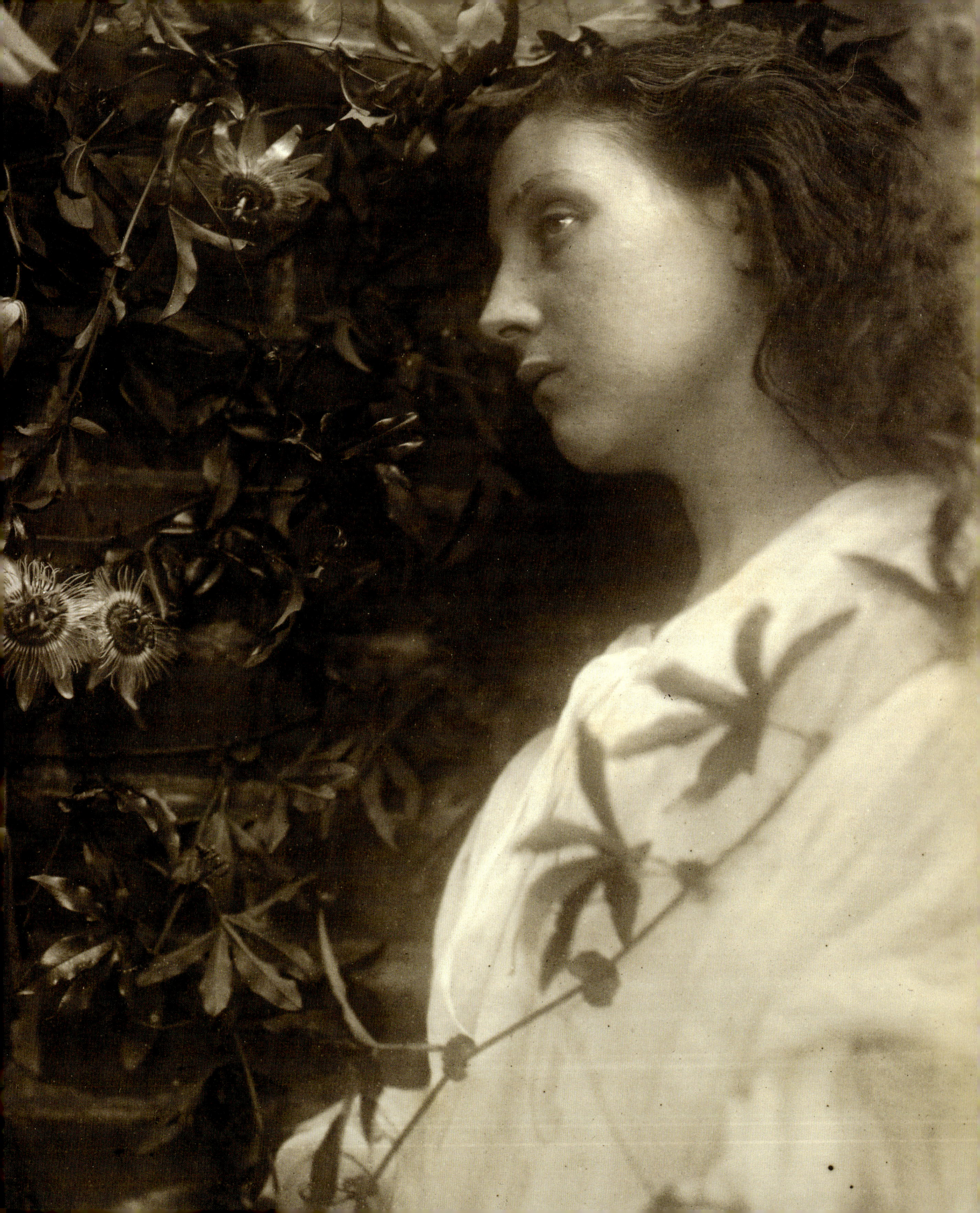

Madonnas, May queens and virgins Ever since Julia Margaret began to take genre pictures – illustrations of biblical, classical and literary narratives, in which women frequently played the most prominent roles – they have been regularly dismissed. Helmut Gernsheim, whose 1948 monograph was largely responsible for bringing about the rediscovery of Julia Margaret and her work in the second half of the twentieth century, called them 'affected, ludicrous and amateur',[1] and Roger Fry, writing in 1926, thought them all 'failures from an aesthetic viewpoint'.[2]

Nowadays, we are willing to reassess such illustrations, just as we have done with Victorian paintings of the same genre. It is easier for us to comprehend, however, that paintings are works of the imagination, while feeling instinctively that photographs merely record what is seen through a camera viewfinder and lens. But the greatest photographers imagine – or visualise – what they will photograph before doing so and Julia Margaret seems to have acquired this ability almost at once. She dressed up her female and child models in costume from the very beginning, 'making endless Madonnas and May Queens and Foolish Virgins and Wise Virgins, and I know not what besides,'[3] as Emily Tennyson wrote to Edward Lear in 1865. Julia Margaret's ambition is surely praiseworthy, and it is clear that her heart was in these illustrations at least as much as it was in her portraits. It is only that sometimes the very realism of the photographic medium defeated her.

Even as a young woman in India, Julia Margaret had been known as a '*bas bleu*' (bluestocking).[4] She was steeped in literature, the visual arts and the Bible, the stories in which she knew so intimately that she could readily draw on them as source material for her pictures. She read daily, particularly poetry, organised readings, and wrote poetry herself, believing that 'Deep feeling finds its vent in simplest words,' as she put it in the introduction to her translation of Bürger's *Lenore*.[5] It is scarcely surprising that she followed in the footsteps of the painters who were her contemporaries, especially the members of the Pre-Raphaelite Brotherhood, who based the majority of their work on narrative (although more than a century later, we rarely know the stories to which their works refer as well as their audiences did at the time). A number of writers, notably Michael Bartram, have pointed out the close parallels between individual Pre-Raphaelite paintings and Julia Margaret's photographs.[6] Her *Mariana*, for instance, has similarities with the painting by Sir John Everett Millais (1829–96) of the same name (now at Tate Britain), and another of her photographs, actually called *A Pre-Raphaelite Study*, bears a close resemblance to Holman Hunt's *Isabella and the Pot of Basil* (now at the Delaware Art Museum, USA). There is a paradoxical difference between them. In painters' hands, details are often generalised and blurred. In photographers' hands, they are usually sharp and precise. But the Pre-Raphaelites revelled in painting every detail with clarity, whereas Julia Margaret usually removed detail altogether, or, as we have seen, at least blurred it.

Julia Margaret evidently knew her Old Master paintings well, as can be judged by the names of artists whose works she draws upon in her 'After the manner of ...' pictures, such as

Maud, 1875
Mary Ann Hillier (detail from p.191)
The J. Paul Getty Museum, Los Angeles

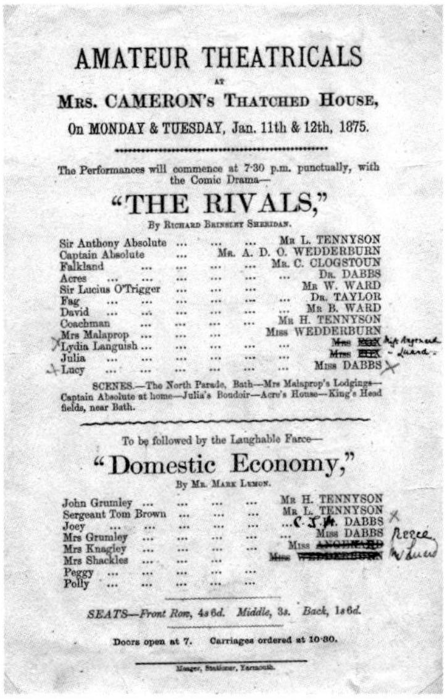

AMATEUR THEATRICALS

AT

MRS. CAMERON'S THATCHED HOUSE,

On MONDAY & TUESDAY, Jan. 11th & 12th, 1875.

The Performances will commence at 7·30 p.m. punctually, with the Comic Drama—

"THE RIVALS,"

By RICHARD BRINSLEY SHERIDAN.

Sir Anthony Absolute ...	MR L. TENNYSON
Captain Absolute ...	MR. A. D. O. WEDDERBURN
Falkland ...	MR. C. CLOGSTOUN
Acres ...	DR. DABBS
Sir Lucius O'Trigger ...	MR W. WARD
Fag ...	DR. TAYLOR
David ...	MR B. WARD
Coachman ...	MR H. TENNYSON
Mrs Malaprop ...	MISS WEDDERBURN
Lydia Languish ...	[illegible]
Julia ...	[illegible]
Lucy ...	MISS DABBS

SCENES.—The North Parade, Bath—Mrs Malaprop's Lodgings—Captain Absolute at home—Julia's Boudoir—Acre's House—King's Head fields, near Bath.

To be followed by the Laughable Farce—

"Domestic Economy,"

By MR. MARK LEMON.

John Grumley ...	MR H. TENNYSON
Sergeant Tom Brown ...	MR L. TENNYSON
Joey ...	... DABBS
Mrs Grumley ...	MISS DABBS
Mrs Knagley ...	MISS [illegible]
Mrs Shackles ...	MISS [illegible]
Peggy ...	
Polly ...	

SEATS—*Front Row*, 4s 6d. *Middle*, 3s. *Back*, 1s 6d.

Doors open at 7. Carriages ordered at 10·30.

Manger, Stationer, Yarmouth.

Programme for *The Rivals* at Mrs Cameron's Thatched House Theatre, 1875
Wilson Centre for Photography

Giotto, Perugino and Francia. Her friend Sir Henry Taylor owned a Francia Madonna and Child painting, and there was a fine collection of Renaissance paintings at her sister Virginia's home, Eastnor Castle. Her frequent visual references to Leonardo da Vinci, Raphael, Rembrandt (*The Whisper of the Muse*; see p.108), Guido Reni (*Beatrice*; see pp.182 and 183), Reynolds, Titian, and others, probably owed something to the fact that she subscribed to the Arundel Society (founded by Ruskin, and on the Council of which both Holman Hunt and Watts sat for a time), which distributed fine quality chromolithograph prints of Italian paintings, including numerous Madonna and Child studies by, among others, Giotto, Pinturicchio and Leonardo. Many of these were in the growing collection of the National Gallery in London, founded in 1824, including an early acquisition, Sassoferrato's *The Virgin in Prayer*, the pose and draperies of which bear a close resemblance to those adopted by Julia Margaret. In the collection of the Royal Photographic Society (now in the National Museum of Photography, Film & Television, Bradford) is a photograph, apparently by Julia Margaret, of what seems to be a nineteenth-century marble bas-relief of a Madonna. She even drew a prominent halo on one of her Madonna studies and seems to have read the *Essays on Sacred and Religious Art* by Anna Brownell Jameson (1794–1860), published between 1848 and 1852. All this renders her sources – and ambitions – very clear.

Reviewing Julia Margaret's work in 1868, the *Art Journal* acknowledged these influences: 'In common photographic portraiture, breadth of light is the rule; but it will be understood how much these examples differ from this rule when we say … that the visitor is occasionally reminded of Caravaggio, Tintoretto, Giorgione, Vélazquez, and others of the Princes of Art.'[7] Dante Gabriel Rossetti once thanked her for 'the most beautiful photograph you so kindly sent me. It is like a Lionardo [*sic*].'[8] We do not know which particular photograph this was. At his death, Rossetti owned no fewer than forty-one of Julia Margaret's photographs, which were auctioned for the princely sum of four pounds and thirteen shillings. Presumably, most if not all of these were given to him by the photographer, as part of her long – and unsuccessful – campaign to persuade him to sit for her. Certainly, she seems to have signed most of them.

It seems likely that the organising of these costume pictures took more time, and caused more disruption, than the portraits of occasional visitors. 'Mrs C. and her household take no note of time. Meet girls going upstairs in fancy dresses, Mrs C. has been photographing a group, and appears carrying glass negative in her collodionised hands. "Magnificent! To focus them all in one picture, such an effort",' wrote William Allingham.[9] But Julia Margaret was always the master of ceremonies for the Camerons and Tennysons, and cannot have lacked entrepreneurial and organisational skills, to say nothing of energy:

> *In those days Mrs Cameron seemed to be omnipresent – organising happy things, summoning one person and another, ordering all the day and long into the night, for of an evening came impromptu plays and waltzes in the wooden ballroom, and young partners dancing under the stars. One warm moonlight night I remember the whole company of lads and lasses went streaming away across the fields and downs, past silvery sheep folds to the very cliffs overhanging the sea.*[10]

The Camerons and the Tennysons shared the Victorian predilection for *tableaux vivants* (elaborate 'living picture' games in which people dressed up as the subjects of paintings, statues, or characters from history, that were played at aristocratic, and even royal, parties) and amateur theatricals. As boys, 'one of the main hobbies of the Tennyson children [Alfred and his brothers] was play acting.'[11] In Freshwater, it was Julia Margaret who was the prime animator of such activities, and she even built a theatre ('Mrs Cameron's Thatched House Theatre') in the grounds of her house, where the children of both families became such enthusiasts that the younger sons, Lionel Tennyson and Henry Herschel Hay Cameron, seriously considered going on the professional stage. Lionel Tennyson was 'perhaps, her star performer … indeed he was artistic enough to satisfy anyone'[12] and he seems to have been the only one of her actors whom she photographed in his costume for a play – as the Marquis of St Cast in *Payable on Demand* (see p.174). Lionel was warned off the stage by the disapproval of his parents, but Henry Cameron had a rather unsuccessful career as an actor after giving up his professional portrait studio. Having produced (but not appeared in) a Christmas play at London's Lyceum Theatre in 1899, he played Humpty Dumpty and the Carpenter in the annual stagings of *Alice in Wonderland* in London from 1900 to 1909.

From surviving programmes, we know that the plays performed at Dimbola Lodge were mostly comic and undemanding. Tennyson had long had a taste for popular theatre. His father had a substantial library of play texts, and Tennyson seems to have regularly attended plays on the Lincolnshire touring circuit. He often took his sons Hallam and Lionel to the theatre, where they would have seen just the sort of plays that they were later to act in. *Helping Hands, Ici on Parle Francais, Delicate Ground* (or *Paris in 1793*) and *Box and Cox*, all performed in the Thatched House Theatre, were popular farces which held the stage until the early twentieth century.

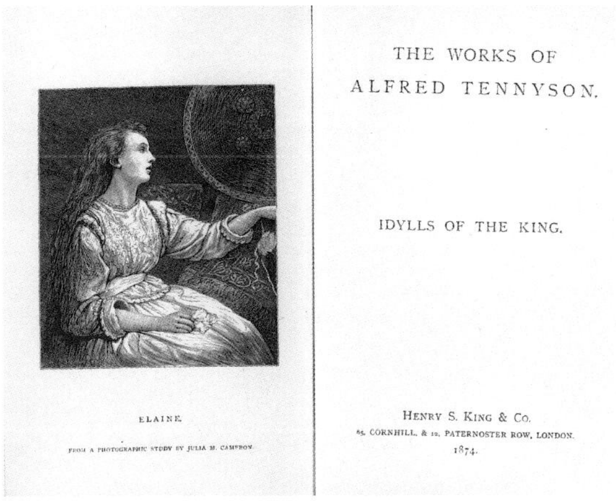

May Prinsep posed as *Elaine*
Frontispiece from *Idylls of the King* by Alfred Tennyson
Engraving after a photograph by Julia Margaret Cameron, published 1874
Julia Margaret Cameron Trust, Isle of Wight

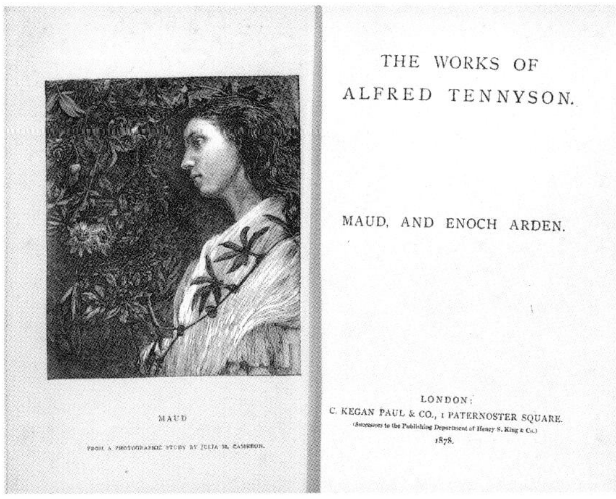

Mary Ann Hillier posed as *Maud*
Frontispiece from *Maud, and Enoch Arden* by Alfred Tennyson
Engraving after a photograph by Julia Margaret Cameron, published 1878
Julia Margaret Cameron Trust, Isle of Wight

The fullest description of one of these productions was written by Edith Nicholl, the daughter of George Granville Bradley, Tennyson's close friend. While staying in one of Tennyson's houses in Freshwater one winter, Edith and her sister joined the Tennyson boys and Henry Cameron in Julia Margaret's production of another farce, *Our Wife*. To Edith, she was

as severely exacting in this direction as she was in her photography … Her excitement and enthusiasm were greater than can be described, the audience was expected to be large, and the tickets were sold rapidly. Her studio was deserted for her parlor, in which daily rehearsals took place. Now the play was a sentimental one, chosen by herself, and there was consequently some rebellion on the part of the performers during these rehearsals. Girls and boys who had been playmates since childhood objected to standing up in the light of day in a commonplace parlor, in their everyday clothes, and making violent love to order – in cold blood too, without paint or powder, or footlights or applause … During some of the rehearsals Mrs Cameron became very much displeased with the backwardness of her troupe in some … of the love-scenes … 'Oh, heavens, Henry!' she cried. 'Do you call that making love? Here – let me show you how to do it!'[13]

Looking at Julia Margaret's set-piece photographs, it is not difficult to imagine her showing her models 'how to do it'!

Young officers of the Royal Artillery, particularly those stationed at Freshwater Redoubt, within sight of Dimbola Lodge, and other visitors – male and female – were also pressed into service. Not that we always know who they are. The Tennyson boys' governess Miss Angenaard appears on one programme; Annie and Lucy Prinsep, May Wedderburn and a 'Miss Dabbs' on others. But on one surviving programme for *Helping Hands*, all the actresses are described merely as 'Miss …'. It was after 'the falling of the curtain on the eventful night that [Julia Margaret's] beaming face and her rapturous embraces of each member of her troupe bore eloquent witness to her final satisfaction.'[14]

Did Julia Margaret's taste for *tableaux vivants* and the theatre lead to her enthusiasm for illustrating literary, classical and biblical stories, or was it the other way round? In the 1870s, her work fully embraced the look and feel of a theatrical performance, as is seen most clearly and consistently in her illustrations for Tennyson's narrative poem of chivalry and illicit love at the court of King Arthur, *Idylls of the King*. Published in 1859, this had crowned the success of his *Poems* (1842) and *In Memoriam* (1850) to make him Britain's most popular and widely read poet. Doubtless, Julia Margaret hoped that being the first photographer to illustrate the *Idylls* (although many painters and illustrators had done so, among them Gustave Doré, Holman Hunt and Millais) would bring her fame too: 'Now *you know*, Alfred, that *I* know that it is immortality to me to be bound up with you …'.[15] Perhaps, too, she saw it as a chance to make a fortune at last.

Tennyson first asked Julia Margaret to make illustrations for a popular ('Cabinet') edition of the *Idylls* in 1874 but, when it appeared, her large-scale photographs had been reduced to small woodcuts, which greatly disappointed

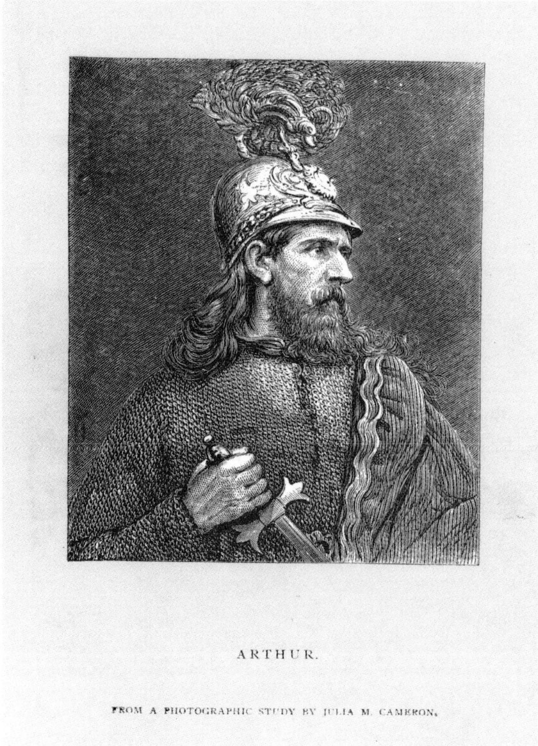

William Warder posed as *King Arthur*
Frontispiece from *Idylls of the King*
Engraving after a photograph by Julia Margaret Cameron, published 1874
Julia Margaret Cameron Trust, Isle of Wight

her. Encouraged by Tennyson, she decided to bring out, at her own expense, a large-format edition with twelve full-size original albumen prints tipped in, depicting characters and incidents from the *Idylls* (see, for instance, *Elaine*, *Maud* and *King Arthur*, pp.190, 191 and 193). There was also a frontispiece (the 'Dirty Monk' portrait of Tennyson). The extracts from the text that are illustrated are written out in Julia Margaret's own hand, and reproduced lithographically. The first volume was published – by Tennyson's own publisher, Henry S. King – in December 1874, and seems deliberately to have been aimed at the Christmas market, being more a pictorial gift book than a book of poems. In preparing it, reported the *Morning Post* a few weeks later, the photographer had

> *spent three months of unceasing care upon the preparation of this volume of photographs, and at what cost they have attained their excellence may be inferred from the fact that, in order to produce even so small a collection, she has had to take quite 200 studies. For one scene alone – that descriptive of the 'Parting between Lancelot and Guinevere' [see p.192] – she took forty-two!*[16]

Although the edition seems to have sold badly, Julia Margaret determined – soon after it received its only other review (in *Anthony's Photographic Bulletin*, April 1875) – to bring out a second volume, which she did in May 1875. This also had a frontispiece portrait of Tennyson and twelve original prints, though only three of the latter are connected with scenes in the *Idylls*. The others accompany other poems by Tennyson, such as *Maud*, *The Princess* and *May Queen*, all once again written out in Julia Margaret's hand. This time, she told her friend Sir Edward Ryan (1793–1875), whom she had first met in India when he was a high-ranking judge, that it took 245 attempts before she got twelve usable pictures. If one ever had doubts as to Julia Margaret's capacity for exaggeration, the fact that no more than three versions of any one of her illustrations to the *Idylls* is known might well resolve them. But there can be no doubt that she worked immensely hard to get the models, the settings, the costumes and the accessories exactly right. Though posterity has sometimes been rather unkind to these pictures, the amount of effort and unceasing experimentation to which they bear witness surely shows that she was aiming to make them at least as good as the work of more traditional book illustrators, and to be the pinnacle of her achievement.

There are a number of variations in the prints pasted into the few surviving copies of Julia Margaret's large-format *Idylls*, as well as in the order in which they are assembled. There also survive a handful of 'miniature editions', which have a mixture of images from the two large-format books with some variants and two new images, one a version of the *The Gardener's Daughter* (the first and most well-known is on p.127). Both versions take as their cue the lines describing the scene which meets the narrator of the poem as he enters a garden, drawn by tales of a beautiful maiden within, hidden from the temptations of the world: 'One arm aloft – / Gown'd in pure white, that fitted to the shape – / Holding the bush to fix it back, she stood'. It had become a favourite image for painters and photographers alike. The young Frank Meadow Sutcliffe (1853–1941), for instance, best remembered for his photographs of the fishing community in Whitby, Yorkshire, made his own version at about the time of publication of Julia Margaret's second volume (it was probably taken on the estate of the Marquis of Normanby).

Few of Julia Margaret's Tennyson illustrations have any similarity to those of other illustrators. For one thing, like Pre-Raphaelite painters, she tended to portray her characters in soulful, melancholy moments. But the poetry itself is often soulful and melancholy. Julia Margaret's *Lady of Shalott* is perhaps rather closer than she might have admitted to the treatment of the same subject by Henry Peach Robinson (1830–1901), whose photographs

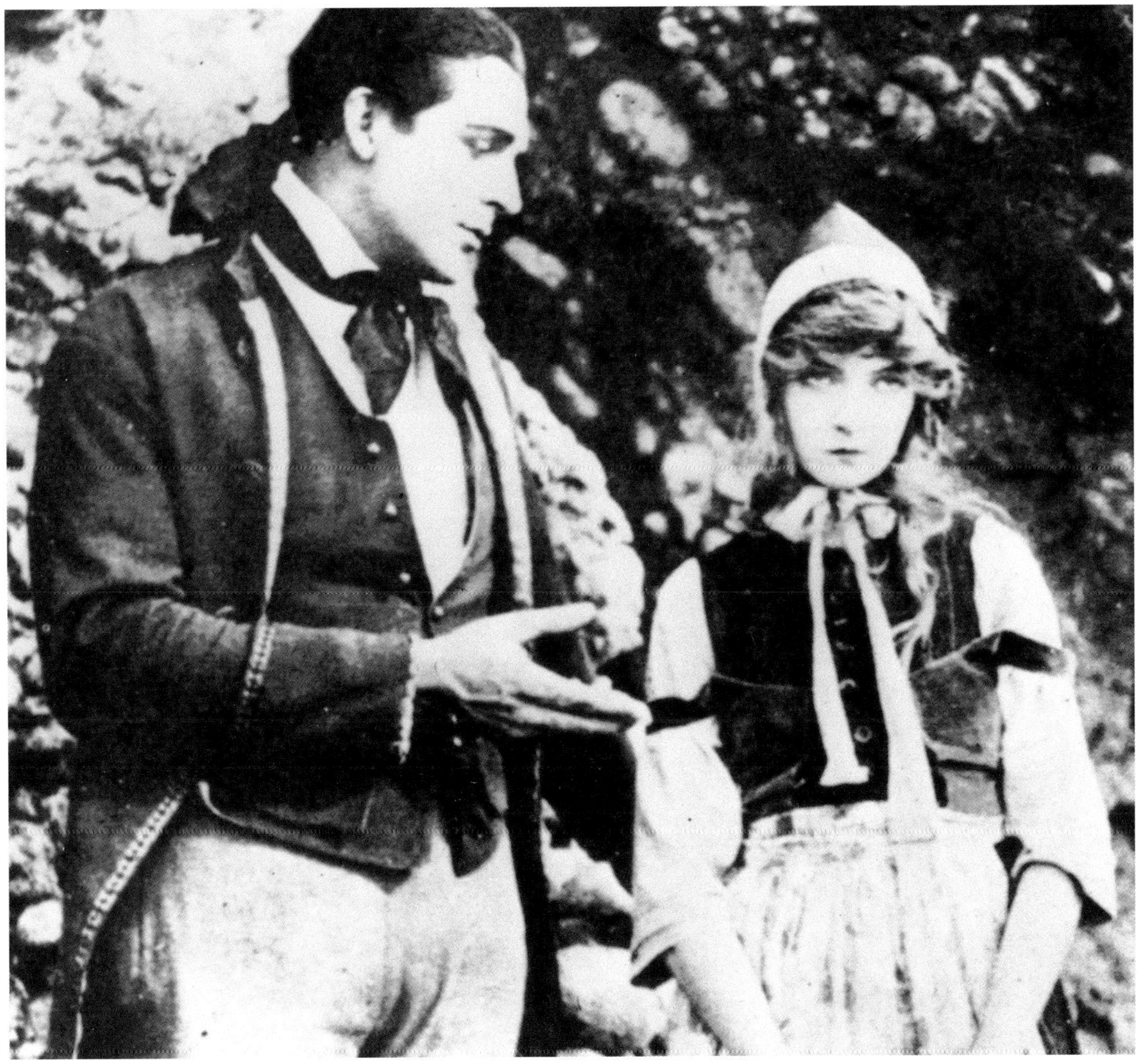

Still from D.W. Griffith's *Enoch Arden* (1915)
Modern copy print, 203 x 253mm (8 x 10")
British Film Institute Collections

were not generally to her taste, or to Millais' *Ophelia*. *The Passing of Arthur* bears a striking resemblance to Daniel Maclise's (1806–70) illustration of the same incident in the celebrated 1857 Moxon illustrated edition of Tennyson. As Julia Margaret had worked with Maclise when he illustrated her translation of *Lenore* (which Julia Margaret translated as *Leonora*), perhaps the imitation was deliberate flattery. But these were exceptions. In most of her illustrations, she went very much her own way.

To modern eyes, accustomed to the convincing reality of film and television, with their actual settings and sophisticated special effects, Julia Margaret's home-made scenarios and heightened gestures may seem to inhabit a rather amateurish world. But it is also a very Victorian world: they look just like photographs of nineteenth-century professional theatre productions, even of silent filmmakers two decades later. Tennyson's *Enoch Arden* (1864) was a frequent source for early filmmakers, being made some half-a-dozen times, twice by the Hollywood pioneer D.W. Griffith (1875–1948); the 1911 version was his first two-reel film. Griffith's 1920 'simple story of plain people', *Way Down East*, is essentially a typical Victorian melodrama. Its characteristic theme is that of a fallen woman who repents, and it even makes use of a scene of baptising an illegitimate baby, just like that in Thomas Hardy's *Tess of the D'Urbervilles* (1891). Audiences shared Griffiths's taste for such Victorian themes, and the film was almost as popular as his epic work *The Birth of a Nation* (1915). In one scene in *Way Down East*, the heroine (played by Lillian Gish, who also played Annie Lee in one of Griffith's versions of *Enoch Arden*), dressed in romantically draped white robes, is told 'In your beauty lives again Elaine, the lily maid, love dreaming at Astolat.'

Julia Margaret was certainly interested in at least two plays of loftier intellectual ambition. *The Cenci* (1819) by Percy Bysshe Shelley (1792–1822) – about a 16-year-old Roman girl who killed her father after he had brutally raped her – was popular with readers, but was not performed until after Cameron's death (by the Shelley Society in 1886). Its problem, as

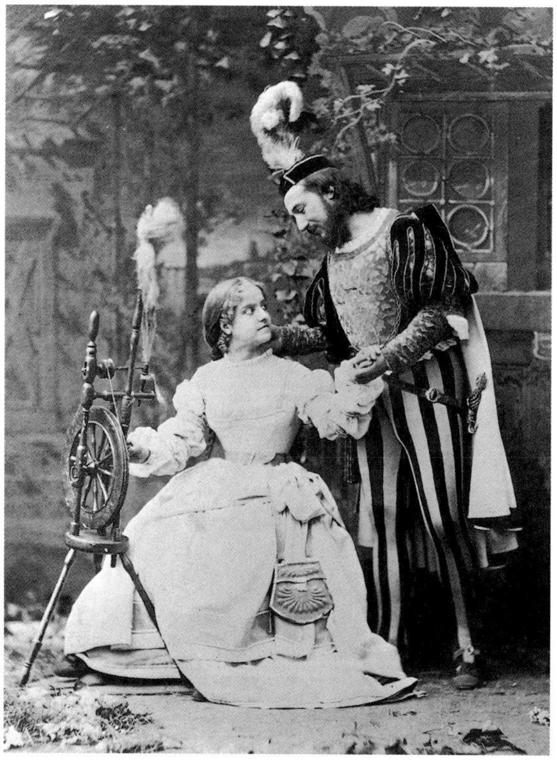

Madame Adelina Patti (1843–1919) *as Marguerite and Giovanni Mario* (1810–83) *as Faust* in Gounod's opera *Faust*, Covent Garden
Caldesi & Co., July 1864
Albumen print, 336 x 241mm (13¼ x 9½")
Guy Little Collection, Theatre Museum

with so much poetic drama, is that, as the drama critic William Hazlitt (1778–1830) put it, 'The boards of a theatre and the regions of fancy are not the same thing.'[17] But it still inspired Julia Margaret. Over a period of four or five years, she photographed half-a-dozen versions of the subject, modelled by May Prinsep and Kate Keown (see pp.182 and 183), despite the fact that the latter was only ten years old at the time.

Hazlitt's stricture might equally well be applied to Sir Henry Taylor's two-part play *Philip van Artevelde*, his most popular work. Written in 1834, it was based on the real-life story of a Flemish hero, and was a deliberate attempt to revive Elizabethan blank verse drama. Part One was adapted for the stage by one of the most intellectual of the Victorian actor managers, William Macready (1793–1873), and opened at the Princess's Theatre, London, on 11 November 1847. Despite the fact that the play closed after only five performances, Julia Margaret admired it unreservedly, arranging private readings of it, sending copies to Robert Browning (1812–89) and the poet and critic Matthew Arnold (1822–88), and even commissioning a German translation, which she distributed far and wide among friends and acquaintances. She always addressed Taylor as Philip – as did many of his friends – and subtitled at least one of her portraits of him 'Philip van Artevelde'.

Tennyson was chiefly a lyrical poet, though – as we have seen – he loved the theatre. Dramatic narrative and dialogue often feature in his poetry, and a poem such as *Enoch Arden* (which Julia Margaret illustrated) is very close to popular drama in form and manner. But he did not start to write plays until he was sixty-five. Indeed, in 1854, he wrote that 'I cannot be considered as a good judge of how a play might tell in being acted.'[18] Perhaps it was all those performances in Julia Margaret's theatre which changed his mind. Sir Henry Irving produced Tennyson's first play *Queen Mary* at the Royal Lyceum Theatre, London, in 1876, despite once complaining to Wilfrid Ward that 'Tennyson is a great poet, but he cannot write plays; what a pity he tries, they are the greatest rubbish.'[19] One of the reasons given for its failure was the disappointing performance of Kate Bateman, the sister of one of Julia Margaret's models, Isabel. Tennyson spent much of the next few years writing half-a-dozen more plays. Like Sir Henry Taylor, he never quite succeeded in blending poetry and drama, and three of the plays were never performed. Two more were staged by Irving – *The Cup* (1881) and *Becket* (finished in 1879, but only staged – heavily cut – in 1892). The latter was such a triumph (with Ellen Terry as Rosamund) that Irving continued to play it until the end of his life – literally, as he died after a performance of the play at the Theatre Royal, Bradford.

Julia Margaret left Freshwater in the same year that Tennyson began writing for the theatre, so it was too late for her to illustrate his rather self-conscious continuations of Shakespeare's history canon (though her son Henry made a famous photograph portrait of Irving as Becket in 1892/3). We can only guess at what she might have made of the plays, and what influence her Thatched House Theatre had on them and the other now largely forgotten verse dramas of Tennyson's later years. We can only guess, too, at how her photography might have developed had she stayed on.

The most affectionate, and funny, description of life in Freshwater at its intellectual, cultural and photographic peak, was written by Virginia Woolf:

> *I must note for future use, the superb possibilities of Freshwater, for a comedy. Old Cameron dressed in a blue dressing gown & not going beyond his garden for 12 years, suddenly borrows his son's coat, & walks down to the sea. Then they decide to proceed to Ceylon, taking their coffins with them, & the last sight of Aunt Julia is on board ship, presenting porters with large photographs of Sir Henry Taylor & the Madonna in default of small change.*[20]

And that is exactly what happened.

NOTES

1. Gernsheim, 1948; second edition 1975, p.83.
2. Fry and Woolf, 1926; second edition 1973, p.25.
3. Letter dated 17 February 1865 from Emily Tennyson to Edward Lear, quoted in Hoge, 1974, p.188.
4. Pemble, 1985, p.98.
5. Gottfried August Bürger, *Leonora*, translated by Julia Margaret Cameron and illustrated by Daniel Maclise (Longman, Brown, Green & Longmans, London, 1847).
6. Bartram, 1985.
7. *Art Journal*, February 1868.
8. Letter written on a 'Sunday night' in mid-January 1866, Collection of John Windle, San Francisco.
9. Allingham and Radford, 1907; second edition 1985, p.182.
10. Thackeray Fuller and Hammersley, 1951, p.111.
11. G. Moore, quoted in Scott, 1970, p.18.
12. Ellison, 1907, p.74.
13. Ellison, 1907, pp.77–79.
14. Ellison, 1907, pp.80–81.
15. Gernsheim,1948; second edition 1975, p.42.
16. *Morning* Post, 11 January 1875.
17. Jackson, 1989, p.1.
18. Letter dated 18 September 1854, Henry E. Huntington Library (San Marino, California), quoted in Martin, 1980, p.526.
19. Quoted in Martin, 1980, p. 523.
20. Diary entry for 31 January 1919, Bell, 1977, p.237.

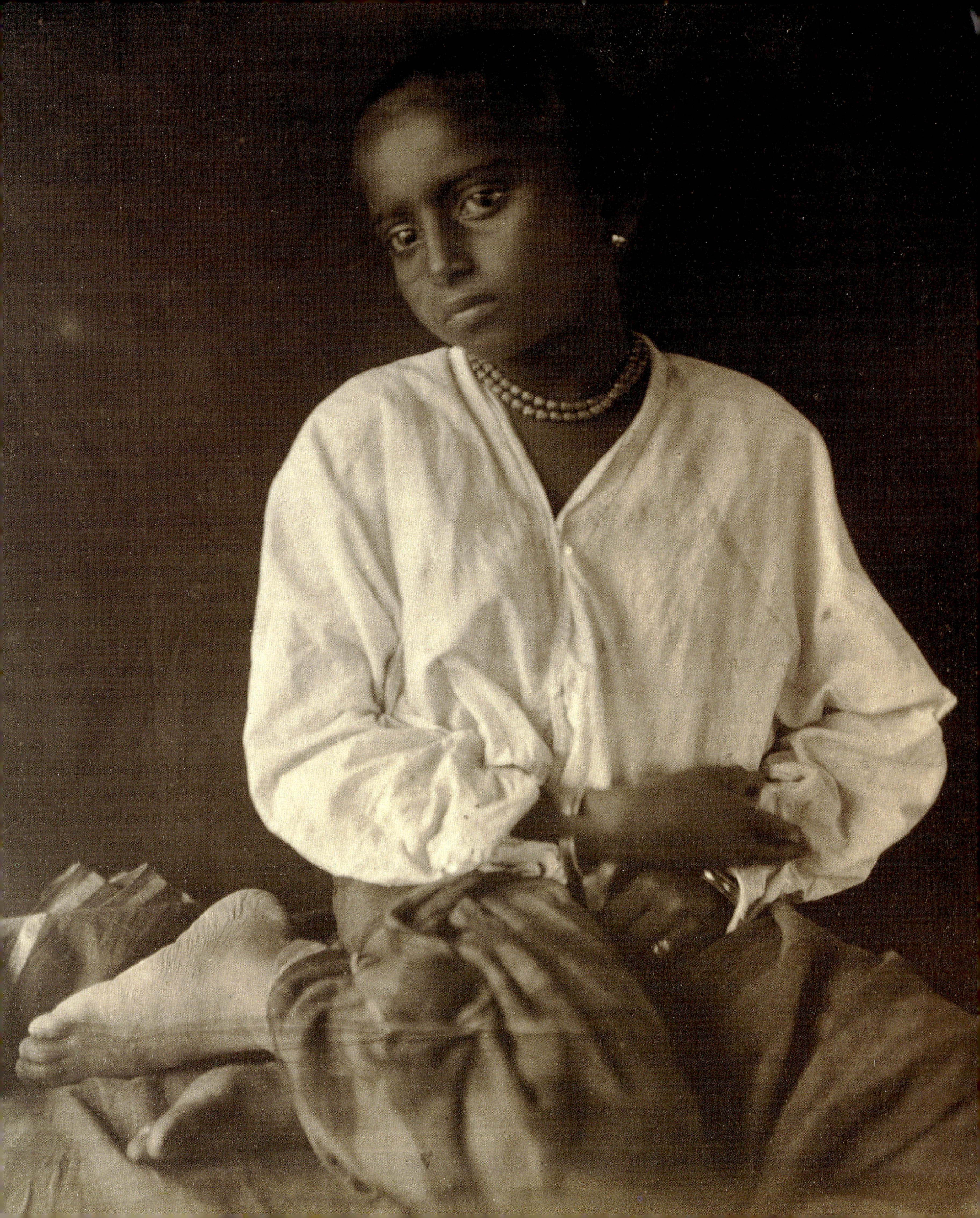

Ceylon The early 1870s were in many ways the pinnacle of Julia Margaret's artistic achievement. The two volumes of Tennyson's *Idylls of the King* illustrated with her photographs were published in 1874 and a poem of her own, 'On a Portrait', written in 1875, appeared in *Macmillan's Magazine* in February 1876. Her prints had been exhibited in London and Bournemouth, and she had entered into a contract for the manufacture and sale of permanent carbon prints of her favourite pictures:

> *She selected prints from some seventy of her best subjects, and applied to the Autotype Company for aid in producing from these, new negatives. The task was accomplished to her satisfaction, ingenious devices being adopted to get rid of spots and stains and to secure good printing density, so that from negatives so reproduced, prints in sepiae and engraving black, were obtained superior, in her judgement, to the original prints in silver.*[1]

In Ceylon, however, three of the Camerons' sons were struggling to make ends meet. The country was in serious economic decline, its coffee plantations being destroyed by fungal disease for the third time in less than fifty years. The Camerons – like the Prinseps and many others – faced the prospect of their income disappearing. On a previous occasion, Julia Margaret had tried to distract her husband from worrying about the situation ('Charles speaks to me of the flower of the coffee plant. I tell him that the eyes of the first grandchild should be more beautiful than any flower'[2]) and to discourage him from travelling out to the estates from which he derived his income. But he insisted 'that the sea voyage is the best thing for him, and Ceylon is the cure for all things'.[3]

In 1875, however, planters were going bankrupt and Charles decided it was time for a permanent return to the island he had first visited in 1831. His friend Henry Taylor believed that Cameron 'never ceased to yearn after the island as his place of abode, and thither in his eighty-first year he has betaken himself, with a strange joy'.[4]

Once the decision had been made that the family would accompany Charles, preparations were made in great haste, probably because another son, Hardinge, then private secretary to the Governor of Ceylon, was about to return to the island from leave in England. The contents of Dimbola Lodge were hurriedly assembled (some of them packed in the coffins mentioned by Virginia Woolf in *The Searchlight*) and in 1875 the family set sail from Dover on the SS *Mirzapor*, perhaps with the evocative words describing a farewell to the Isle of Wight by Tennyson's brother Charles running through their minds:

Silent I gazed upon our foaming wake,
And silent on the Island hills I gazed,
As up the ebbing stream we bore to make
Our harbour, while the West athwart us blazed.
Keen were my thoughts: my memory wandered back
To those fair shores – the Needles and the Downs;
The happy woodlands and the little towns,
For every day a new and pleasant track.
... The shadows of our mast
And sail ran sadly o'er the fruitless ooze
A sunset, as between the banks we passed
Of that tide falling river, speeding fast
To land, and further from those fond adieus.[5]

Reaching Ceylon rather more quickly than they used to, because the recent opening

Untitled (Ceylon), 1875–9 (detail from p.197)
The J. Paul Getty Museum, Los Angeles

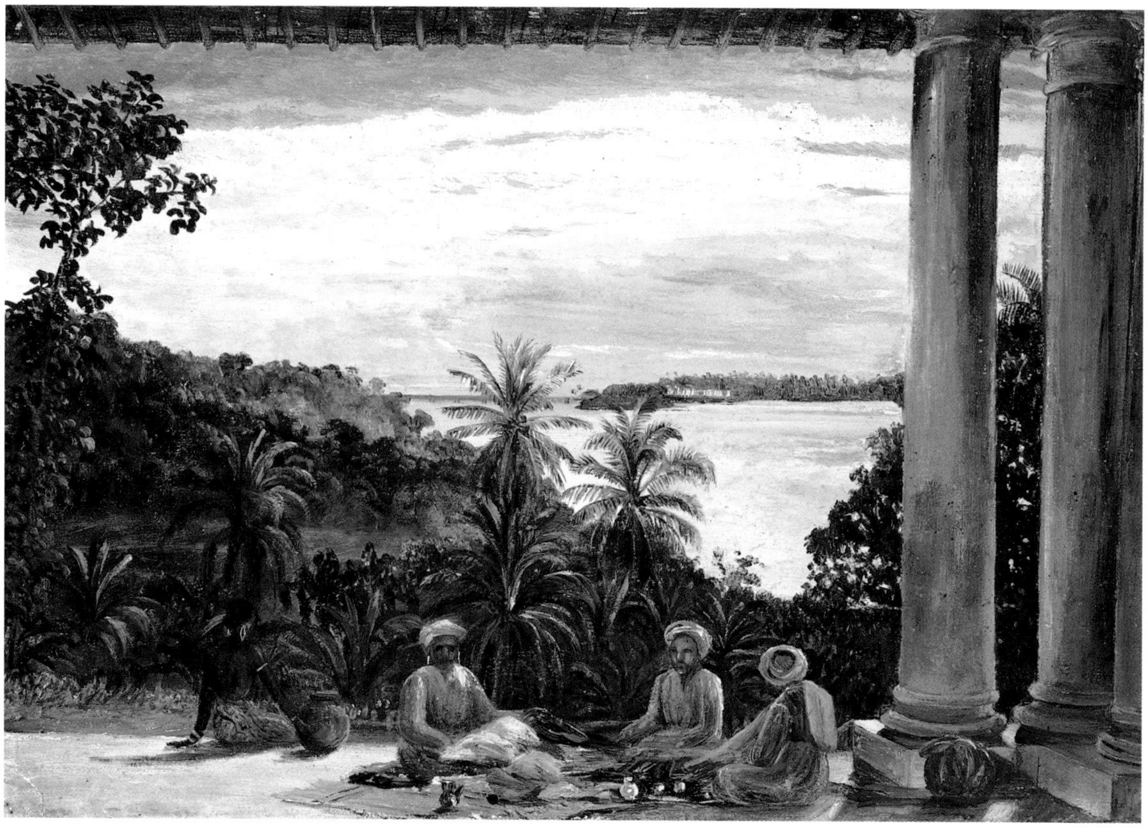

Bombay Pedlars on Mrs Cameron's Verandah, Kalutara
Marianne North, January 1877
Oil on paperboard, 240 x 345mm (9½ x 13⅝")
Royal Botanic Gardens, Kew

of the Suez Canal (in 1869) had reduced the length of the voyage considerably, the Camerons stayed for a time at Hardinge's cottage in Kalutara, before settling with one of their adopted daughters, Mary Clogstoun, and a maid, Ellen Ottington (always known to the family as 'Little E') at Balmoral Cottage, Lindula. Here, Julia Margaret continued to take photographs, mostly of the Tamils who worked for the family. These photographs have often been dismissed as inferior to her work in Britain but by reproducing almost all of the small number known to survive, I hope to show that this is not true. The pictures (see pp.194–203) exhibit exactly the same understanding of how to fill the frame with human figures, how to define their presence with careful control of light and shade, and how to give them dignity – even if Julia Margaret did refer to her sitters as 'natives', just as she had called the local residents at Freshwater 'peasants'. Of course, the sunlight in Ceylon was consistently brighter than in even the southernmost part of England and this inevitably meant that Julia Margaret was able to use shorter exposure time, the sitters did not have to keep still for so punishingly long a time, and the pictures are relatively sharply focused.

In 1876 and 1877, the botanical painter Marianne North went to stay with Julia Margaret at Kalutara: 'I had long known her glorious photographs, but had never met her. She had sent me many warm invitations to come when she heard I was in Ceylon.'[6]

North found that the health of Julia Margaret's husband had indeed improved on his return to Ceylon:

for ten years he had never moved from his room. At last she made up her mind to go and live near her sons in Ceylon. Every one had said it would be impossible; but when told of what she was going to do, he said that the one wish he had was to die in Ceylon! He got up and walked, and had been better ever since. He was eighty-four, perfectly upright, with long white hair over his shoulders. He read all day long, taking walks round and round the verandah at Kalutara with a long staff in his hand, perfectly happy, and ready to enjoy any joke or enter into any talk which went on around him.

Julia Margaret was active too:

The walls of the room were covered with magnificent photographs; others were tumbling about the tables, chairs, and floors with quantities of damp books, all untidy and picturesque; the lady herself with a lace veil on her head and flowing draperies. Her oddities were most refreshing.

Nor had the photographer lost her admiration for physical beauty:

She also made some studies of natives while I was there, and took such a fancy to the back of one of them (which she said was absolutely superb) that she insisted on her son retaining him as her gardener, though she had no garden and he did not know even the meaning of the word.[7]

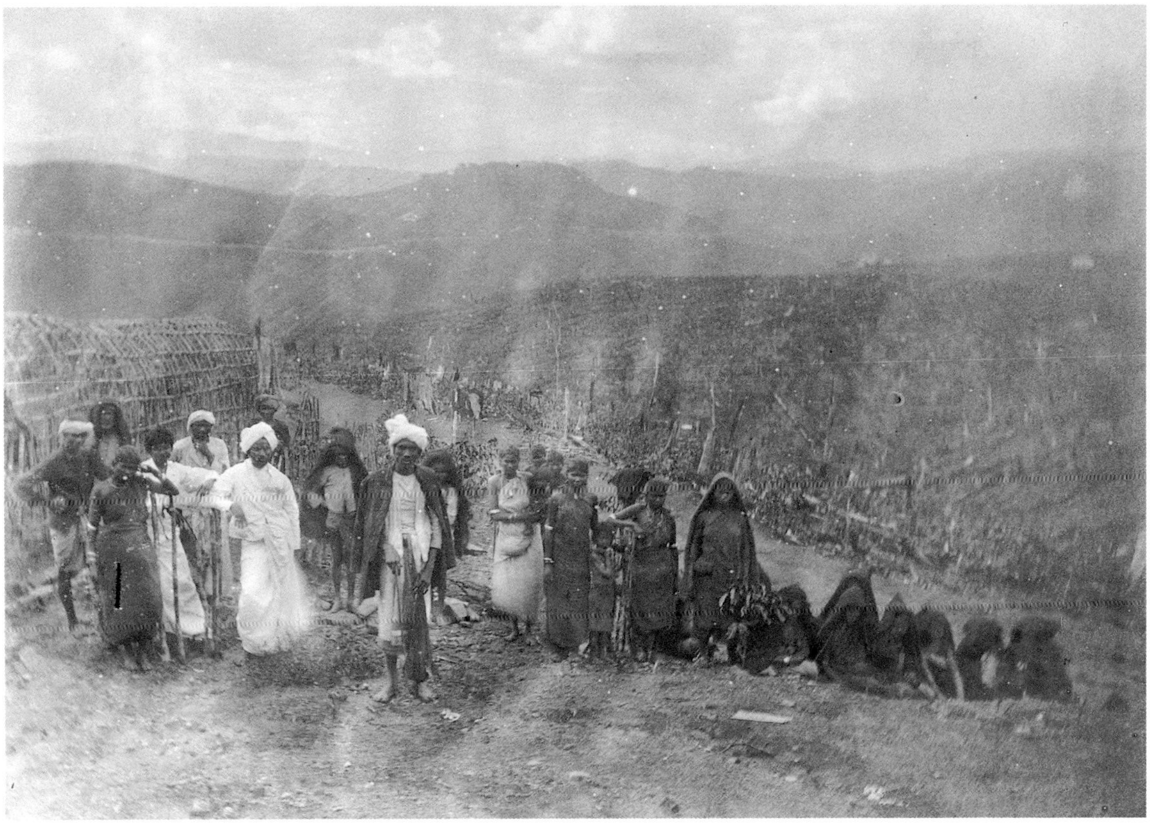

Estate workers (Ceylon)
Julia Margaret Cameron, 1875–9
Albumen print, 186 x 249mm (7¼ x 9½")
National Museum of Photography, Film & Television, Bradford

North described the idyllic situation of the Camerons' home, and commemorated it in some atmospheric paintings, which can now be seen in the Marianne North Gallery devoted to 832 of her works at the Royal Botanic Gardens, Kew:

*Their house stood on a small hill, jutting out into the great river which ran into the sea a quarter of a mile below the house. It was surrounded by cocoa-nuts, casuarinas, mangoes, and breadfruit trees; tame rabbits, squirrels, and mainah-birds [*sic*] ran in and out without the slightest fear, while a beautiful tame stag guarded the entrance; monkeys with gray whiskers, and all sort of fowls, were outside.*[8]

North was, as far as we know, the only well-known figure photographed by Julia Margaret in Ceylon:

She made her mind up at once she would photograph me, and for three days she kept herself in a fever of excitement about it, but the results have not been approved at home since. She dressed me up in flowing draperies of cashmere wool, let down my hair, and made me stand with spiky cocoa-nut branches running into my head, the noonday sun's rays between the leaves as the slight breeze moved them, and told me to look perfectly natural (with a thermometer standing at 96°)! Then she tried me with a background of breadfruit leaves and fruit, nailed flat against a window shutter, and told them *to look natural, but both failed; and though she wasted twelve plates, and enormous amount of trouble, it was all in vain, she could only get a perfectly uninteresting and commonplace person in her glasses, which refused to flatter.*[9]

Julia Margaret made four portraits of North, of which perhaps the most interesting is the unusual study, for her, of a subject at work – the painter at her easel on the terrace of the Camerons' house (see p.194). North's visit probably inspired what is, as far as I know, Julia Margaret's nearest photograph to a landscape, a group of estate workers (or possibly itinerant peddlers) close to the veranda of her home.

After two years in Ceylon, the Camerons returned briefly to England in 1878 for four weeks 'of turmoil, sickness, sorrows, marriages, and deaths', again accompanied by Hardinge. The main purpose was to seek urgent medical treatment for Charles, but the marriage of Julia Margaret's god-daughter Julia Herschel to Captain John Maclear, son of Her Majesty's Astronomer in Cape Town, whom the Herschels had first met there forty years earlier, at the beginning of our story, must have been a very pleasant distraction. The Camerons presumably also attended the second marriage of their son-in-law Charles Norman, who had been left a widower when their daughter Julia died in 1873.

On their return to Ceylon, it seems that the medical treatment Charles had received in London had met with some success, and he was able to walk round the veranda, read, talk and joke with visitors. But Hardinge's health suffered in the damp coastal air and because of this the family soon moved up to its Glencairn estate in the mountains, which was being managed by Henry Herschel Hay Cameron and the young Charles Hay Cameron. Julia Margaret caught a chill after this sudden change of climate but, a caring mother to the last, she continued to nurse Hardinge. It was a mistake and, within days, she died, on 26 January 1879, aged only sixty-three. Her last word, we are told by Henry Cameron, who was at her side, was 'beautiful'.[11]

Years before, Charles had told Sir Henry Taylor that: 'I have long contemplated Ceylon as my final resting place and fixed the site of my tomb.'[12] That site was St Mary's Church, Bogawantala, consecrated in 1876, the building and maintenance of which had been supported by the Cameron family. Julia Margaret's coffin was taken on the sixteen-mile journey to its churchyard, drawn on an open cart by white oxen. Though twenty years older than his wife, and an invalid, Charles survived her by two years before dying in a hilltop sanatorium at Nuwara Eliya, on 8 May 1881 (though his tombstone says '1880').

Julia Margaret and her husband were the subjects of lengthy obituaries in *The Times*. Julia Margaret's appeared on 4 March 1879, and commemorated her character as much as her artistic achievement:

Mrs Cameron's singular ardour of enthusiasm, the energy with which she flung herself into whatever she undertook, her rare forgetfulness of self and readiness to help others, endeared her to a wide circle of friends, while her devotion to her family was for her a love which nothing ever diminished – not even her departure for a distant island, whither her affection for her children carried her, at a time of life when the long journey and the difficulties and discomforts of forming a new home would to most women have been insurmountable.

The Times also paid tribute to Julia Margaret's photography:

Mrs Cameron appealed to a still wider public by her perfectly original and unique photographic work and subject pictures, in which, after a daring fashion of her own, forfeiting the sharpness of definition which ordinary photographers strive for, and which is one of the things artists most dislike in photographic portraiture, and having the advantage of sitters usually distinguished for intellectual gifts or personal graces, she produced a series of heads and groups quite unique in their suggestiveness, the most picture-like photographs certainly which have been given to the world, and some of them among the best extant portraits of their distinguished originals.

Later, the Camerons would be the only husband and wife to be accorded separate entries in the *Dictionary of National Biography*, and Julia Margaret the sole photographer in its pages (in a volume which listed only eighteen women out of 420 entries). This undoubtedly owed something to the fact that the dictionary was founded and edited by Leslie Stephen, whose wife, Julia, was Julia Margaret's niece and a favourite photographic model. It was Julia who wrote the entry on her aunt, which described how: 'At the age of fifty she took up photography, which in her hands became truly artistic, instead of possessing merely mechanical excellence.'[13] The Stephens' daughter Virginia (later Virginia Woolf), was always fascinated by the story of her great-aunt and, as we have already seen, later wrote a one act farce, *Freshwater*, in which she was a central character. She also clearly drew on Julia Margaret for a character in her short story *The Searchlight* who, 'with clenched fist and threats of damnation', tried to 'force those around her to hold still' with the rhetorical question 'surely you can put up with a little discomfort in the cause of Art?'[14]

Within her family, and the art world, Julia Margaret and her work were held in high regard at the time of her death. But the photography world was less certain, and it took almost a century to change its mind.

NOTES

1. W.S. Bird, *Autotype Notes*, 11, 21 April 1879.
2. Letter from Julia Margaret to the Tennysons, quoted in Gernsheim, 1948; second edition 1975, p.23.
3. Gernsheim, 1948; second edition 1975, p.23.
4. Quoted in Hopkinson, 1986, p.80.
5. Charles Tennyson Turner's sonnet is quoted by Anne Thackeray Ritchie in Thackeray Ritchie and Cameron, 1893, p.16. The complete sonnet is in F.B. and M. Pinion, 1988, p.146.
6. North, I, 1892, p.314.
7. North, I, 1892, p.315.
8. North, I, 1892, p.314.
9. North, I, 1892, p.315.
10. Taylor, II, 1885, p.44.
11. Quoted in Hopkinson, 1986, p.93.
12. Letter from Charles Hay Cameron to Taylor, written on the eve of the Camerons' embarkation for Ceylon, quoted in Taylor, II, 1885, p.44.
13. Sir Leslie Stephen (ed.), *Dictionary of National Biography* (Smith, Elder & Co., London, 1882–1900), p.300.
14. Quoted in Hopkinson, 1986, p.136.

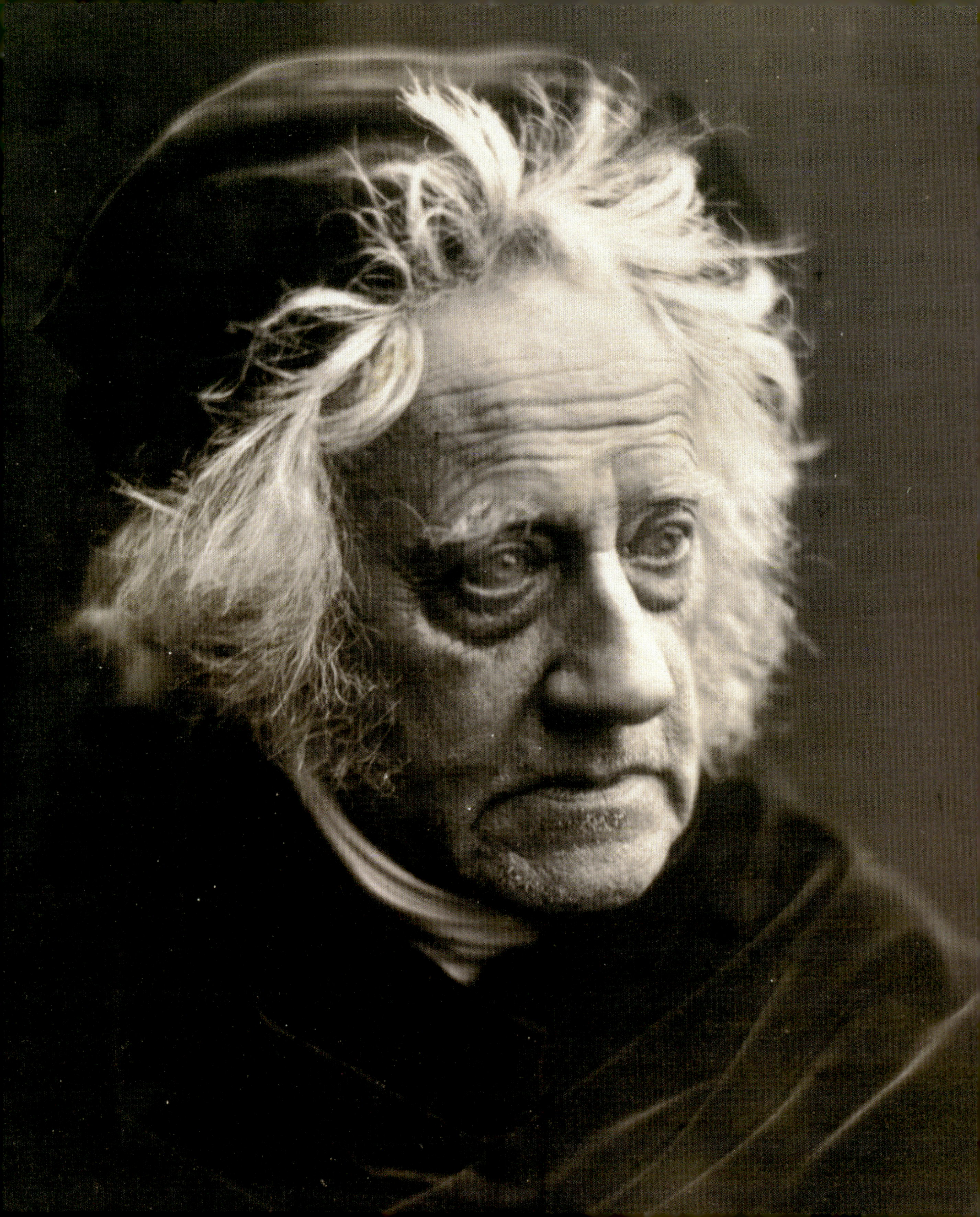

Epilogue: genius and love

'My aspirations are to ennoble Photography and to secure for it the character and uses of High Art by combining the real & Ideal & sacrificing nothing of Truth by all possible devotion to Poetry & beauty,'[1] wrote Julia Margaret to Sir John Herschel in 1864, sending him an album of her work on the last day of her first year of photography. The cumulative force of the pictures in this book certainly demonstrates that she succeeded in achieving this lofty ambition, but such a view has not always been shared in the 140 years since she embraced that manifesto.

In Julia Margaret's lifetime, as we have seen, artists and art critics were generous in their praise of her work. But the photography world was nearly always discouraging. In her first year, 1864, she joined both the London and Scottish Photographic Societies and submitted prints to their exhibitions. In 1864, the jury of the tenth annual Photographic Society of London exhibition, which contained five of her prints, recommended that 'She should not let herself be misled by the indiscriminate praise bestowed upon her by the non-photographic press and she should do much better when she has learnt the proper use of her apparatus.'[2] Undeterred, she sent twenty-three prints to the Scottish Society's ninth annual exhibition: 'a Head of Henry Taylor with the light illumining the countenance in a way that cannot be ~~surpassed~~ described & a Raphaelesque La Madonna Aspettante, these photographs still exist & I think they cannot be surpassed.' She was not best pleased that it was the photographer Henry Peach Robinson who won rather than her: 'The picture that did receive the prize called Brenda, clearly proved to me that detail of Table cover chair & crinoline skirt were essentials to the Judges of the Art.'[3] The disapproval was mutual: Robinson was to write of the 'photographs by a lady, many of them failures from every point of view … *it is not the mission of photography to produce smudges*.'[4] The *Photographic Journal* weighed in, having lavished praise on Robinson:

> *Mrs Cameron exhibits her series of out-of-focus portraits of celebrities. We must give this lady credit for daring originality, but at the expense of all other photographic qualities. A true artist would employ all the resources at his disposal, in whatever branch of art he might practise. In these pictures all that is good in photography has been neglected, and the shortcomings of the art are prominently exhibited. We are sorry to speak thus severely on the works of a lady, but we feel compelled to do so in the interests of art.*[5]

This attack, typical of criticisms of her work, failed to deter Julia Margaret. She sent prints to exhibitions in London, Paris, Berlin, Dublin and even to Sydney, Australia. In none of these did the photographic press praise her, and the first real public support for her art from a photographer came more than a decade after her death, when Peter H. Emerson wrote the commentary ('a labour of love', he called it) accompanying a portfolio of four of her pictures – portraits of Herschel and Tennyson, as well as *The Dream* and *The Kiss of Peace* (see p.149) – in the fifth issue of the journal of art photography, *Sun Artists*.

Sir John Herschel with Cap, April 1867
(detail from p.100)
National Portrait Gallery, London (NPG P213)

Had Mrs Cameron been well-advised, she would never have entered for these contemptible competitions, the judges were incompetent, her competitors beneath contempt, and her public uneducated. The majority of her competitors were banded together by class instincts, and trade interests, and one is filled with scorn, on turning back to the photographic journalism of the period.

After much more in the same tone, and a detailed critique of a number of pictures, Emerson concluded that 'Of the crowd of dark-box bearers now with the shades, the most successful was Mrs Cameron, whose pictures alone are worth preserving.'[6]

Nearly a decade later, in 1898, the Royal Photographic Society (as the Photographic Society of London had become in 1894) included work by her in an international exhibition and catalogue:

Nowadays the advocates of what is styled diffusion of focus' may be numbered by thousands, but in the seventies, they were few and far between. The calotype workers were to some extent compelled to give their pictures breadth and vigour by the very nature of the process, but the advent of the collodion film with its delicacy and almost microscopic structure gave an impetus in the other direction to photography, the reaction from which is largely due to two artists, Mrs Cameron and O.G. Rejlander.

But the writer cannot avoid a professional sneer: 'Unfortunately her technical skill was not equal to her artistic ability, and many otherwise fine productions were marred by defects in photographic manipulation.'[7]

In the early years of the twentieth century, much of the impetus to take, collect, and write about art photography crossed the Atlantic. In 1913, the American photographer, critic and dealer Alfred Stieglitz (1864–1946) reproduced in photogravure carbon prints of Julia Margaret's two portraits of Carlyle, and one each of Herschel, Joseph Joachim and Ellen Terry. 'Mrs Cameron,' he wrote, 'is one of photography's few "classics".'[8] In 1926, as we have seen, Roger Fry wrote an admiring essay in which he said that 'Mrs Cameron's photographs bid fair to outlive most of the works of the artists who were her contemporaries.'[9]

To understand why Julia Margaret Cameron is such a 'classic', one needs to know a little more of the history of photography, and of the practitioners who helped to shape it. A surprisingly large percentage of the greatest of these – women and men who used what was basically a recording device to make art and to open the eyes of their generation to a new way of seeing their world – worked in the sixty years from the invention of photography to the beginning of the twentieth century. Many were, solely or principally, portraitists.

Almost from the beginning, portraiture was the *raison d'être* of photography – the qualifying 'almost' being solely because of practical and technical restrictions. When Arago told the Académie des Sciences on 7 January 1839 about the wonderful new invention of the daguerreotype, he said 'The time needed to take a picture ... varies according to the brightness of the light and, thus, according to the season and the time of day. In summer, and at midday, eight to ten minutes is sufficient.'[10] It seems likely that the French inventor of photography, Daguerre, recorded his first human subject almost by accident – when he uncovered his lens to take a photograph of the Boulevard du Temple in Paris, a boot-black and his customer imprinted themselves on his shiny silver plate because they kept more or less still throughout Daguerre's minutes-long exposure.

When Daguerre's English counterpart, Fox Talbot, described his paper-based negatives and positives (at first called 'photogenic drawings', later calotypes) to the British Association for the Advancement of Science conference in August 1839, he observed: 'I have said nothing of perhaps the most important application of which the new art is susceptible (that of taking portraits with a camera obscura), because I have not yet accomplished this, although I see no reason to doubt its practicability.'[11] Fox Talbot's view was that, in really sunny conditions, one might get exposure down to two or three minutes.

In 1840, the inventors of both processes found ways to accelerate the response of their photosensitive chemicals, and portraiture became viable. In June or July, the Englishman John William Draper took a daguerreotype portrait of his sister Dorothy in New York. Three or four months later, Fox Talbot took one of his wife Constance. By 1841, portraits – and portraitists – were everywhere. Two of the first portrait studios in London were on a rooftop a few hundred yards from the National Portrait Gallery, opened by the Frenchman Antoine Claudet (1798–1867) in 1841, and at the Royal Polytechnic Institution in Regent Street, operated by Richard Beard (1801 or 2–85).

Having one's picture taken in such a studio was a real business, in both senses of the word. The operators were principally interested in making profits and the procedure they inflicted on their sitters must have been agonising. The subject of one of the earliest photographic images in the National Portrait Gallery's collection, taken in 1841 by Richard Beard of the Irish novelist Maria Edgeworth (1768–1849), makes that clear enough:

It is a wonderful mysterious operation. You are taken from one room into another upstairs and down and you see various people whispering and hear them in neighbouring passages and rooms unseen and the whole apparatus and stool on a high platform under a glass dome casting a snapdragon blue light making all look like spectres and the men in black gliding about like &c.[12]

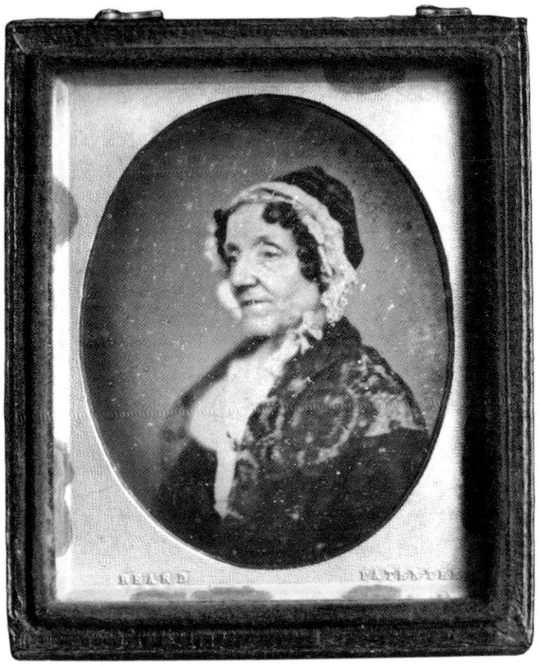

Maria Edgeworth (1768–1849)
Richard Beard, 1841
Daguerreotype, 54 x 44mm (2⅛ x 1¾")
National Portrait Gallery, London (NPG P5)

In the circumstances, Beard's daguerreotype of Edgeworth looks almost human, but not quite. It might just as well depict a waxwork. To avoid this lifelessness, what was needed was a photographer – or photographers – who were not driven by profit, and who could take all the time and trouble in the world to get things right. The first who appeared on the scene – in the mid-1840s – were neither English nor French, but Scottish; two men very different in age and background who came together in a partnership to produce perhaps the first masterpieces in the history of the medium.

At the time, Scotland was enjoying an intellectual, scientific and artistic boom. One of the leaders of this renaissance was Sir David Brewster (1781–1868), Principal of the University of St Andrews. Brewster knew Fox Talbot well and had encouraged experimentation with calotypes at the university. When Fox Talbot asked Brewster whether he should patent his process in Scotland, Brewster advised him against the trouble and expense. He recommended that the young, rather delicate Robert Adamson (1821–48), brother of one of Brewster's university colleagues, should be trained to take up photography as a profession. Adamson went to Edinburgh on 10 May 1843 to set up a studio, just eight days before the 'Free' Church of Scotland was established. This was perhaps the most important occasion in the history of Scotland between the signing of the Act of Union in 1707 and the creation of the Scottish Parliament in 1999. Indeed, so important a historical moment was it, and so spectacular a piece of carefully staged public relations, that the secretary of the Royal Scottish Academy of Fine Arts, David Octavius Hill (1802–70), made up his mind to paint a monumental picture commemorating the event. As a landscape painter, he well knew the difficulty of the essential first step – making sketches of the nearly 500 people who participated in the ceremonies before they left the city (some had travelled from different parts of the ever-growing British Empire). Brewster put Hill in touch with Adamson, and within weeks they were making calotype studies for the grand picture, as well as planning 'to apply the Calotype to many other general purposes of a very popular kind', as Brewster wrote to Fox Talbot.[13]

The art world – in Scotland at least – was bowled over by Hill and Adamson's pictures, even comparing them to paintings by Rembrandt. As early as April 1839, Fox Talbot had called his best results 'Rembrandtish' and some of Adamson's pictures taken before he met Hill had already been praised for having 'all the force and beauty of the Sketches of Rembrandt'.[14] Now, the Edinburgh painter John Harden (1772–1847) thought the partnerships' results 'as Rembrandt's but improved'.[15] The marine and landscape painter and stage designer Clarkson Stanfield (1793–1867) declared that he would 'rather have a set of them than the finest Rembrandt's I ever saw'.[16] Is this hyperbole, or do such views remind us of the shock of the new – the sensation for these Victorians that they were seeing something they had never seen before? For the rest of the century, and even into the twentieth, photographers claimed Rembrandt as their aesthetic forebear; Julia Margaret 'declared she could make a quite Rembrandt-like picture',[17] and professional studio portraitists advertised their mastery of the 'Rembrandt effect'.

Comparisons were made with even older artistic models. A critic writing in April 1846 wrote of the calotypes:

These clean, sonsy, caller, comely, substantial fishwives – what a refreshing sight! As easy, as unconfined, as deep-bosomed and ample, as any Grecian matron. Indeed, we have often been struck, when seeing them sitting together round their oyster creels, with their likeness to those awful and majestic women, the 'Fates' of the Elgin Marbles, the casts of which are in the Gallery of the Royal Institution.[18]

The artist who had persuaded the British Museum to buy the marbles from Lord Elgin for £35,000 was Benjamin Robert Haydon (1786–1846), who thought them 'the true beau ideal, of which nature alone is the basis'. Even he wrote to Hill to compare his calotypes favourably with the marbles.

While all this was going on, a young Scotswoman, Clementina Elphinstone-Fleeming (1822–67), born in Cumbernauld House, near Glasgow, was being wooed by the heir to the Hawarden title and estates. In 1857, on the death of her father-in-law, Clementina became Lady Hawarden and moved to Dundrum House in Tipperary, Ireland. With time, and means, she took up photography and over the next seven years made an extraordinary series of photographs, the majority using her eight children as models. A year before Julia Margaret submitted photographs to the Photographic Society of London's exhibition in 1864, Hawarden won the prize for the best amateur exhibitor. A year later, she won the medal for the best composition from a single negative. Another amateur, who had taken up photography in the same year as Hawarden, wrote in his diary 'I did *not* admire Mrs Cameron's large heads taken out of focus. The best of the life-ones were Lady Hawarden's.'[19] The writer was Lewis Carroll.

We have already met Carroll at Freshwater, and he and Julia Margaret knew each other's work well. We have also seen the work of another of Julia Margaret's contemporaries, David Wilkie Wynfield, from whom she had one lesson in photography. If Carroll's portraits, many of which were of young girls, are the most natural and relaxed photographs of children to come down to us from the nineteenth century, Wynfield's costumed pictures of his fellow artists are more painterly, and have much more in common with Julia Margaret's fancy dress illustrations.

At the beginning of December 1863, just before Julia Margaret was given her first camera, Jabez Hughes (1819–84), a pro fessional photographer who lived on the Isle of Wight, wrote in the *British Journal of Photography*:

Though the extensive diffusion and numerous applications of the art depend upon the professional, yet it must be always borne in mind that the original discoveries – marked improvements – are made by the amateur … It is scarcely to be wondered at that the impulses forward should emanate rather from the amateur than the professional. The former pursues the art for pleasure, the latter for profit. The one can try all manner of experiments, and whether he succeeds or fails, he secures his object – agreeable occupation. The professional has all his energies directed to make things pay. He has too much at stake to speculate.[20]

Had Hughes met Julia Margaret on the Isle of Wight? Had he seen any of her early photographic experiments? Was she at all influenced by his views? Three months later, might he have referred to amateurs as 'he or she' rather than just 'he'? Hughes' views seem to me to be prescient. Perhaps his word 'amateur' needs defining – the photographers to whom he refers are no mere 'Sunday painters', playing with the medium, and failing more often than succeeding. These amateurs are characterised by a love for their medium, by a will to work very hard at it, sometimes by a wish to make money from it (usually disappointed) and by the very highest professional standards. They were amateurs in the sense that gentlemen 'amateurs' used to be separated from professional 'players' in national cricket teams. Like cricketers, amateur photographers often outperformed their professional colleagues; certainly the small group I have named all made major contributions to the development of the medium, and all can claim to have been artists in their own right.

These amateur ladies and gentlemen also found the technology difficult to handle. In December 1857, not long before Lewis Carroll took up photography, he wrote a parody of Longfellow's narrative poem *Hiawatha*, that included a surprisingly full description of the wet collodion process:

First, a piece of glass he coated
With collodion, and plunged it
In a bath of lunar caustic
Carefully dissolved in water –
There he left it certain minutes.
Secondly, my Hiawatha
Made with cunning hand a mixture
Of the acid pyrro-gallic;
And of glacial-acetic,
And of alcohol and water –
This developed all the picture.

Finally, he fixed each picture
With a saturate solution
Which was made of hyposulphite,
Which, again, was made of soda.[21]

No wonder that Julia Margaret's first recorded attempt to master all this took her seven hours from start to finish. This struggle to master the chemistry, and the technology, seems to me to be another factor separating these 'amateurs' from their more practised professional colleagues – who often had assistants to carry out the darkroom processes for them.

The photographers I have mentioned have a number of other things in common. To begin with, they all (with the exception of Carroll) seem to have been largely uninterested in sharp focus. We already know that technical and practical reasons – her lens, her camera, perhaps even her own eyes – made it difficult for Julia Margaret to get sharply focused results. But 'What a fallacy it is to suppose that the camera makes the portrait! Was it the camera alone that made the immortal portraits of DAVID OCTAVIUS HILL and JULIA MARGARET CAMERON?'[22] asked the twentieth-century photographer Emil Otto Hoppé (1878–1972) in 1945. Coincidentally, Hoppé lived and worked in the Kensington home of Millais perhaps used by Julia Margaret for photography. The answer to his rhetorical question is that immortal portraits call for very conscious artistic decisions. Julia Margaret had already asked Herschel: 'What is focus – & who has a right to say what focus is the legitimate focus?'[23]

This interest in a creative and unconventional use of focus, and in the manipulation of light and shade, derives from a profound belief that photography was an art form, in which differences in focus could be exploited like brushstrokes, pencil shadings, or chisel marks. Writing in the *Illustrated London News*, a perceptive critic of the 1865 Photographic Society of London exhibition, was on Julia Margaret's side:

Light, instead of being the greatest friend is, we verily believe, the greatest enemy to the mass of photographers; and until we see three-fourths of their glass houses bricked up they will never be able to secure the one great charm of art within their reach, the broad, simple, and regulated chiaroscuro of Rembrandt, Correggio and Velasquez [sic]. *The nearest approach to art, or rather the most bold and successful application of the principles of fine Art to photography, will be found in several portraits of literary men and painters, and studios from women and children, intended as illustrations of 'Faith', 'Hope', 'Charity', &c., by Miss Julia Cameron.*[24]

All this, and more, was quoted in the *Photographic Journal*, which by 1867 admitted that, though her 'lens could not do what the lady wanted it to do, and produced an image with a blurred definition,' she 'in many cases succeeds in turning out a head with a good deal of power in it, and with a softness of outline which is in contrast to the ordinary style of photographs'.[25]

The creative use of soft focus, by Julia Margaret and a handful of others, led to the long-lived 'Pictorialist' movement, which, at its best, produced some of the most beautiful photographs ever taken. The text accompanying Stieglitz's publication in 1913 of photogravures of Julia Margaret's prints in his influential *Camera Work* magazine had no doubt where it all began: 'Those who think that pictorial photography is a product of the last quarter of a century would do well to study the work of David Octavius Hill ... some of his portraits are not surpassed by anything that has been done since.' Of Cameron herself, the writer said: 'Her portrait work is characterized by a breadth of force seen in that of no one else since the time of Hill.'[26] At its worst, especially late in its development, Pictorialism became empty and formulaic – as so often happens with art movements when they outlive their original inspiration.

Another common factor was these photographers' respect for their sitters – colleagues, family members, beautiful men, women and children. Cameron, Carroll and Wynfield eagerly invited heroes to sit for them. In contrast, professional portraitists had to accept whoever came into their studio. The challenge was to get their sitters in and out as quickly as possible, to persuade them that they could make more flattering portraits than any other photographer, and to charge them as much money as possible.

Lady Hawarden and Julia Margaret in particular sought something that was more impersonal, more abstract, perhaps more timeless. Rejlander's obituary of Hawarden declared that 'She aimed at elegant and, if possible, idealised truth.'[27] Neither she nor Julia Margaret were interested in surface reality, but sought to make pictures which penetrated beneath the facial contours. In a way, the results are almost abstracts of greatness. Hill and Adamson, Carroll, and Wynfield's portraits clearly show people from another age; Cameron's and Hawarden's, despite their antique costumes, facial hair and coiffures, seem timeless.

Being ladies and gentlemen, all our photographers were well connected – some even aristocrats, like Lady Hawarden and a number of other women photographers, such as Lady Jocelyn and Lady Mildmay. All were sociable, even Lewis Carroll, though his stutter and his shyness made him feel most relaxed in the company of children. Hill and Adamson seem to have tried to make their sittings cheerful and enjoyable occasions, and when they made one of their very few photographic forays out of Edinburgh – to an 1844 meeting of the British Association for the Advancement of Science in York – Hill was far from comfortable working among people who did not know him well, or were not in sympathy with him: 'Coldness on the part of those to be calotyped unmans me quite.'[28] Those portrayed in Hill and Adamson's portraits look natural, relaxed, and comfortable – occasionally, they even smile – a difficult achievement given the length of time they had to sit absolutely still.

Another shared interest was in literature. All these photographers were well read, and many of their pictures illustrated moments in literature or the Bible. Indeed, a paradoxical common factor is that photography, for all of them, was only one element in their crowded lives. Biographers of any of these figures must of necessity write thousands of words which have nothing to do with photography at all (as I have done). Dinner table conversation at Dimbola and Farringford, at Hill and Adamson's Rock House, Lewis Carroll's Christ Church, Lady Hawarden's Dundrum or Cromwell Place, and Wynfield's St John's Wood, was not about photography so much as about religion, politics, literature, science, spiritualism, theatre, the Elgin Marbles, and other cultural matters.

Where Julia Margaret Cameron was concerned, one can be confident that a constant element of her conversation, as it was of her whole life, was the search for 'Beauty' as her poem 'On a Portrait', written in September 1875, shortly before she and her husband left England for Ceylon attests:

Oh, mystery of Beauty! Who can tell
Thy mighty influence? Who can best descry
How secret, swift, and subtle is the spell
Wherein the music of thy voice doth lie?

The last few lines of Julia Margaret's poem seem exactly the right place to leave our remarkable little group of portraitists, and the heroine of this extraordinary period of just thirteen years in the history of photography, Julia Margaret Cameron:

Genius and love have each fulfilled their part,
And both unite with force and equal grace,
Whilst all that we love best in classic art
Is stamped for ever on the immortal face.[29]

NOTES

1. Letter from Julia Margaret to Herschel, 31 December 1864, National Museum of Photography, Film & Television, Bradford.
2. *Photographic Journal*, 15 August 1864, pp.86–8.
3. 'Annals of my Glass House', p.9.
4. H.P. Robinson, *Pictorial Effect in Photography*, quoted in Gernsheim, 1948; second edition 1975, p.68.
5. *Photographic Journal*, 15 January 1865, p.191.
6. P.H. Emerson, 'Mrs Julia Margaret Cameron', *Sun Artists*, 5, October 1890 (Kegan Paul, Trench, Trübner & Co., London), p.38.
7. The 1898 Royal Photographic Society International Exhibition was at the Crystal Palace, South London. The work of Julia Margaret and Rejlander was included, Mozley, 1974, p.59.
8. Stieglitz, *Camera Work*, 41, January 1913.
9. Fry and Woolf, 1926; second edition 1973, p.28.
10. *Comptes Rendus Hebdomadaires des Séances de l'Académie des Sciences*, VIII, January–June 1839.
11. *Notices and Abstracts of Communications to the British Association for the Advancement of Science at the Birmingham Meeting*, August 1839.
12. Colvin, 1971, pp.593–4. The author points out that the portrait, reproduced as the frontispiece of her book, shows Edgeworth wearing a dark wig.
13. Letter from Brewster to Fox Talbot dated 13 July 1843, National Museum of Photography, Film & Television, Bradford.
14. *Edinburgh Review*, January 1843.
15. Letter to his married daughter Mrs Jane Barker, 23 November 1843.
16. Quoted in Ford and Strong, 1976, p.39.
17. According to Weld, 1902, p.68.
18. Dr John Brown reviewing the Royal Scottish Academy exhibition in *The Witness*, 22 April 1846, quoted in Stevenson, 2002, p.133.
19. Diary entry for 23 June 1864, Wakeling, IV, 1997, p.315.
20. 'A Tribute to Amateurs', *British Journal of Photography*, 1 December 1863, pp.466–7.
21. Lewis Carroll's *Hiawatha's Photographing* was published in three versions between 1857 and 1883. The lines about wet collodion were omitted from the final version (in his *Rhyme? And Reason?*, Macmillan & Co., London, 1883) as by then the process had largely been superseded by dry-plate photography.
22. Hoppé, 1945, p.44.
23. Letter from Julia Margaret to Herschel, 31 December 1864, National Museum of Photography, Film & Television, Bradford.
24. The *Illustrated London News* review was reprinted in the July 1865 issue of the *Photographic Journal*, p.117.
25. Stieglitz, op.cit.
26. Stieglitz, op.cit.
27. O.G. Rejlander, 'In Memoriam', quoted in Dodier, 1999, p.106.
28. Stevenson, 2002, p.133.
29. Written in September 1875, published in *Macmillan's Magazine*, XXXIII, February 1876, p.372.

Plates

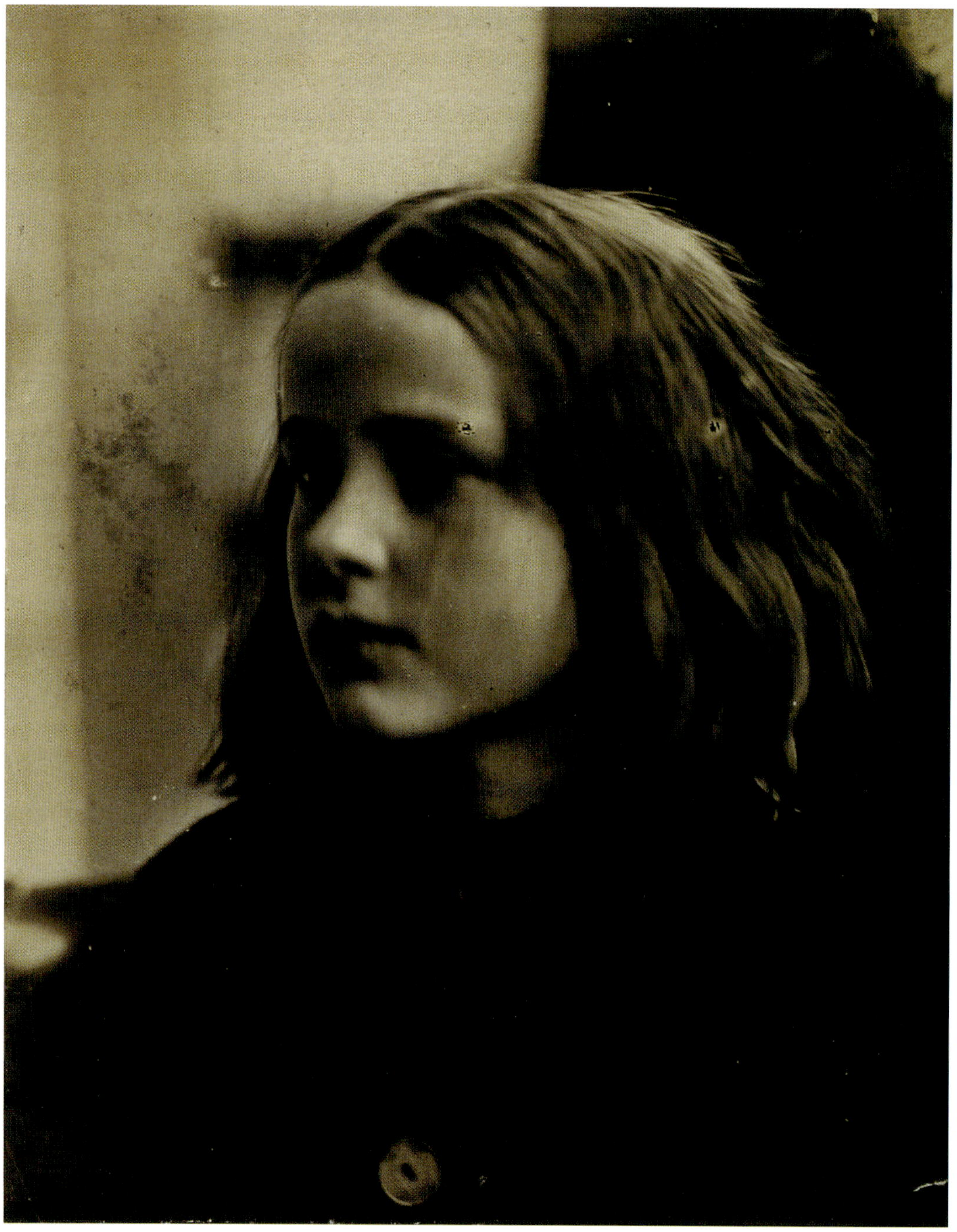

Annie my first success, 29 January 1864
Annie Wilhelmina Philpot
Albumen print, 188 x 145mm (7⅜ x 5¾")
National Museum of Photography, Film & Television, Bradford

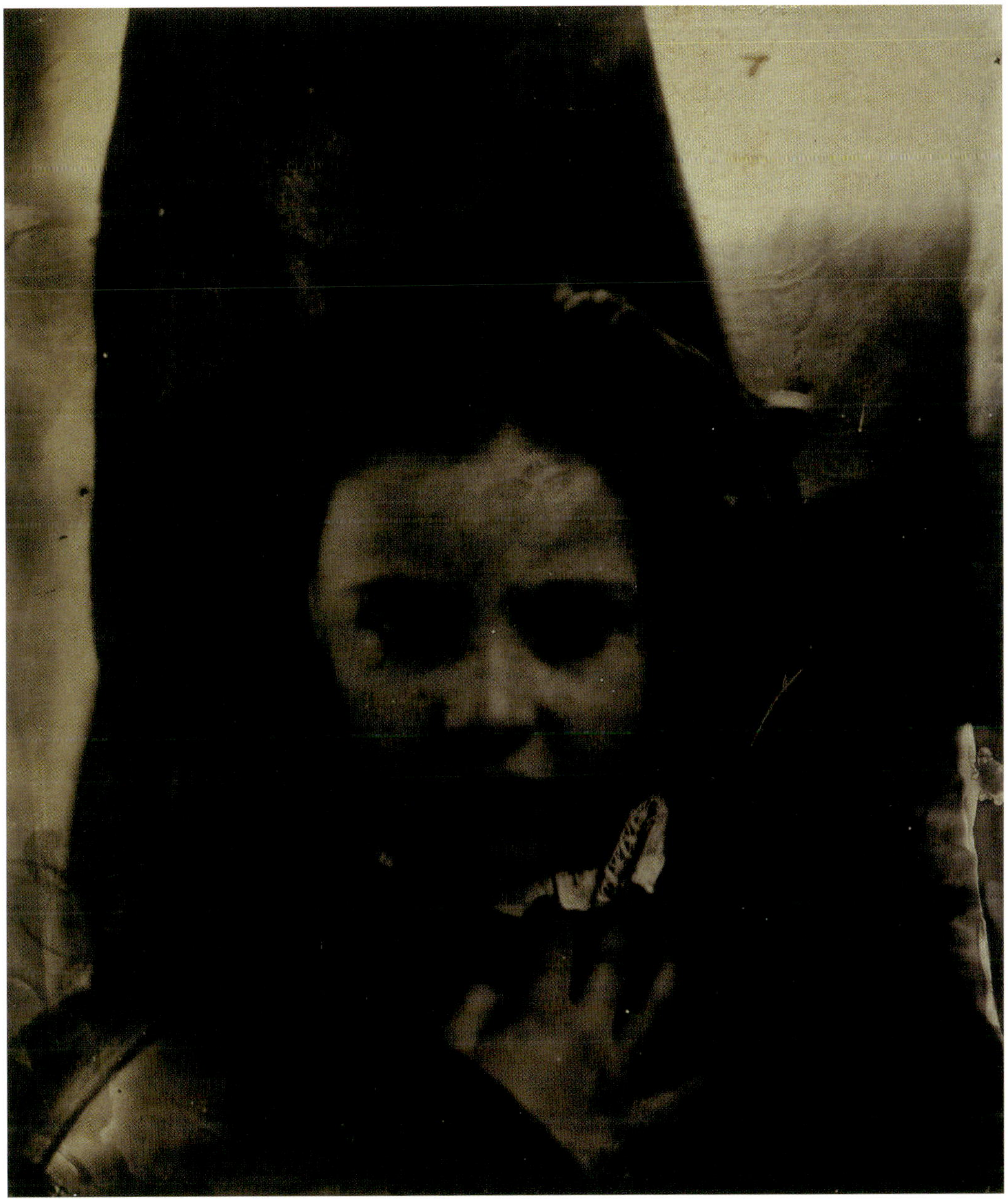

Daisy, January 1864
Margaret Louisa Bradley
Albumen print, 179 x 149mm (7 x 5⅞")
National Museum of Photography, Film & Television, Bradford

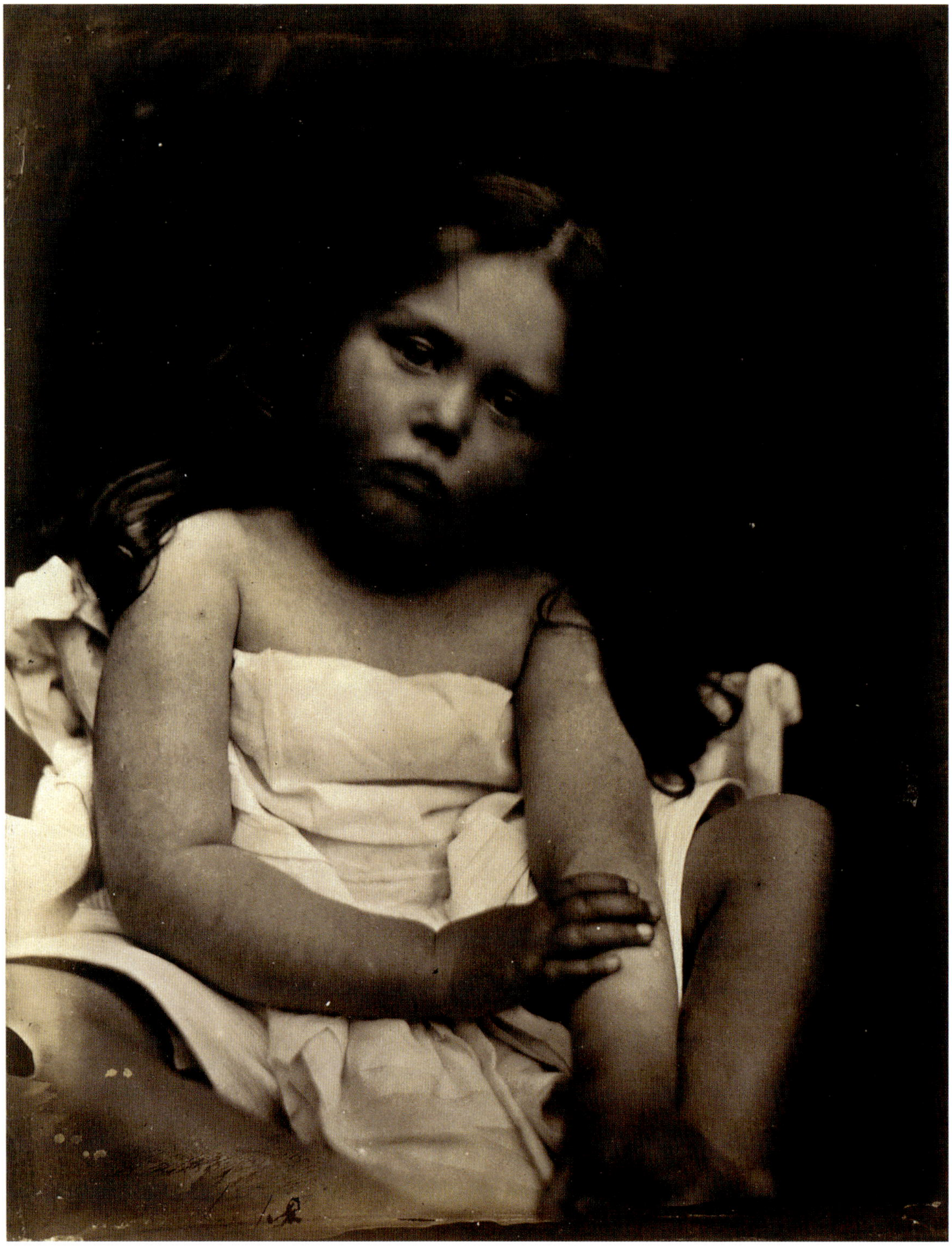

Alice, 1864
Alice du Cane
Albumen print, 274 x 207mm (10¾ x 8⅛")
National Museum of Photography, Film & Television, Bradford

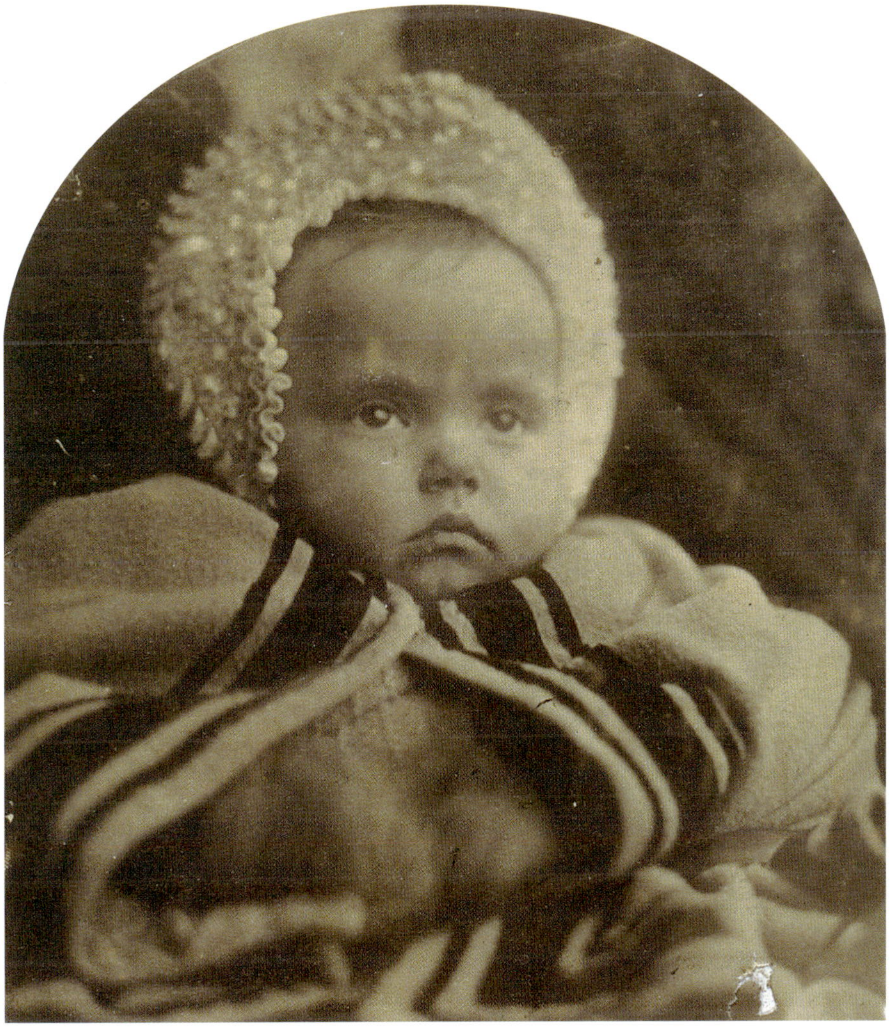

Baby 'Pictet', April 1864
'One year Old Infant shipwrecked once in the Madras Surf
& again in the wreck of the Colombo Steamer'
Georgina Anna Mary Pictet
Albumen print, 172 x 148mm (6¾ x 5⅞")
National Museum of Photography, Film & Television, Bradford

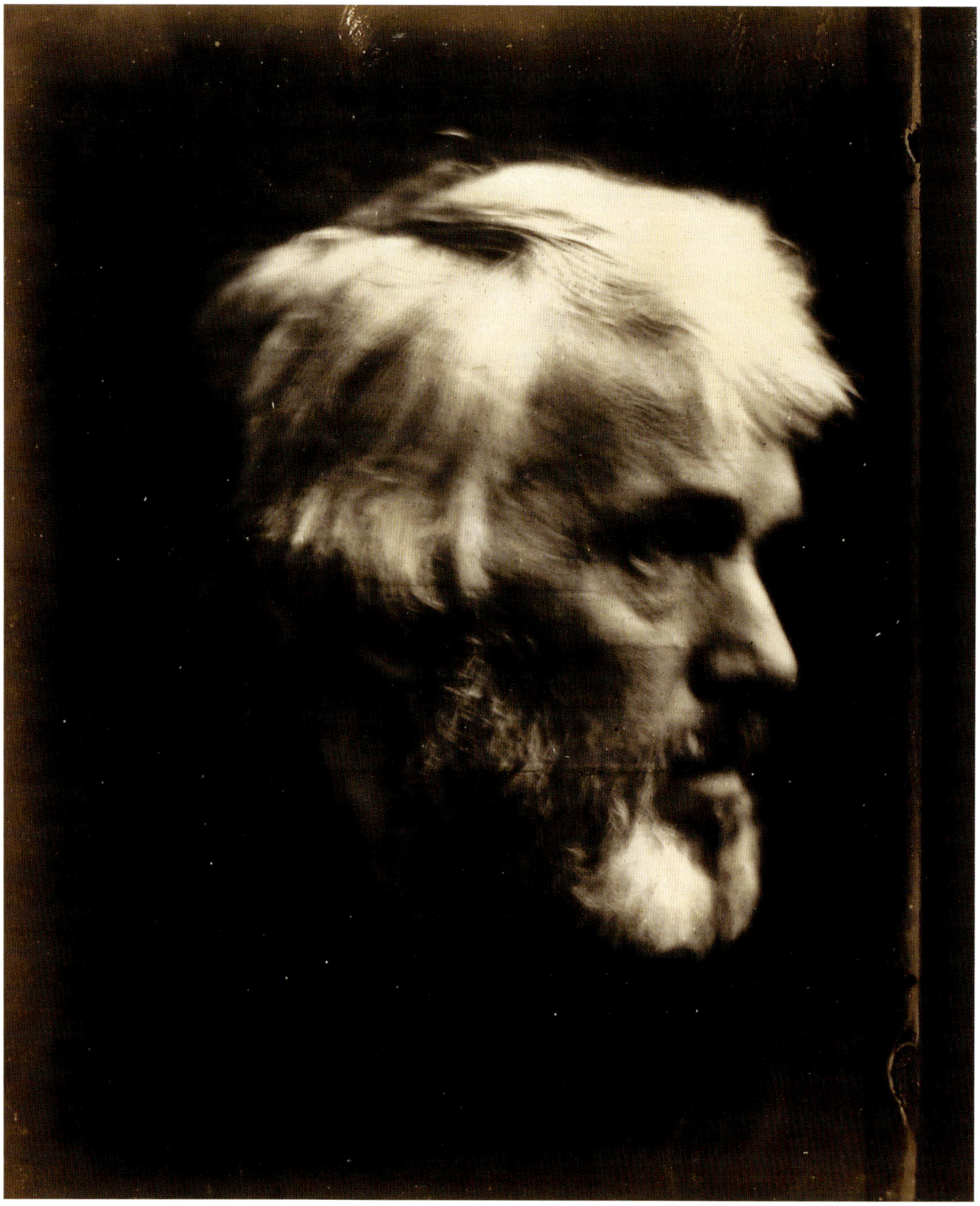

Thomas Carlyle profile, 1867
Albumen print, 320 x 257mm (12⅝ x 10⅛")
National Museum of Photography, Film & Television, Bradford

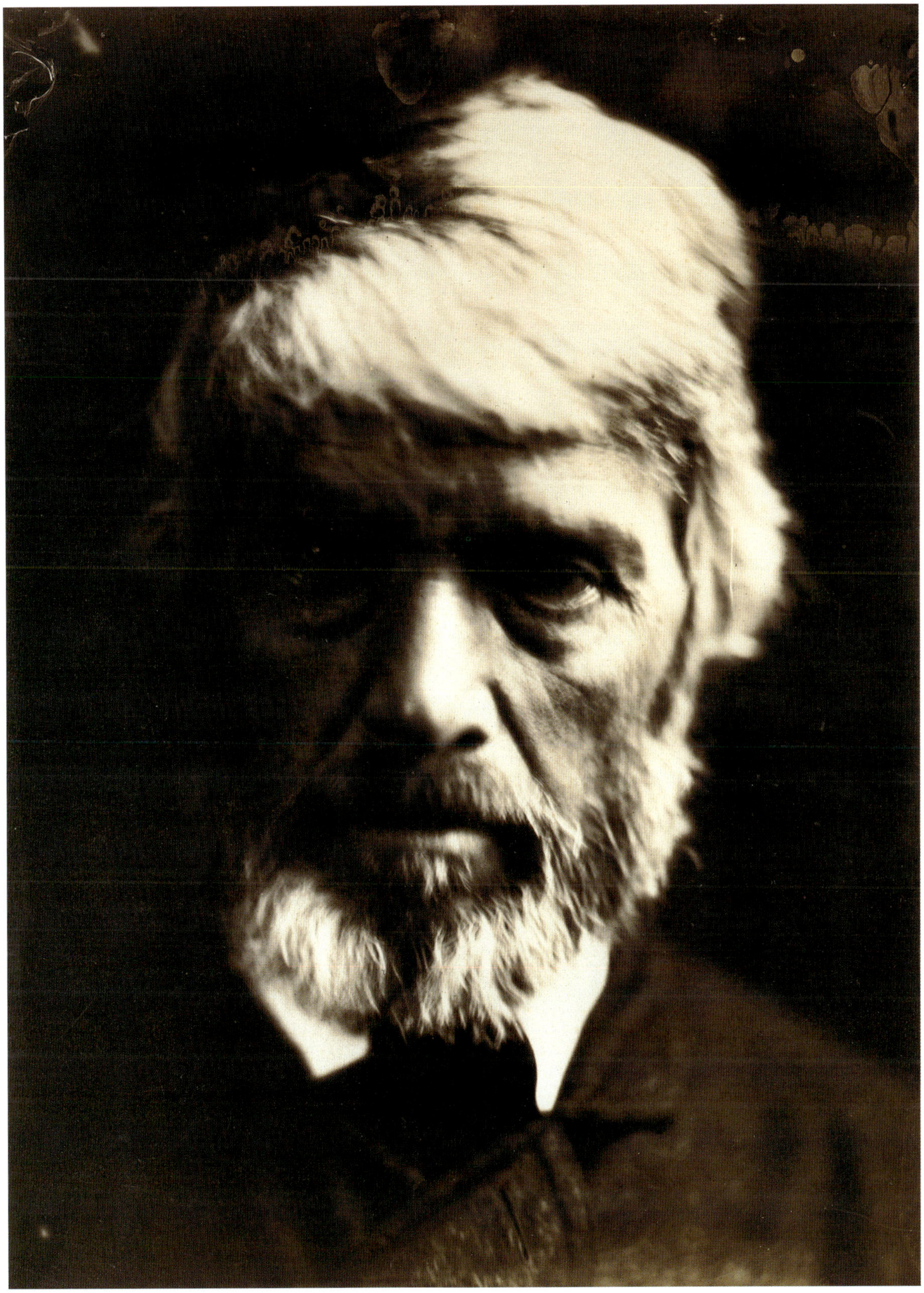

Carlyle like a rough block of Michael Angelo's sculpture, 1867
Thomas Carlyle
Albumen print, 364 x 258mm (14⅜ x 10⅛")
The J. Paul Getty Museum, Los Angeles

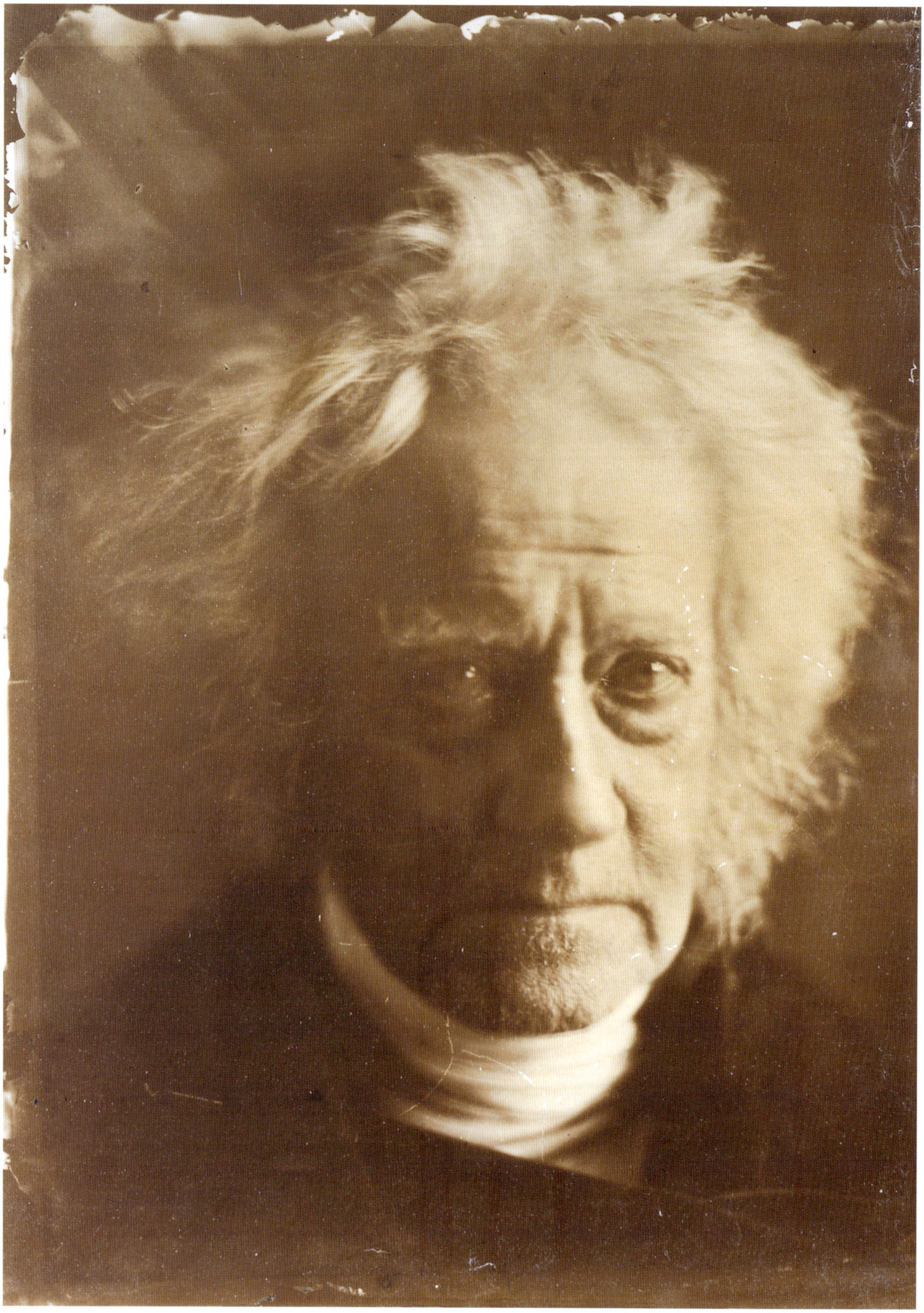

Sir John Herschel, April 1867
Albumen print, 384 x 279mm (15⅛ x 11")
National Portrait Gallery, London (NPG P201)

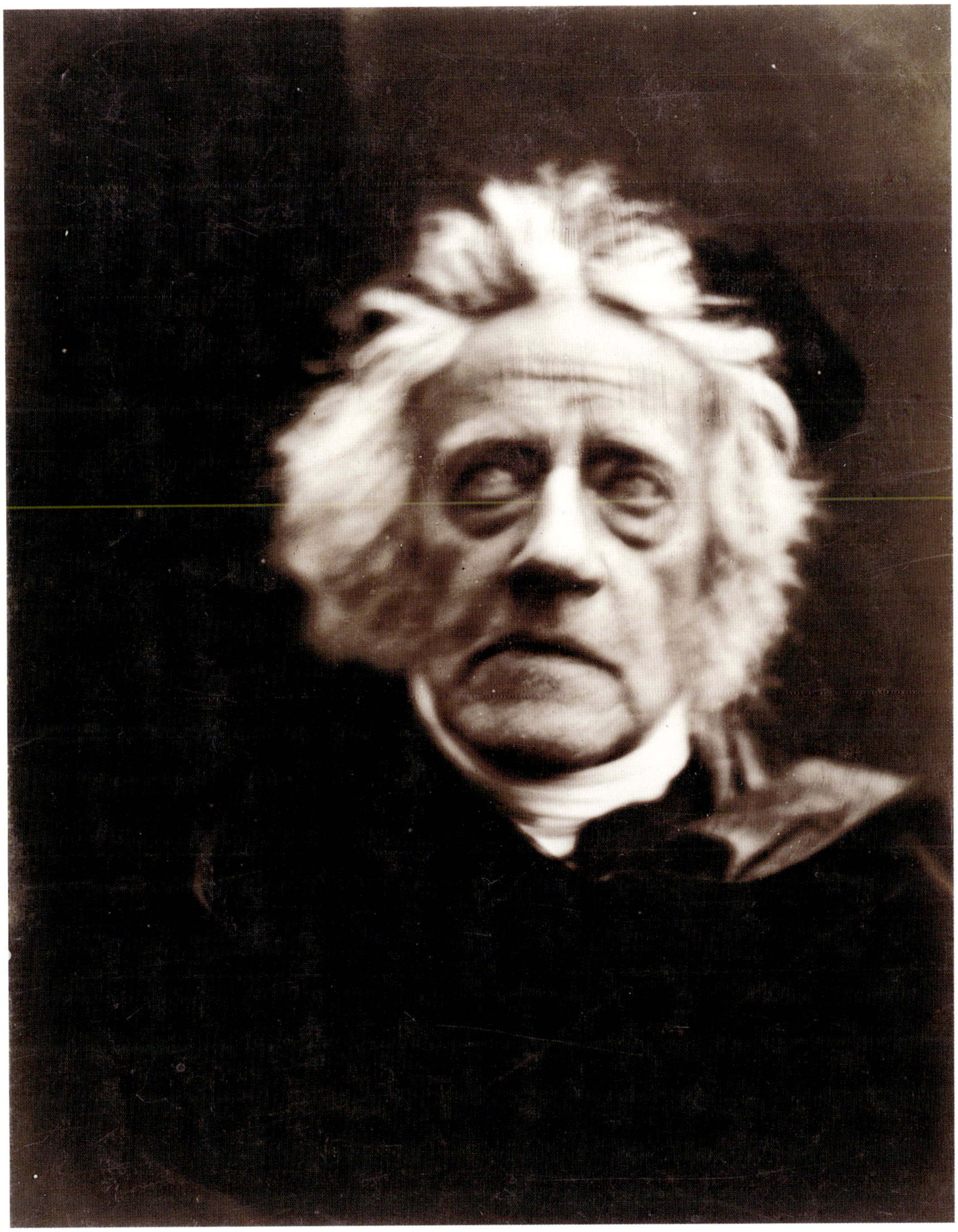

The Astronomer, April 1867
Sir John Herschel
Albumen print, 302 x 232mm (11⅞ x 9⅛")
Royal Photographic Society

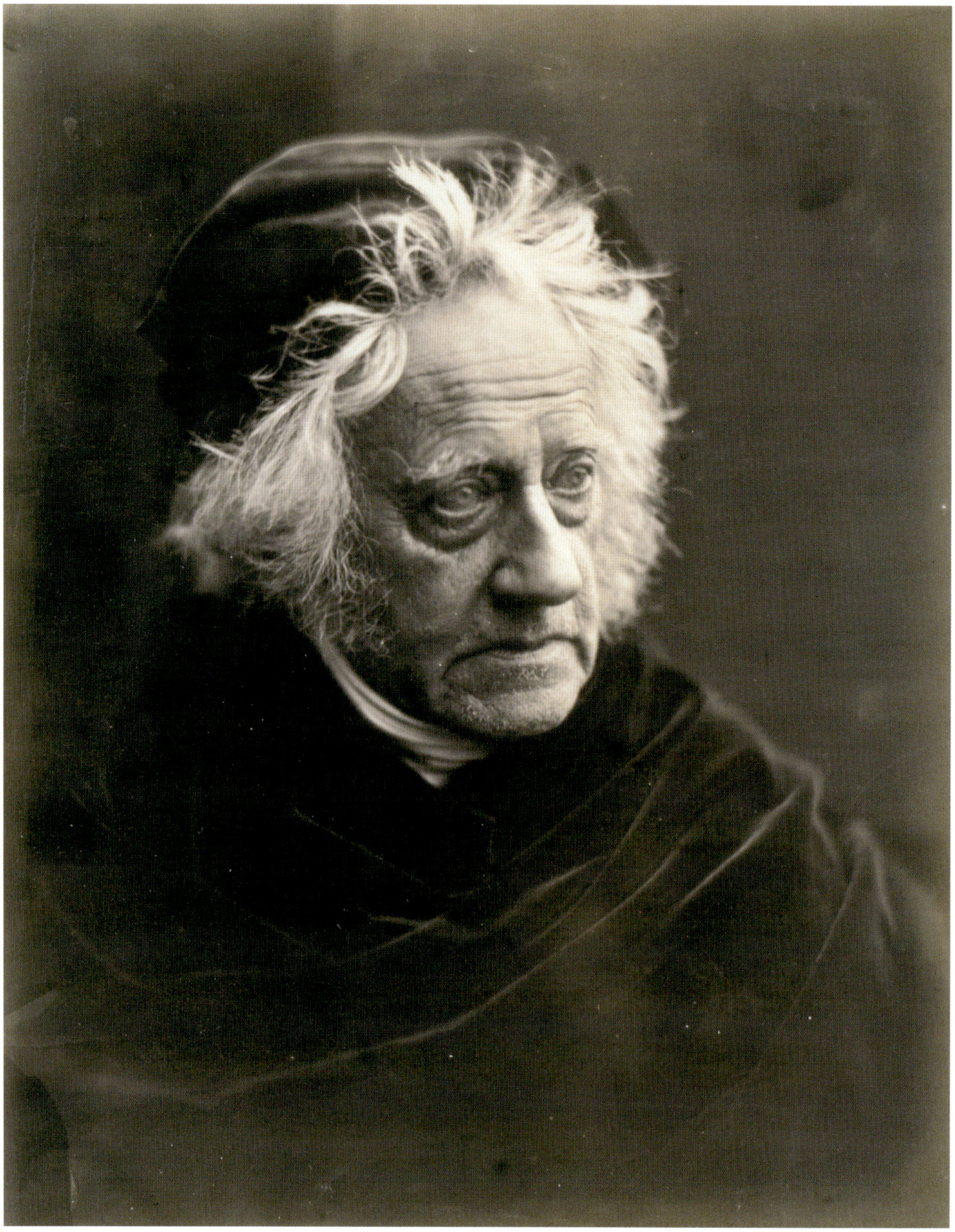

Sir John Herschel with Cap, April 1867
Albumen print, 340 x 264mm (13⅜ x 10⅜")
National Portrait Gallery, London (NPG P213)

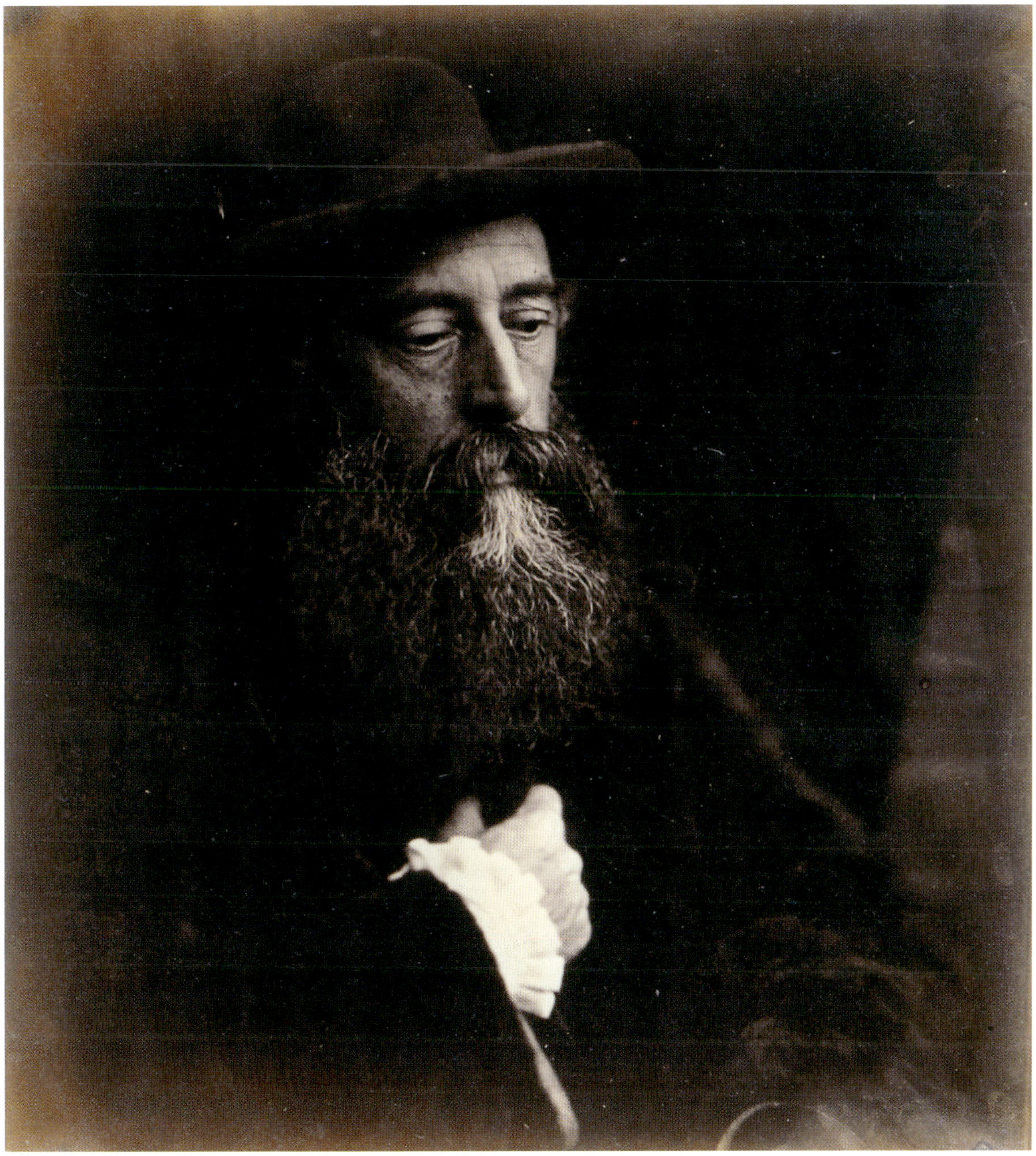

G.F. Watts with hat, 1864
Albumen print, 248 x 219mm (9¾ x 8⅝")
National Museum of Photography, Film & Television, Bradford

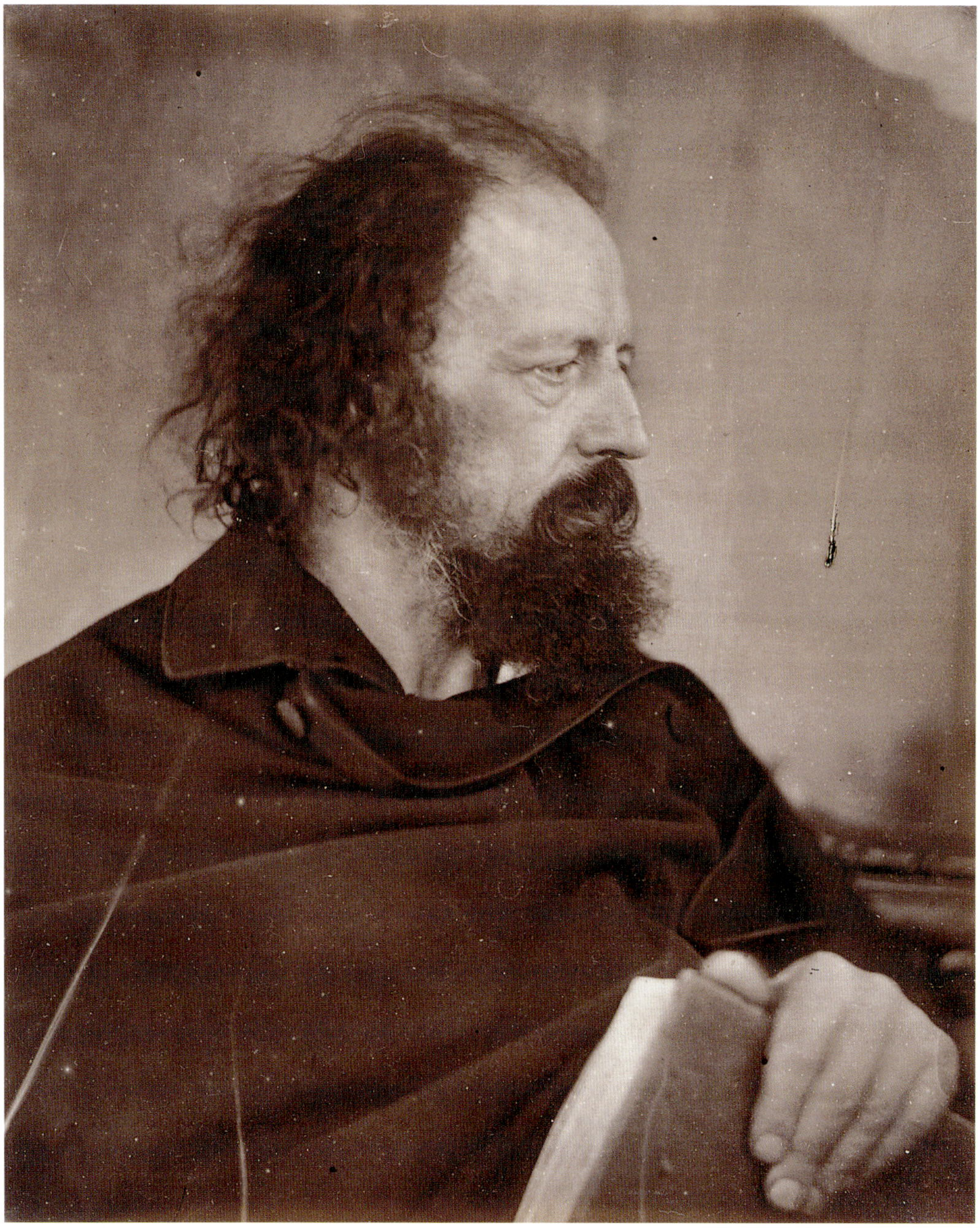

Alfred Tennyson with book, May 1865
(Tennyson dubbed this portrait 'The Dirty Monk')
Albumen print, 252 x 200mm (9⅞ x 7⅞")
National Museum of Photography, Film & Television, Bradford

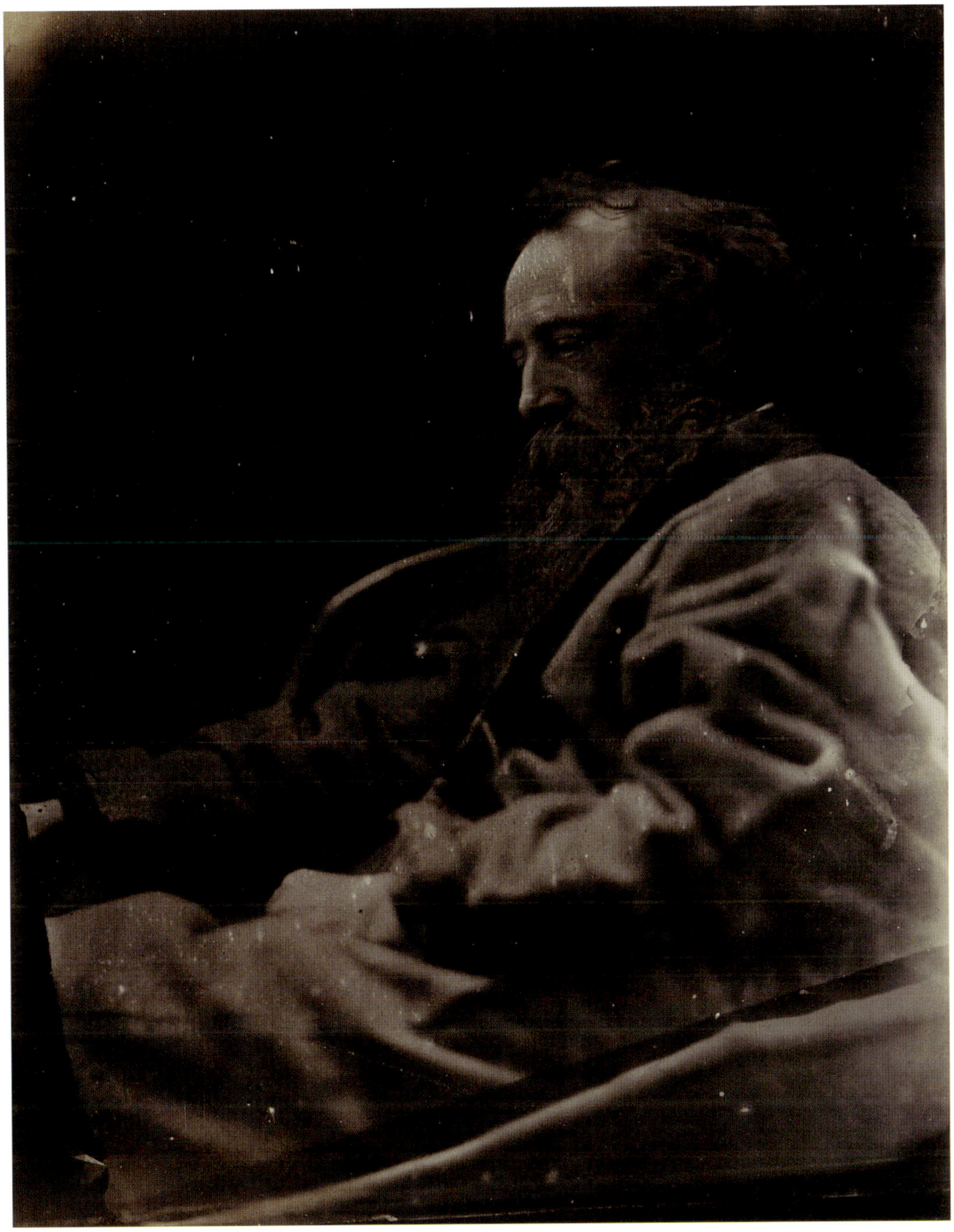

G.F. Watts profile, 1864
Albumen print, 273 x 210mm (10¾ x 8¼")
National Museum of Photography, Film & Television, Bradford

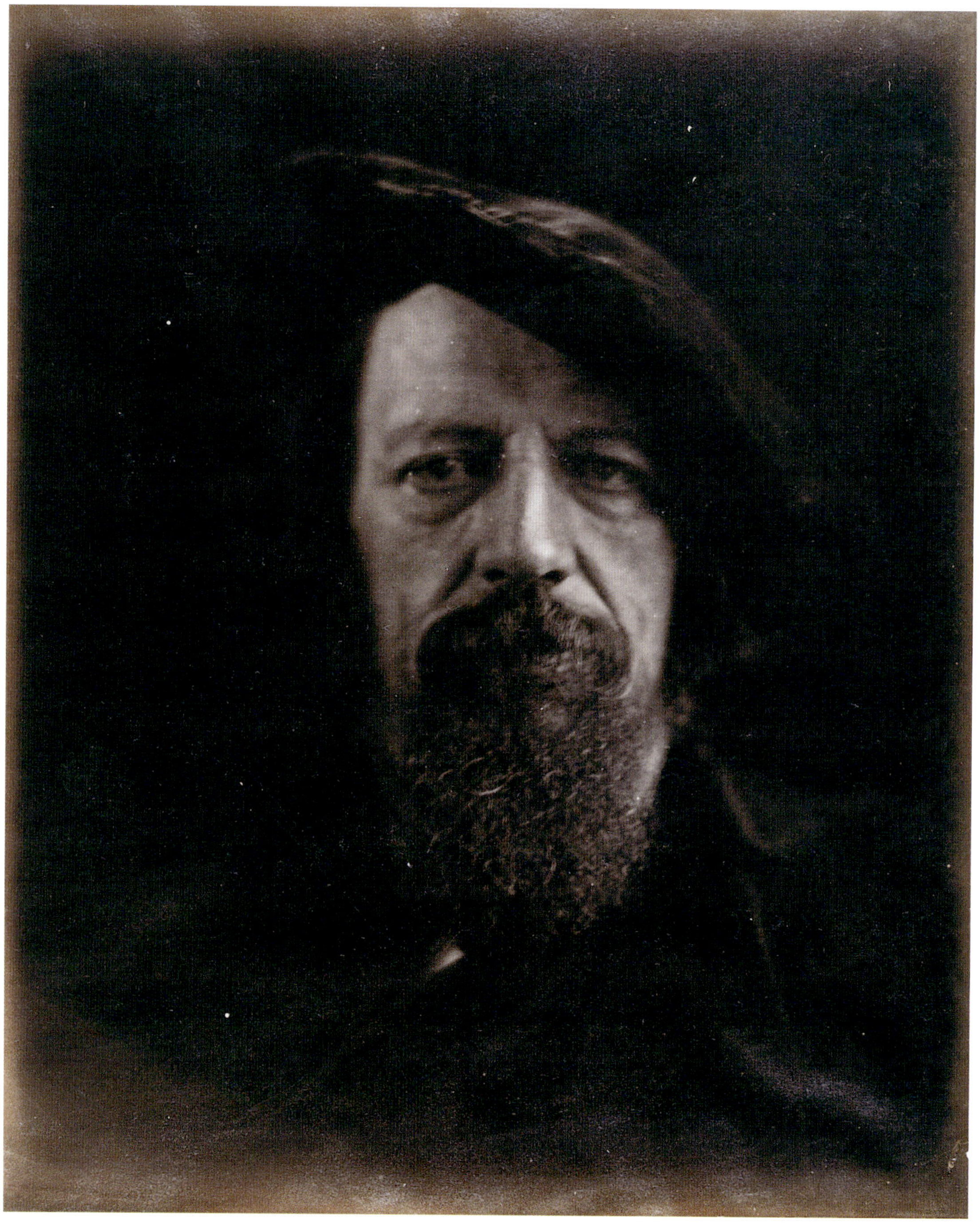

Alfred Tennyson, 1866
Albumen print, 328 x 260mm (13 x 10¼")
National Museum of Photography, Film & Television, Bradford

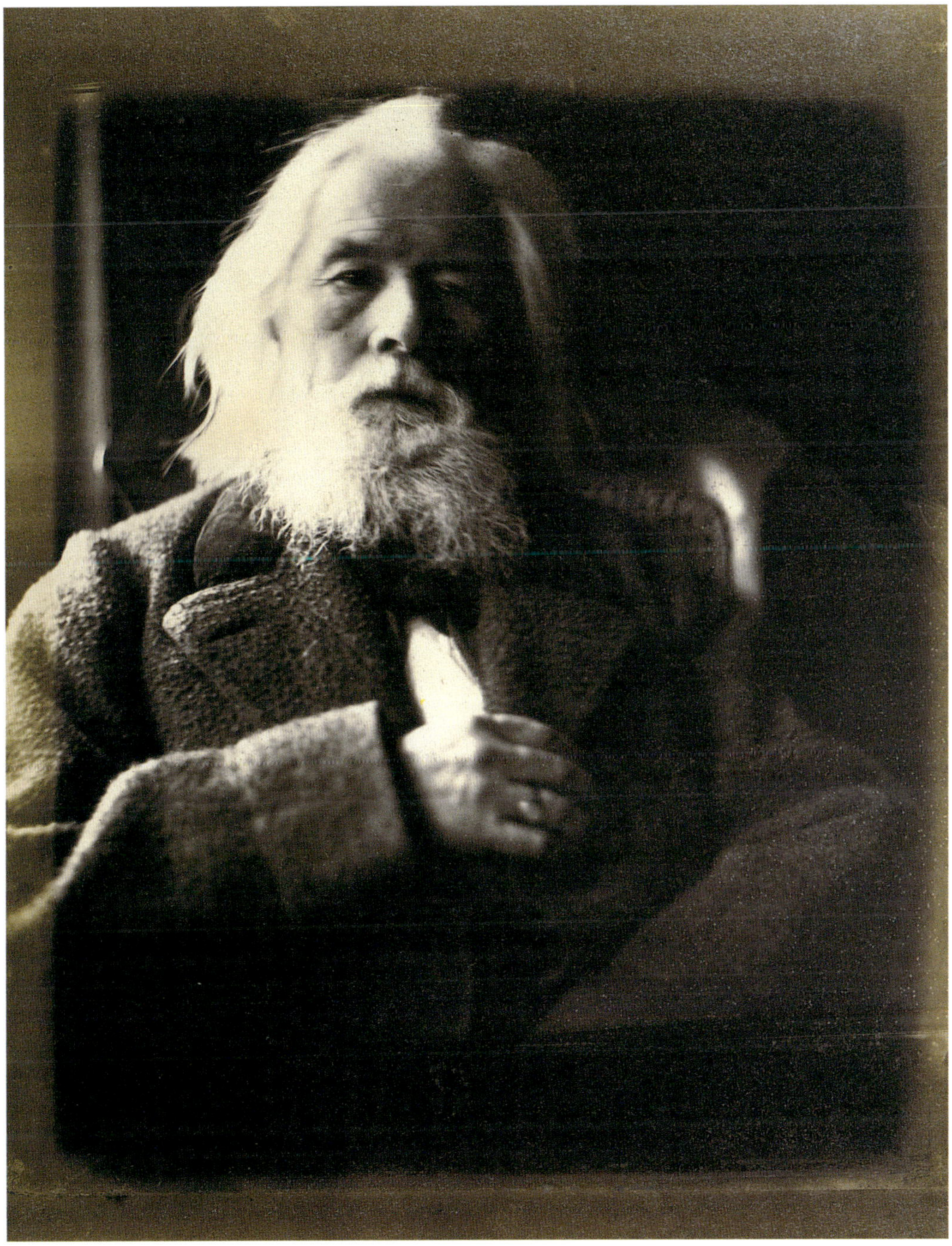

Charles Hay Cameron, 1864
Albumen print, 291 x 223mm (11½ x 8¾")
The J. Paul Getty Museum, Los Angeles

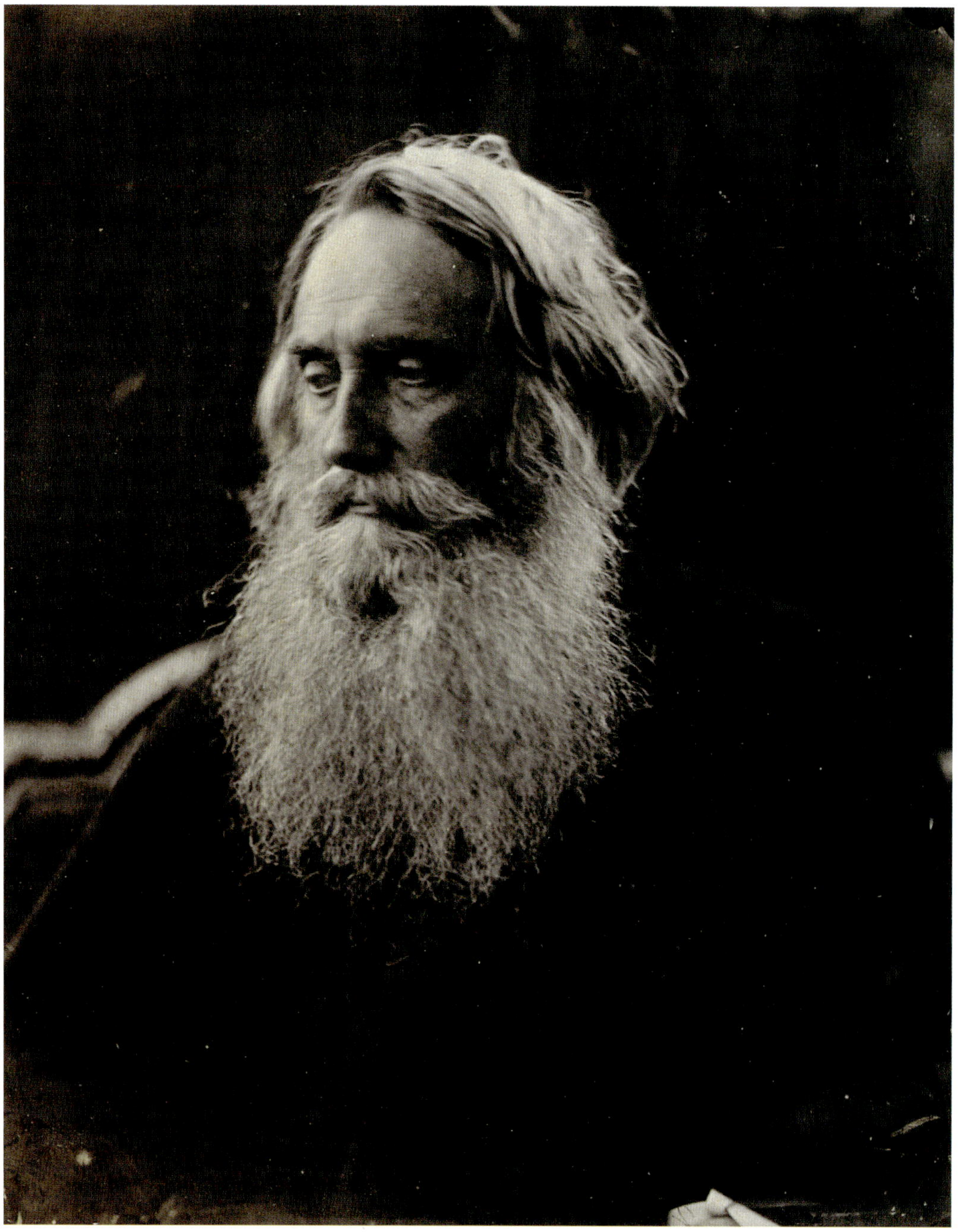

Henry Taylor Philip Van Artevelde, 1864
Albumen print, 270 x 209mm (10⅝ x 8¼")
National Museum of Photography, Film & Television, Bradford

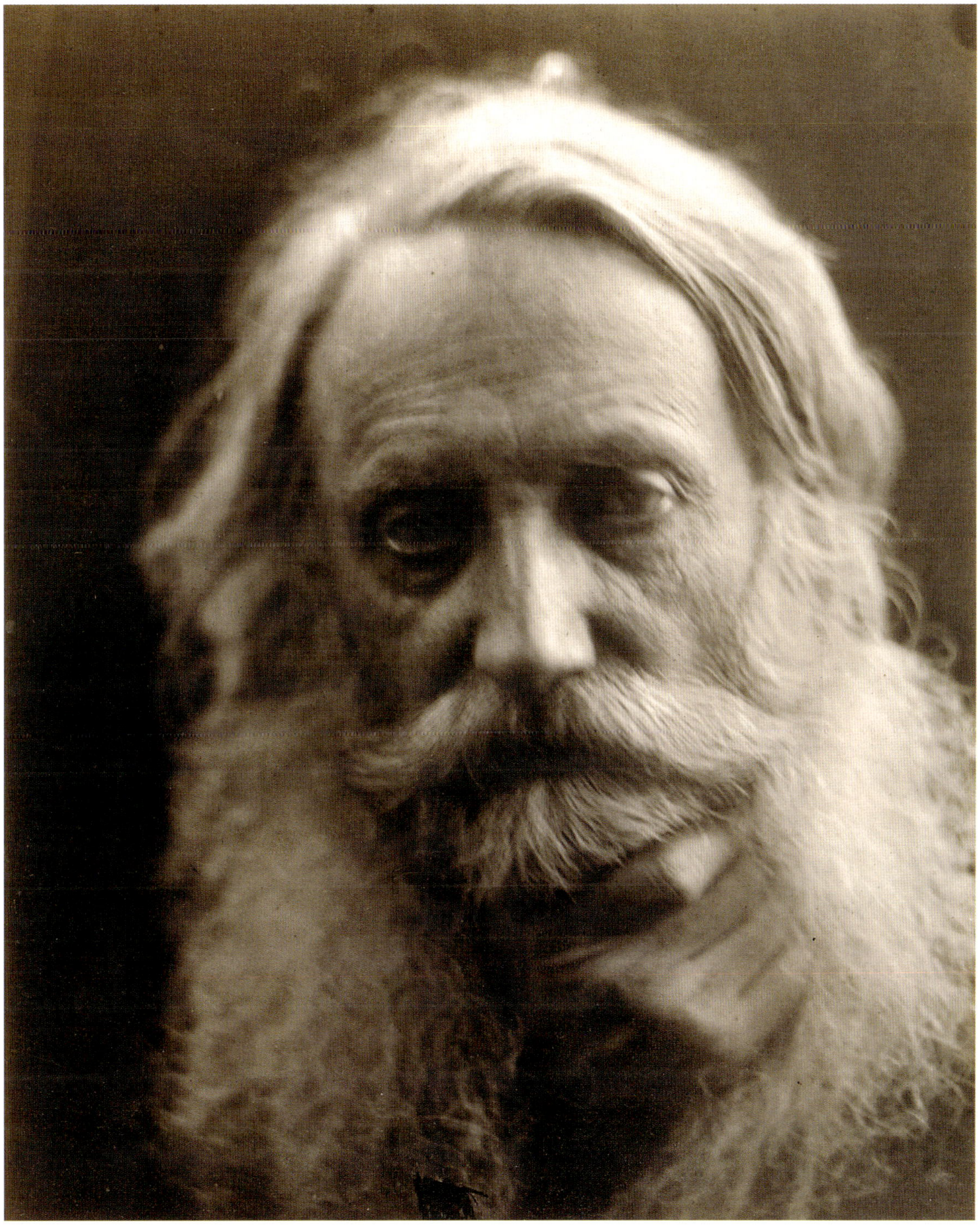

Sir Henry Taylor, 10 October 1867
Albumen print, 344 x 269mm (13½ x 10⅝")
The J. Paul Getty Museum, Los Angeles

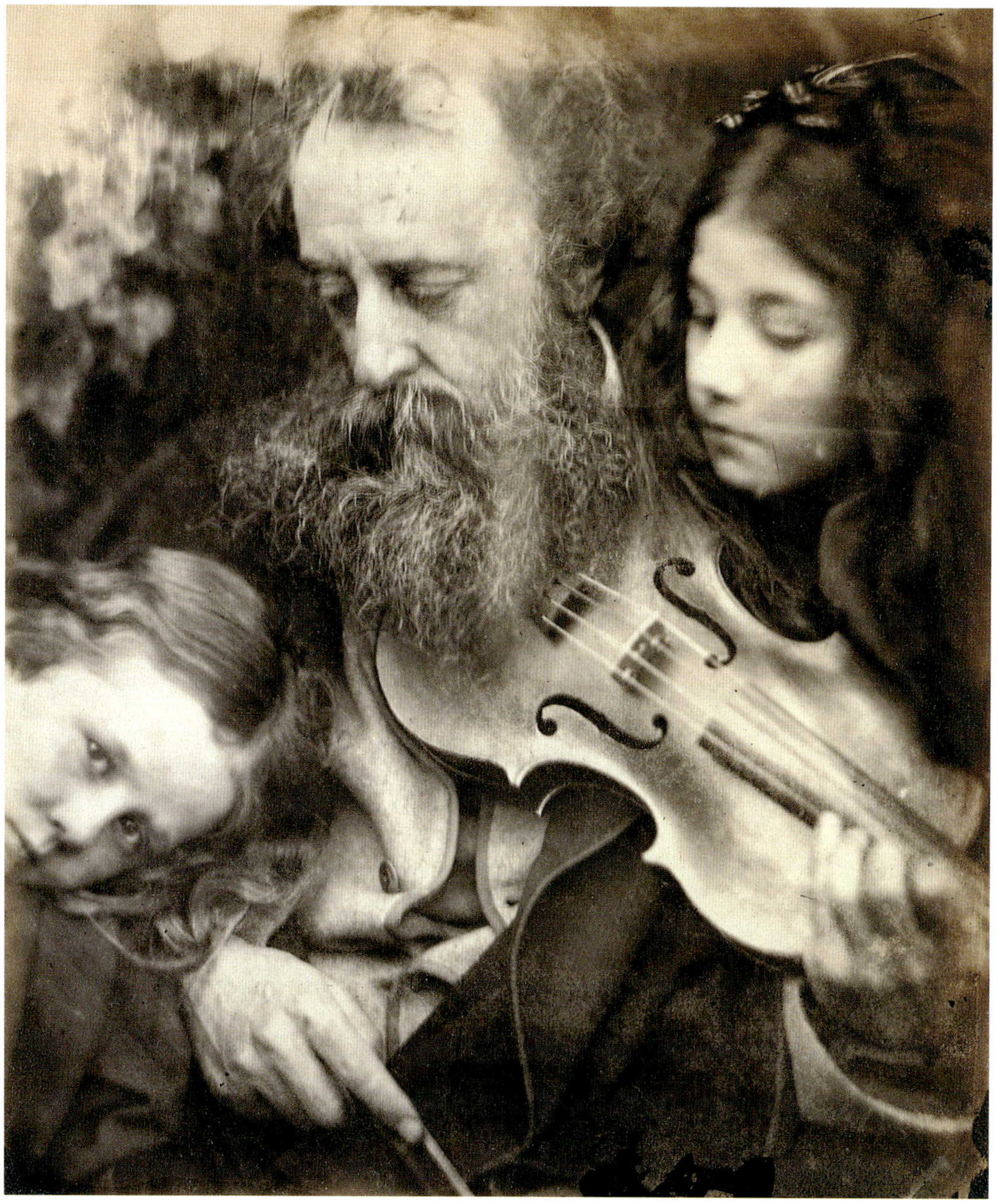

The Whisper of the Muse, April 1865
Elizabeth Keown, G.F. Watts and Kate Keown
Albumen print, 261 x 215mm (10¼ x 8½")
The J. Paul Getty Museum, Los Angeles

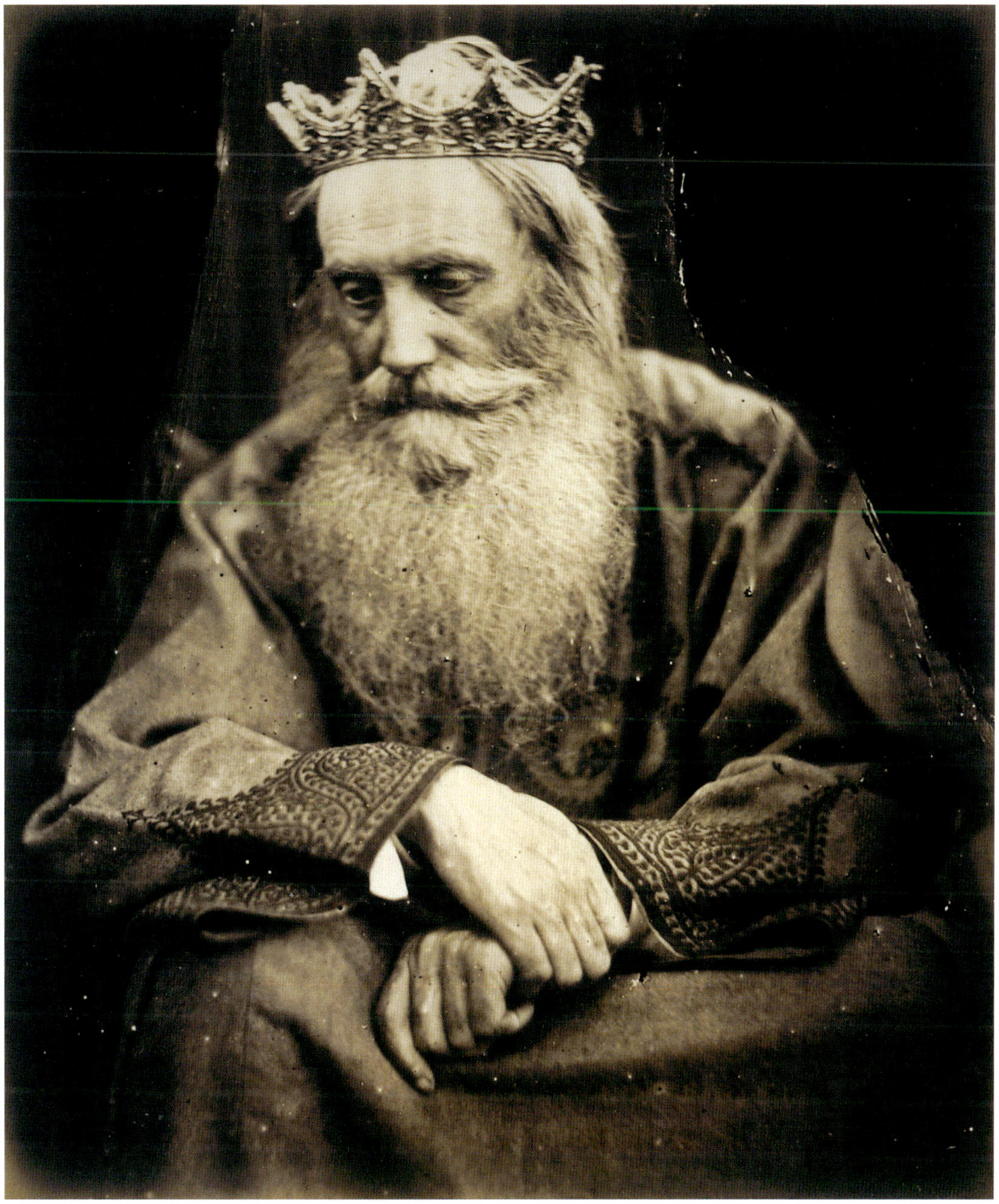

Study of King David, 1866
Henry Taylor
Albumen print, 272 x 225mm (10¾ x 8⅞")
National Museum of Photography, Film & Television, Bradford

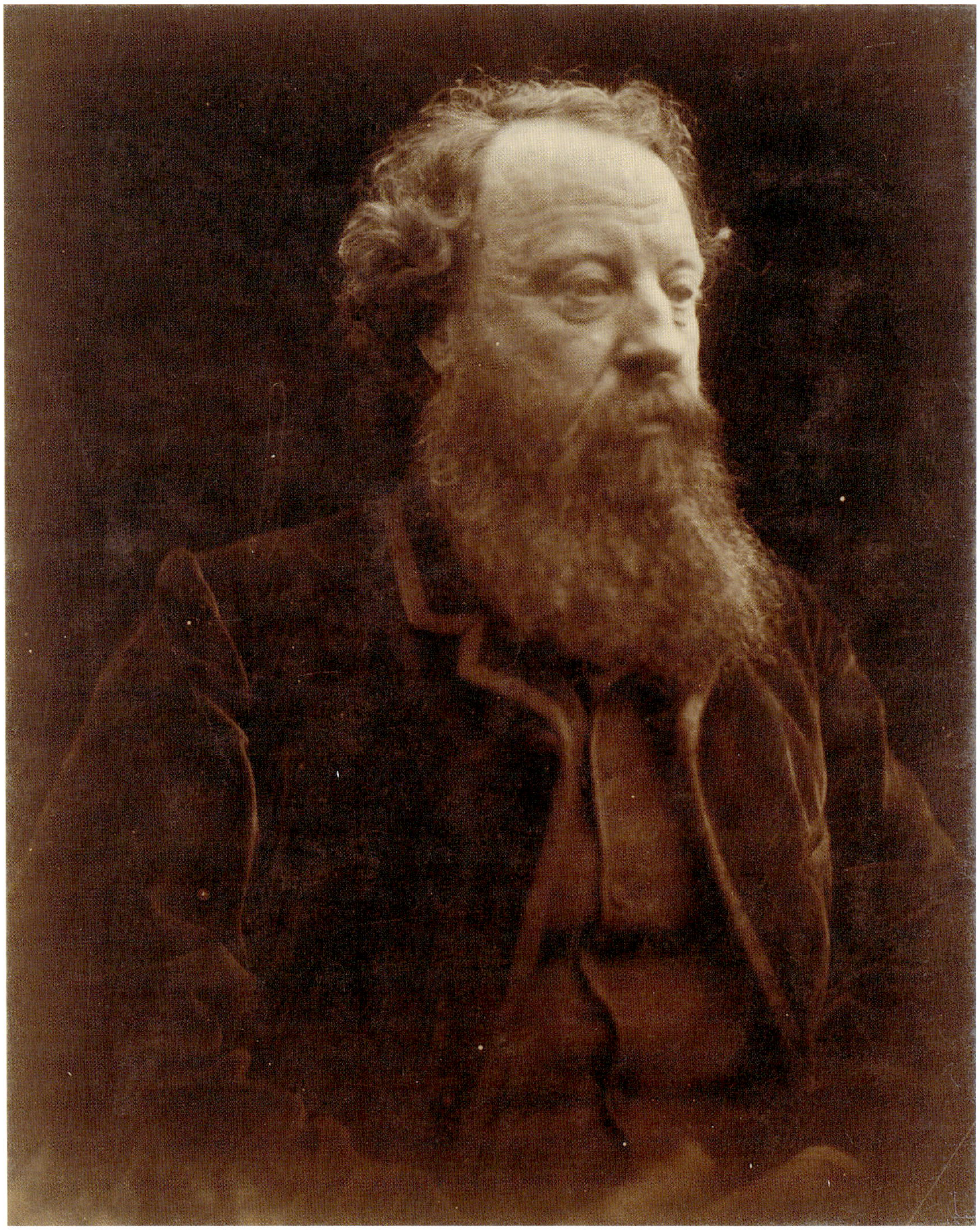

Sir John Simeon (Bart), 1870
Albumen print, 303 x 240mm (11⅞ x 9½")
Royal Photographic Society

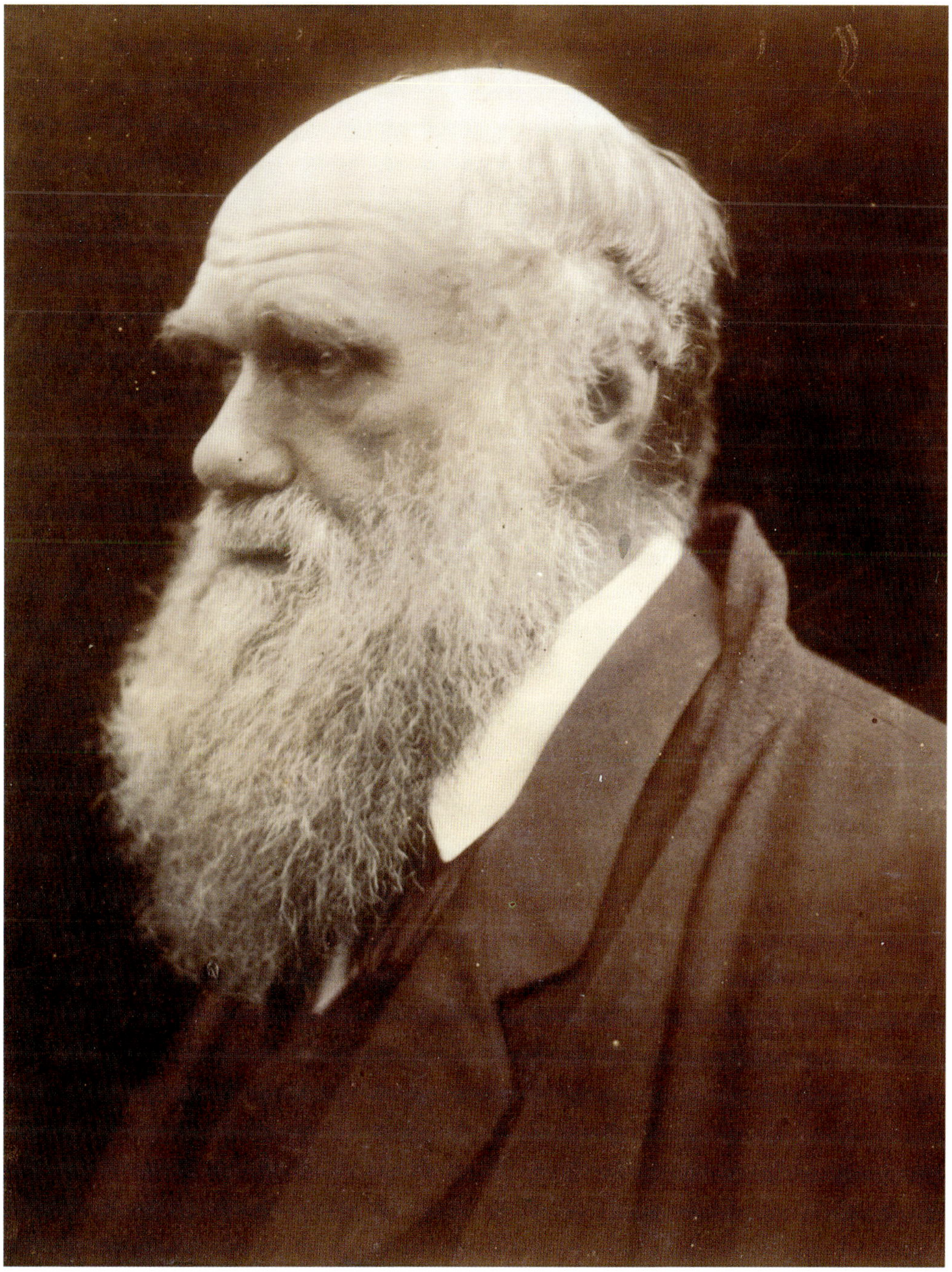

Charles Darwin, 1868–9
Albumen print, 251 x 210mm (9⅞ x 8¼")
Royal Photographic Society

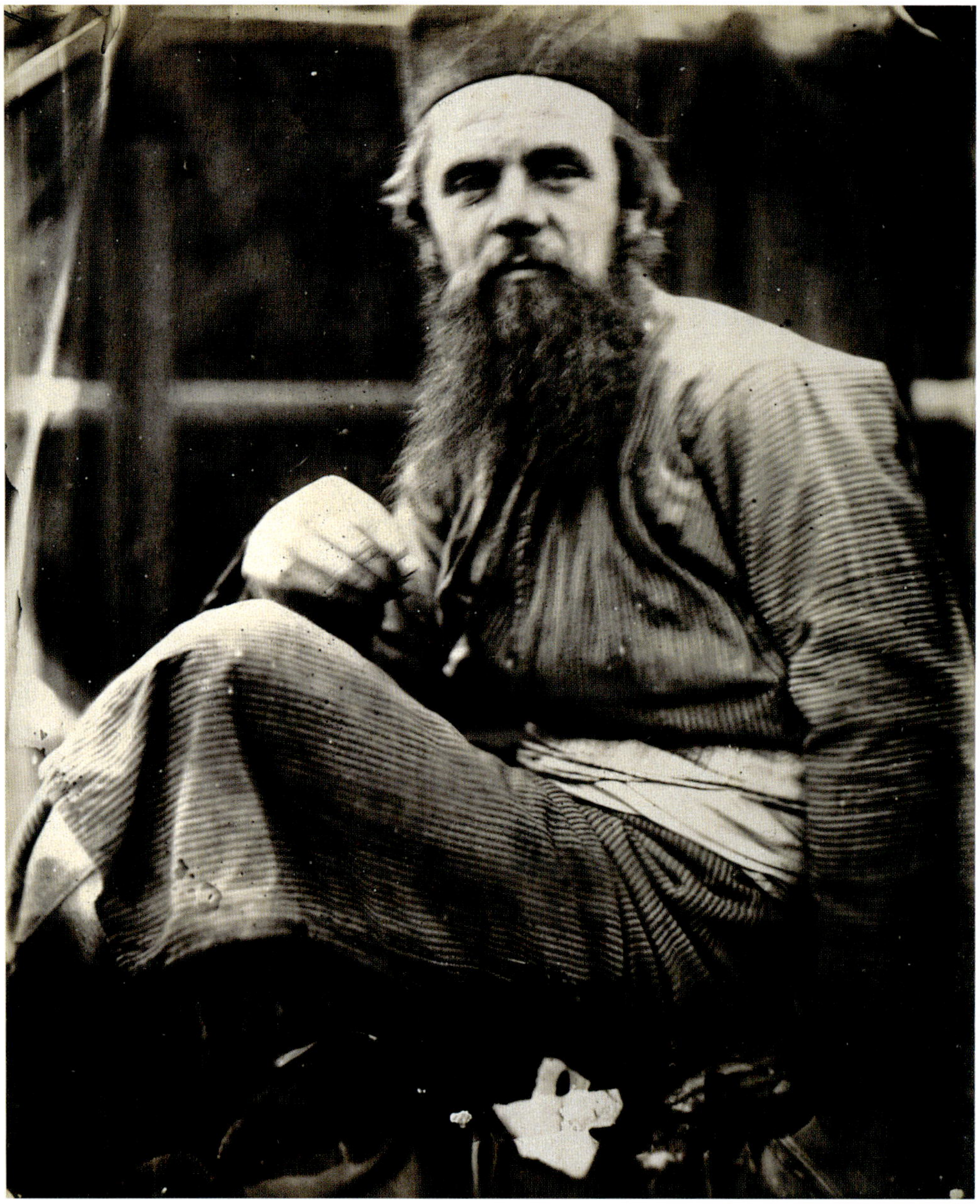

William Holman Hunt in his Eastern Dress, May 1864
(Taken on the lawn of Brent Lodge, Hendon)
Albumen print, 259 x 208mm (10¼ x 8¼")
National Museum of Photography, Film & Television, Bradford

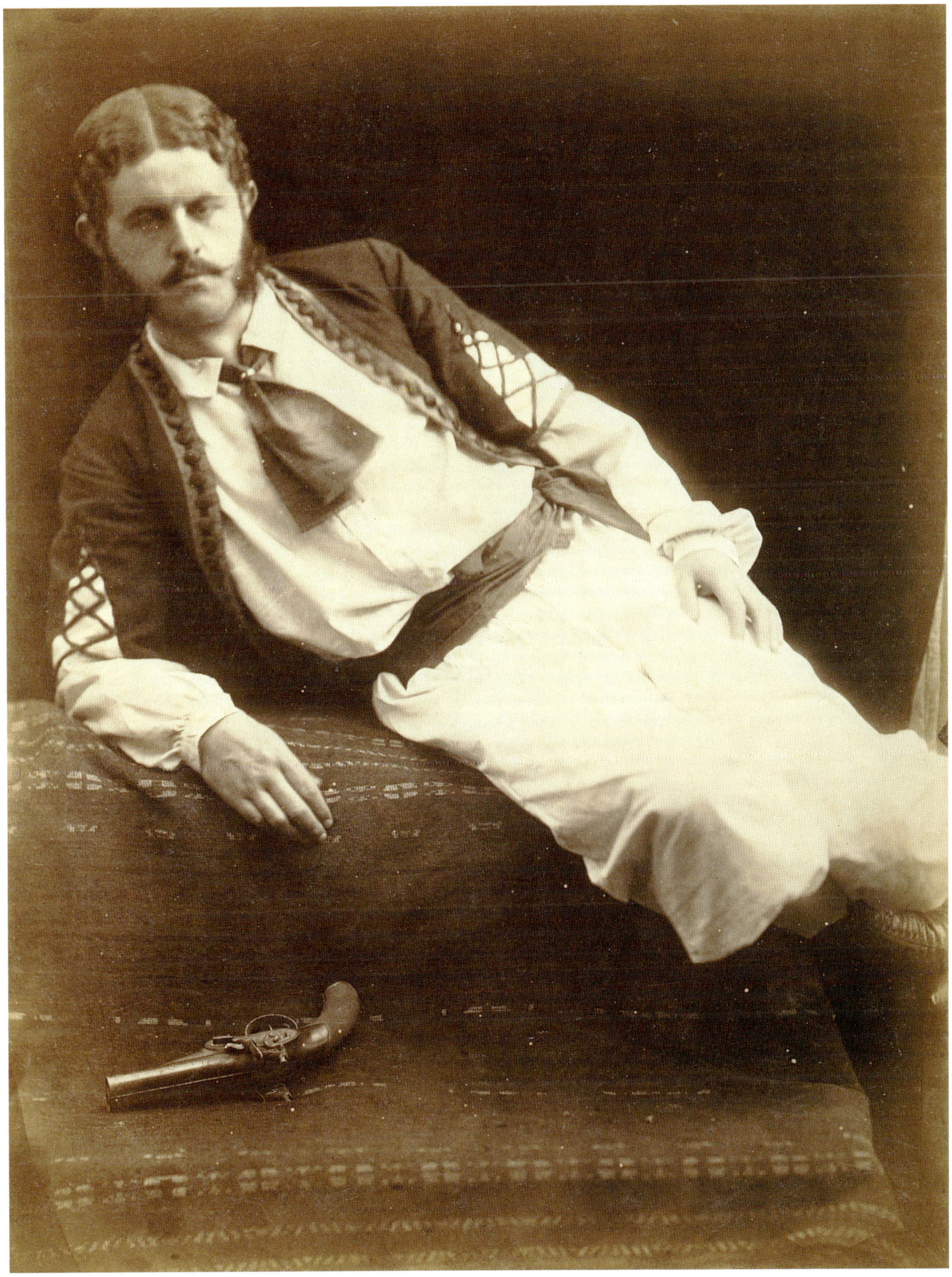

Unknown Man, 1868–74
Albumen print, 346 x 258mm (13⅝ x 10⅛")
Royal Photographic Society

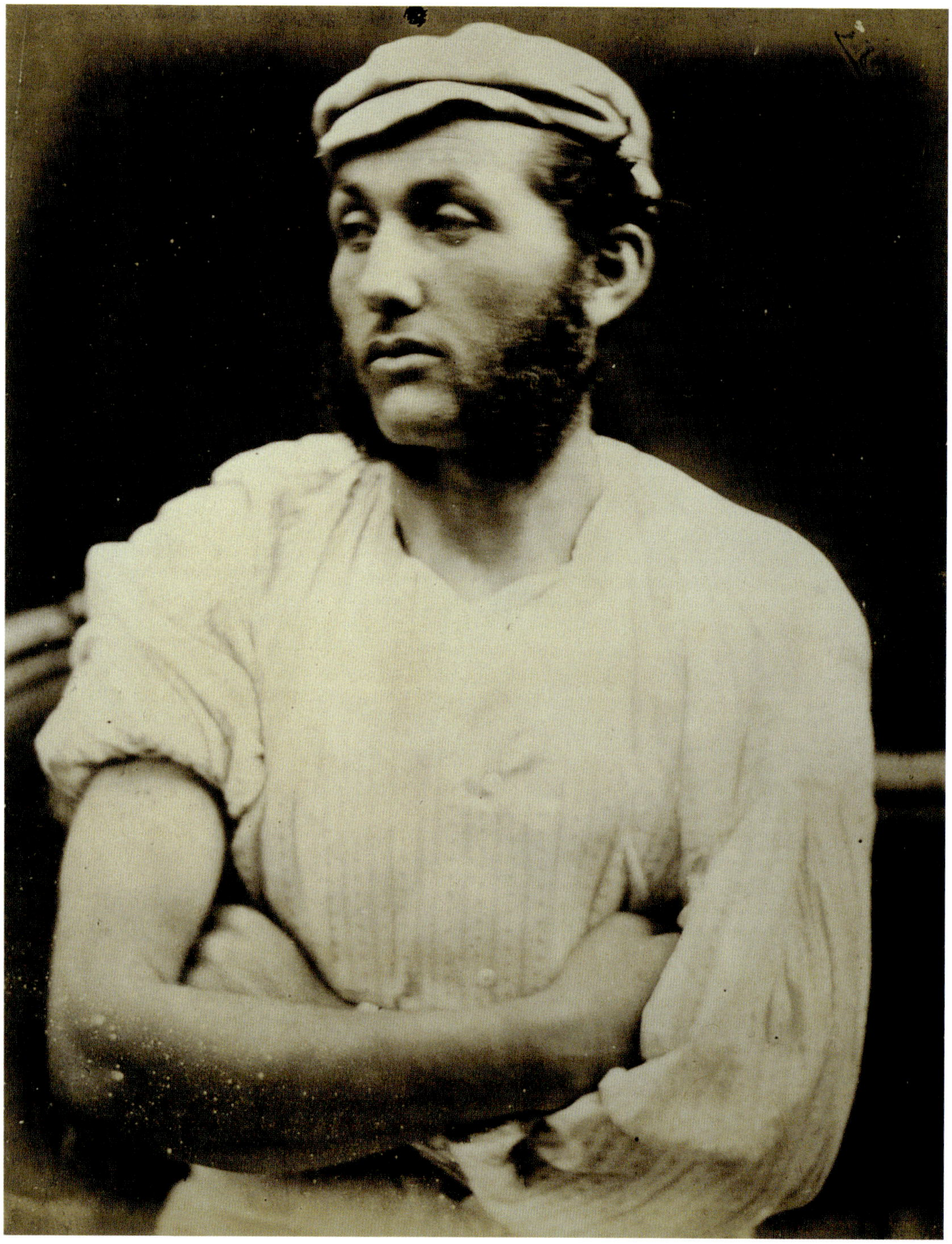

Connor of the Royal Artillery Winner of Prizes at the R.A. Games at FreshWater, October 1864
Gunner Patrick Connors?
Albumen print, 263 x 200mm (10⅜ x 7⅞")
National Museum of Photography, Film & Television, Bradford

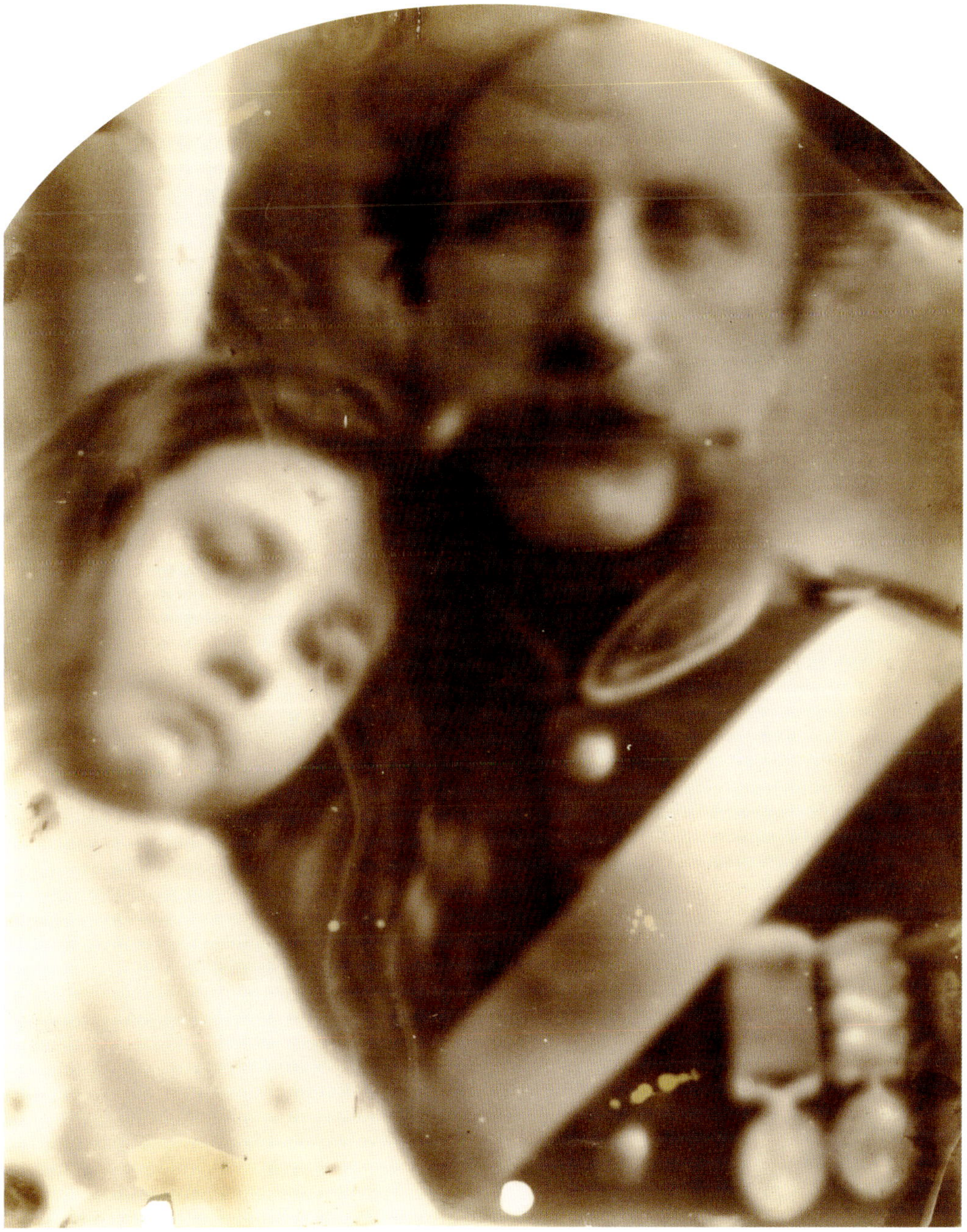

Kate Keown & Her Father, 1864
Kate Keown and Thomas Keown
Albumen print, 207 x 162mm (8½ x 6⅜")
Courtesy George Eastman House

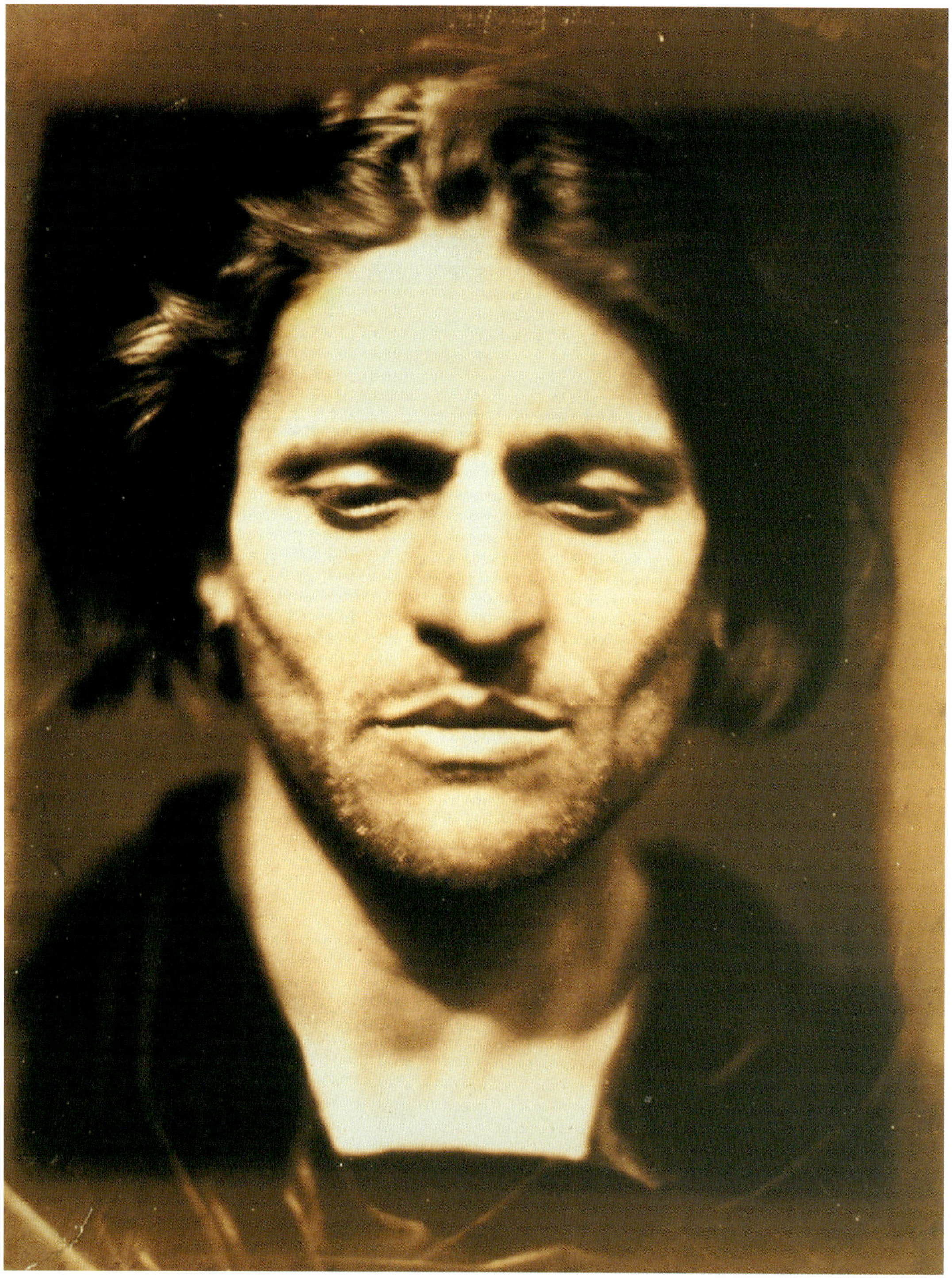

Iago, Study from an Italian, 1867
Angelo Colarossi
Albumen print, 334 x 248mm (13⅛ x 9¾")
National Museum of Photography, Film & Television, Bradford

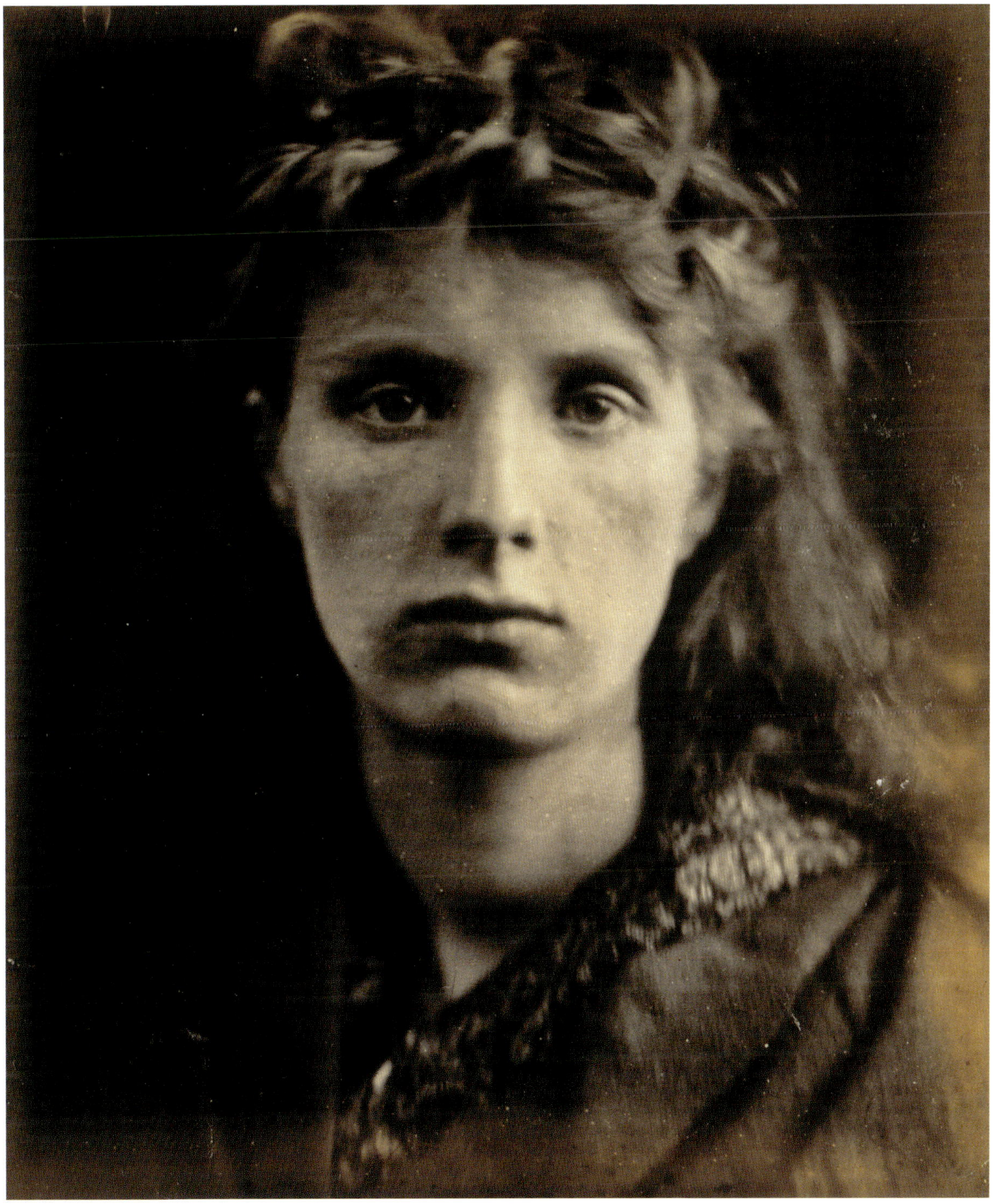

The Mountain Nymph Sweet Liberty, June 1866
Mrs Keene
Albumen print, 360 x 281mm (14⅛ x 11⅛")
Royal Photographic Society

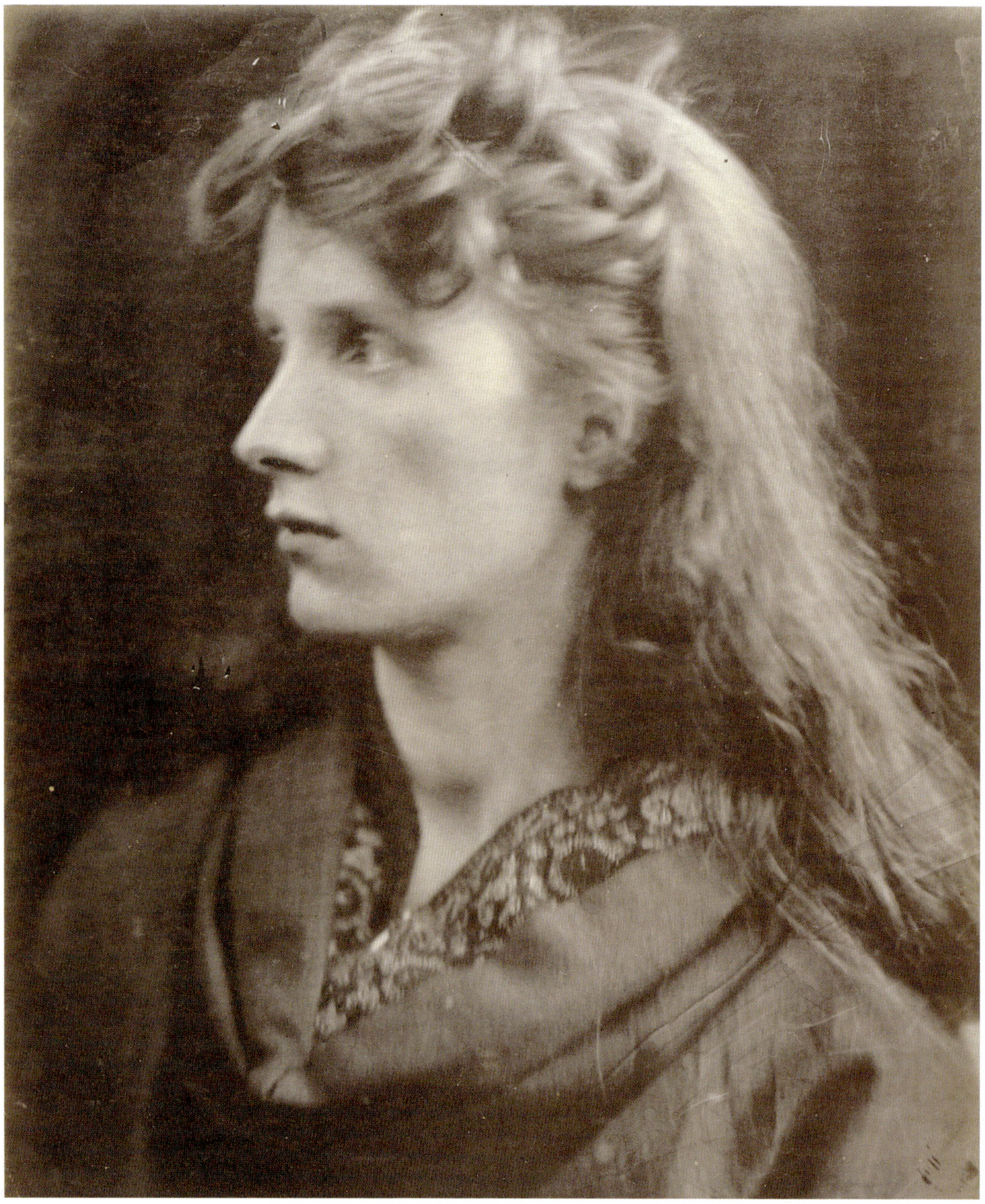

Lady Clara Vere de Vere, 1866
Mrs Keene
Albumen print, 274 x 224mm (10¾ x 8⅞")
Royal Photographic Society

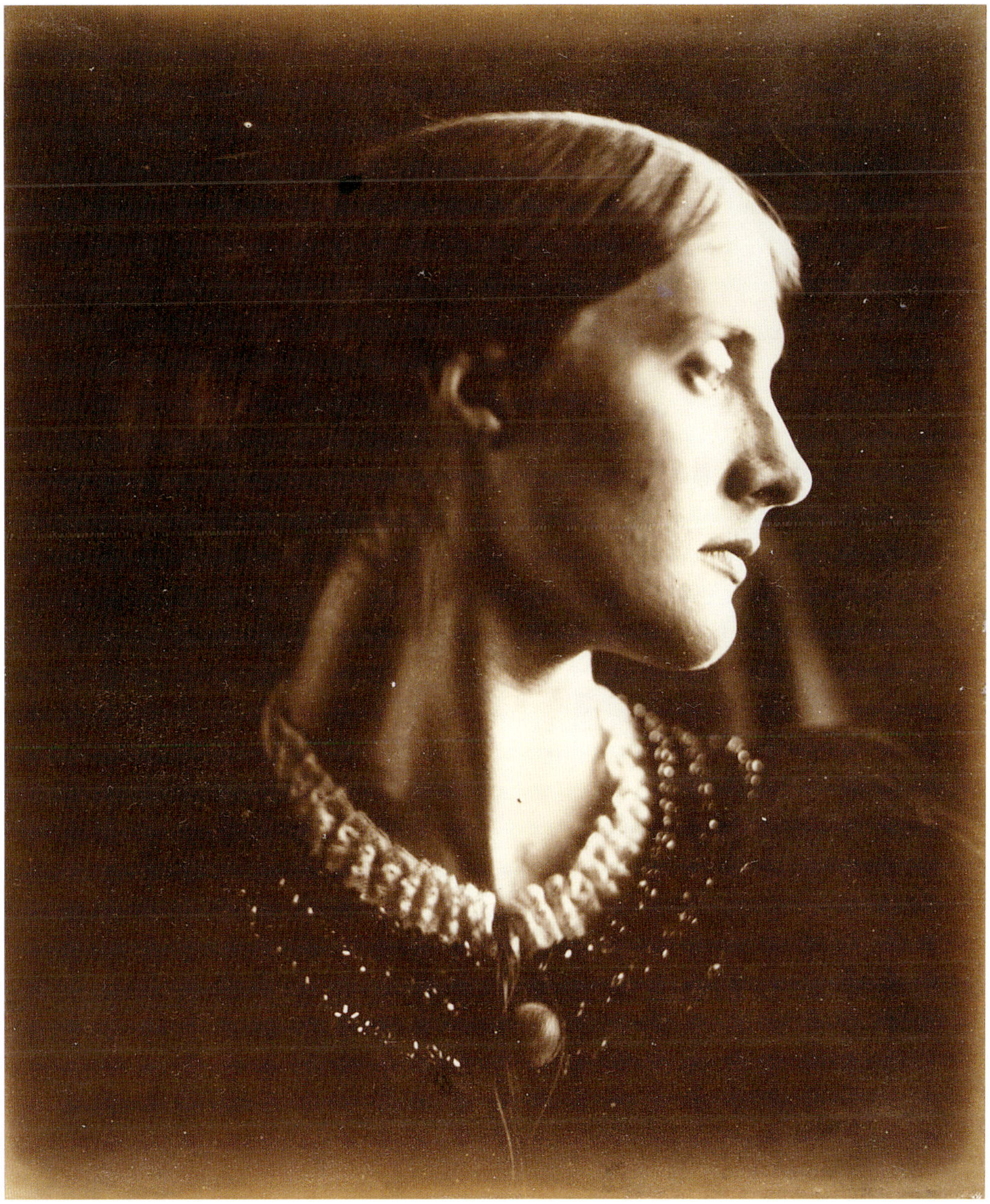

My niece Julia Jackson now Mrs Herbert Duckworth, April 1867
Albumen print, 290 x 234mm (11⅜ x 9¼")
National Museum of Photography, Film & Television, Bradford

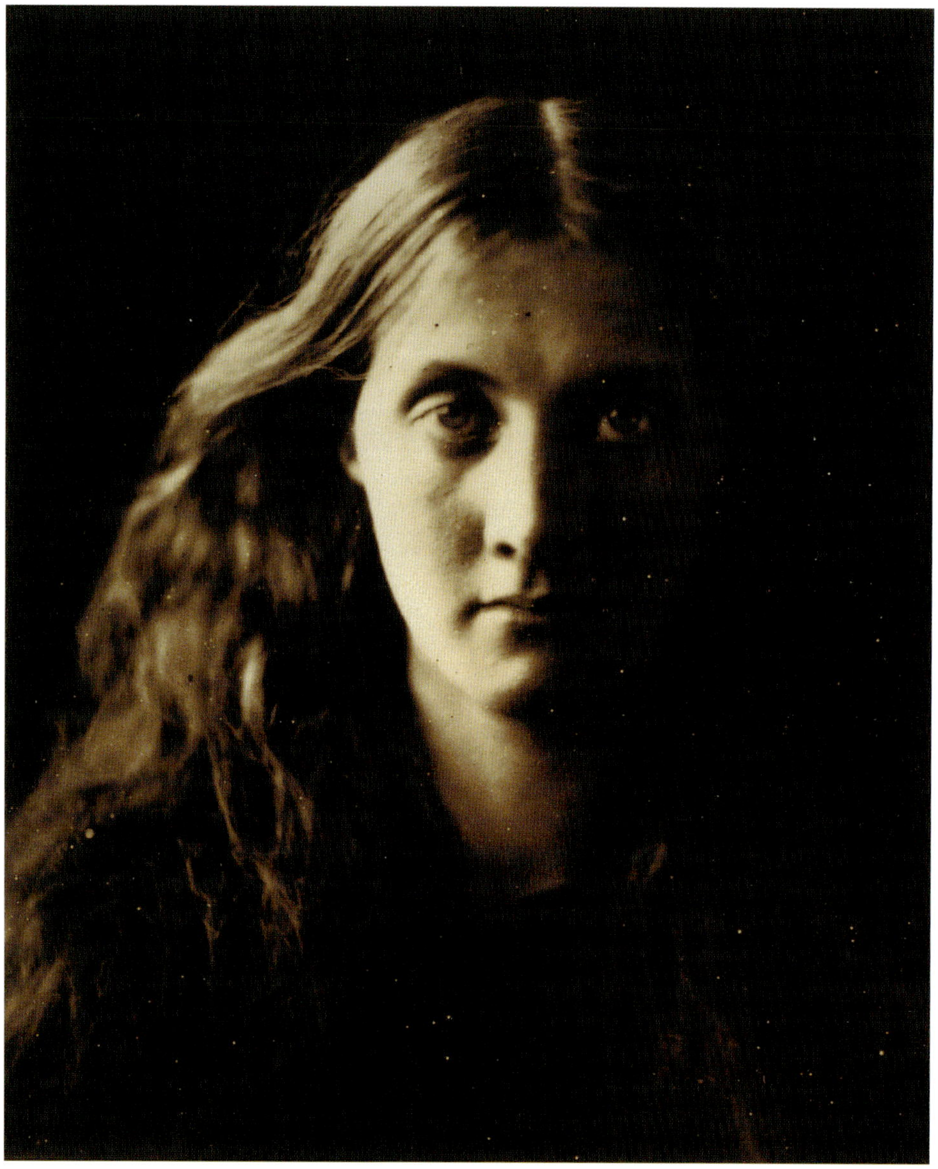

My niece Julia full face, April 1867
Julia Duckworth (née Jackson)
Albumen print, 253 x 201mm (10 x 7⅞")
National Museum of Photography, Film & Television, Bradford

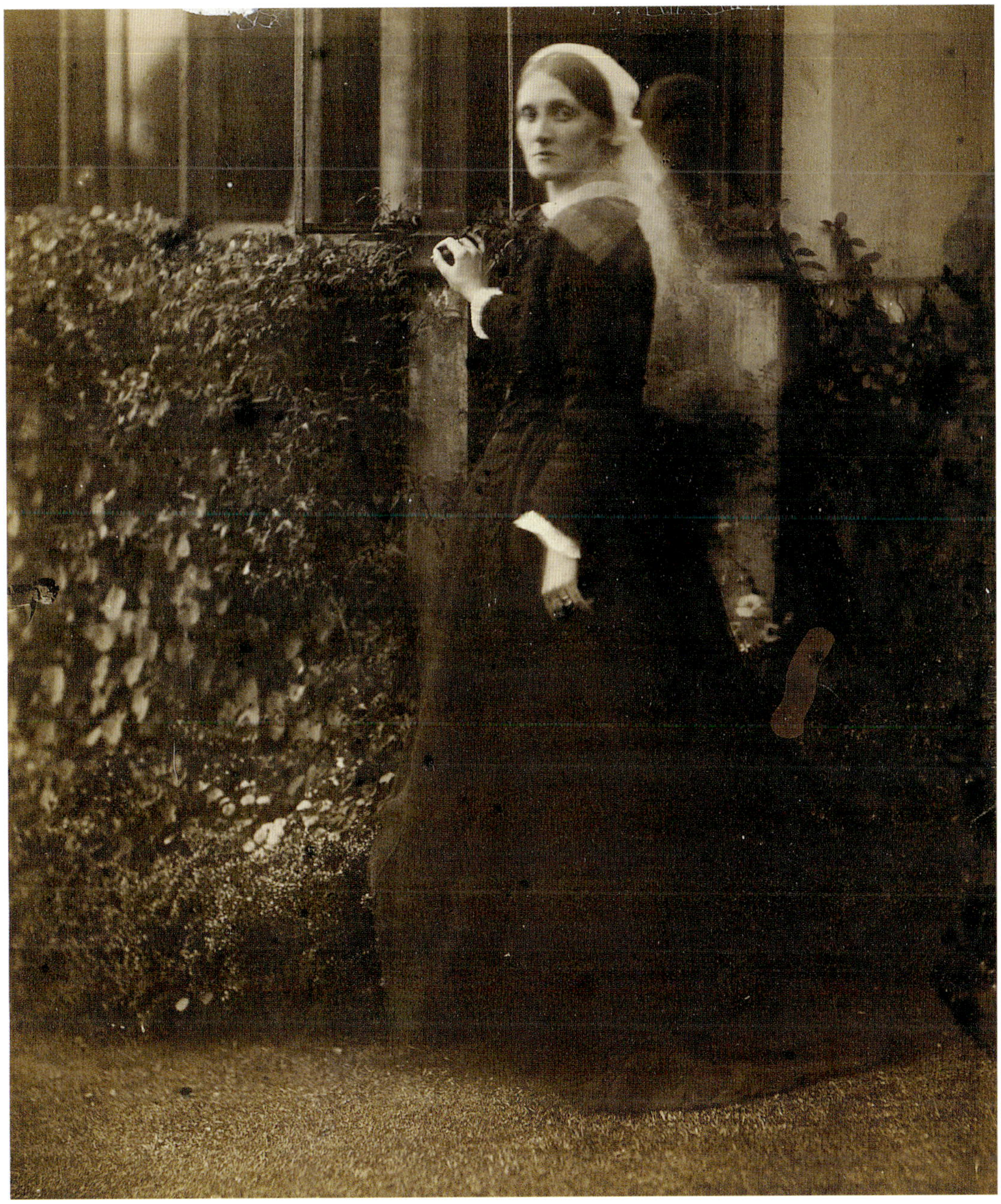

Julia Duckworth in Garden, 1872
Albumen print, 300 x 247mm (11¾ x 9¾")
National Portrait Gallery, London (NPG x18019)

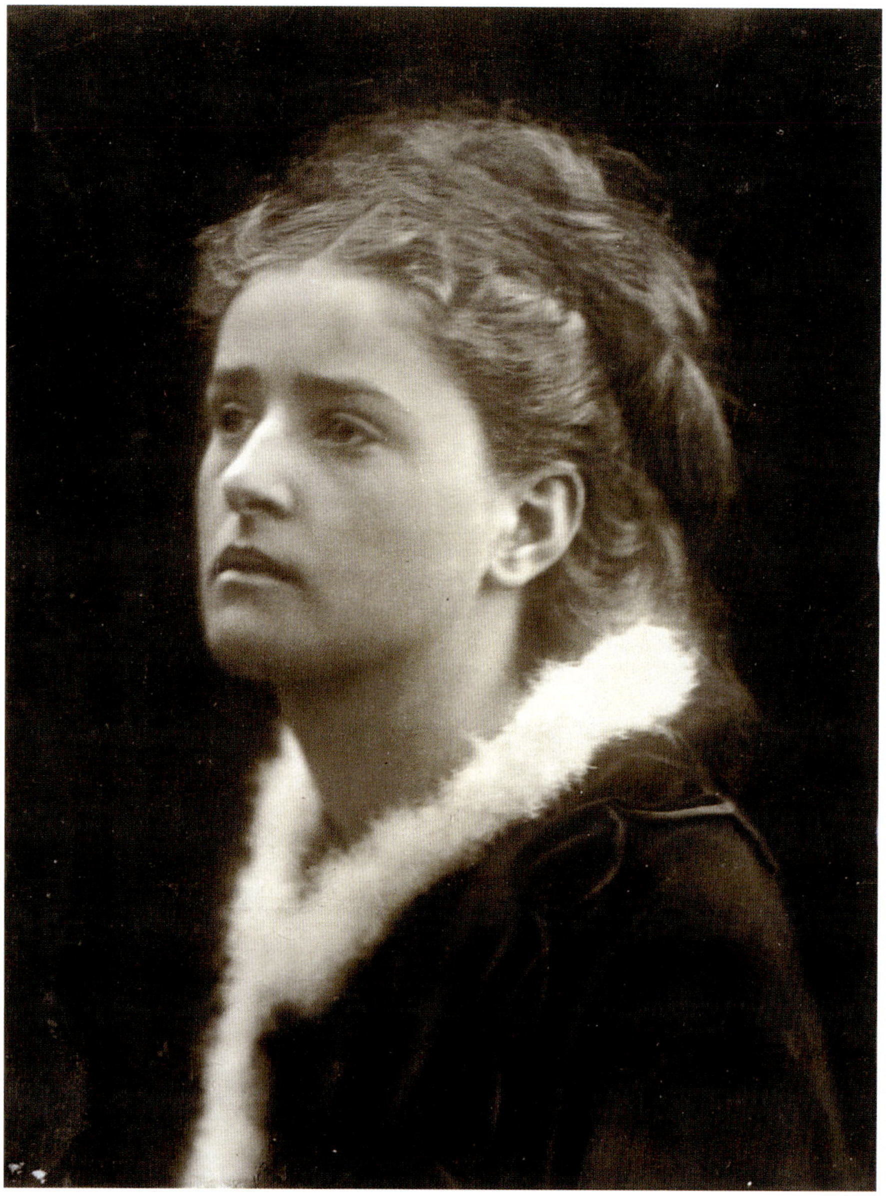

The Angel in the House, 1873
Emily Peacock
Carbon print, 350 x 254mm (13¾ x 10")
The Board of Trustees of the Victoria and Albert Museum, London

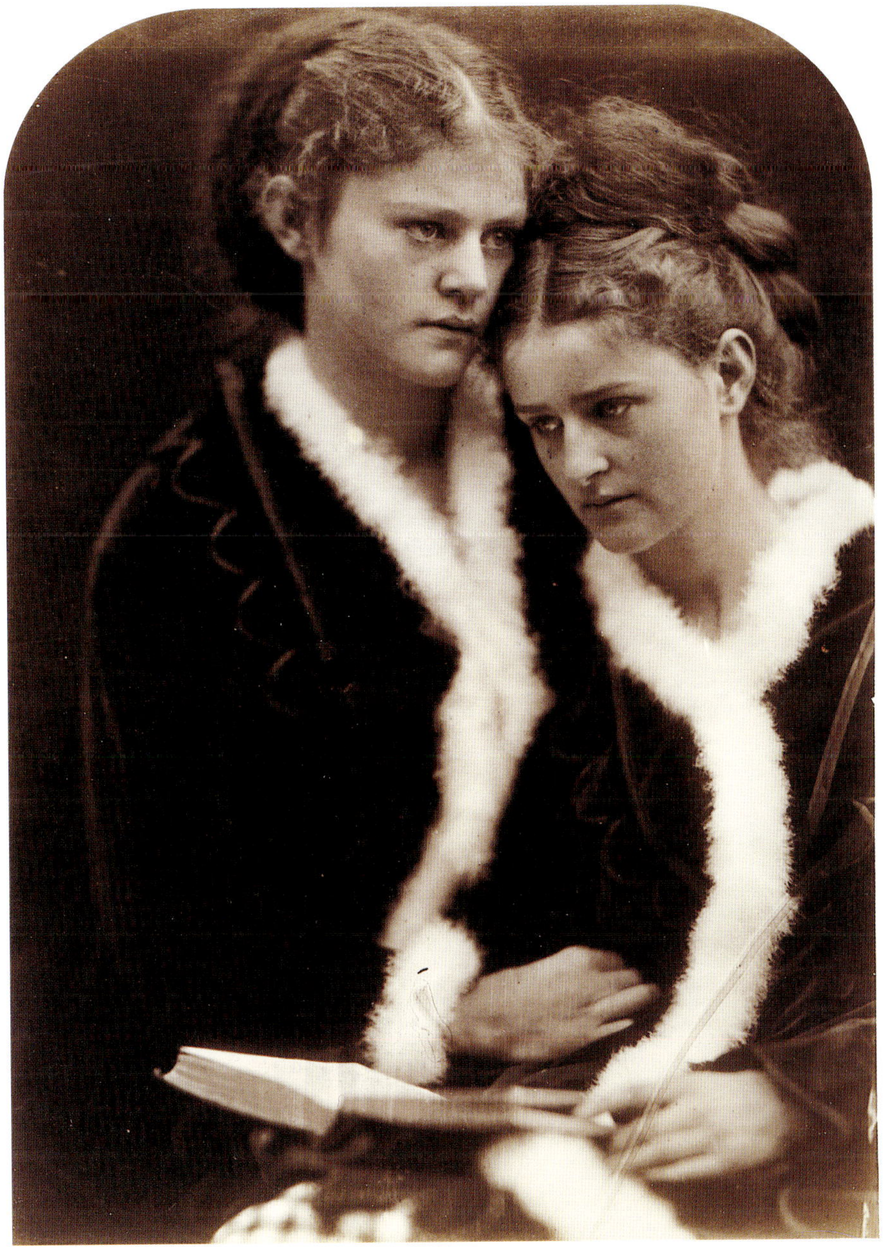

Sisters, 1873
Mary and Emily Peacock
Albumen print, 365 x 253mm (14⅜ x 10")
Wilson Centre for Photography

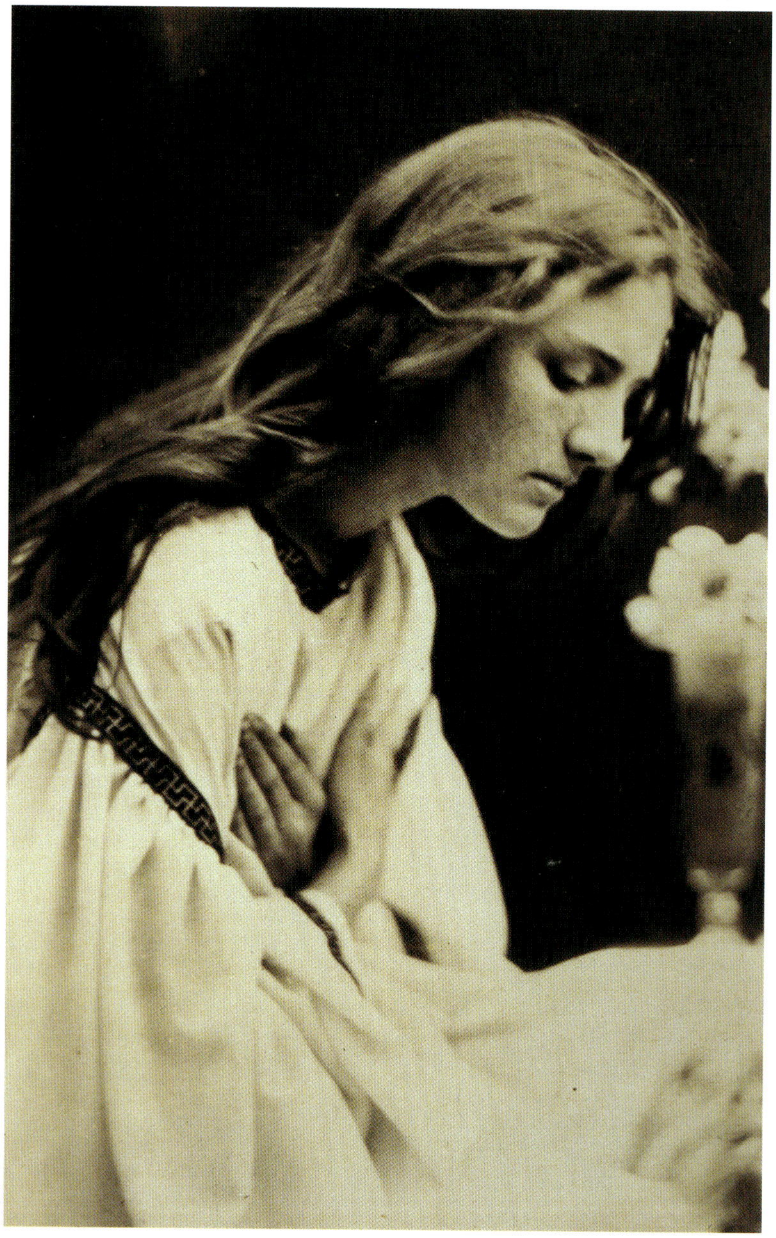

After the manner of Perugino, 1865
Mary Ryan
Albumen print, 208 x 130mm (8¼ x 5⅛")
National Museum of Photography, Film & Television, Bradford

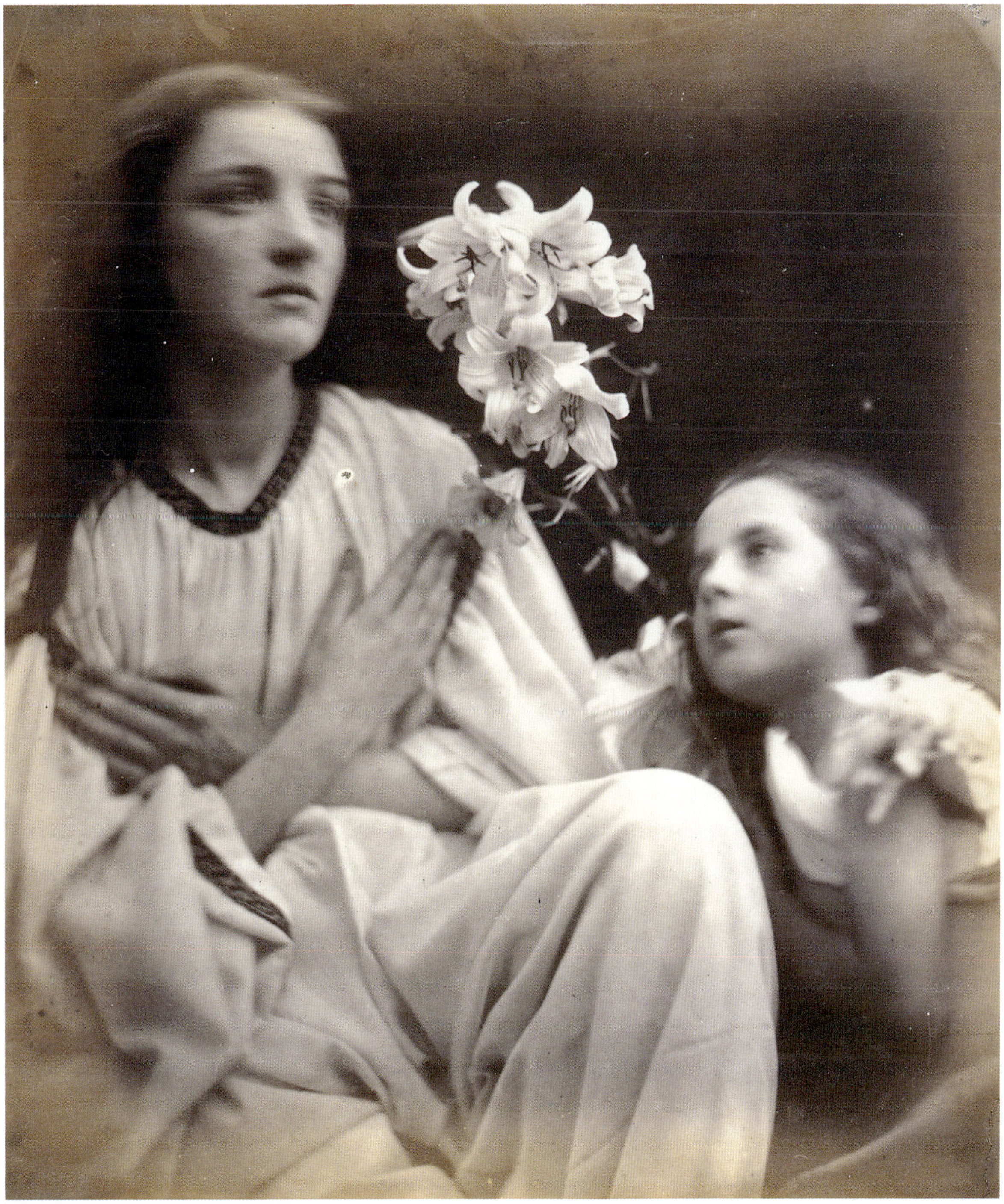

A Study after the manner of Francia, 1865
Mary Ryan and Elizabeth Keown
Albumen print, 305 x 281mm (12 x 11⅛")
National Museum of Photography, Film & Television, Bradford

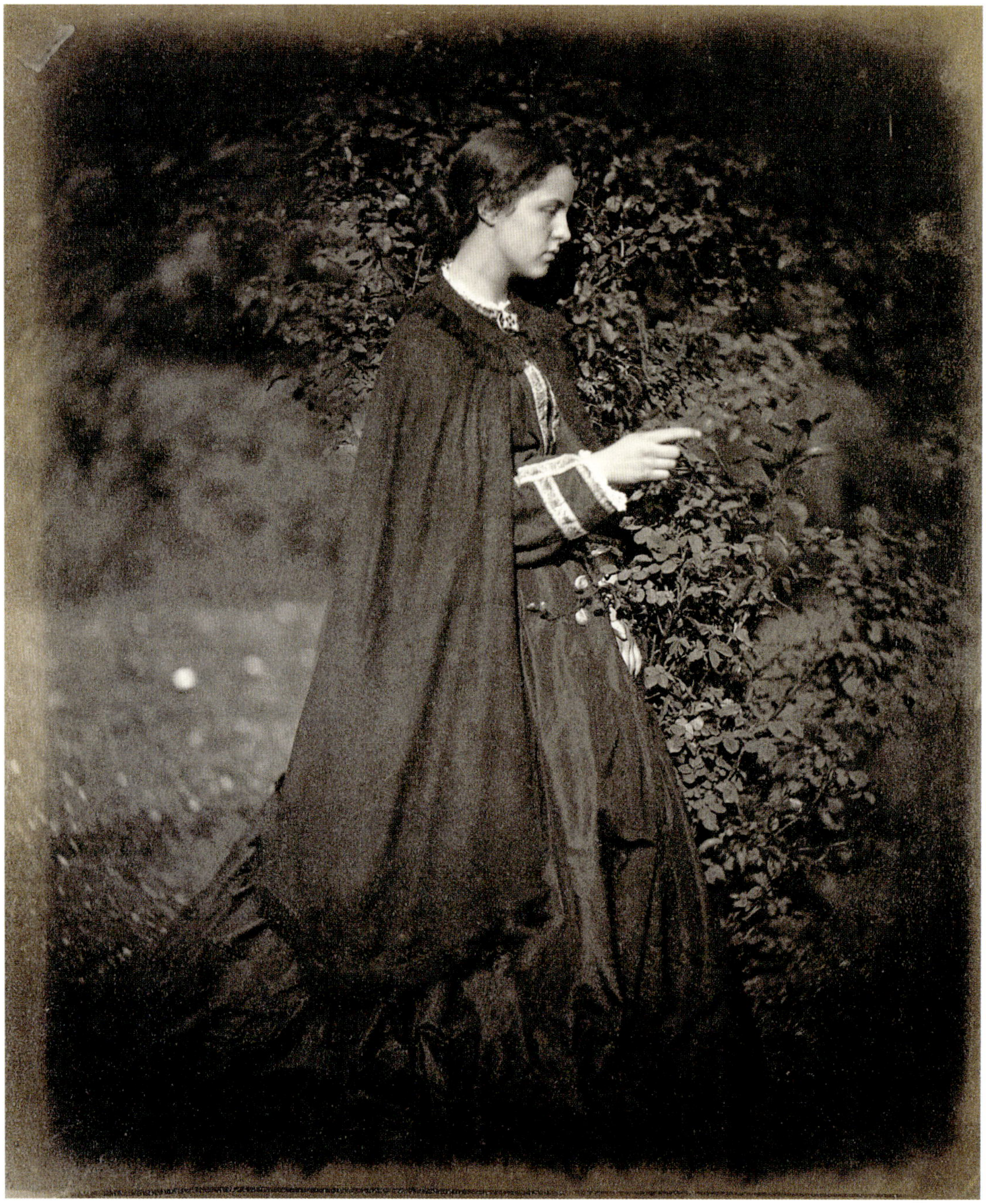

Magdalene Brookfield, May 1865
(Taken on the lawn of Little Holland House)
Albumen print, 271 x 221mm (10⅝ x 8¾")
The J. Paul Getty Museum, Los Angeles

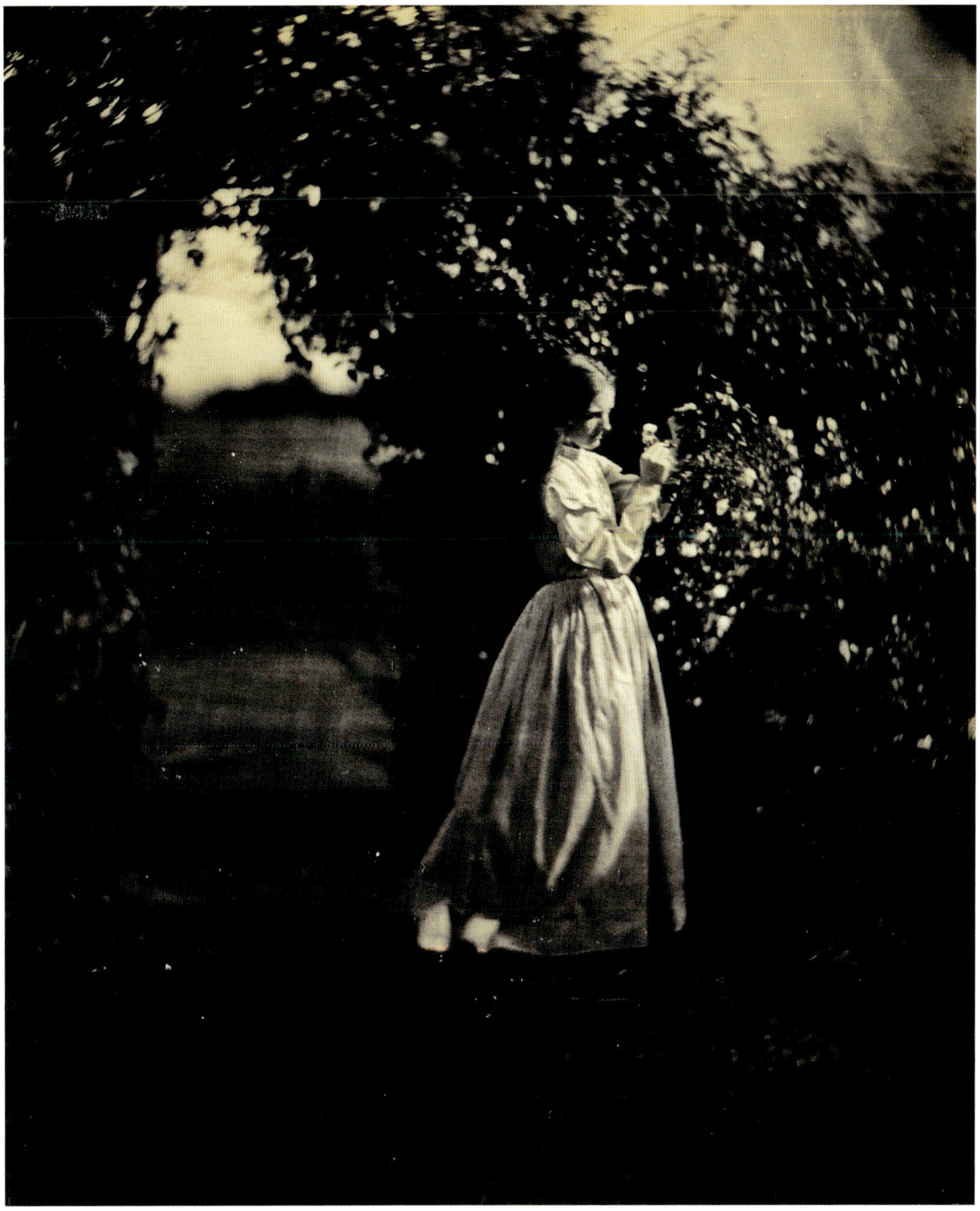

The Gardener's Daughter, 1867
Mary Ryan
Albumen print, 292 x 234mm (11½ x 9¼")
National Museum of Photography, Film & Television, Bradford

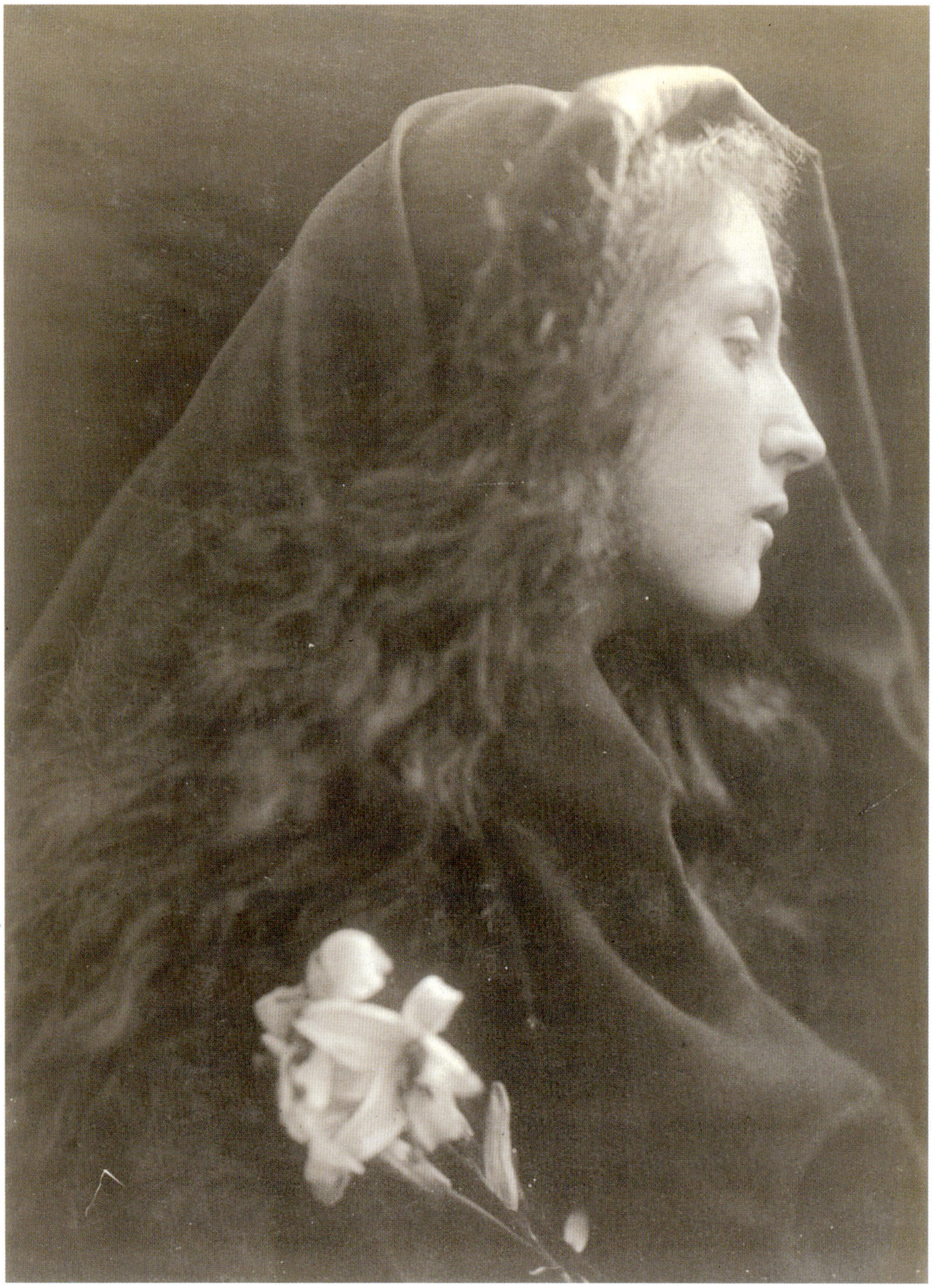

The Angel at the Sepulchre, 1869–70
Mary Ann Hillier
Albumen print, 353 x 256mm (13⅞ x 10⅛")
The Board of Trustees of the Victoria and Albert Museum, London

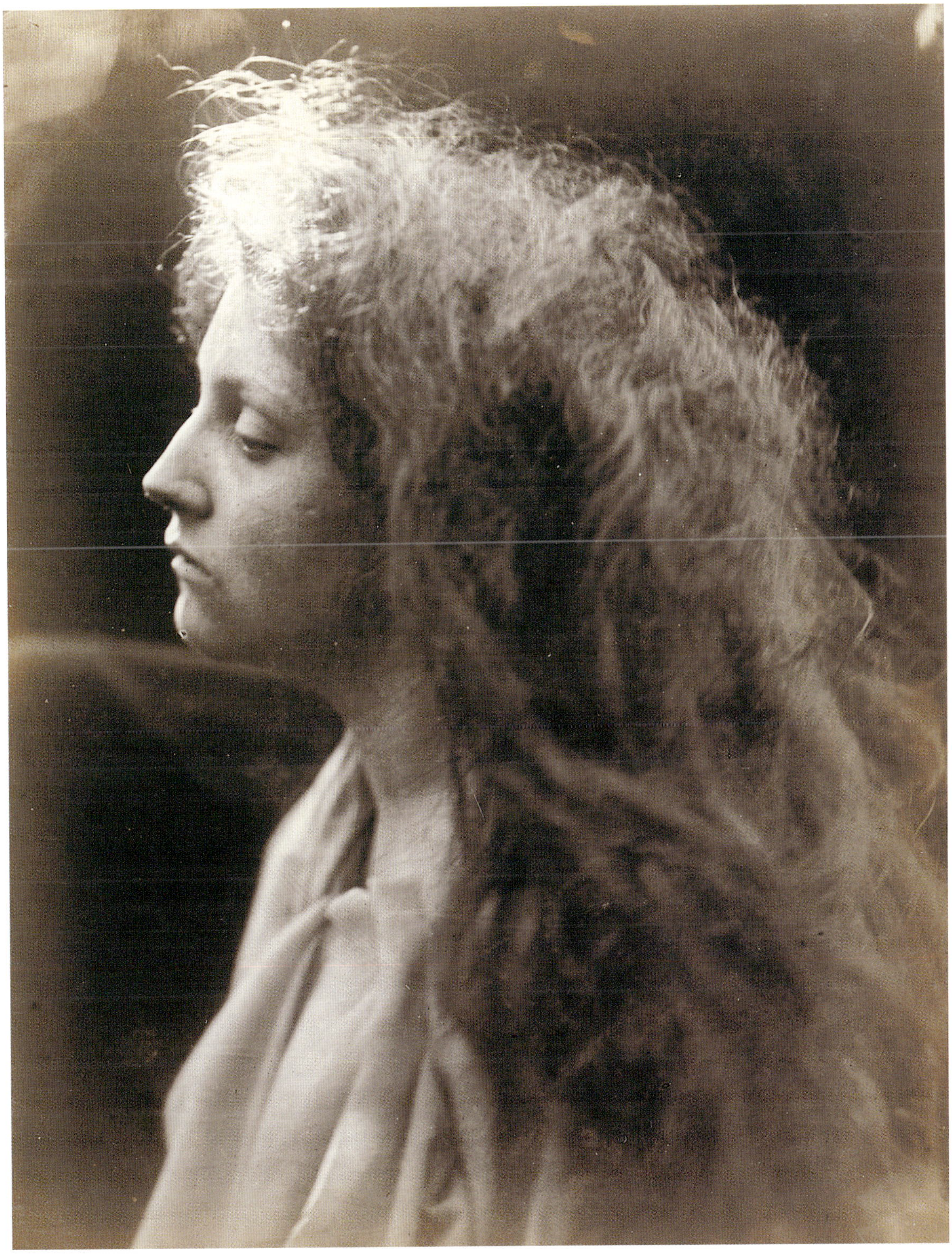

The Angel at the Tomb, 1869–70
Mary Ann Hillier
Albumen print, 340 x 255mm (13⅜ x 10")
Royal Photographic Society

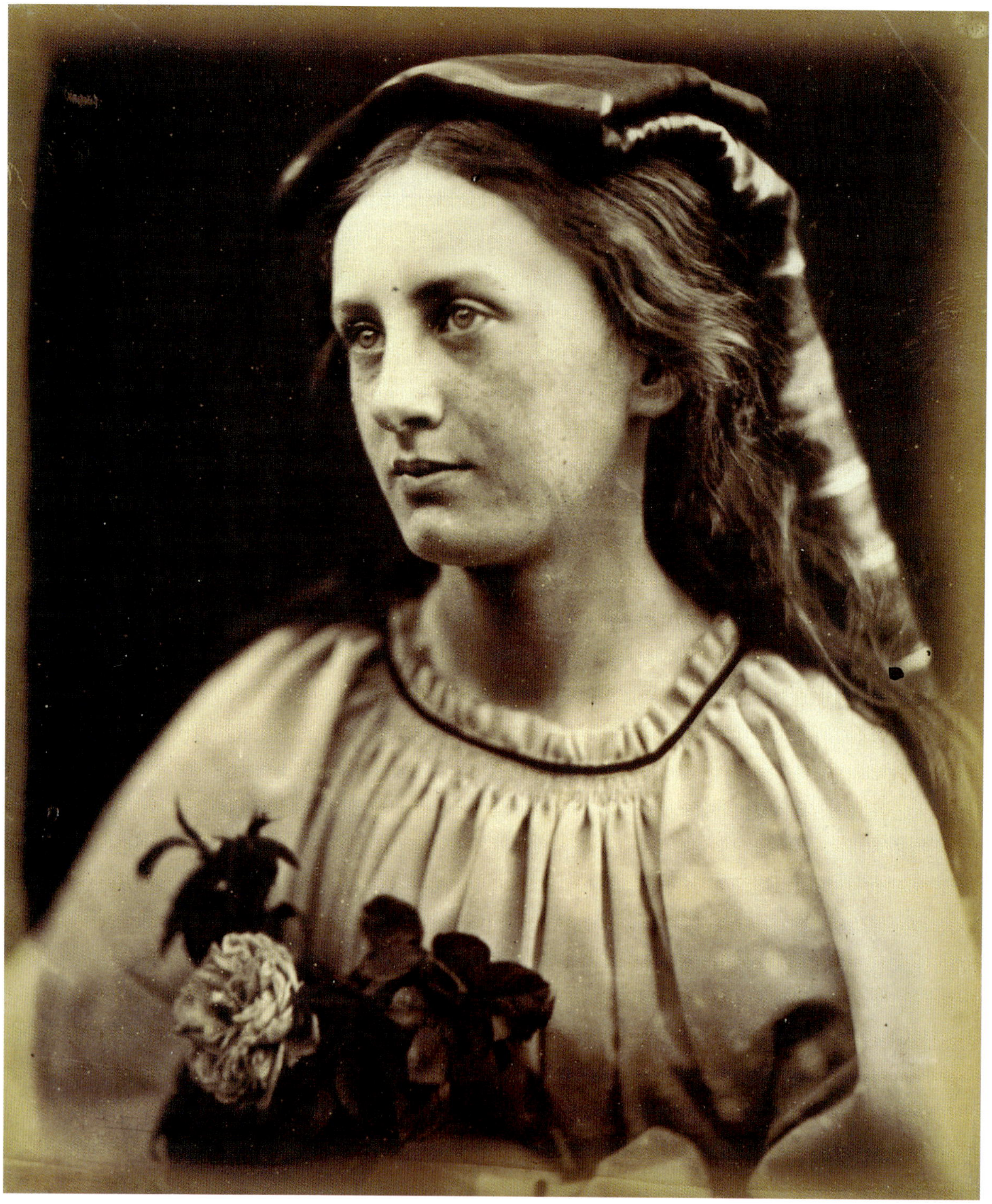

La Contadina, 1866
May Prinsep
Albumen print, 331 x 270mm (13 x 10⅝")
National Museum of Photography, Film & Television, Bradford

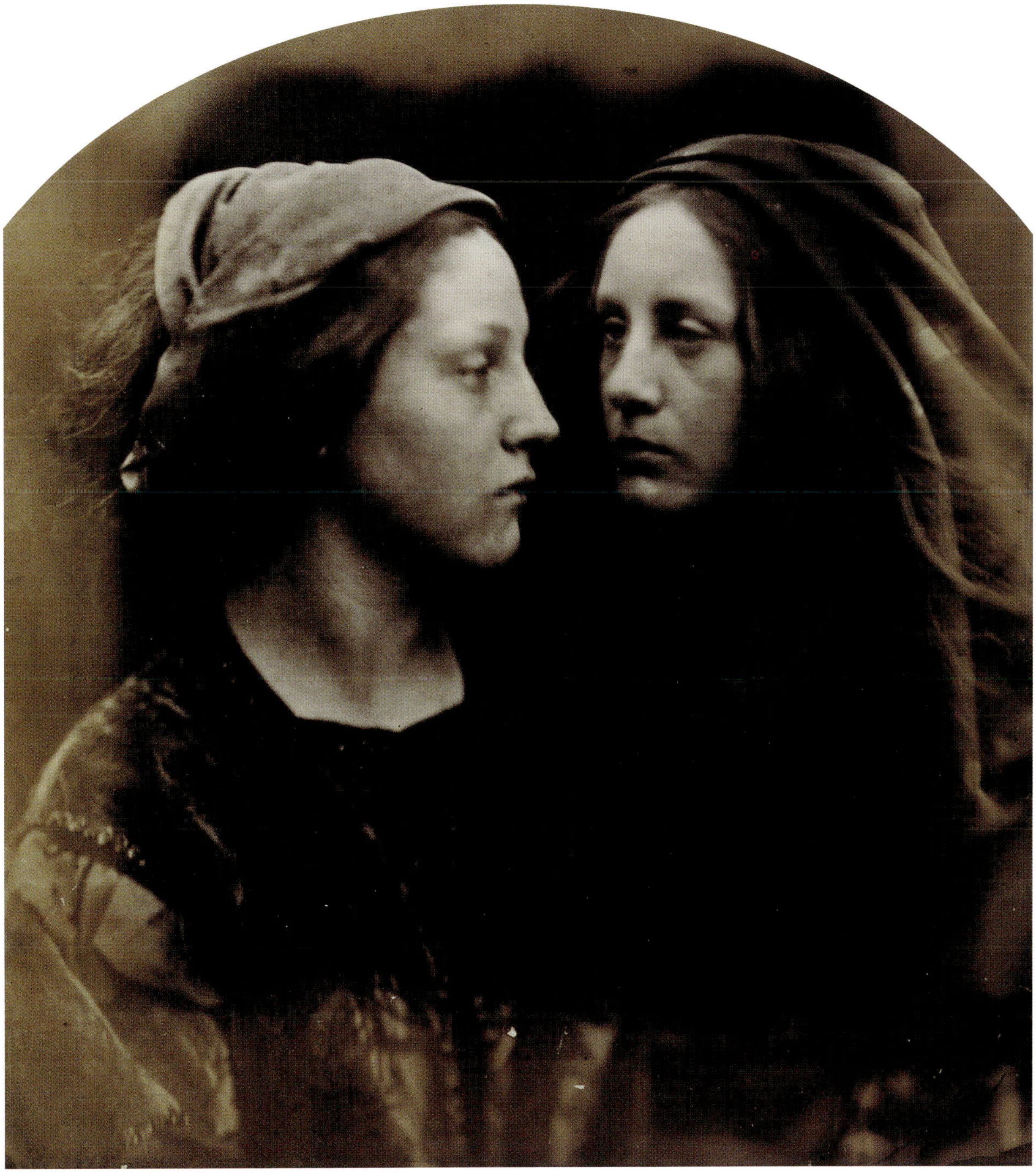

The Dialogue, 1866
Mary Ann Hillier and May Prinsep
Albumen print, 321 x 284mm (12⅝ x 11⅛")
National Museum of Photography, Film & Television, Bradford

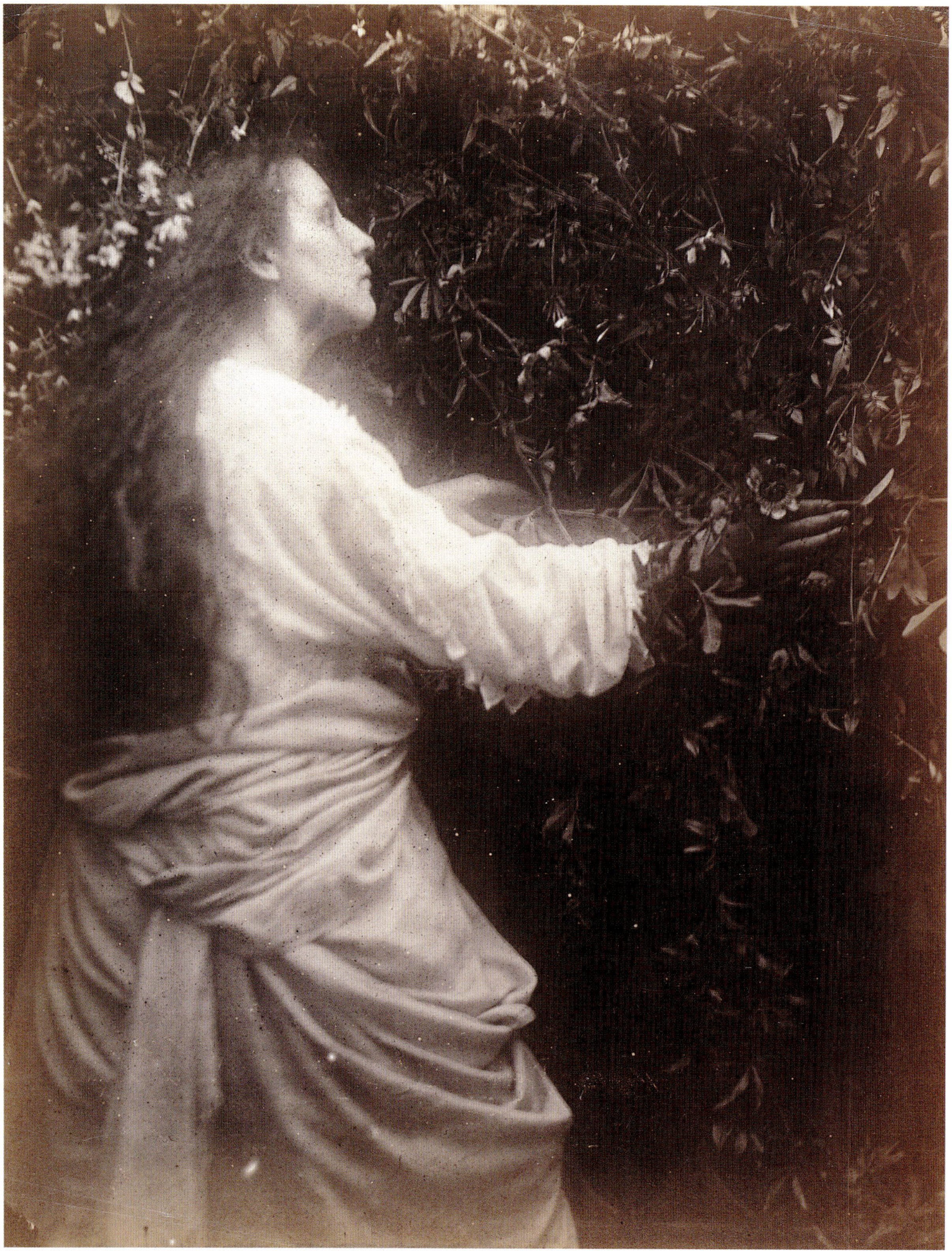

Mary Ann Hillier, 1874
Albumen print, 371 x 281mm (14⅝ x 11⅛")
Royal Photographic Society

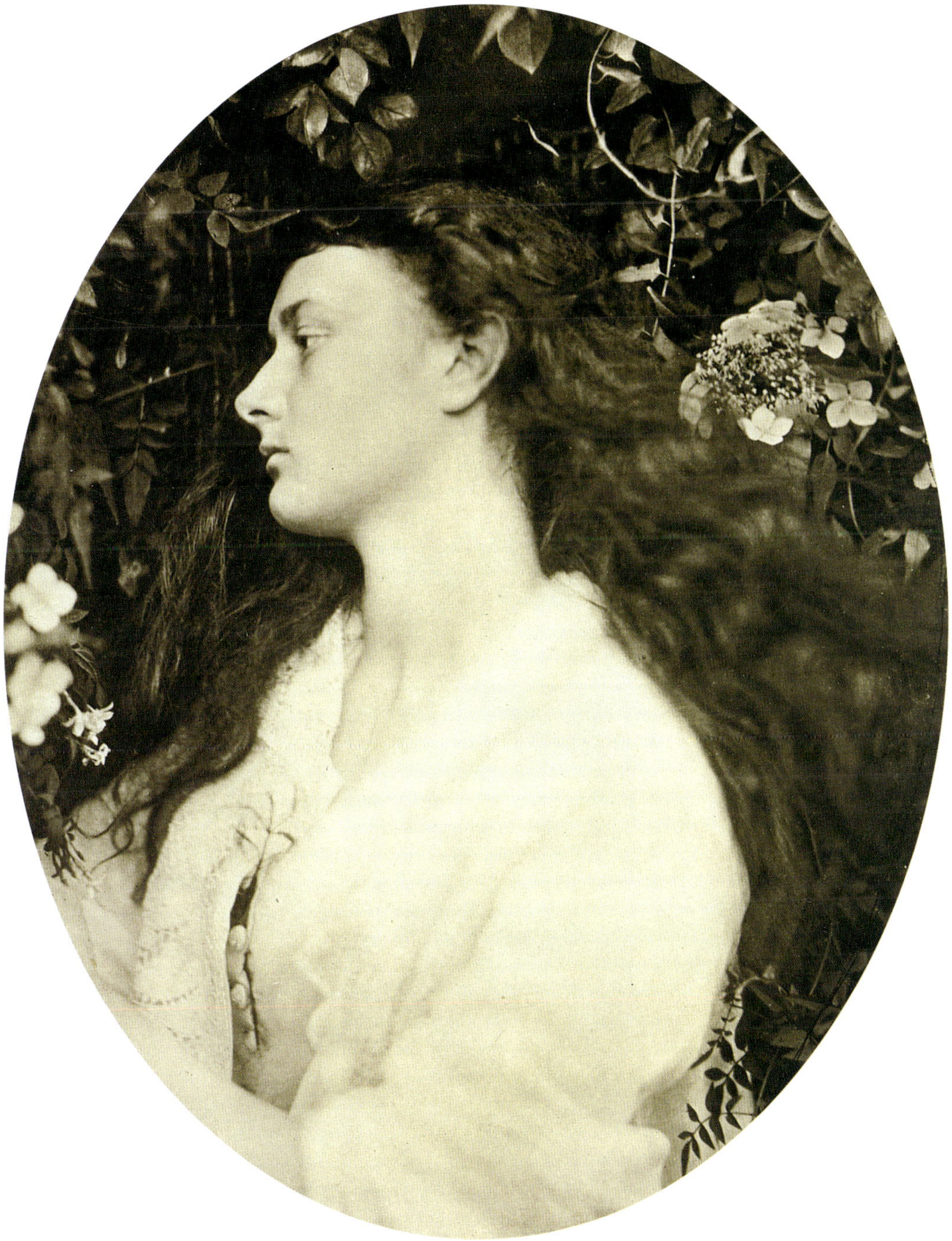

Alethea, 1872
Alice Pleasance Liddell
Carbon print, 333 x 249mm (13⅛ x 9¾")
Royal Photographic Society

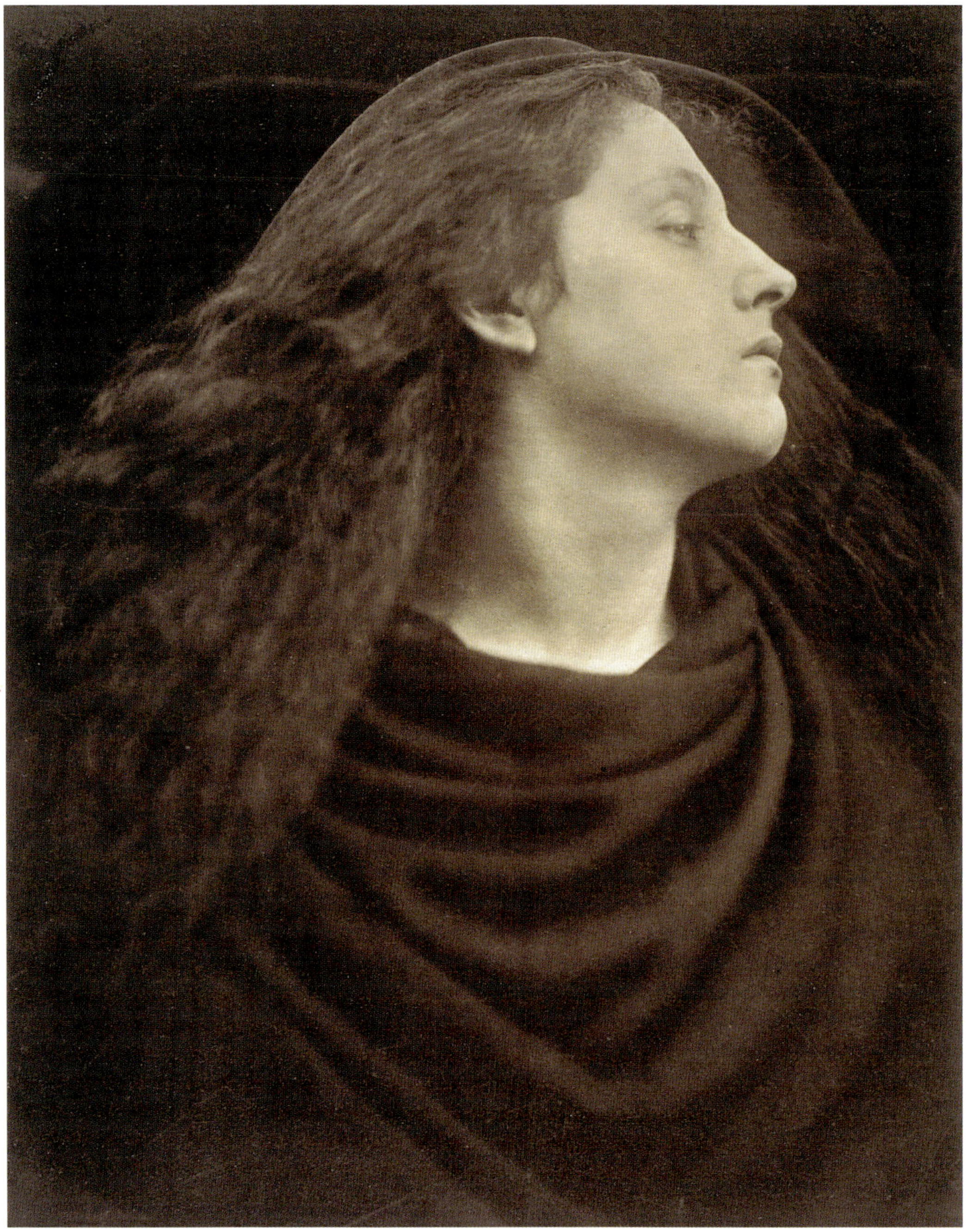

*Call, I Follow, I Follow, Let Me Die, c.*1867
Mary Ann Hillier
Carbon print, 350 x 267mm (13¾ x 10½")
The Board of Trustees of the Victoria and Albert Museum, London

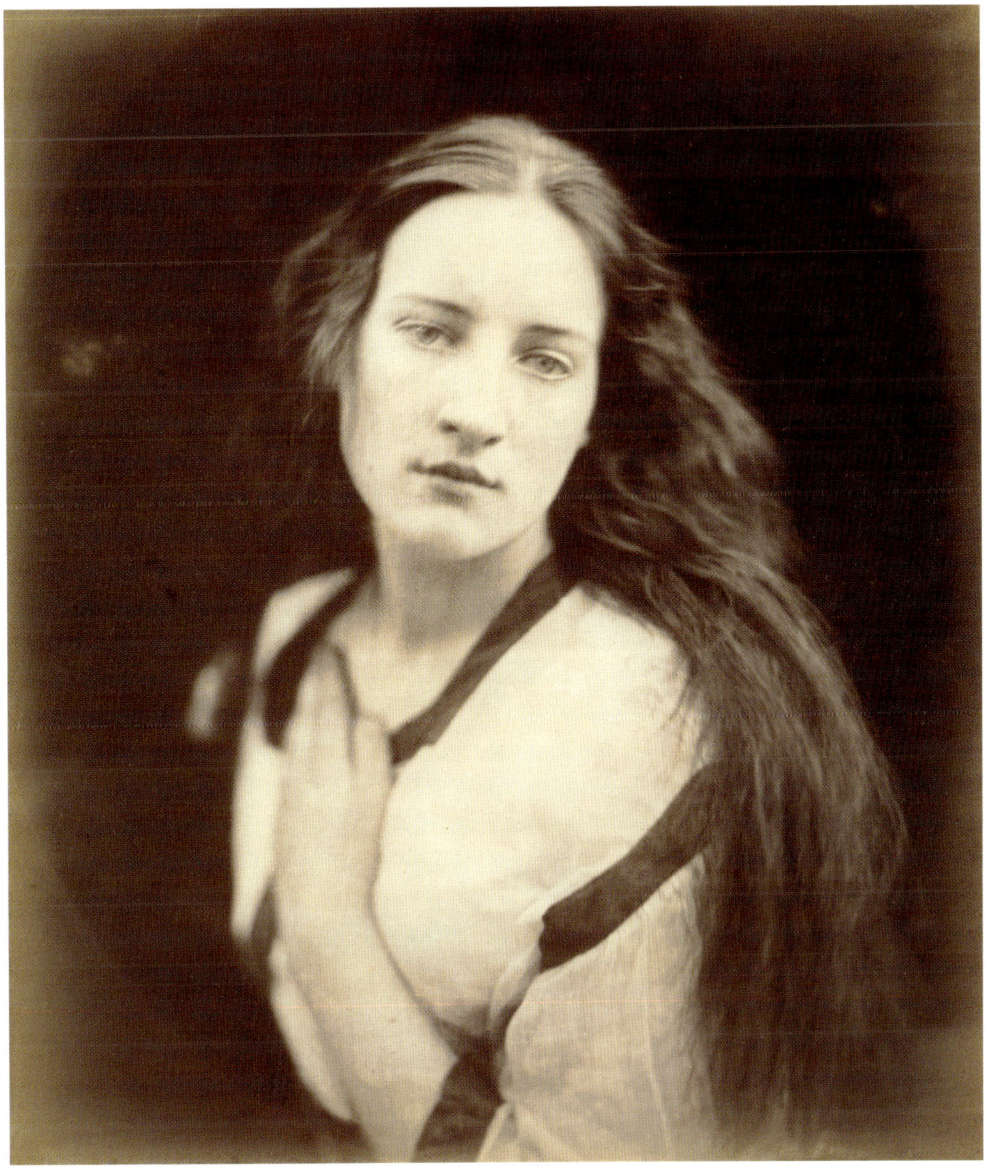

The Echo, 1868
Hatty Campbell
Albumen print, 270 x 226mm (10⅝ x 8⅞")
The J. Paul Getty Museum, Los Angeles

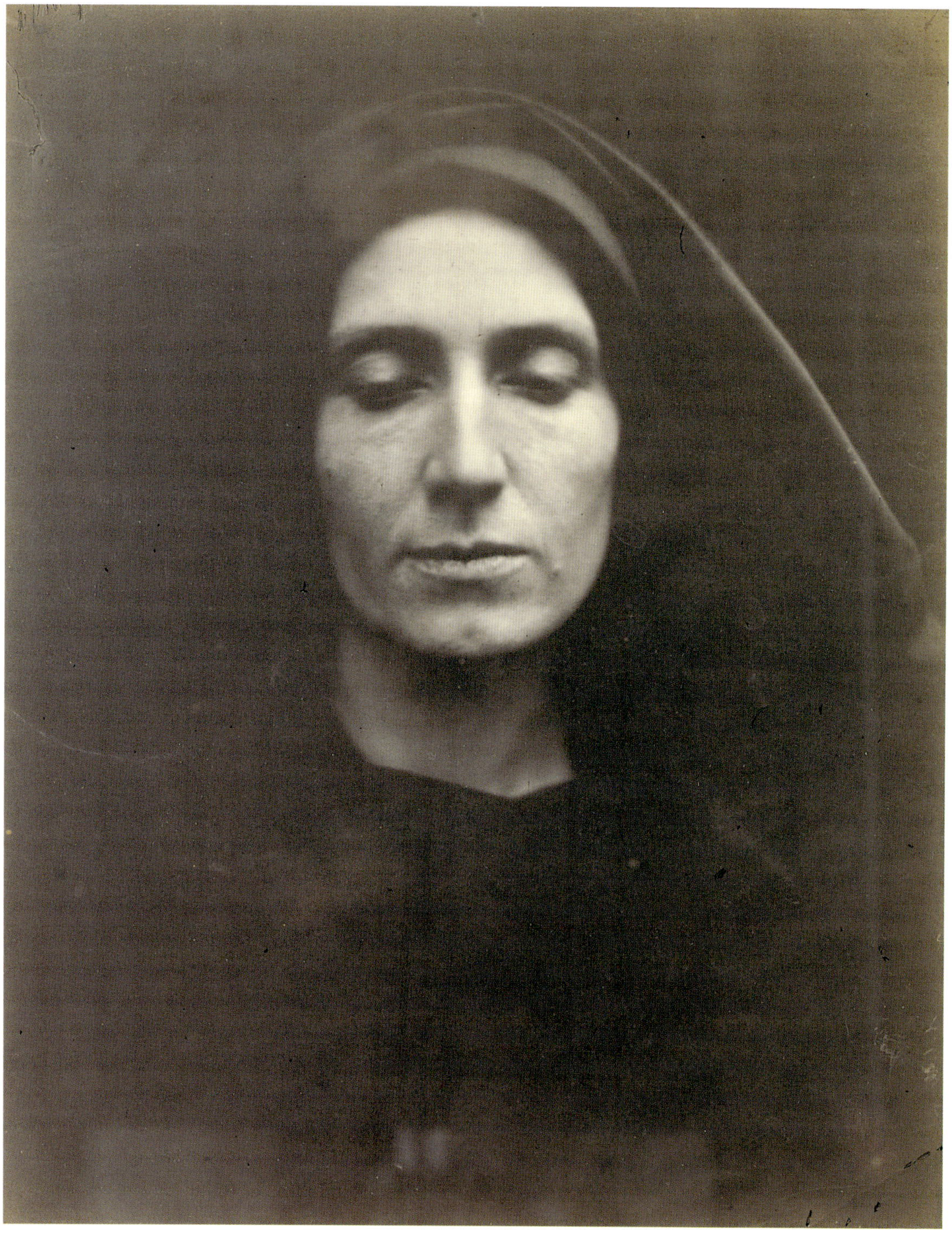

Unknown Woman, March 1868
Albumen print, 344 x 263mm (13½ x 10⅜")
Wilson Centre for Photography

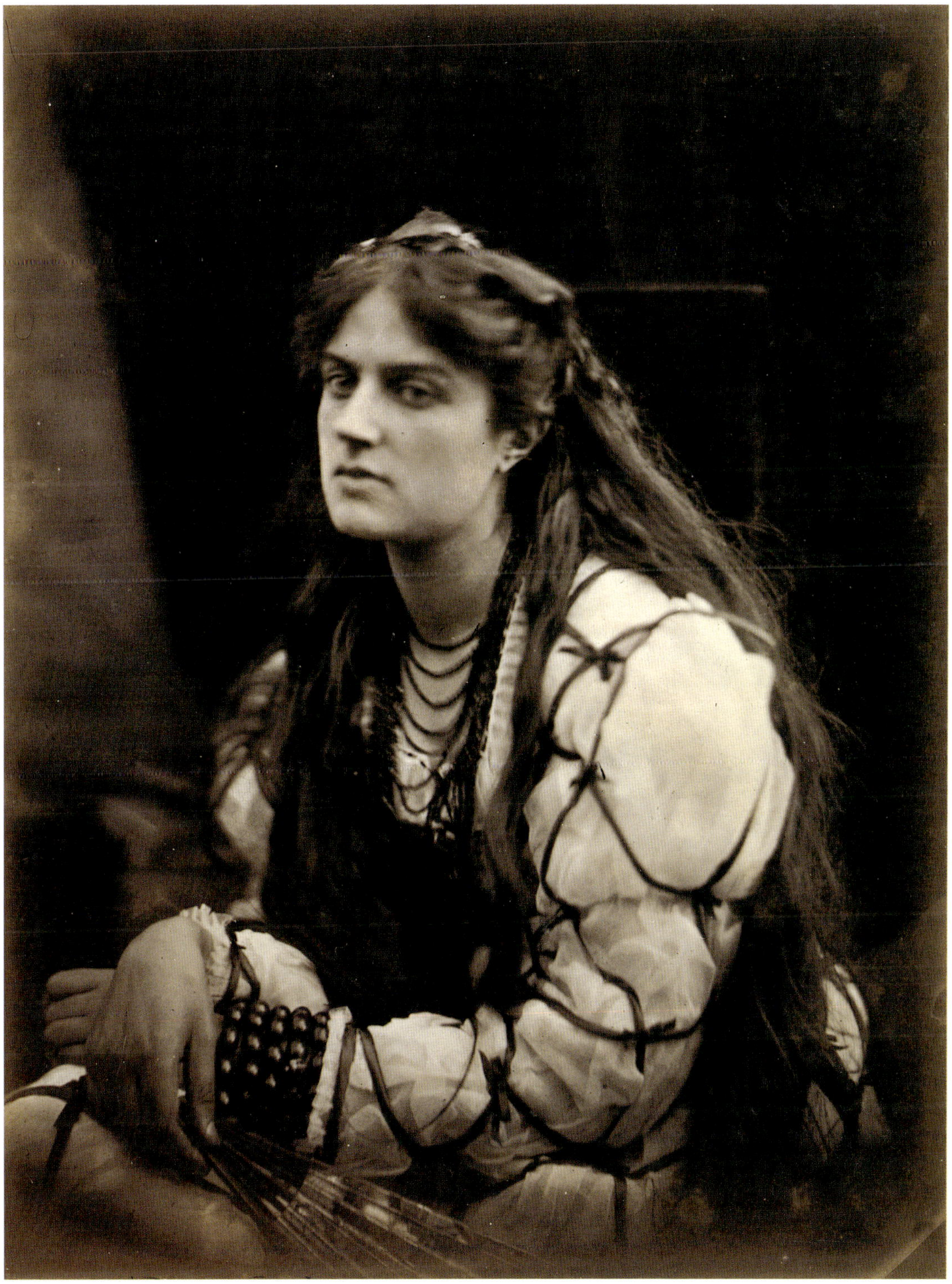

Hypatia, 1867
Marie Spartali
Albumen print, 335 x 246mm (13¼ x 9⅝")
The J. Paul Getty Museum, Los Angeles

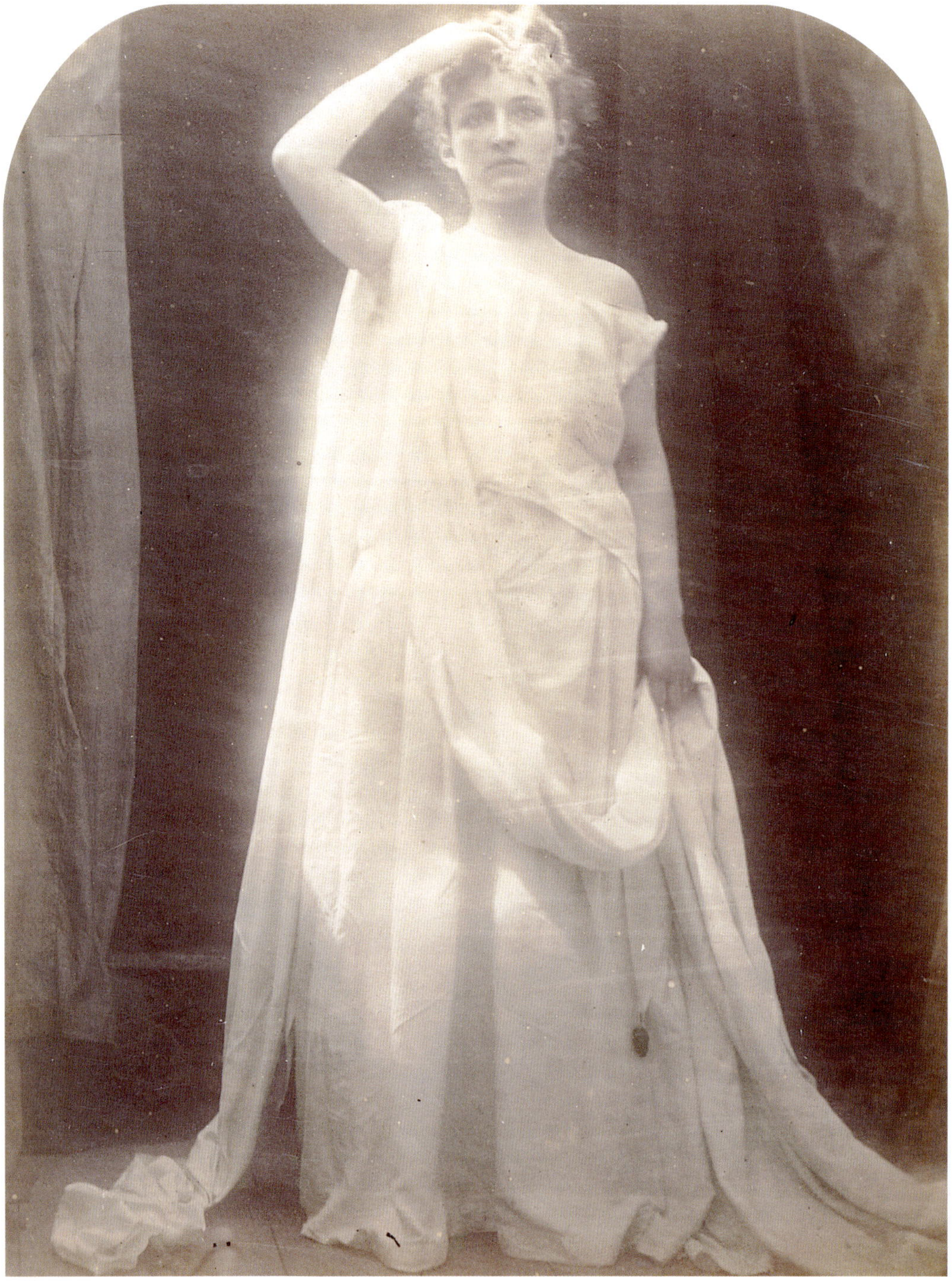

Isabel Bateman, 1874
Albumen print, 359 x 262mm (14⅛ x 10⅜")
Royal Photographic Society

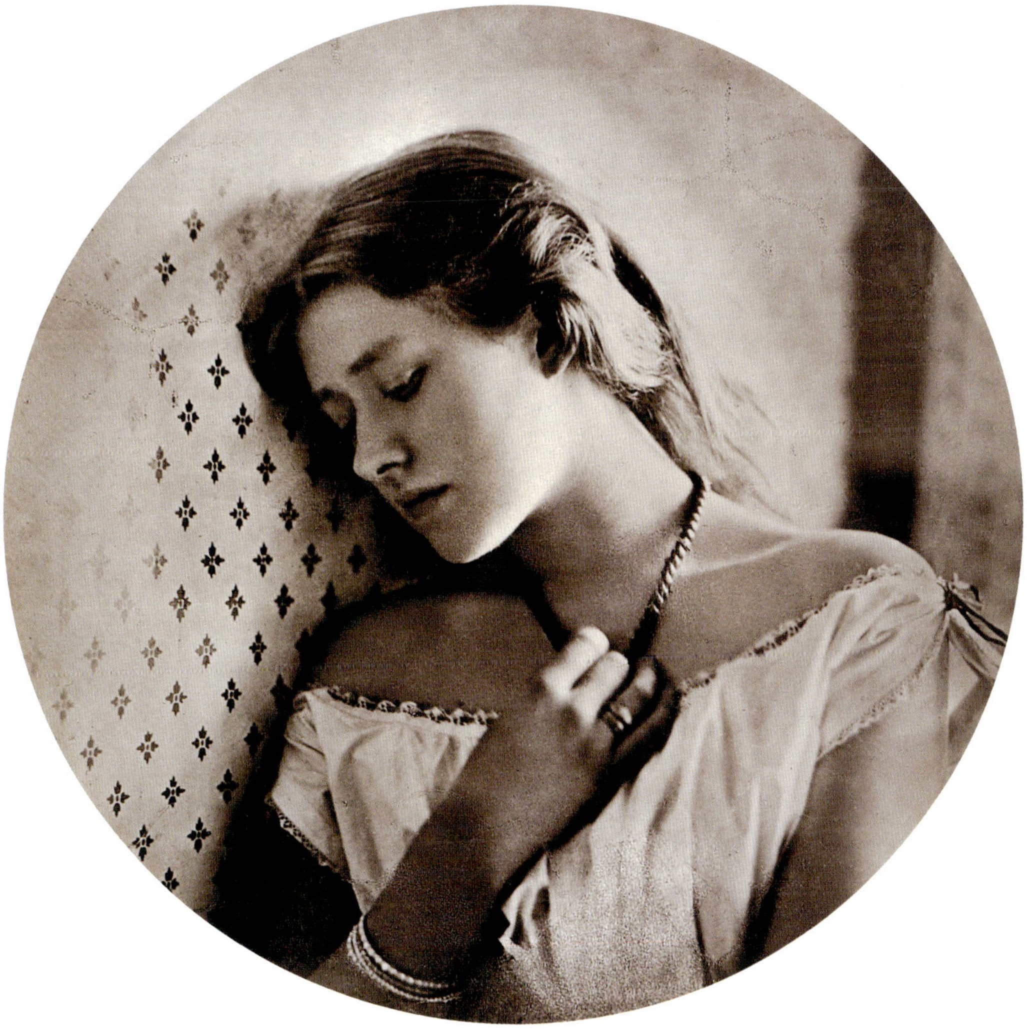

Sadness, 1864
Ellen Terry
Carbon print, 242 x 240mm (9½ x 9½")
Royal Photographic Society

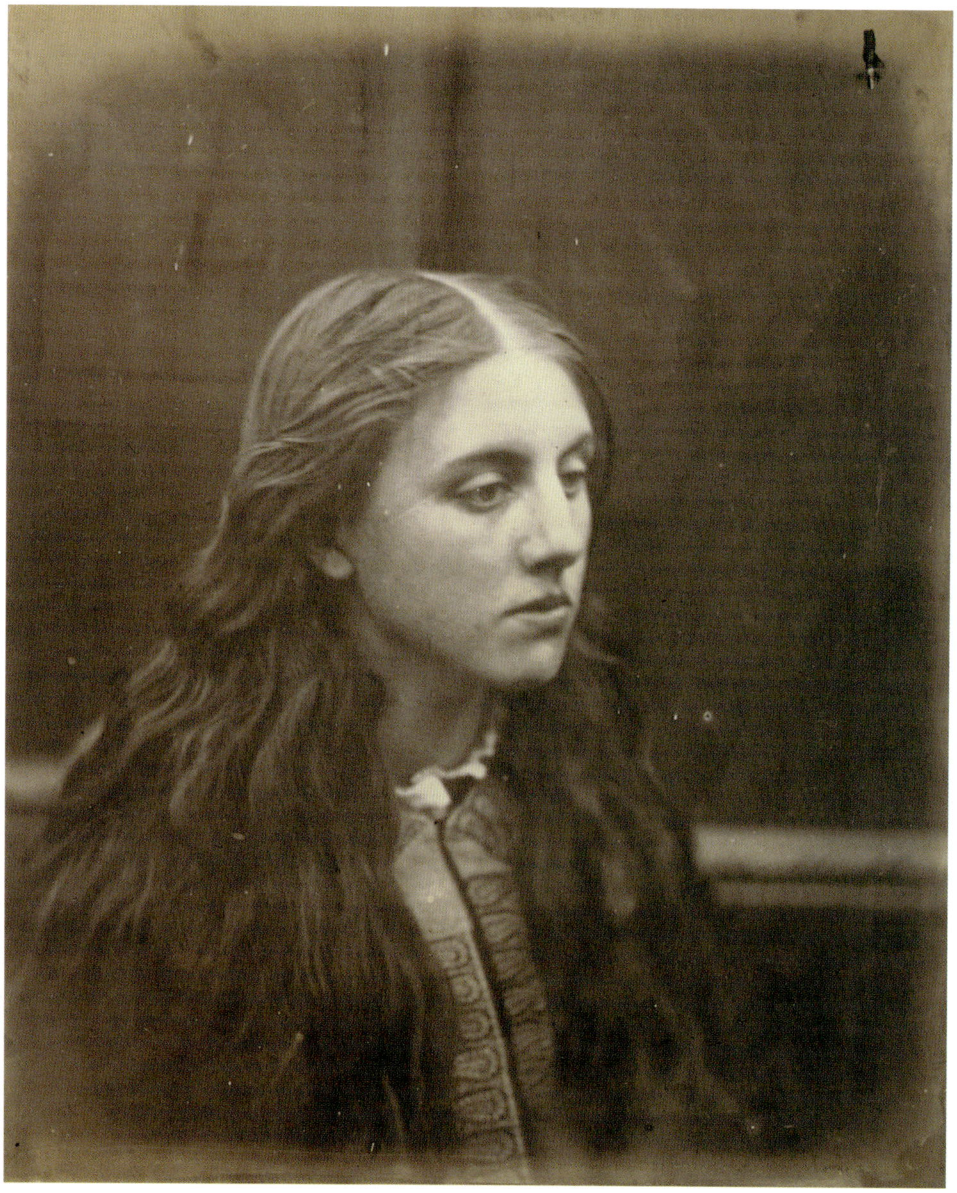

Suspense, 1864
Kate Dore
Albumen print, 260 x 205mm (10¼ x 8⅛")
National Museum of Photography, Film & Television, Bradford

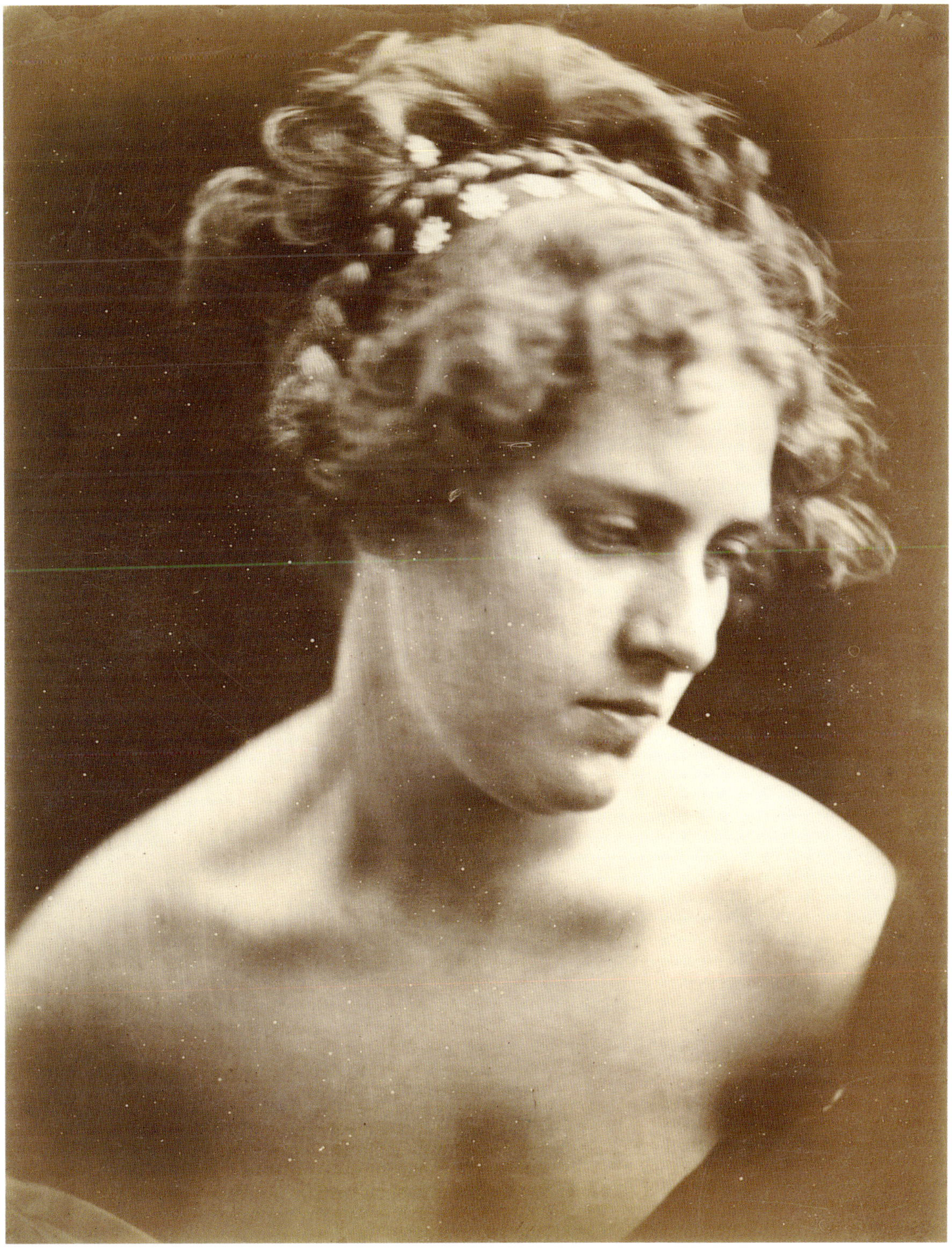

Vectis, 1868
Cyllena Wilson
Albumen print, 351 x 266mm (13⅞ x 10½")
Royal Photographic Society

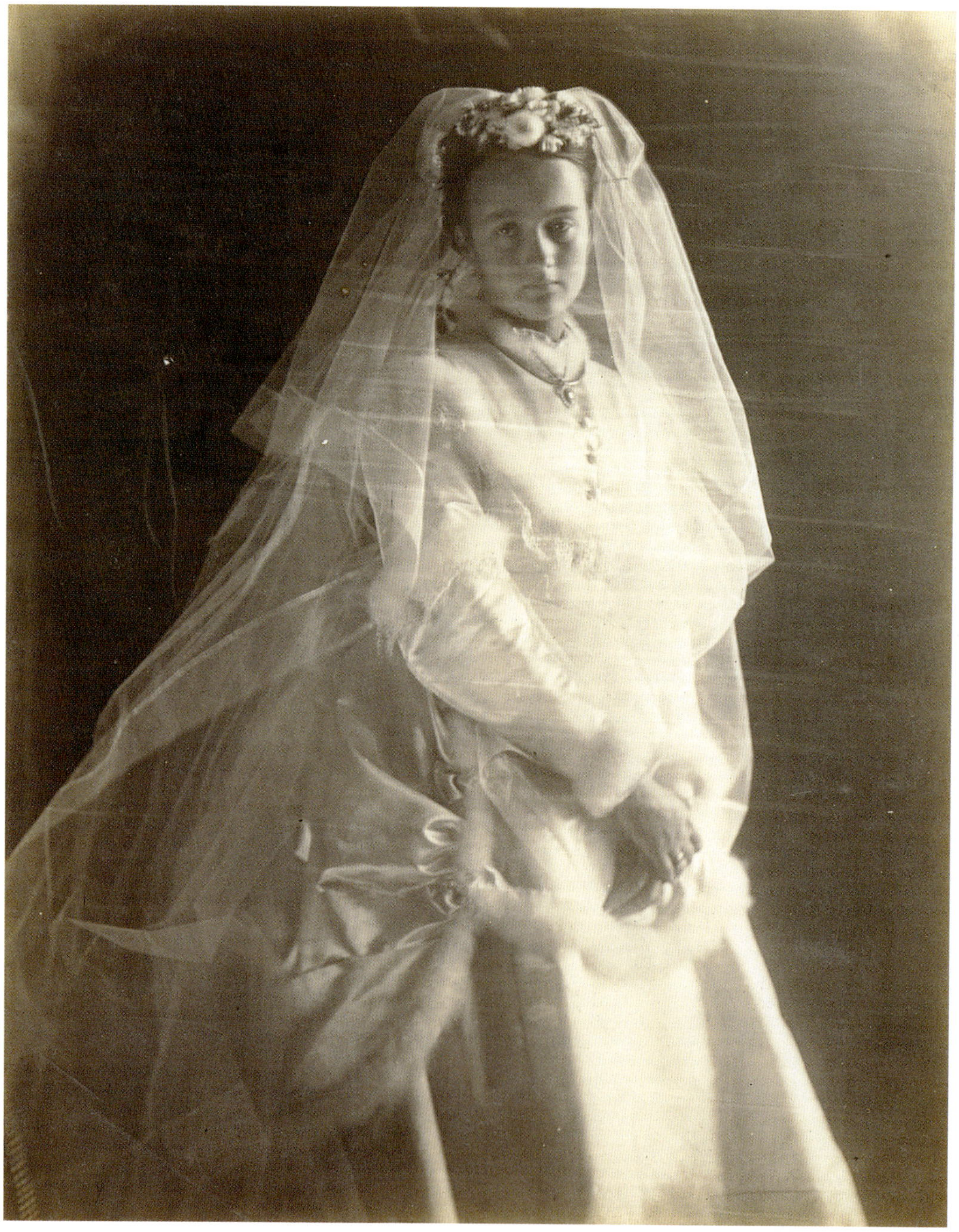

The Bride, 1869
Annie Chinery (Mrs Ewen Cameron)
Albumen print, 323 x 250mm (12¾ x 9⅞")
Royal Photographic Society

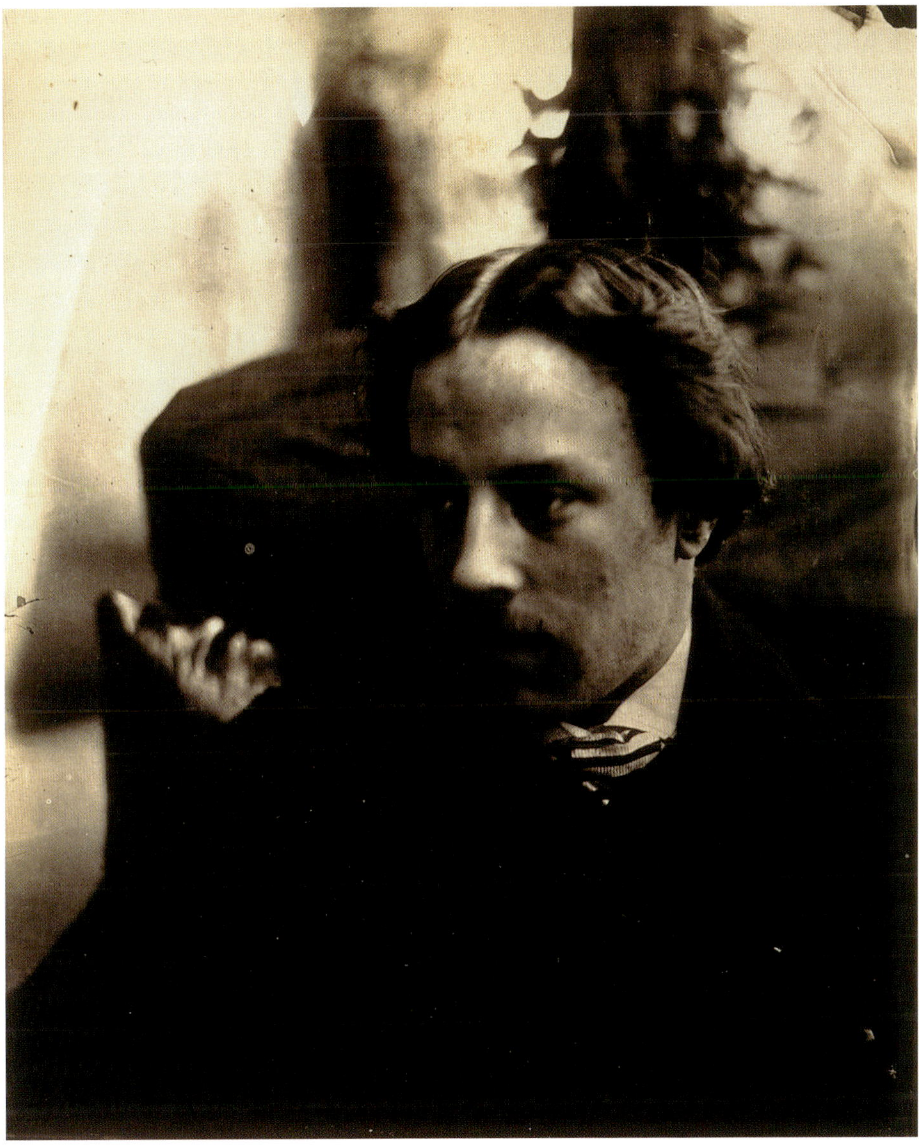

Ewen Wrottesley Hay Cameron, 1864
Albumen print, 265 x 211mm (10½ x 8¼")
National Museum of Photography, Film & Television, Bradford

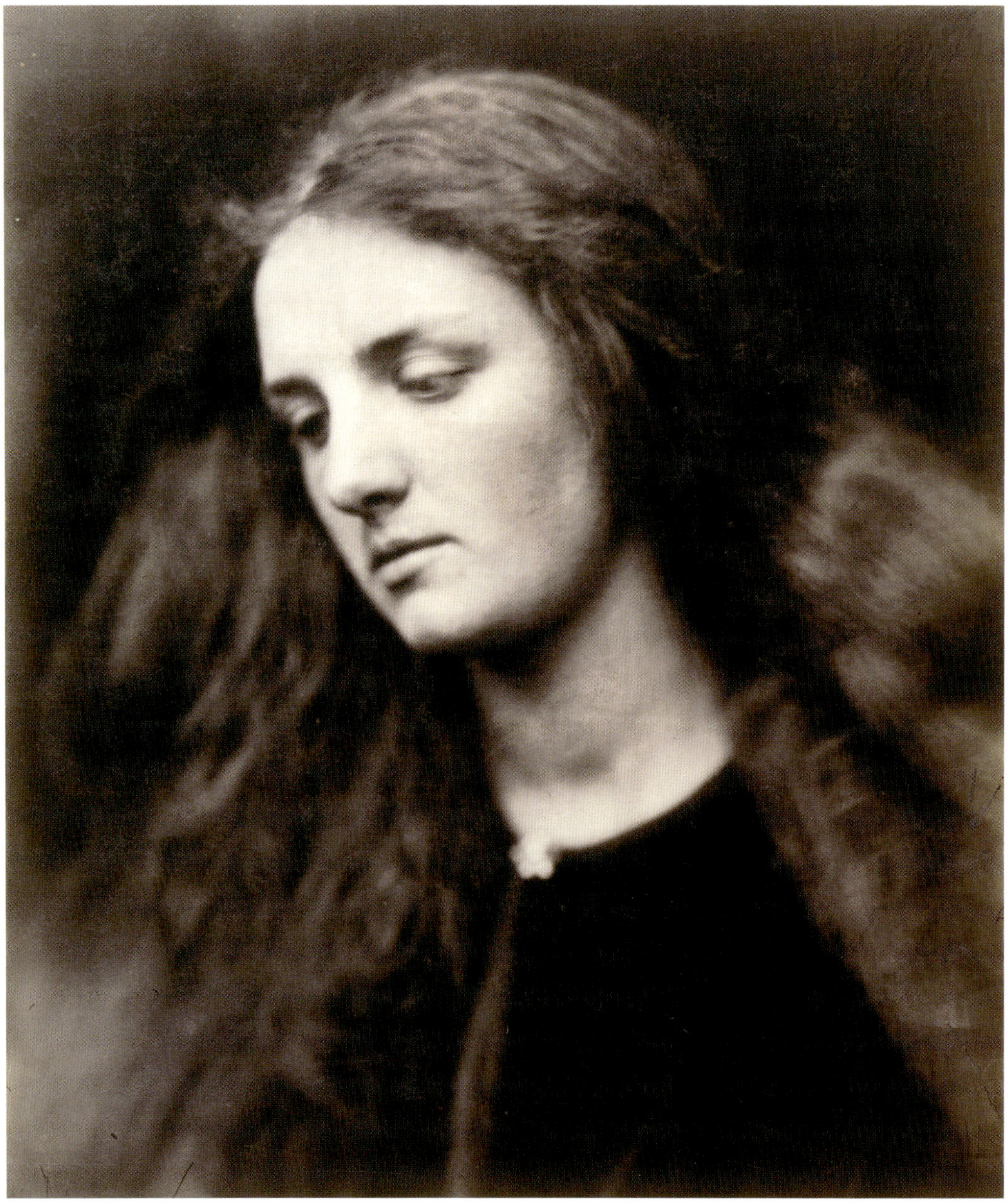

The Wild Flower, 1867
Annie Chinery (Mrs Ewen Cameron)
Albumen print, 292 x 243mm (11½ x 9⅝")
Royal Photographic Society

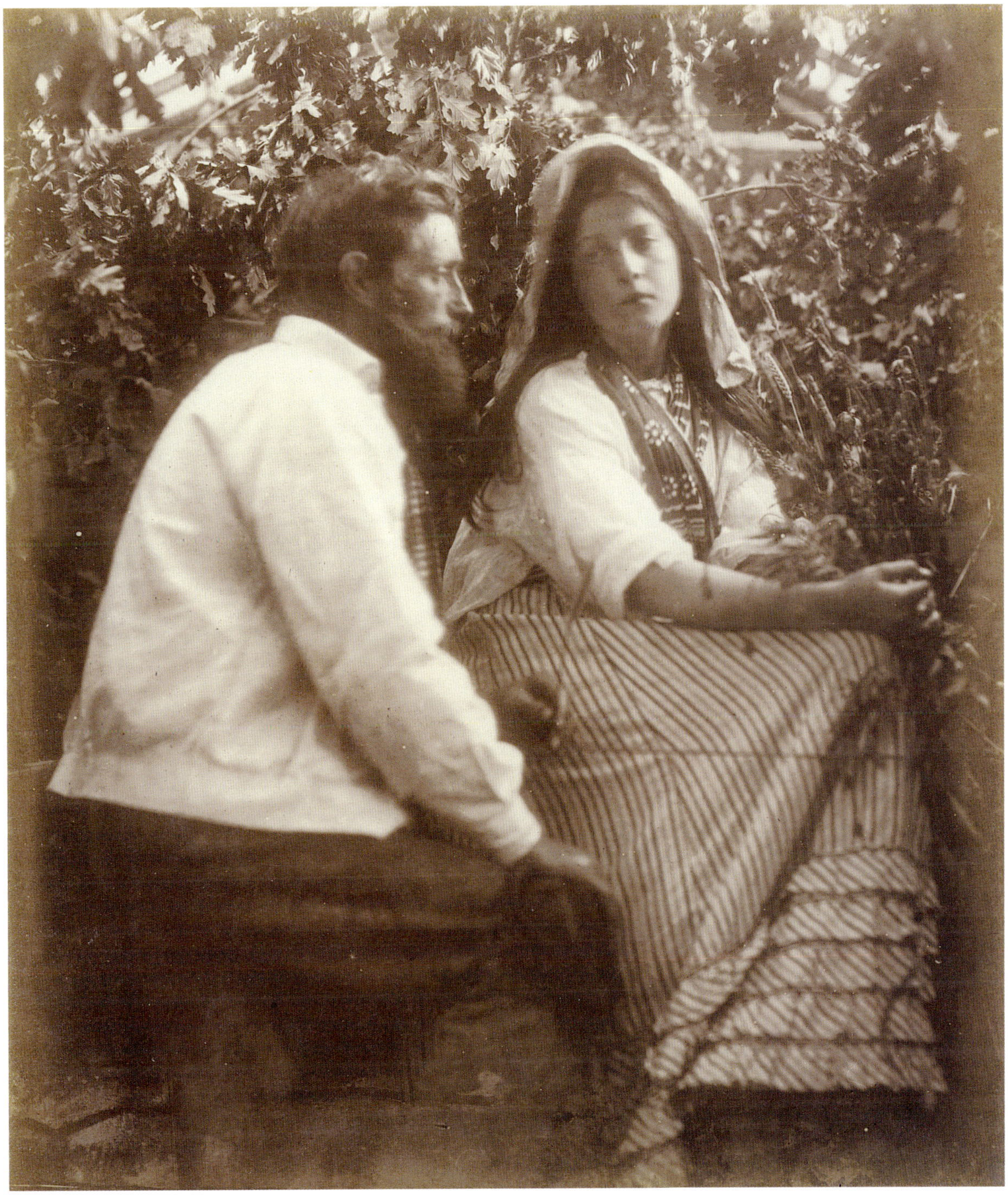

The Twilight hour, 1874
Unknown man and Kate Keown
Albumen print, 333 x 278mm (13⅛ x 11")
Royal Photographic Society

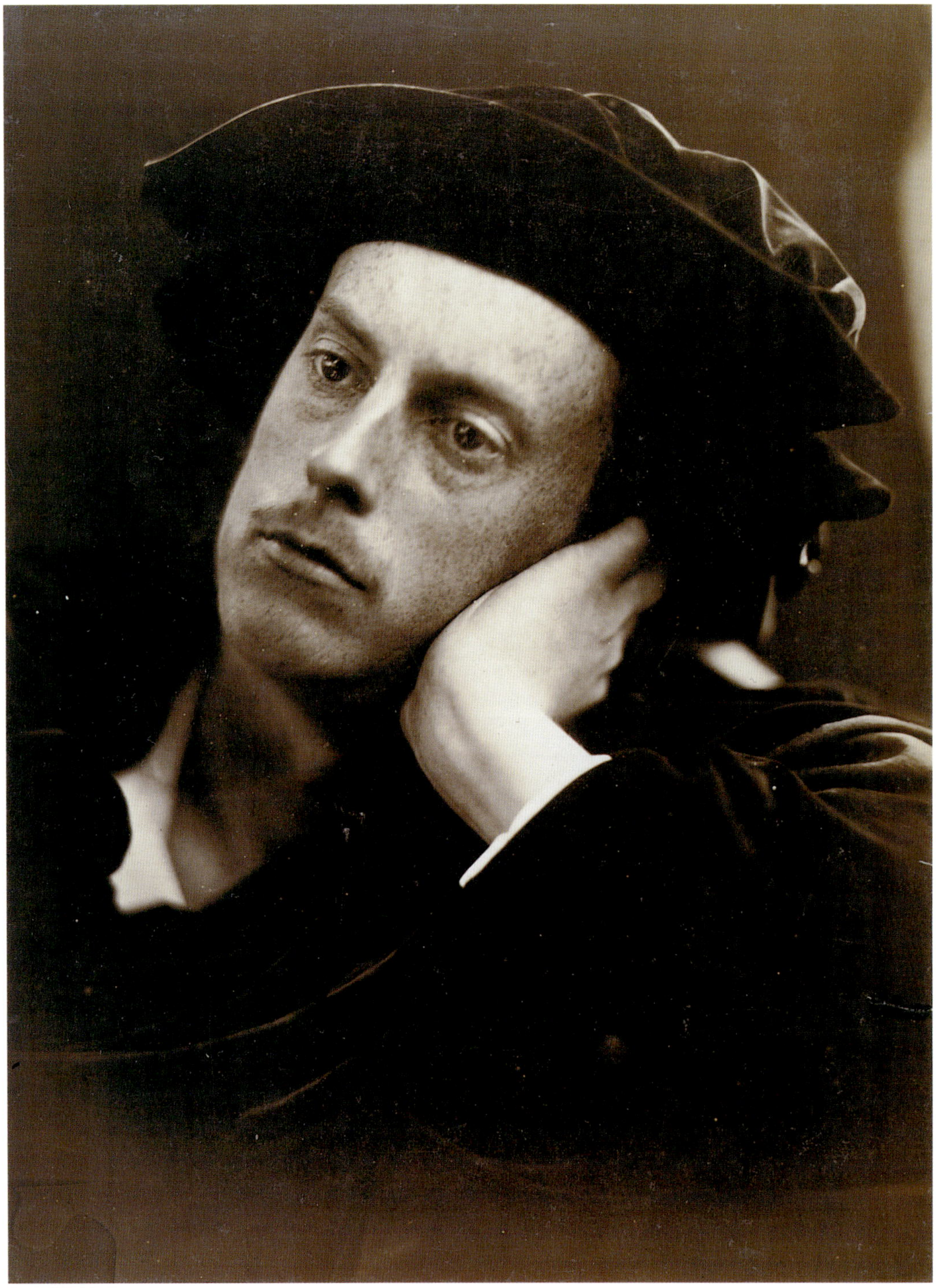

Hon. Frank Charteris, 1867
Albumen print, 332 x 240mm (13⅛ x 10")
Royal Photographic Society

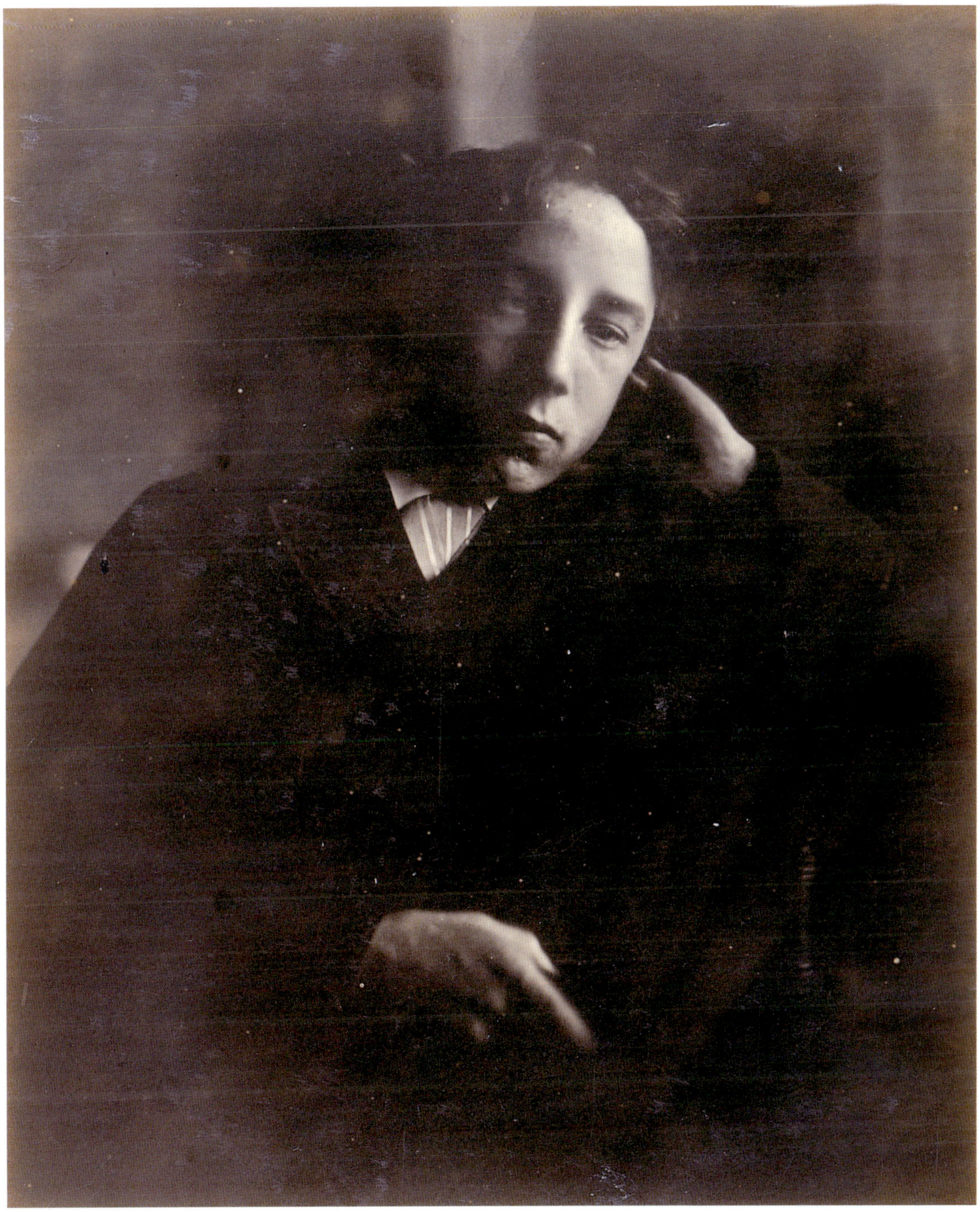

Henry Herschel Hay Cameron, 1867–8
Albumen print, 282 x 226mm (11⅛ x 8⅞")
Royal Photographic Society

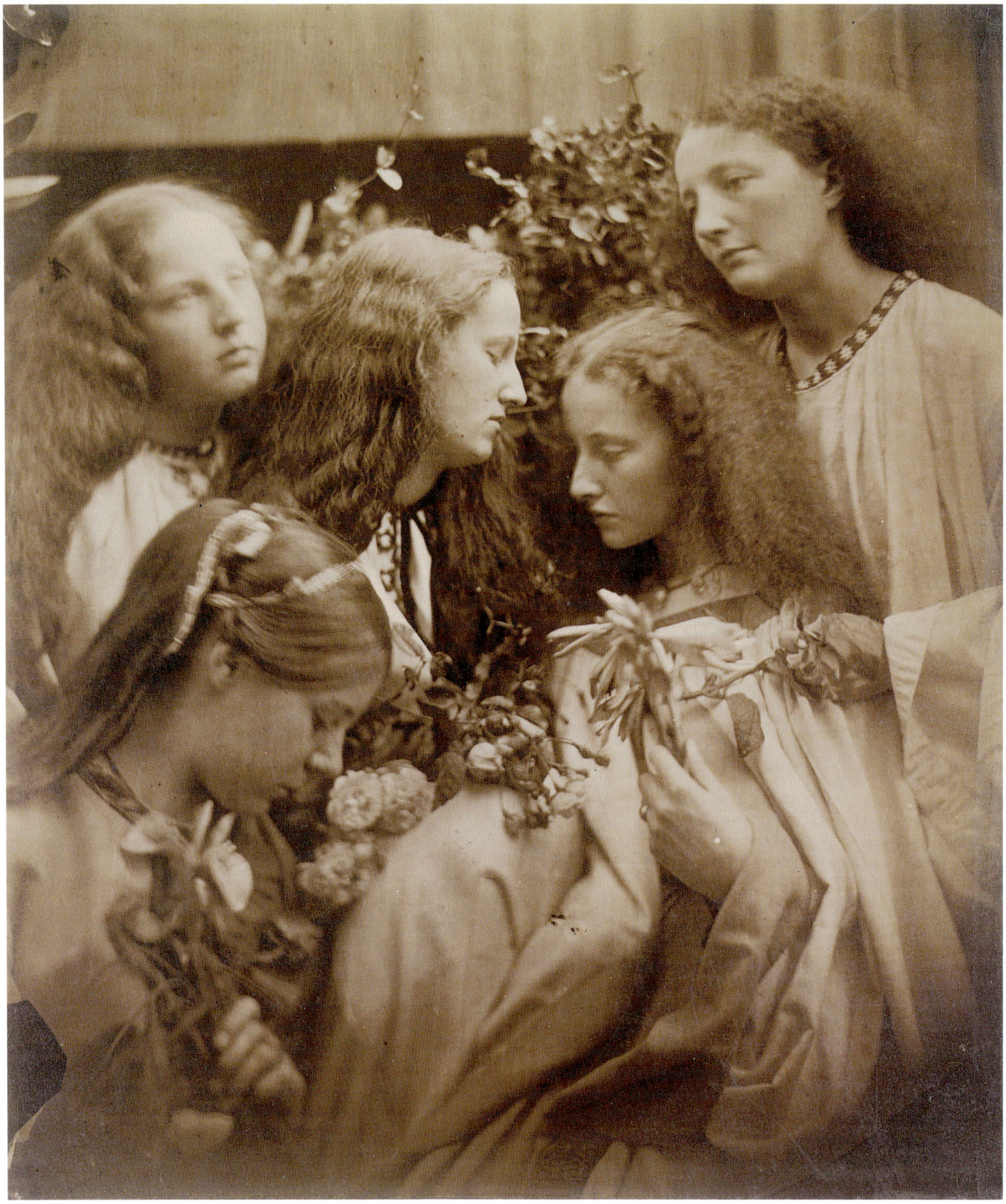

The Rose bud garden of girls, June 1868
Eleanor, Christina, Mary and Ethel Fraser-Tytler
Albumen print, 350 x 292mm (13¾ x 11½")
Royal Photographic Society

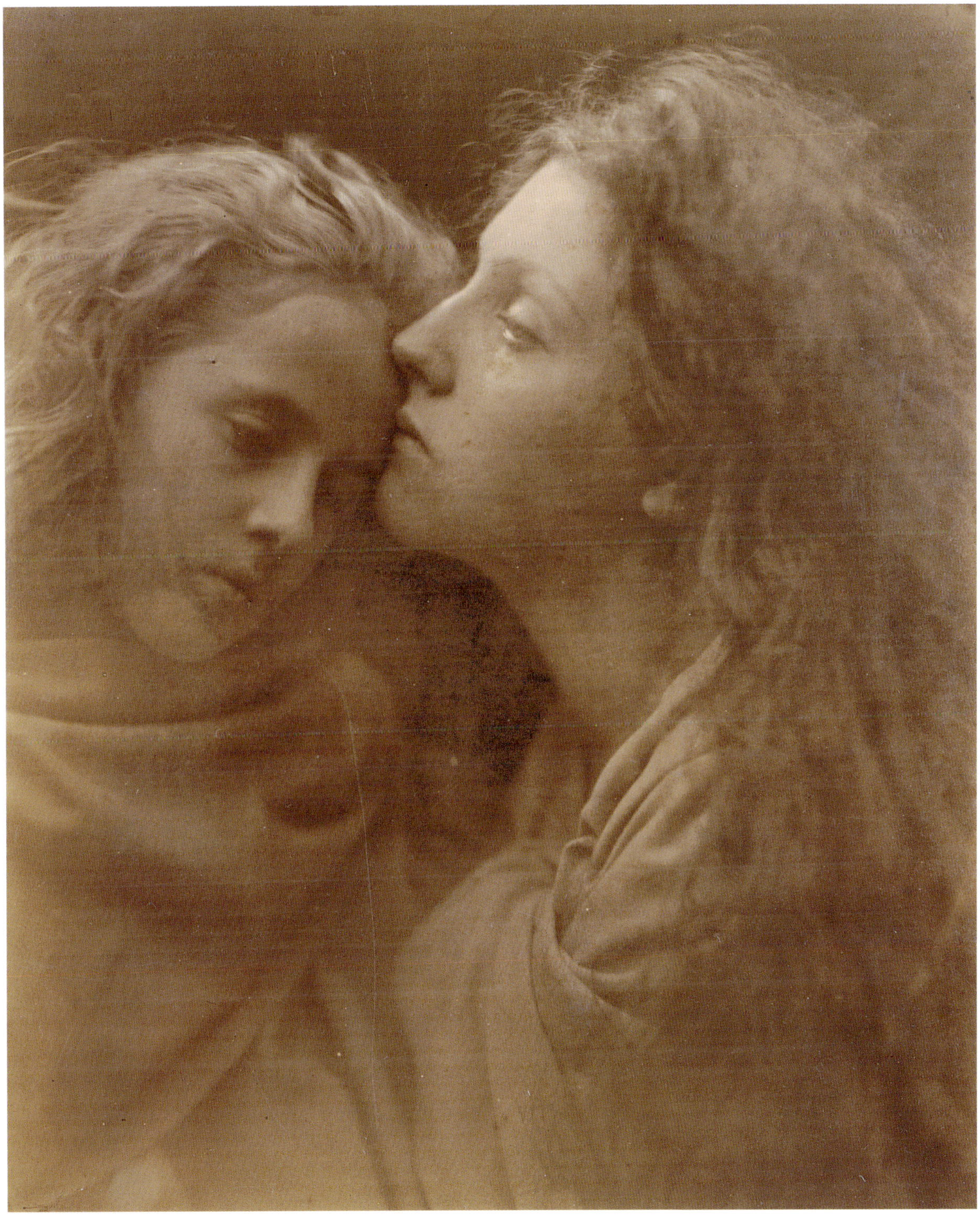

The Kiss of Peace, September 1869
Florence Anson? and Mary Ann Hillier
Albumen print, 345 x 275mm (13⅝ x 10⅞")
Royal Photographic Society

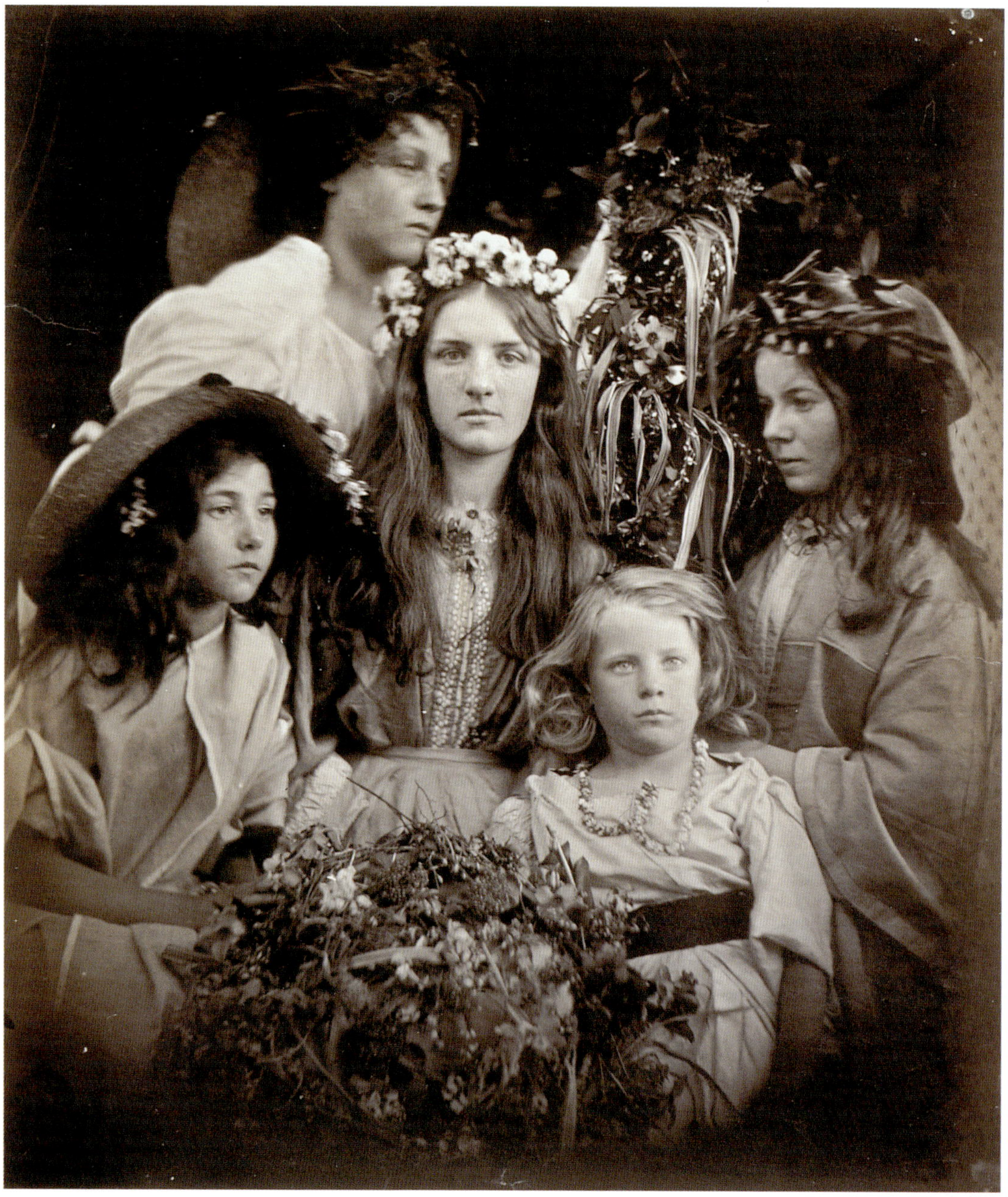

May Day, 1866
Kate Keown, Mary Ann Hillier, Mary Ryan, Freddy Gould and unknown girl
Albumen print, 339 x 286mm (13⅜ x 11¼")
The Board of Trustees of the Victoria and Albert Museum, London

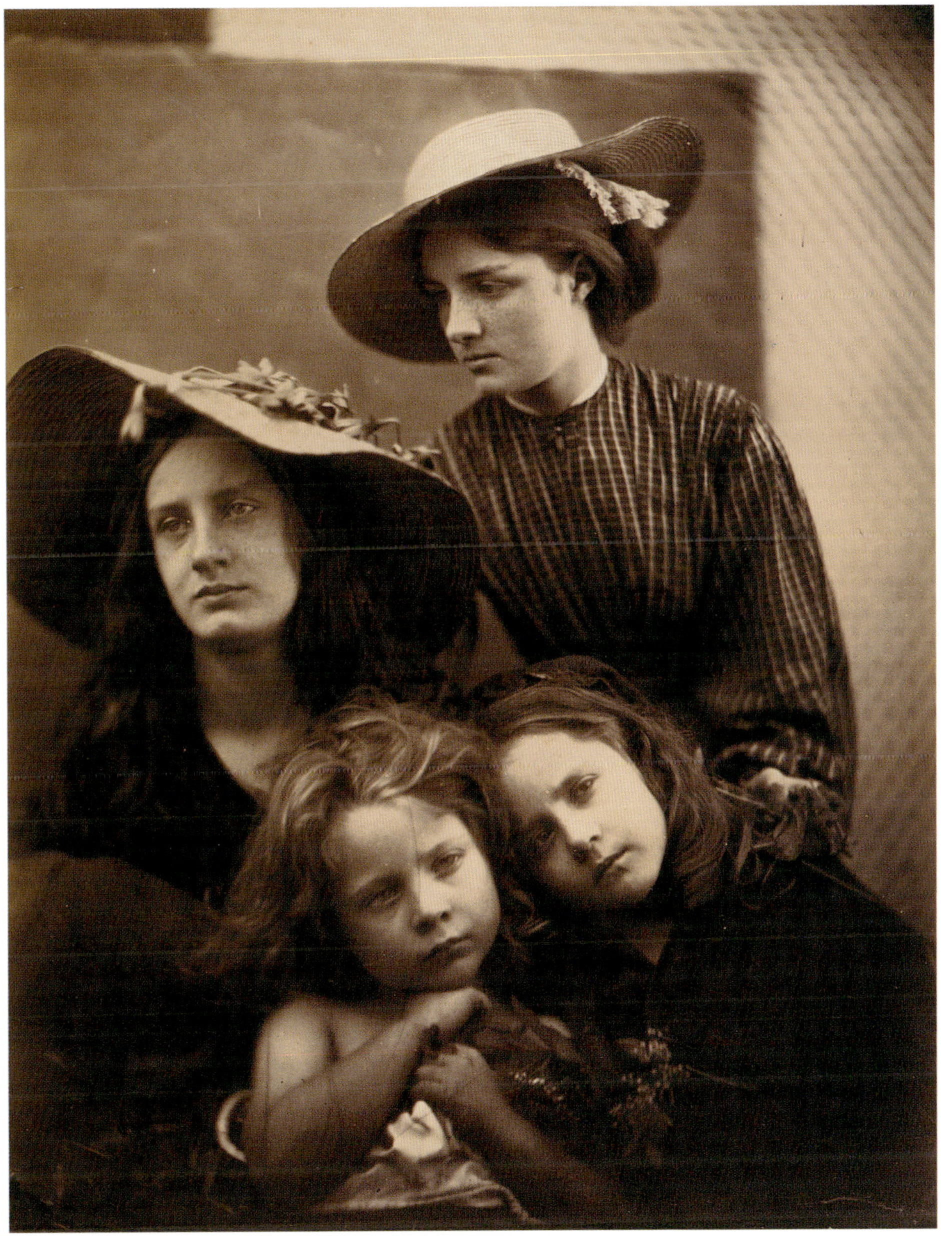

Summer Days, 1866
May Prinsep, Mary Ryan, Freddy Gould and Elizabeth Keown
Albumen print, 353 x 265mm (13⅞ x 10⅜")
Tennyson Research Centre, Lincoln

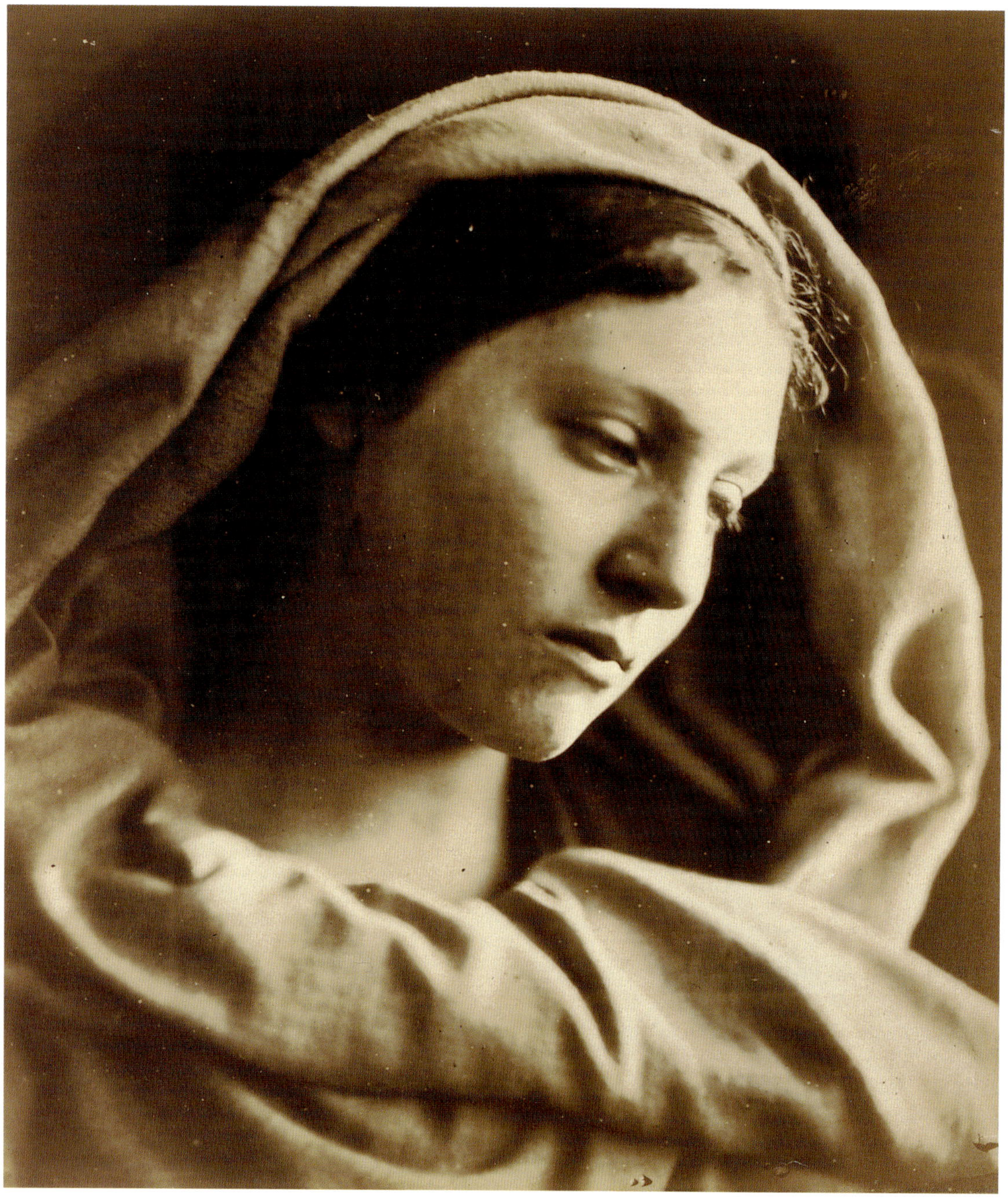

Mary Mother, April 1867
Mary Ann Hillier
Albumen print, 307 x 257mm (12⅛ x 10⅛")
Royal Photographic Society

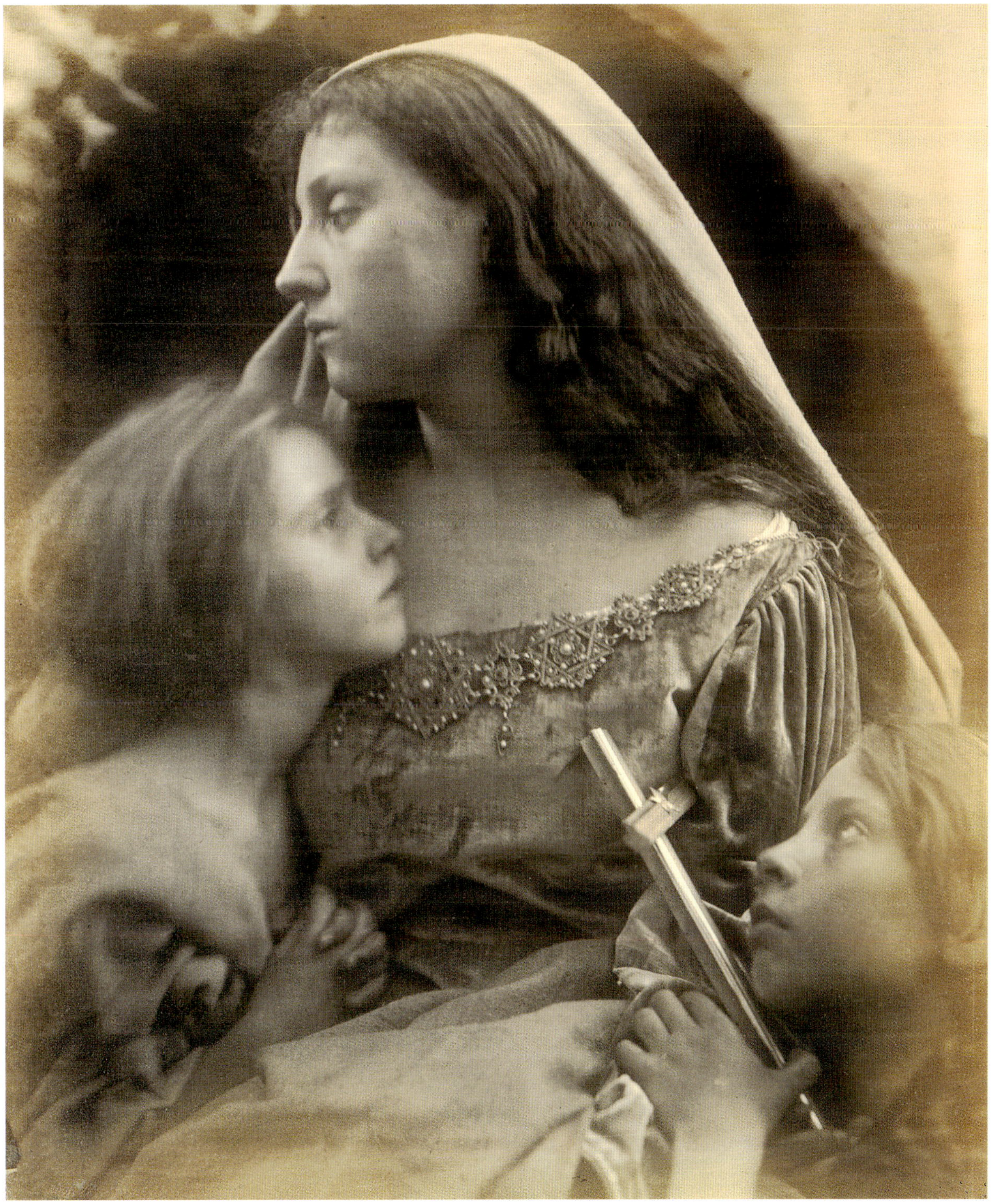

A Holy Family, 1872
Rosie Prince?, Mary Ann Hillier and Freddy Gould
Albumen print, 333 x 269mm (13 x 10⅝")
The J. Paul Getty Museum, Los Angeles

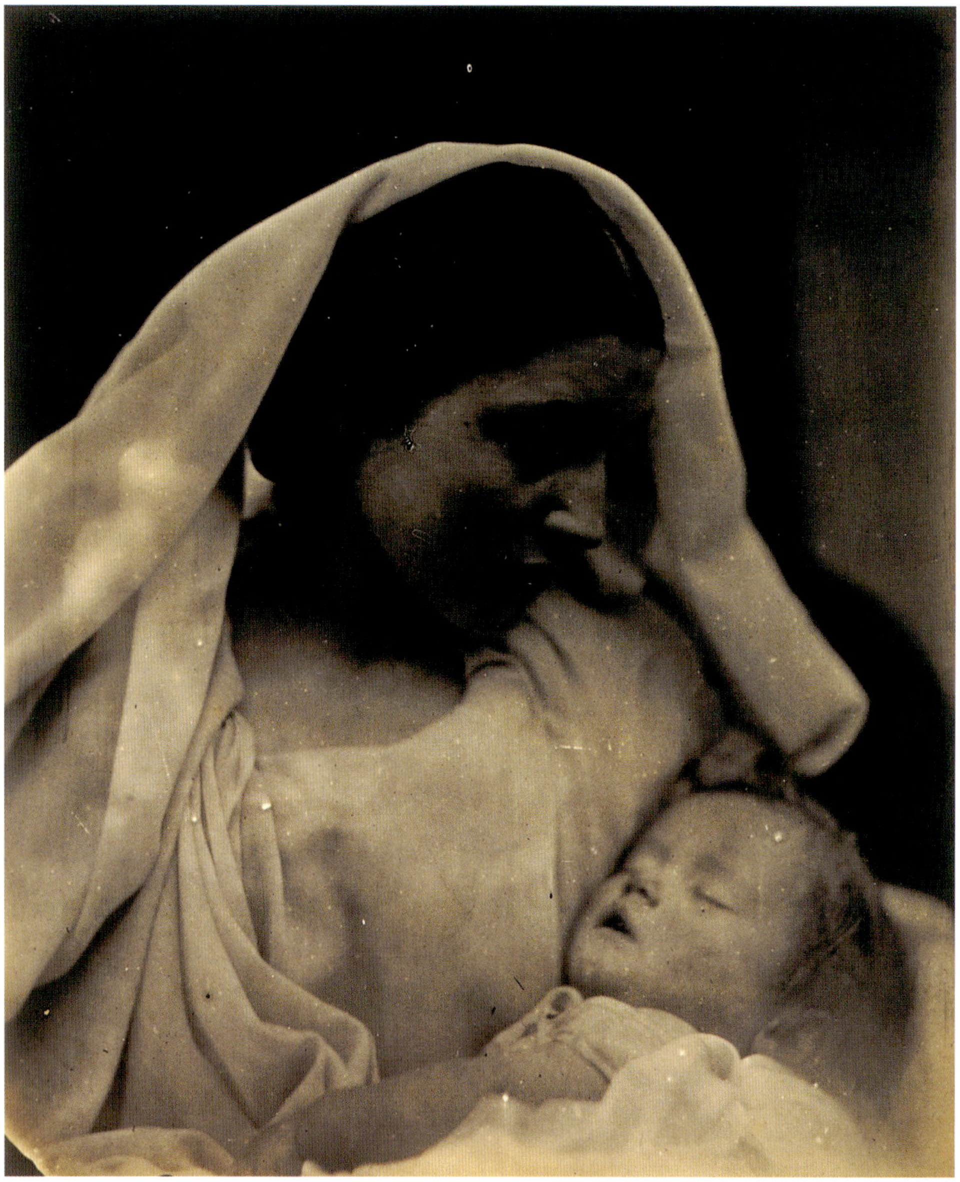

La Madonna Riposata Resting in hope, 1864
Mary Ann Hillier and Percy Seymour Keown
Albumen print, 250 x 202mm (9⅞ x 8")
National Museum of Photography, Film & Television, Bradford

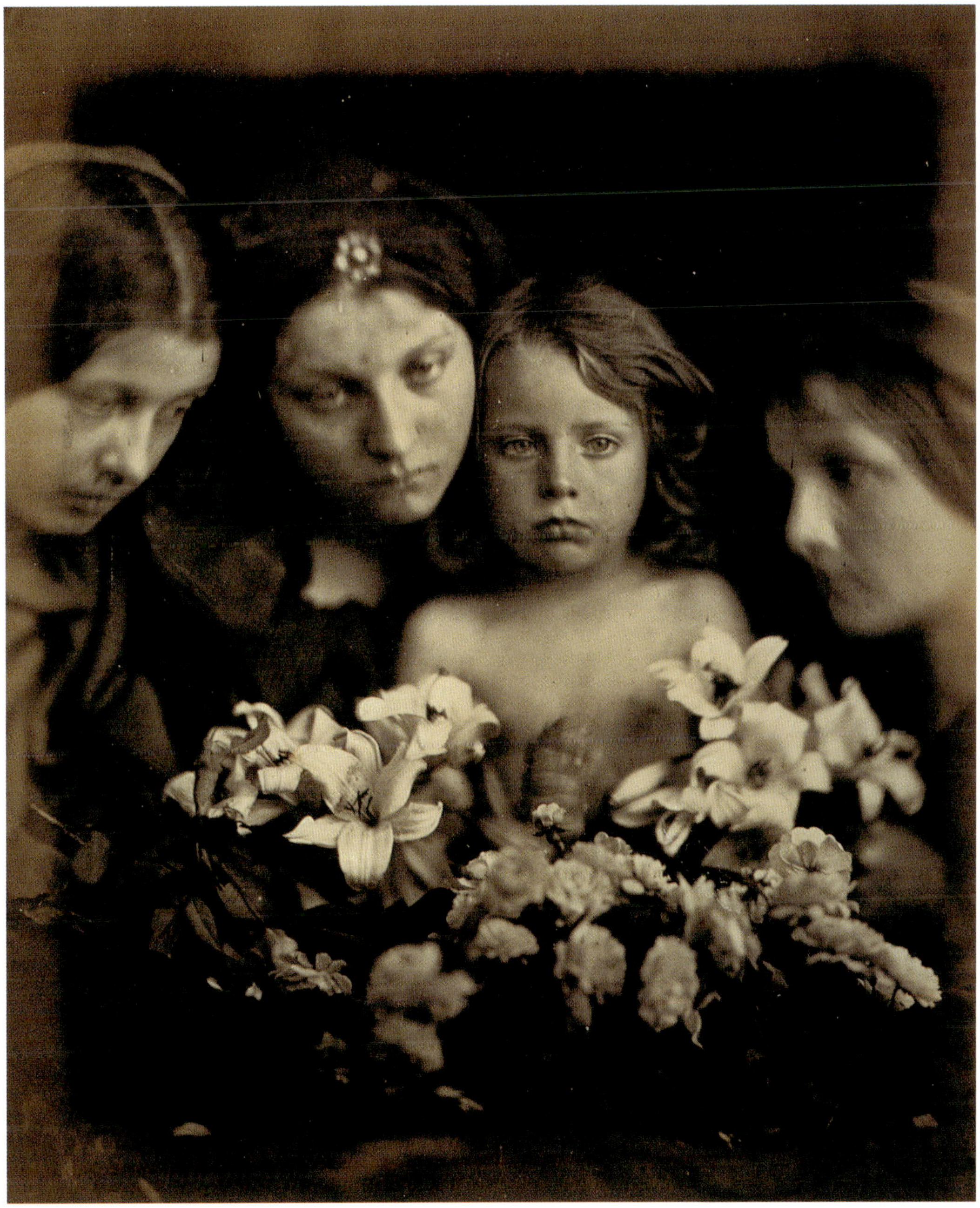

The Return after 3 days, 1865
Mary Kellaway, Mary Ann Hillier, Freddy Gould and Mary Ryan
Albumen print, 308 x 252mm (12⅛ x 9⅞")
National Museum of Photography, Film & Television, Bradford

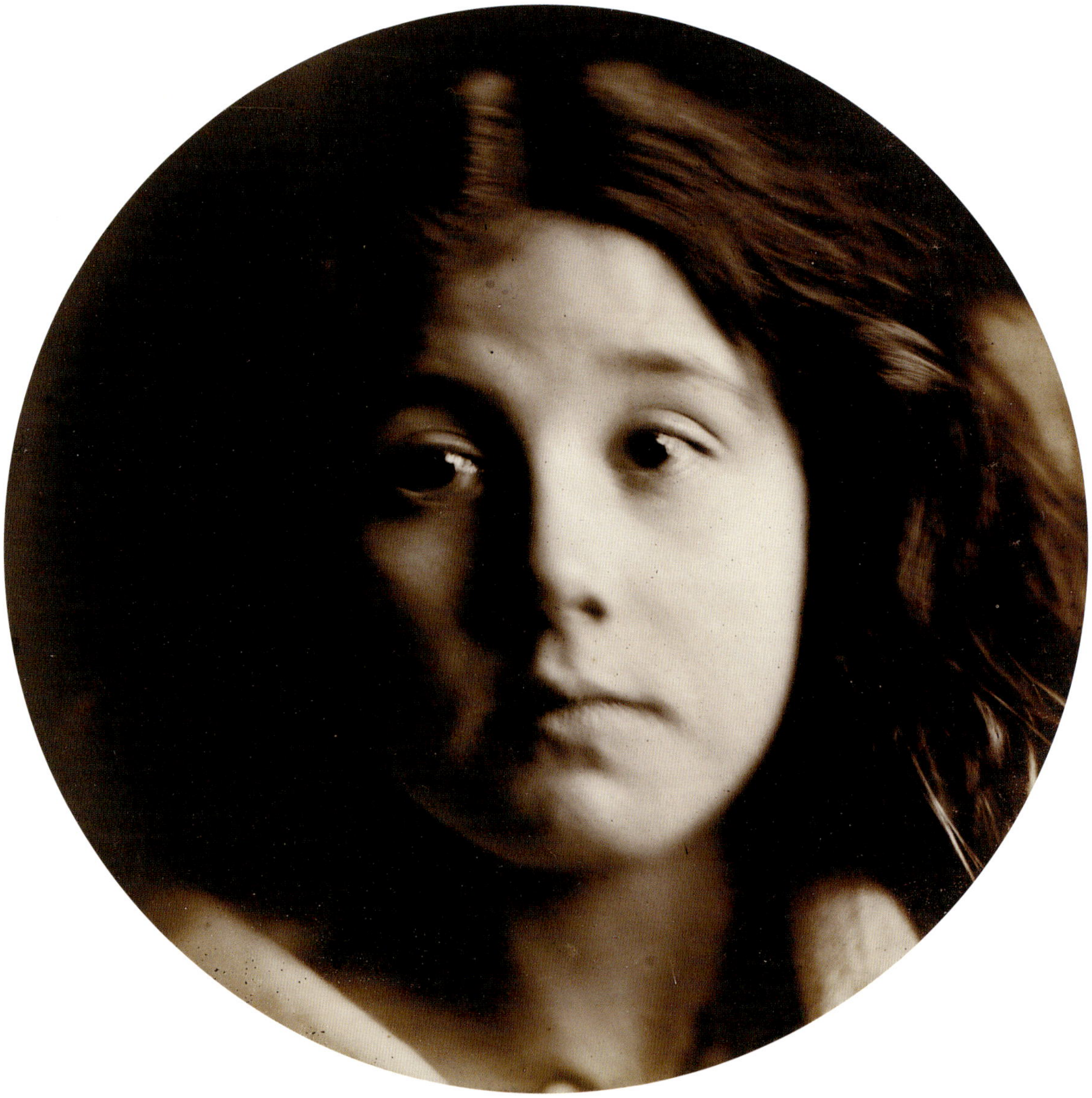

Kate Keown, 1866
Albumen print, diameter 290mm (11⅜")
Wilson Centre for Photography

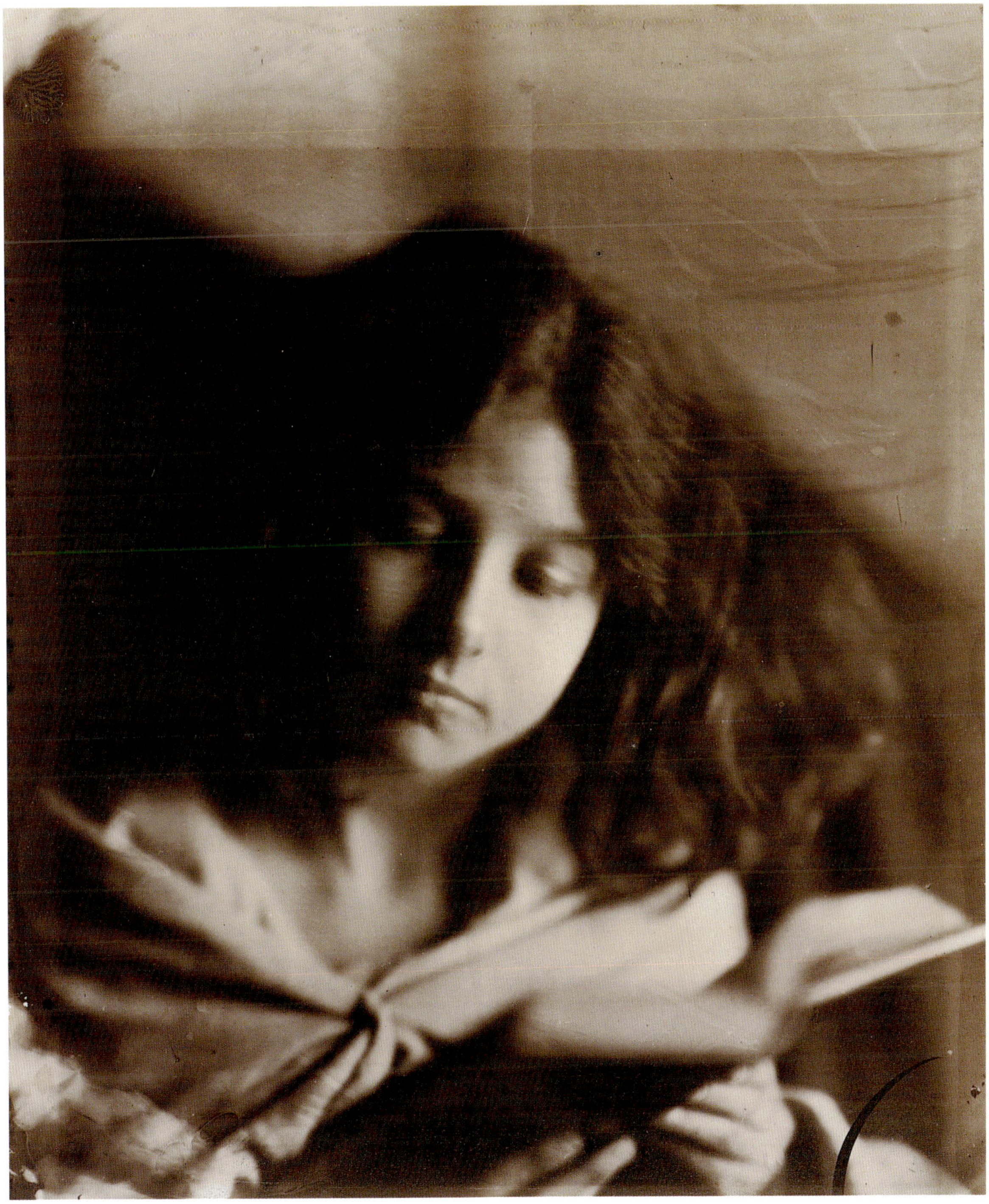

Kate Keown Reading, March 1867
Albumen print, 340 x 280mm (13⅜ x 11")
Wilson Centre for Photography

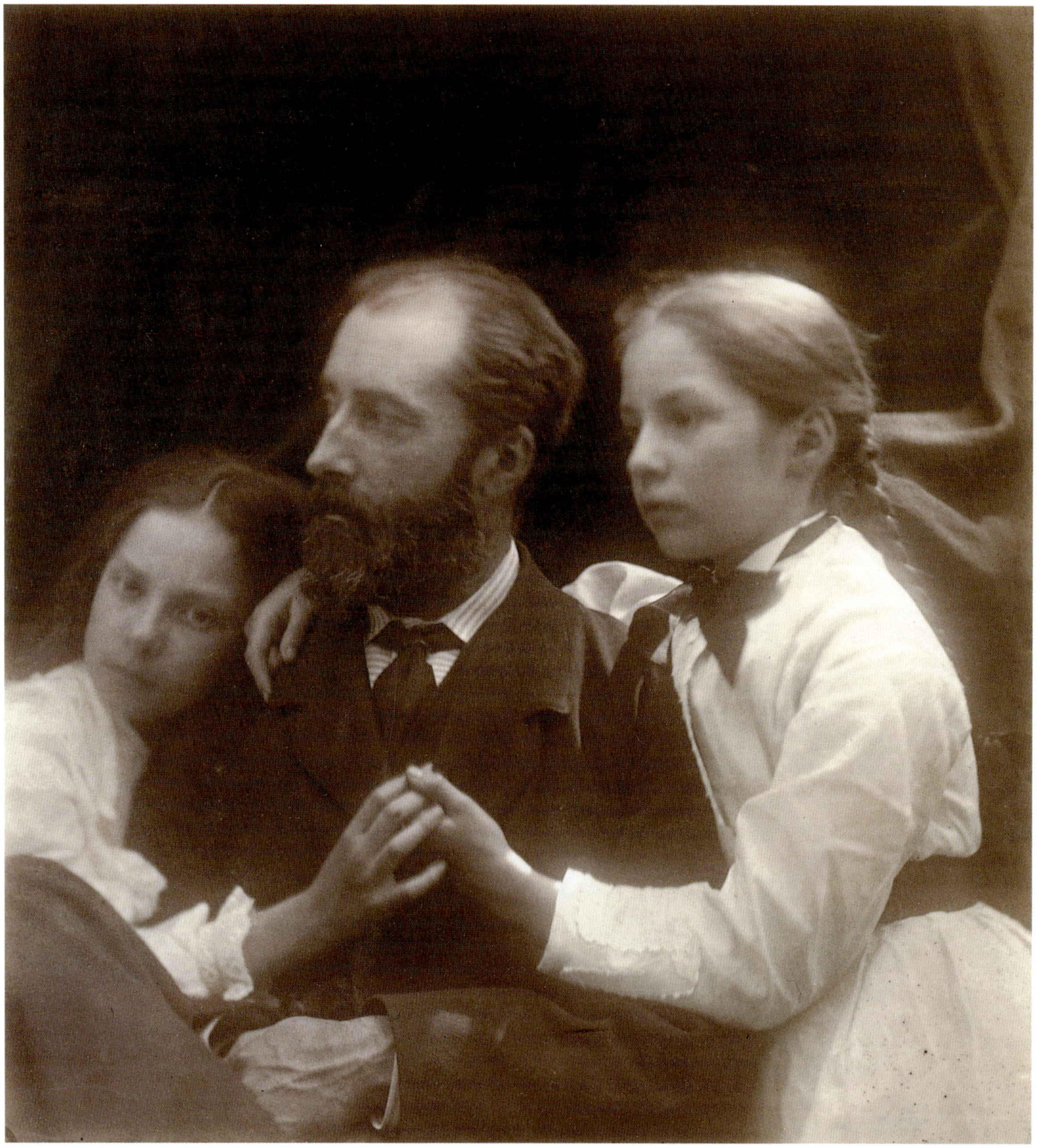

Charles Norman and his Daughters, Adeline and Margaret, July 1874
Albumen print, 297 x 266mm (11¾ x 10½")
The J. Paul Getty Museum, Los Angeles

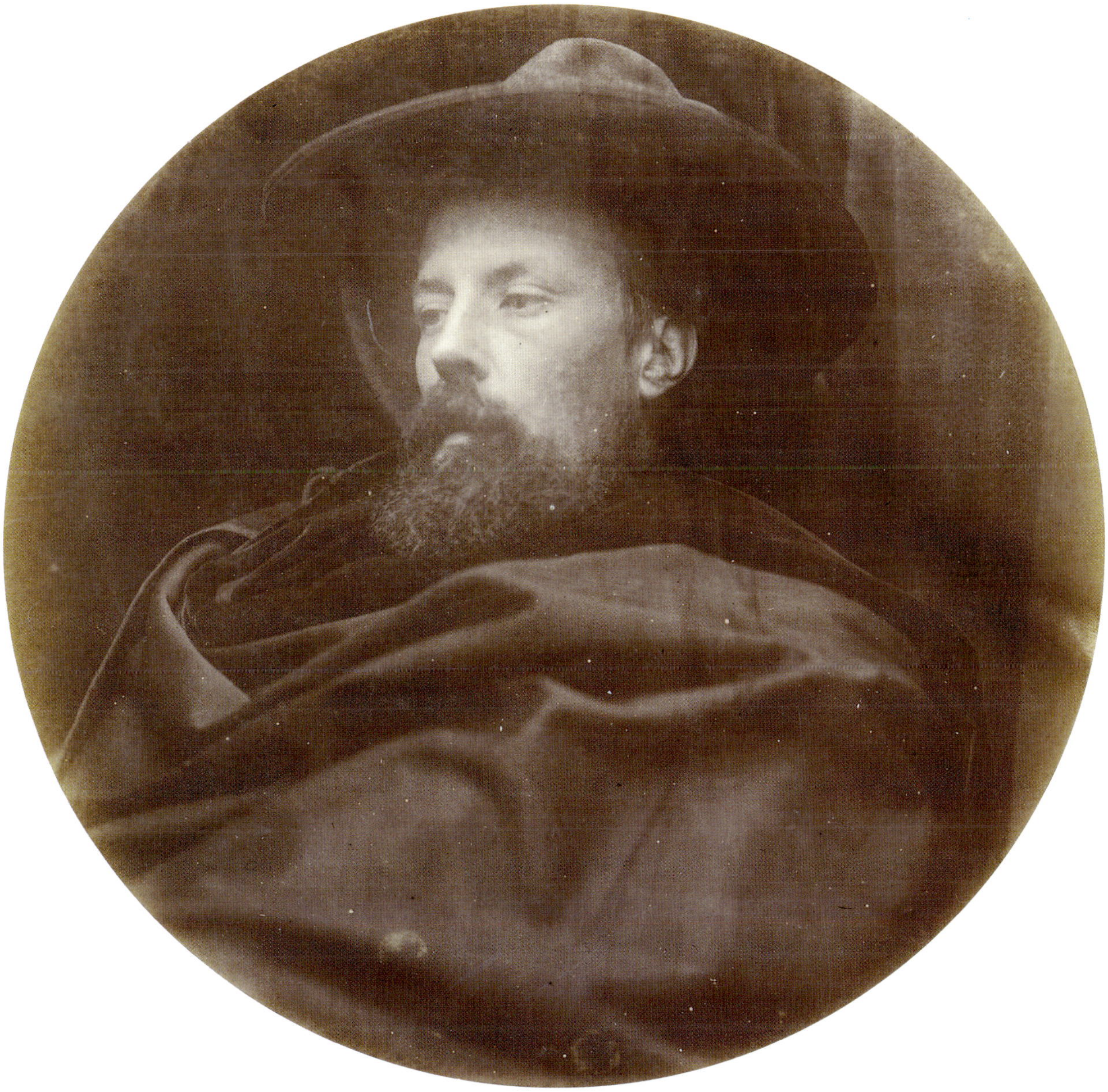

Unknown Man, 1868–72
Albumen print, diameter 278mm (11")
Royal Photographic Society

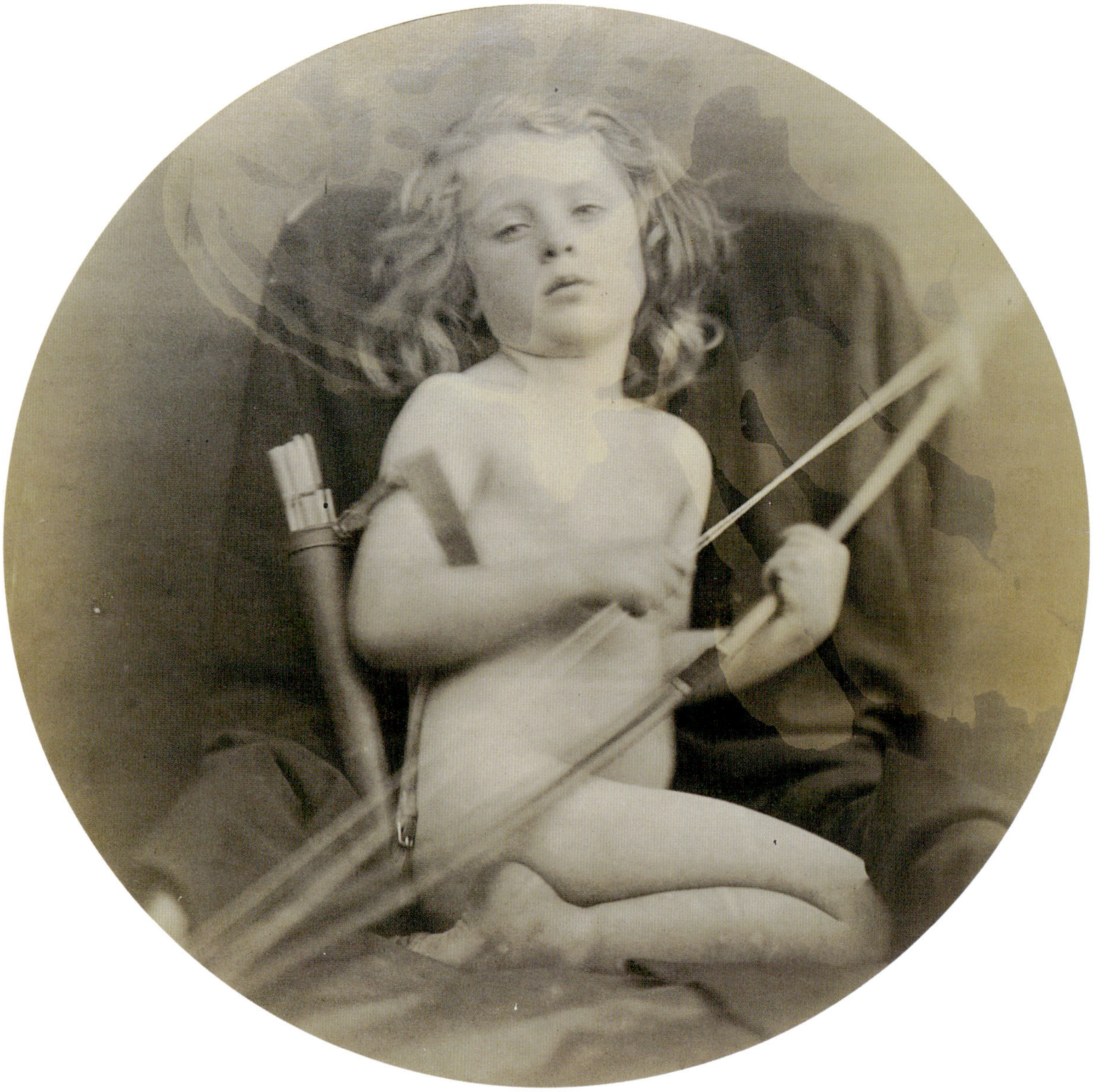

Love in Idleness, *c.*1867
Freddy Gould
Albumen print, diameter 290mm (11⅜")
Liverpool Libraries and Information Services

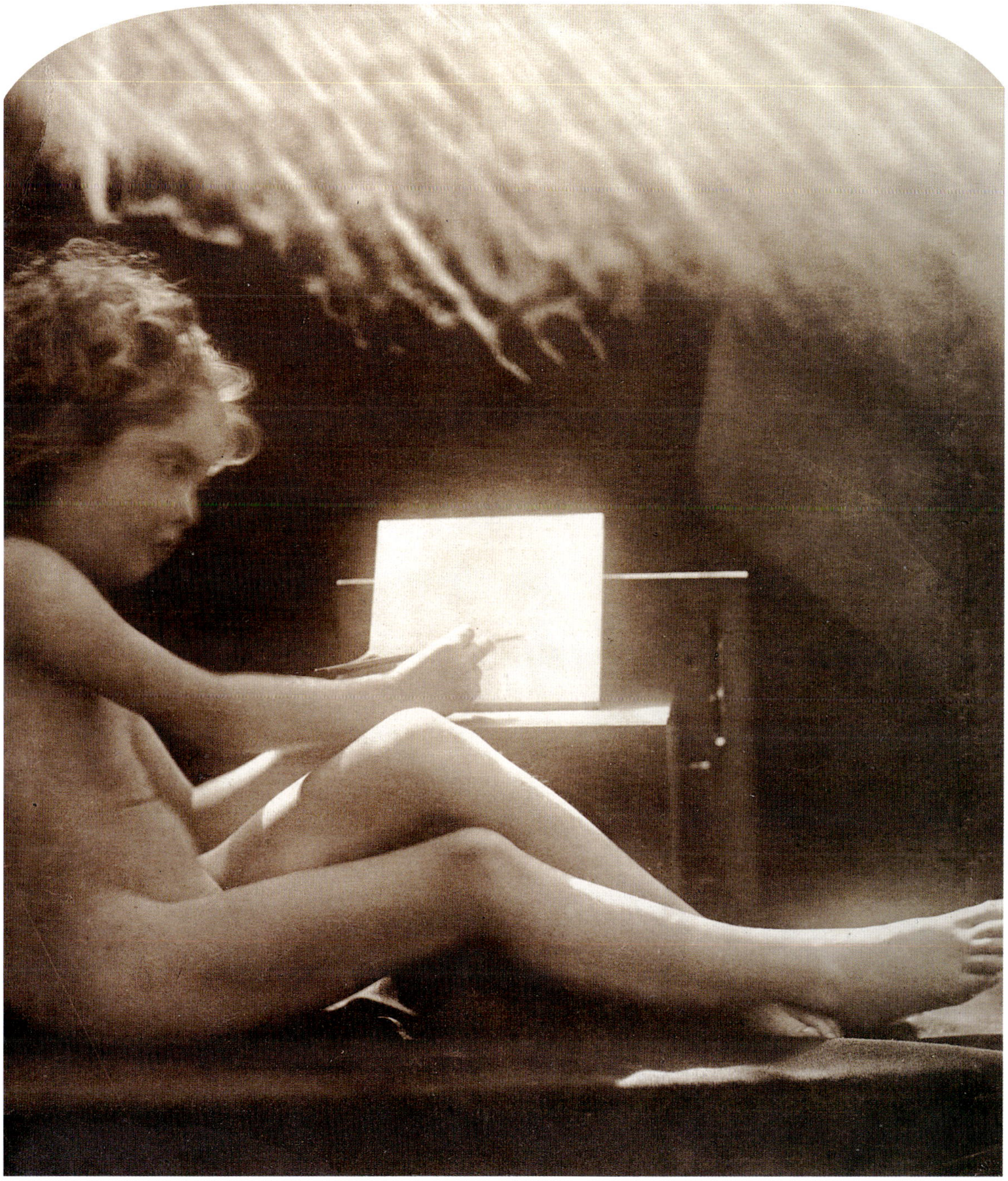

Cupid's Pencil of Light, 1870
Freddy Gould
Carbon print, 320 x 299mm (12⅝ x 11¾")
Royal Photographic Society

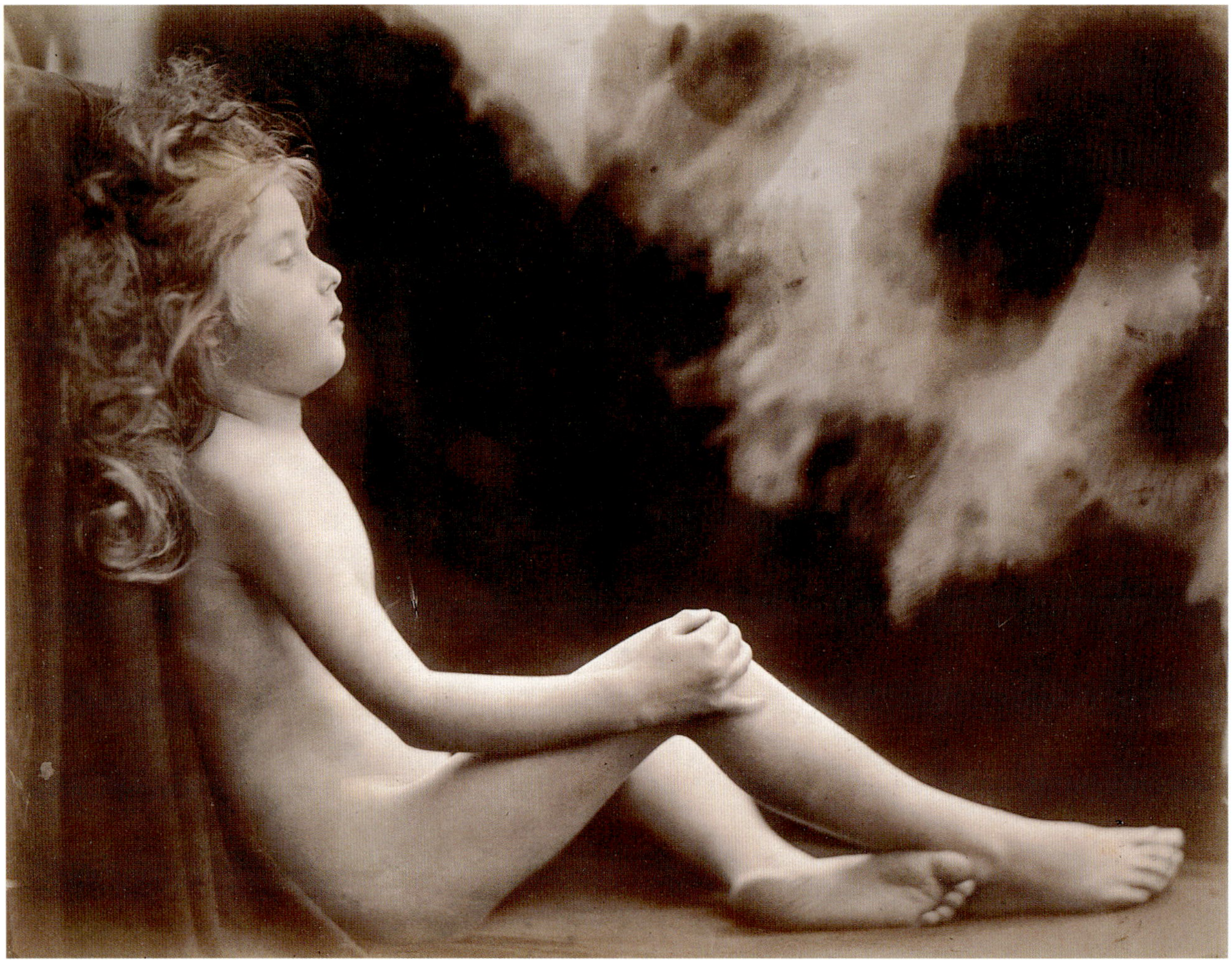

The Young Endymion, September 1873
Freddy Gould
Albumen print, 273 x 348mm (10¾ x 13¾")
Wilson Centre for Photography

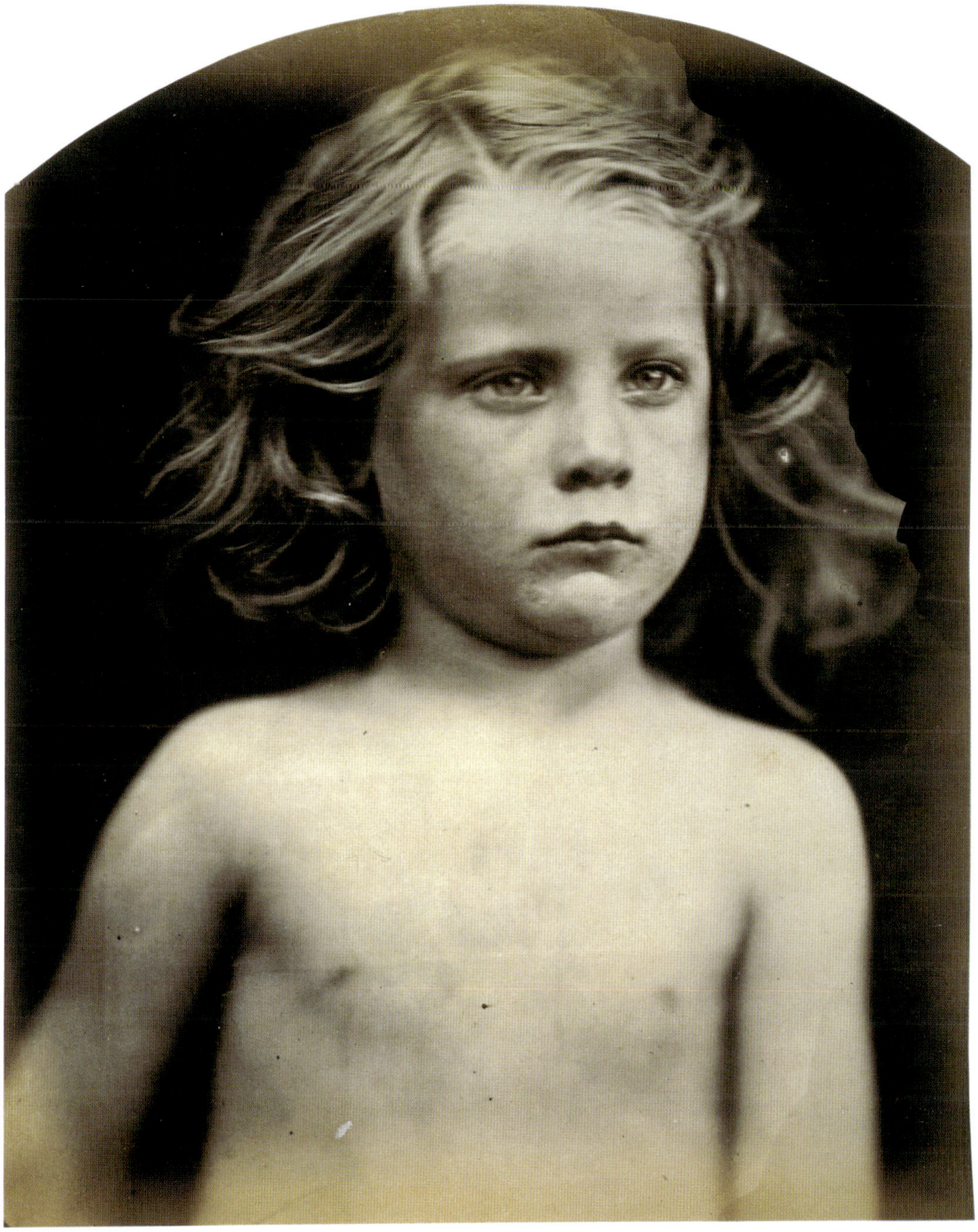

Young Astyanax, 1866
Freddy Gould
Albumen print, 314 x 249mm (12⅜ x 9¾")
National Museum of Photography, Film & Television, Bradford

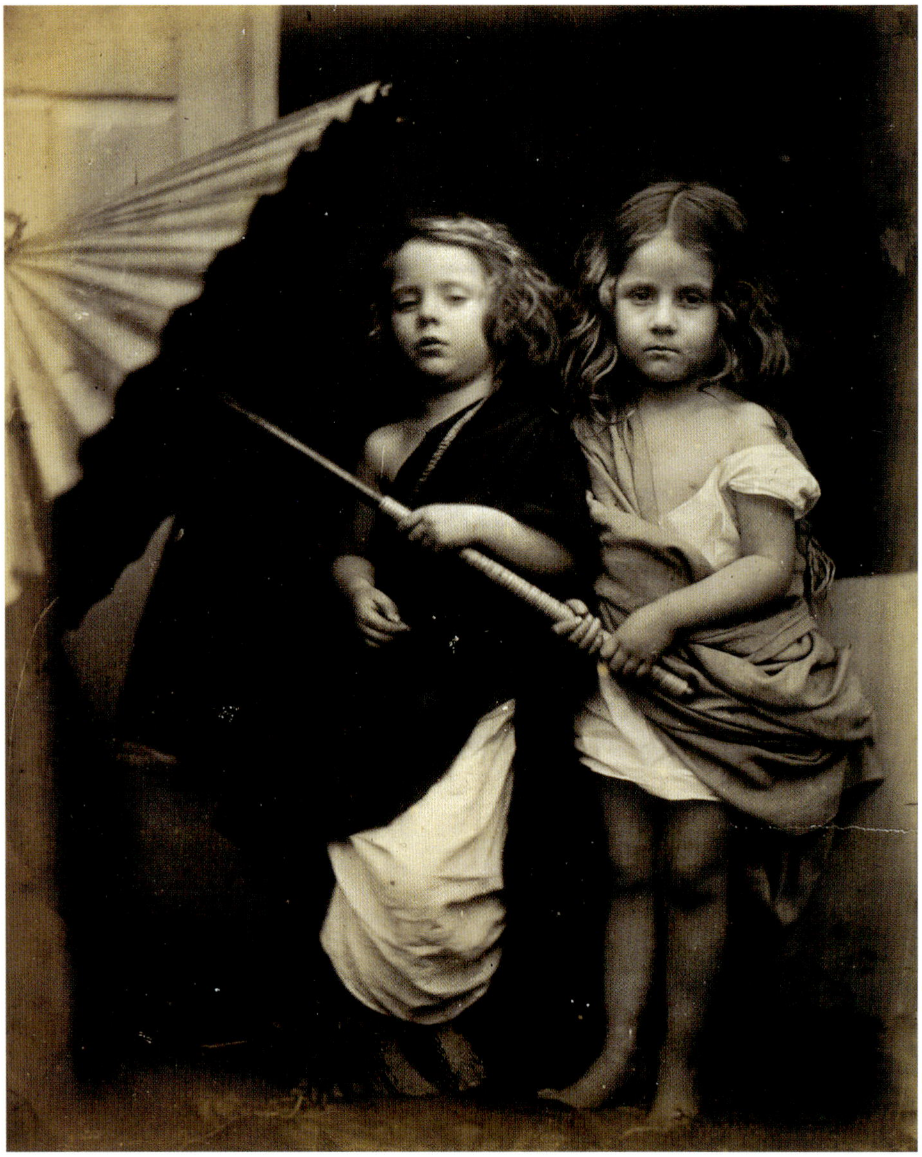

Paul and Virginia, 1864
Freddy Gould and Elizabeth Keown
Albumen print, 270 x 214mm (10⅝ x 8⅜")
National Museum of Photography, Film & Television, Bradford

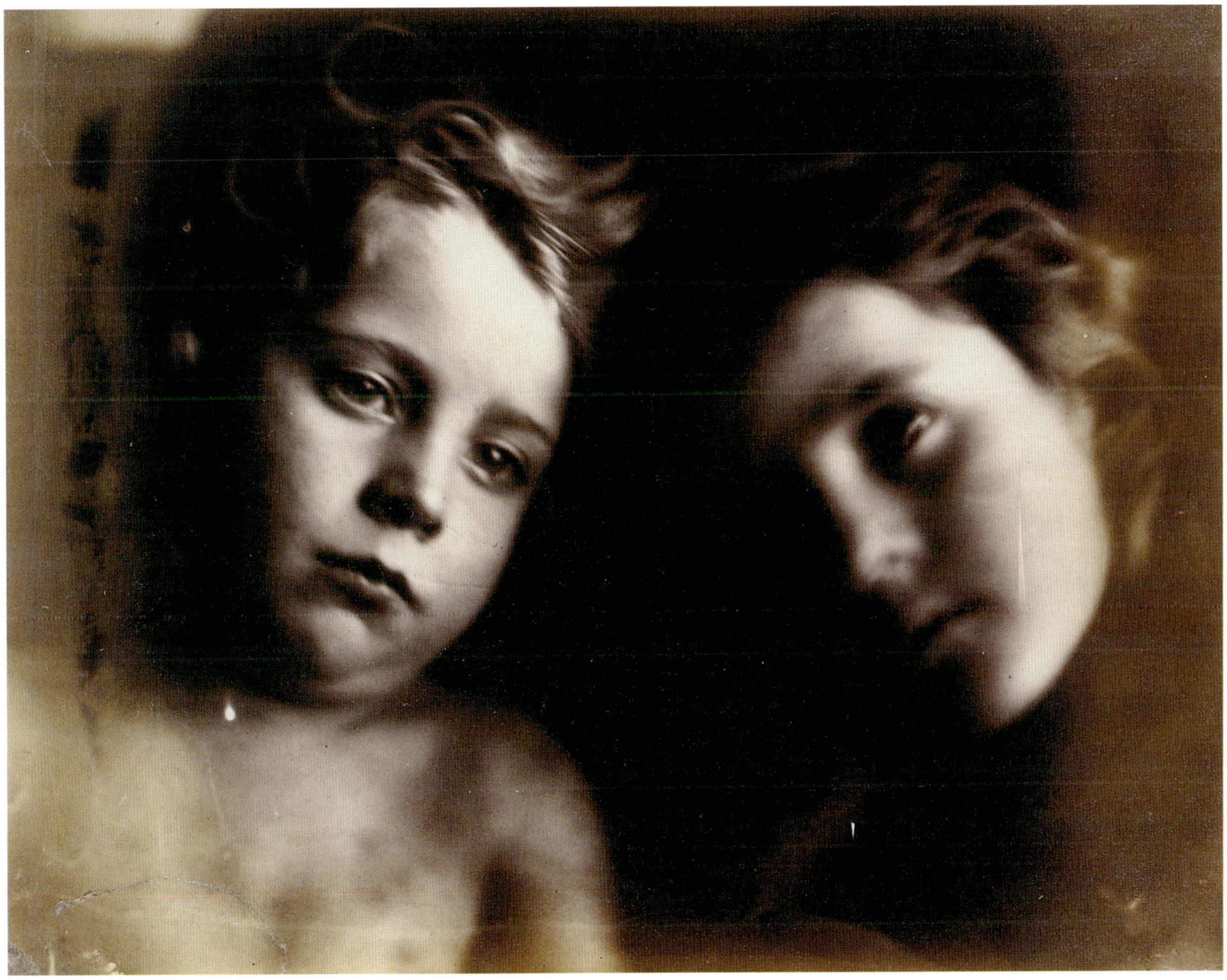

Cherub and Seraph, 1866
Freddy Gould and Elizabeth Keown
Albumen print, 232 x 289mm (9⅛ x 11⅜")
National Museum of Photography, Film & Television, Bradford

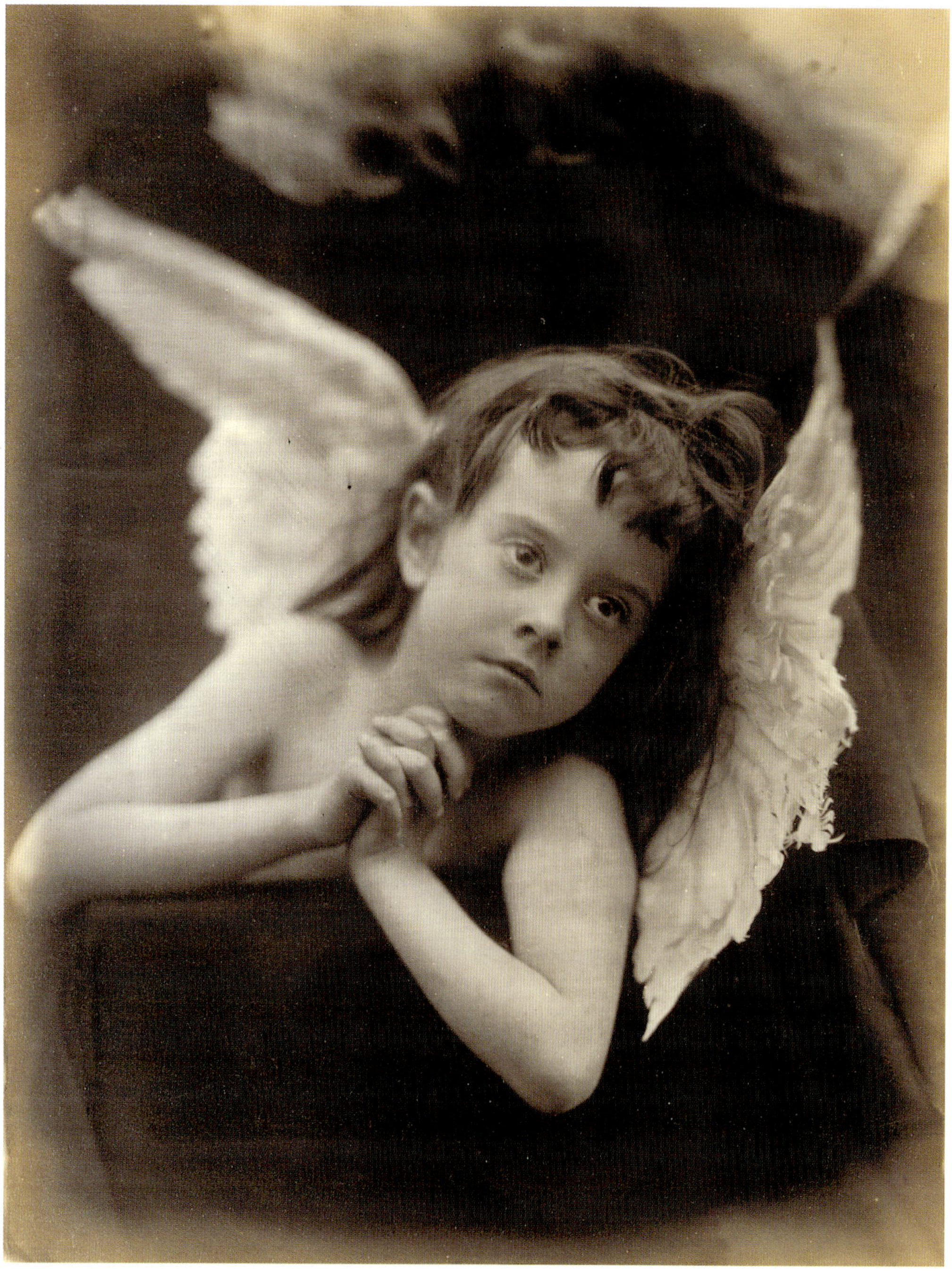

Angel of the Nativity, 1872
Laura Gurney
Albumen print, 327 x 243mm (12⅞ x 9⅝")
The J. Paul Getty Museum, Los Angeles

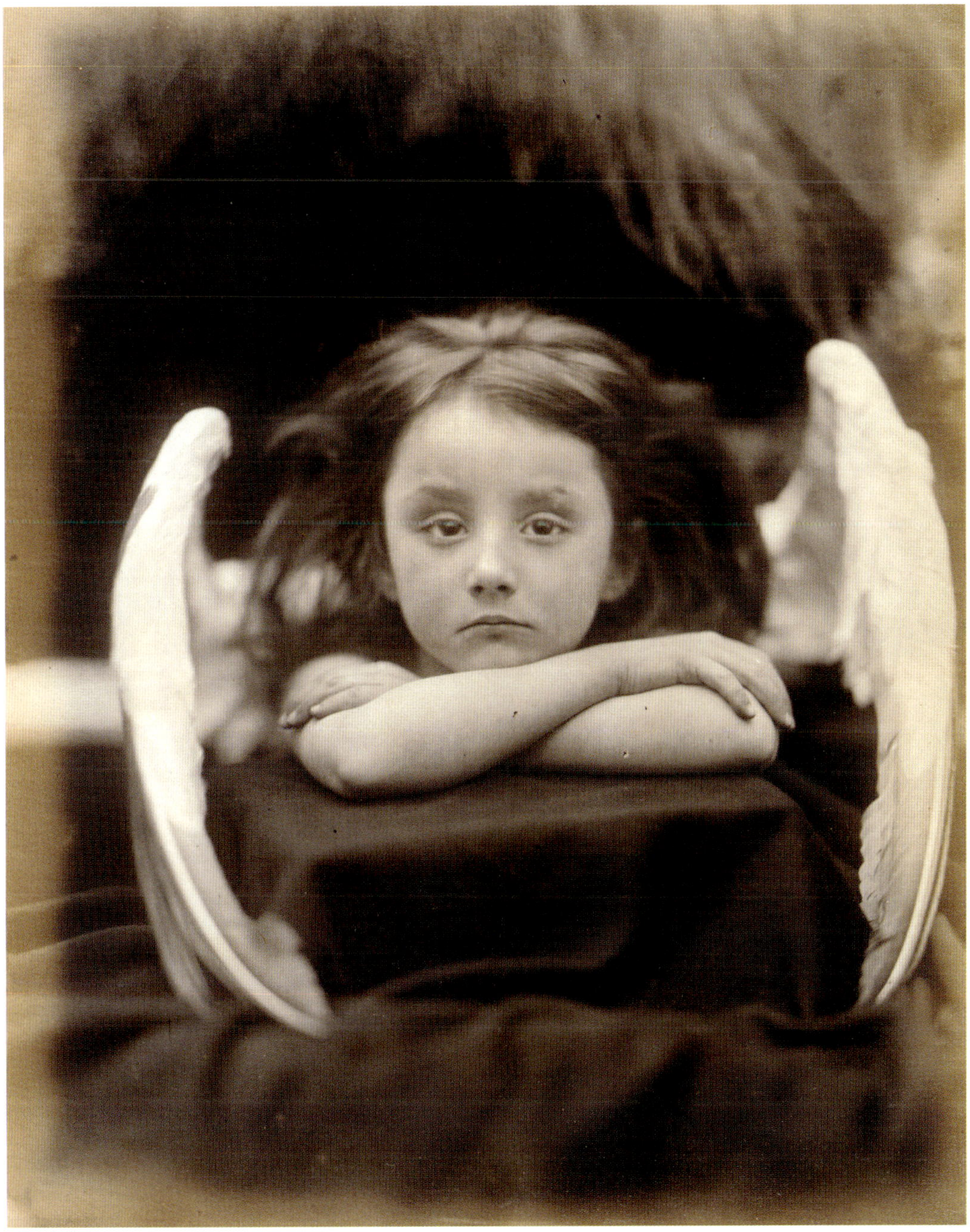

I Wait, 1872
Rachel Gurney
Albumen print, 327 x 254mm (12⅞ x 10")
The J. Paul Getty Museum, Los Angeles

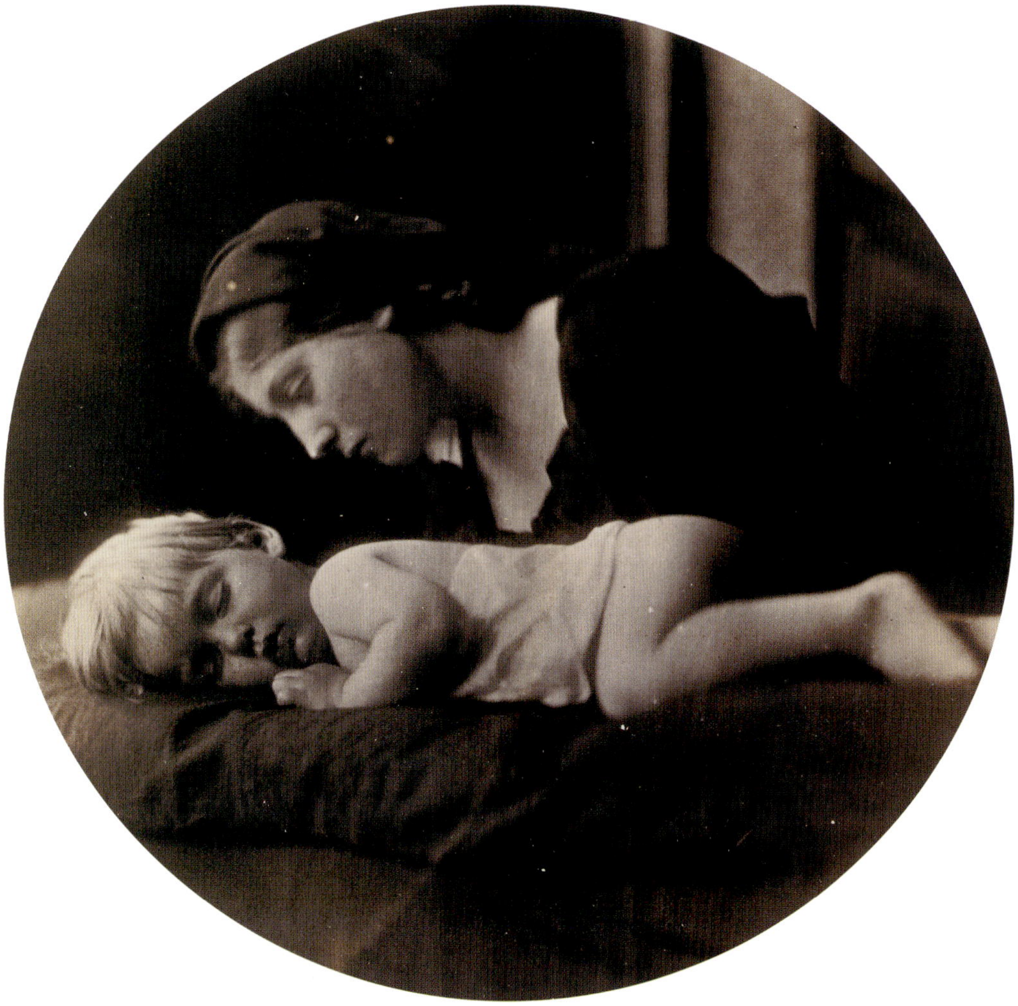

My Grandchild aged 2 years & 3 months, 1865
Mary Ann Hillier and Archibald Cameron
Albumen print, diameter 190mm (7⅛")
Royal Photographic Society

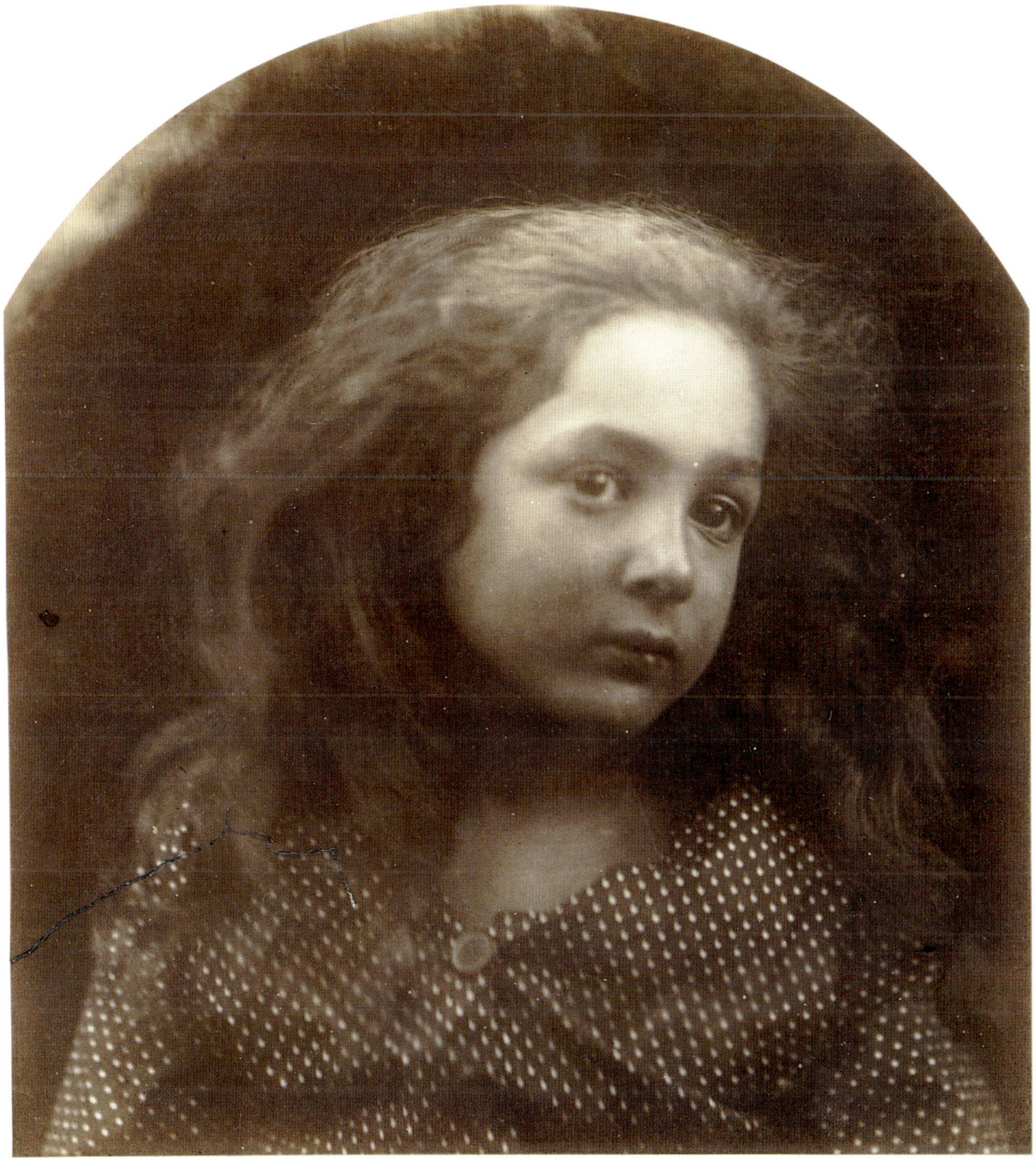

A Child's Head 'Little Bee', August 1874
Beatrice Cameron
Albumen print, 260 x 230mm (10¼ x 9")
Royal Photographic Society

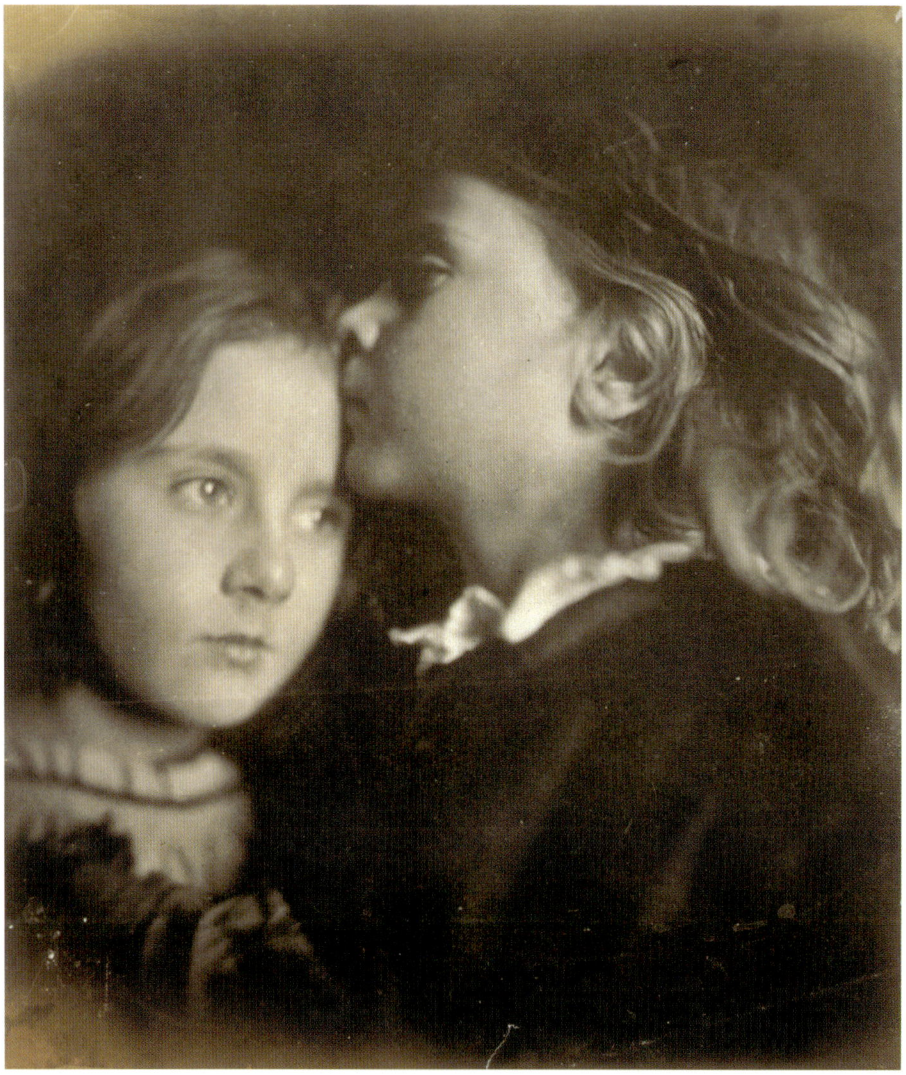

Ernest and Maggie, 1864–5
Unknown sitters
Albumen print, 237 x 200mm (9⅜ x 7⅞")
National Museum of Photography, Film & Television, Bradford

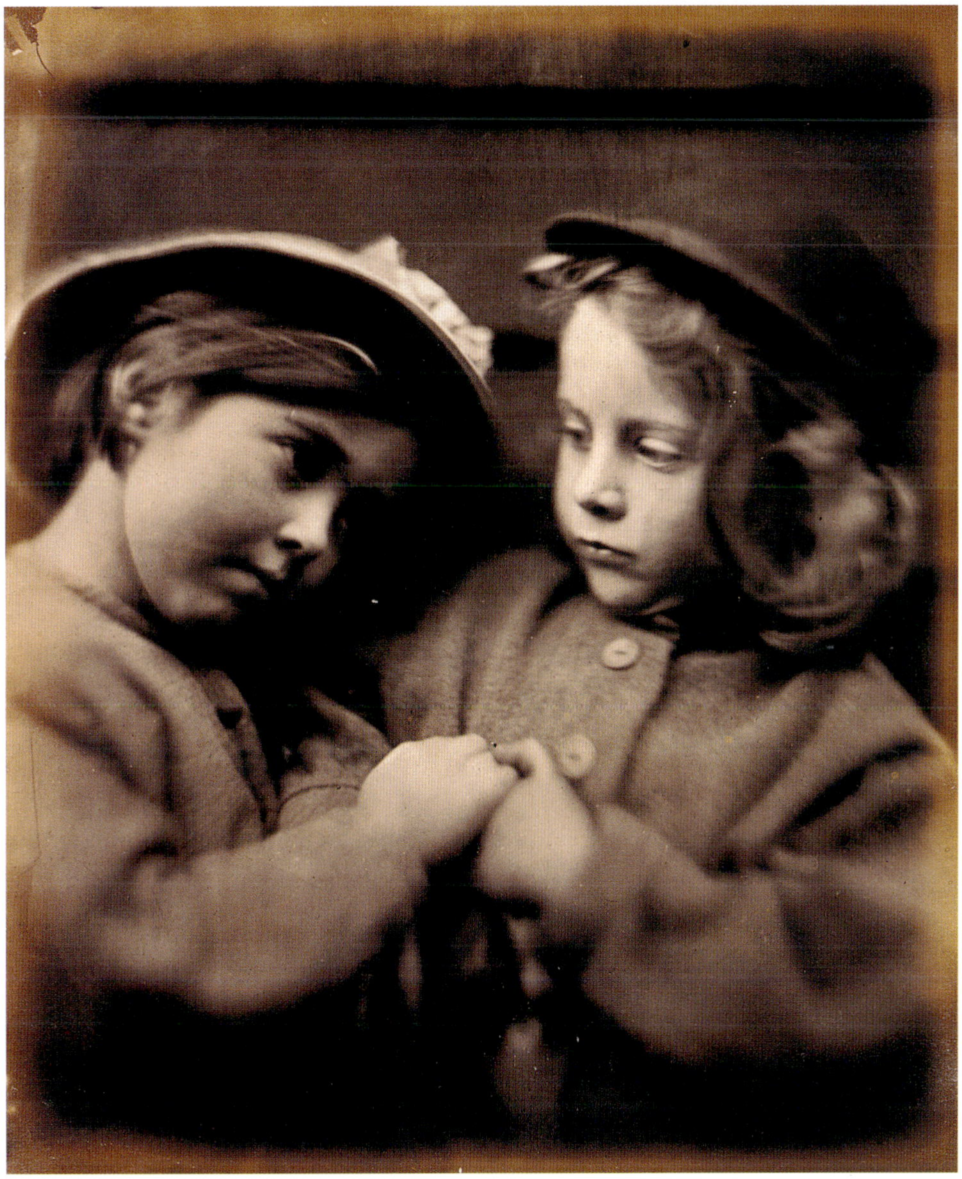

Two Little Girls Wearing Hats, 1864–5
Unknown girl and Freddy Gould
Albumen print, 271 x 219mm (10⅝ x 8⅝")
Tennyson Research Centre, Lincoln

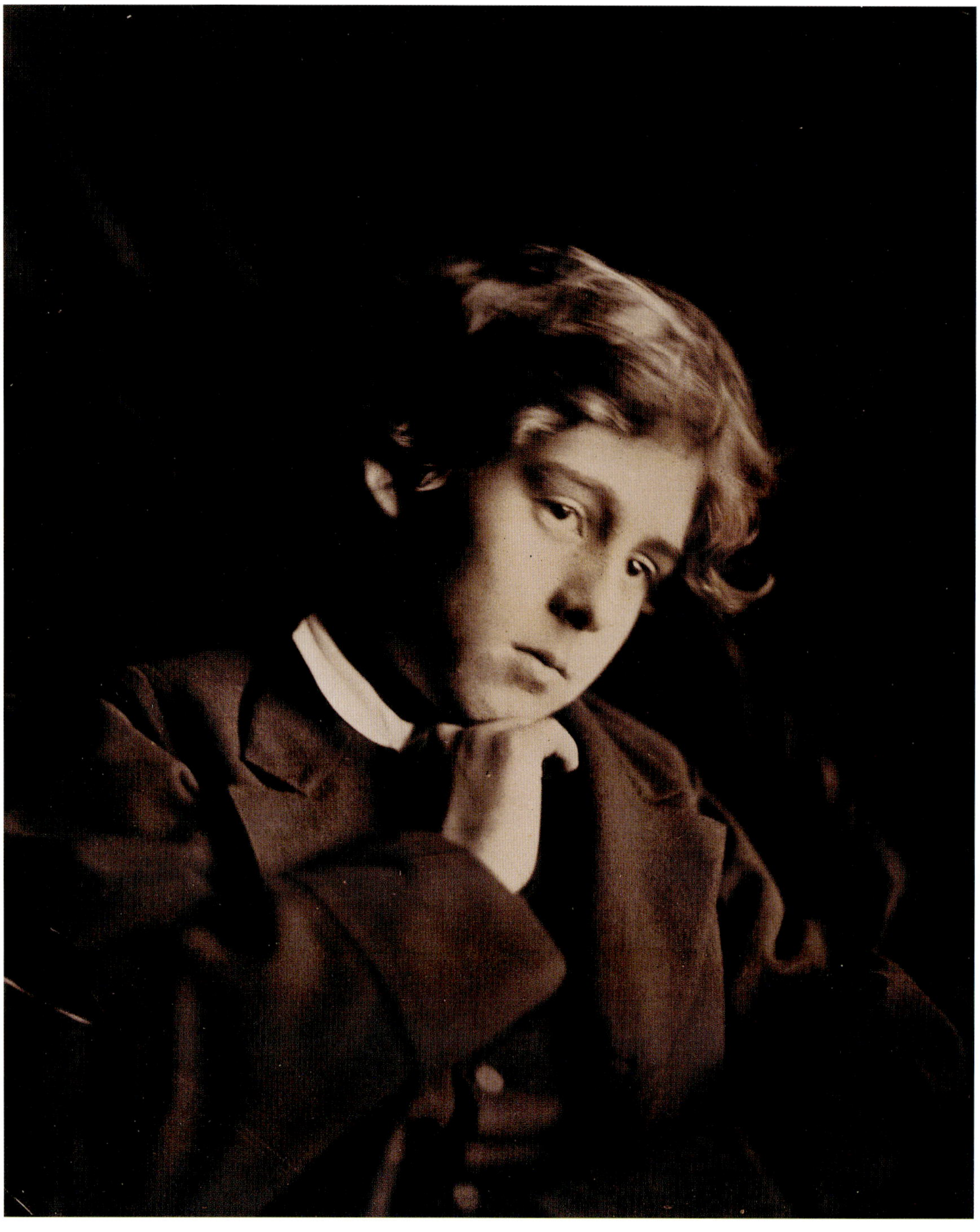

Lionel Tennyson, 1869
Albumen print, 328 x 262mm (12⅞ x 10⅜")
Tennyson Research Centre, Lincoln

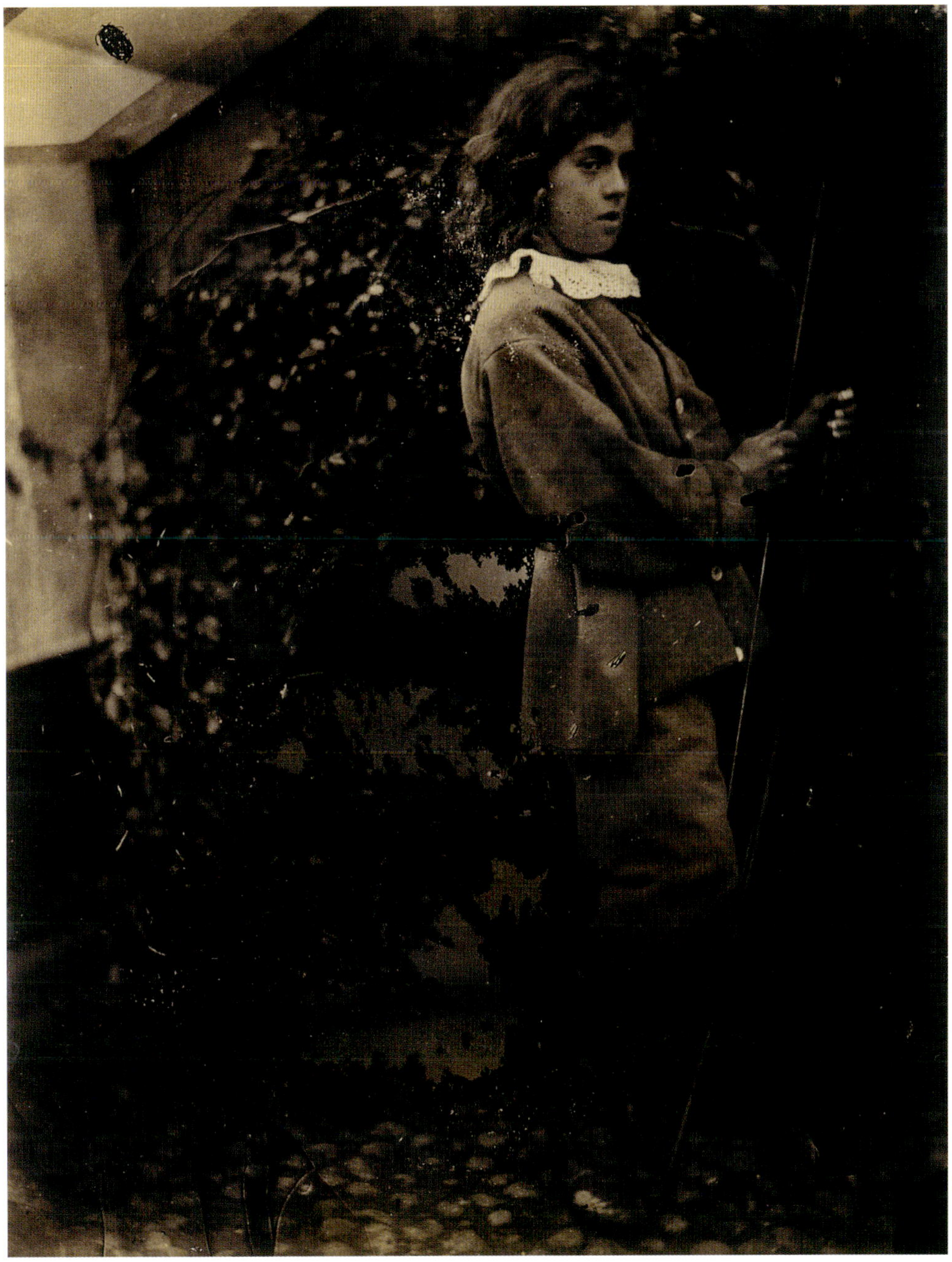

Lionel Tennyson with bow & arrow, 1864
Albumen print, 258 x 193mm (10⅛ x 7⅝")
National Museum of Photography, Film & Television, Bradford

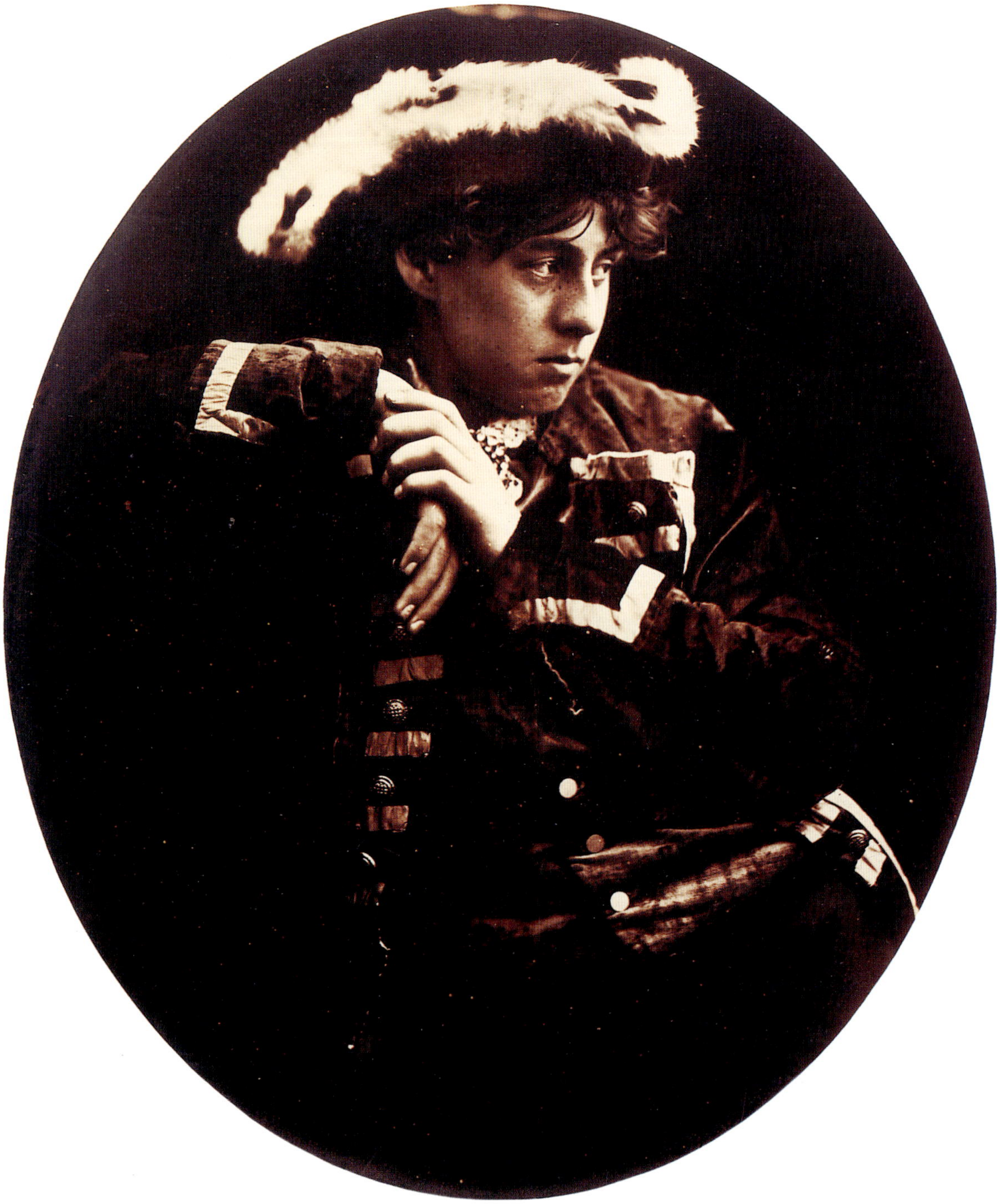

Lionel Tennyson in the character of the Marquis de St Cast, April 1869
Albumen print, 316 x 259mm (12½ x 10¼")
Tennyson Research Centre, Lincoln

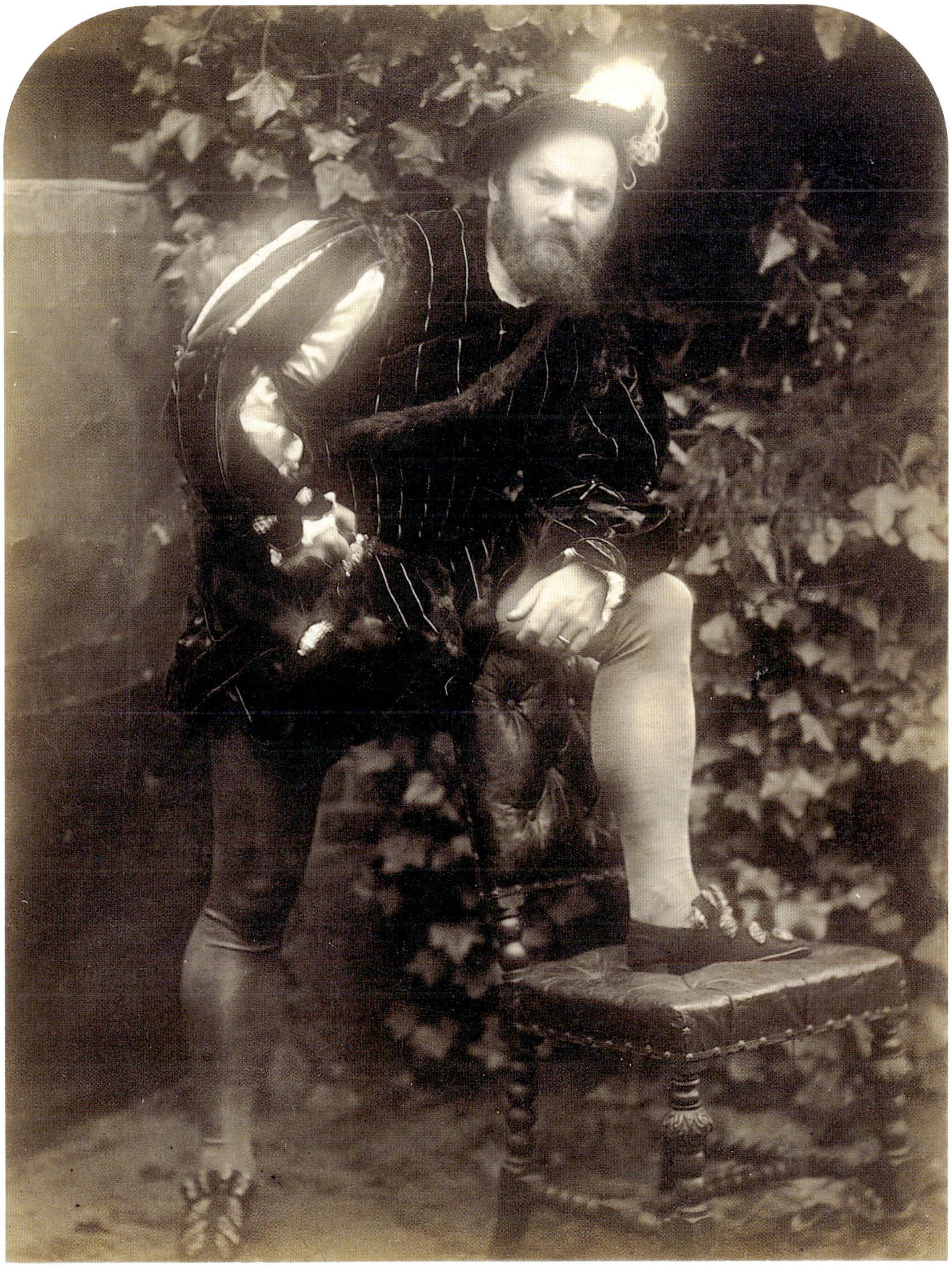

'Our Royal Cousin', September 1874
Val Prinsep as Henry VIII
Albumen print, 438 x 251mm (17¼ x 9⅞")
Royal Photographic Society

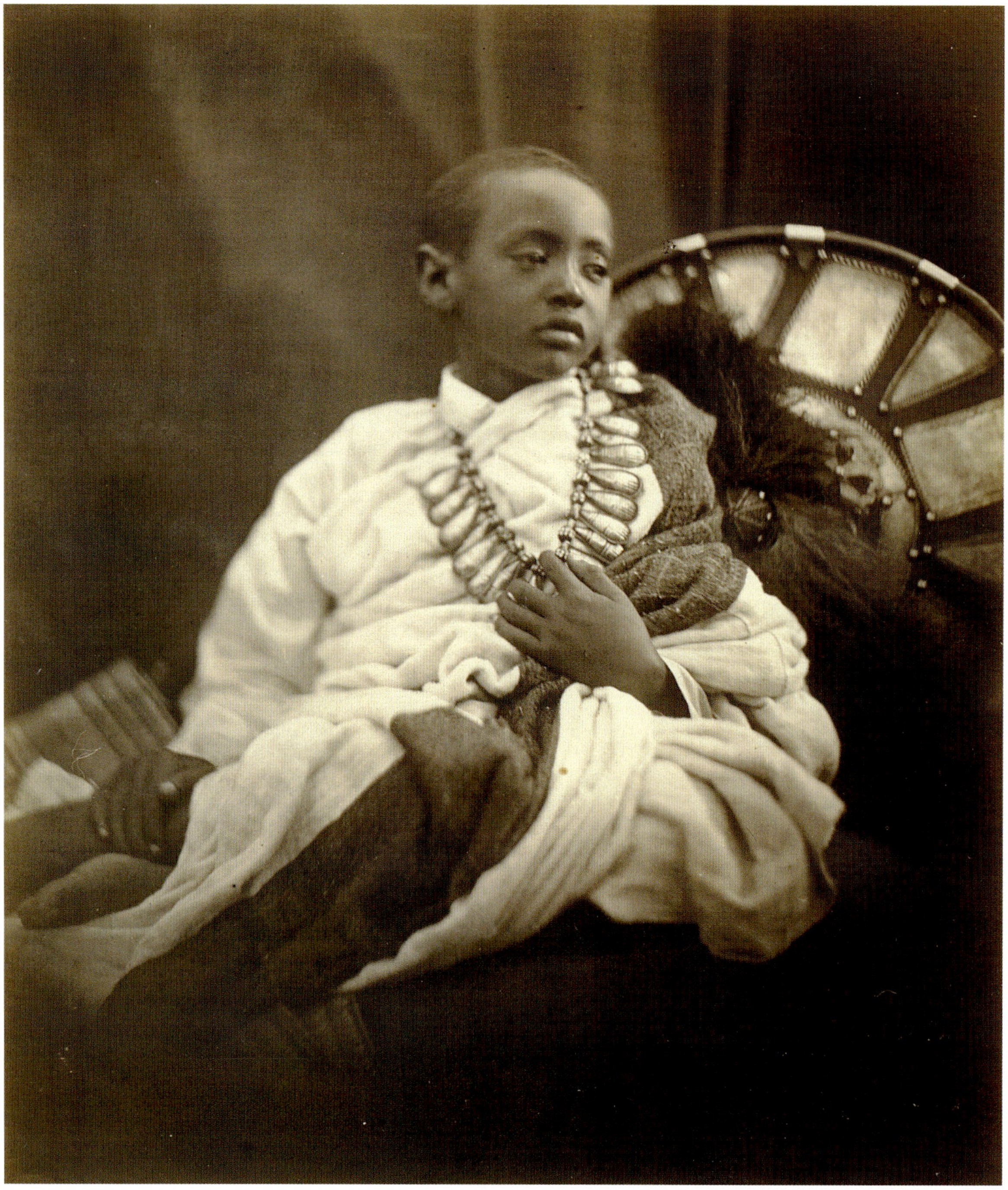

Déjatch Alámayou, King Theodore's Son, July 1868
Albumen silver print, 306 x 256mm (12 x 10⅛")
Collection of JGS, Inc., New York

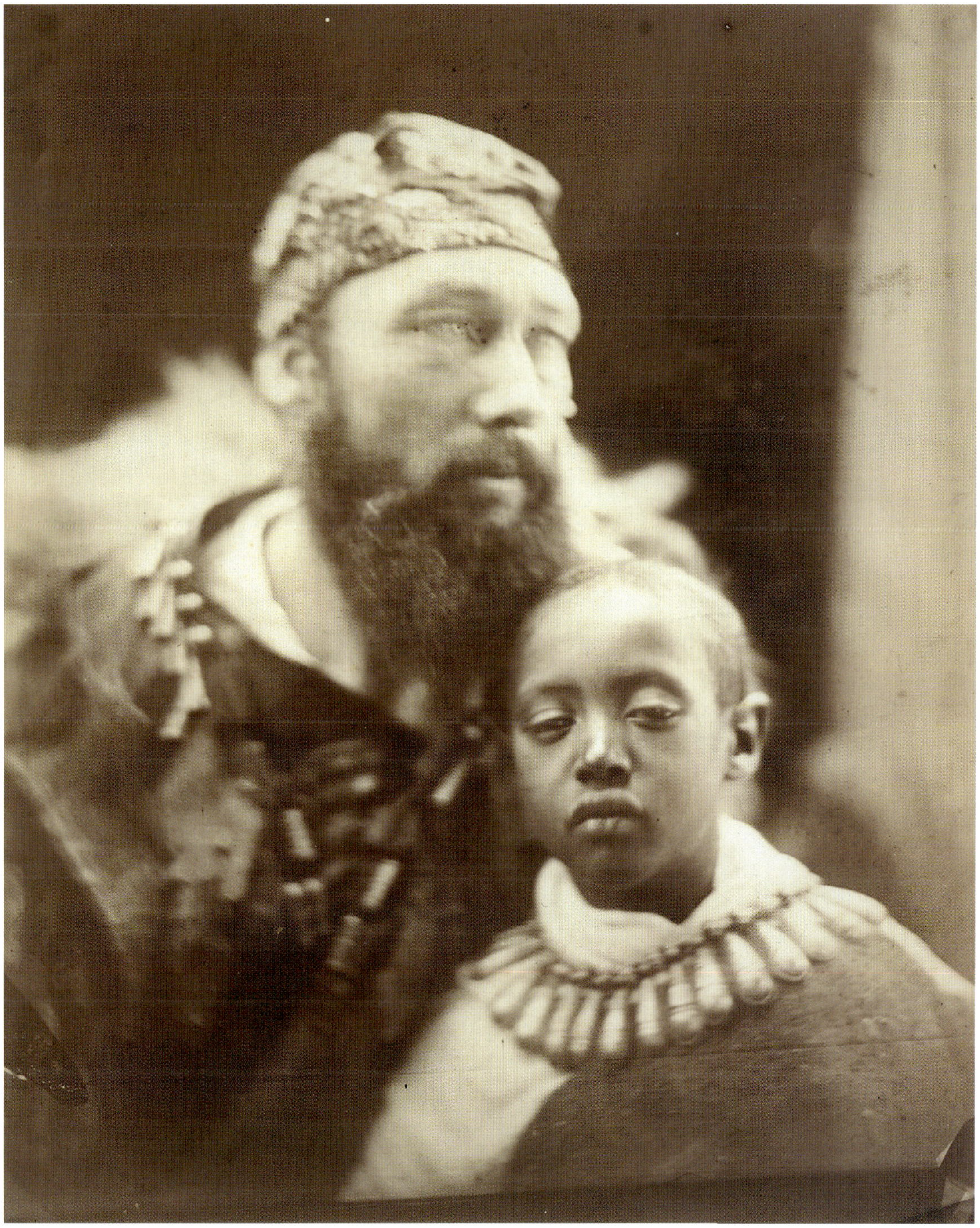

Déjatch Alámayou and Báshá Félika, 20 July 1868
King Theodore's son and Captain Tristram Speedy
Albumen print, 357 x 276mm (13¾ x 10⅞")
National Gallery of Art, Ottawa. Purchased 1967

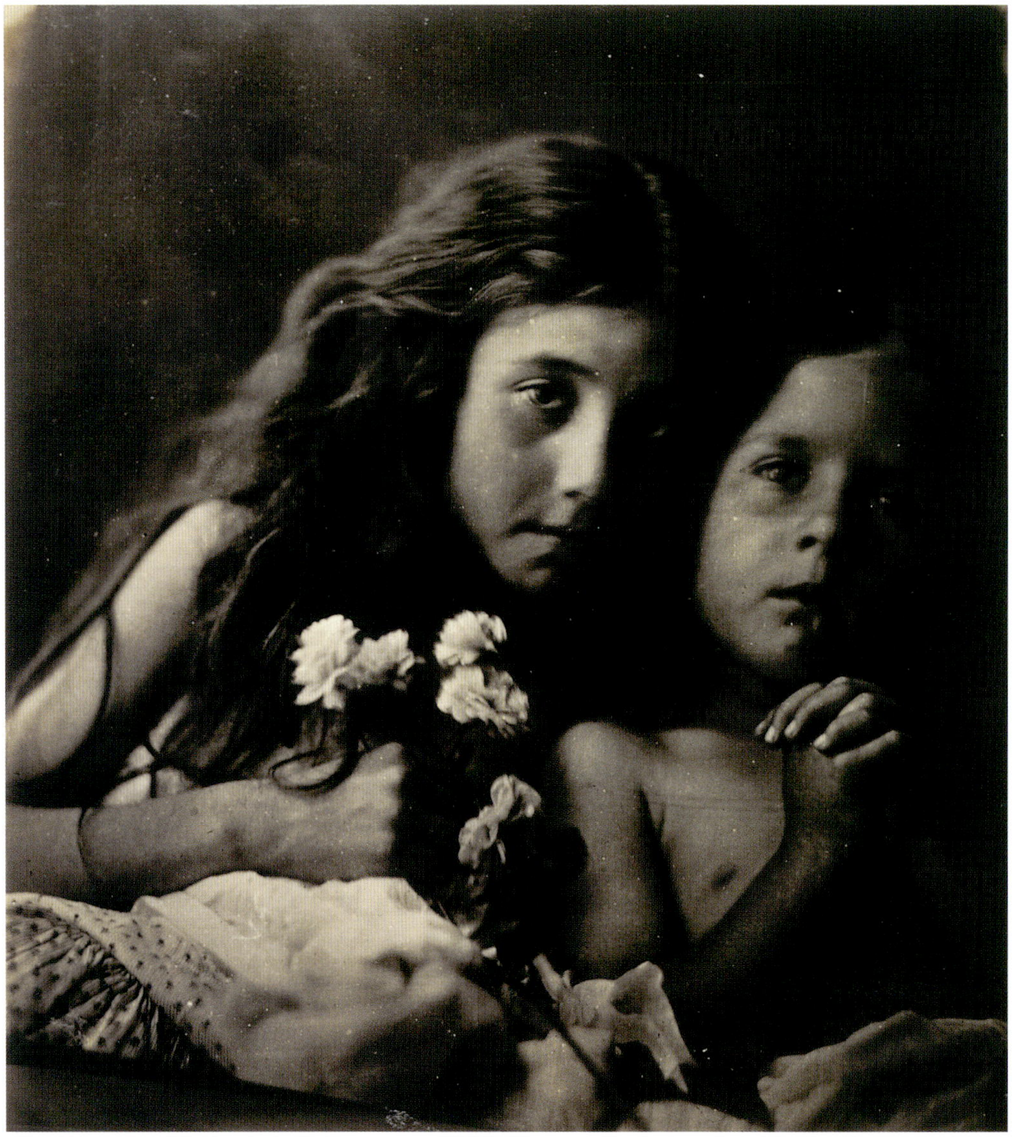

The Red and White Roses, 1865
Kate and Elizabeth Keown
Albumen print, 261 x 234mm (10¼ x 9¼")
National Museum of Photography, Film & Television, Bradford

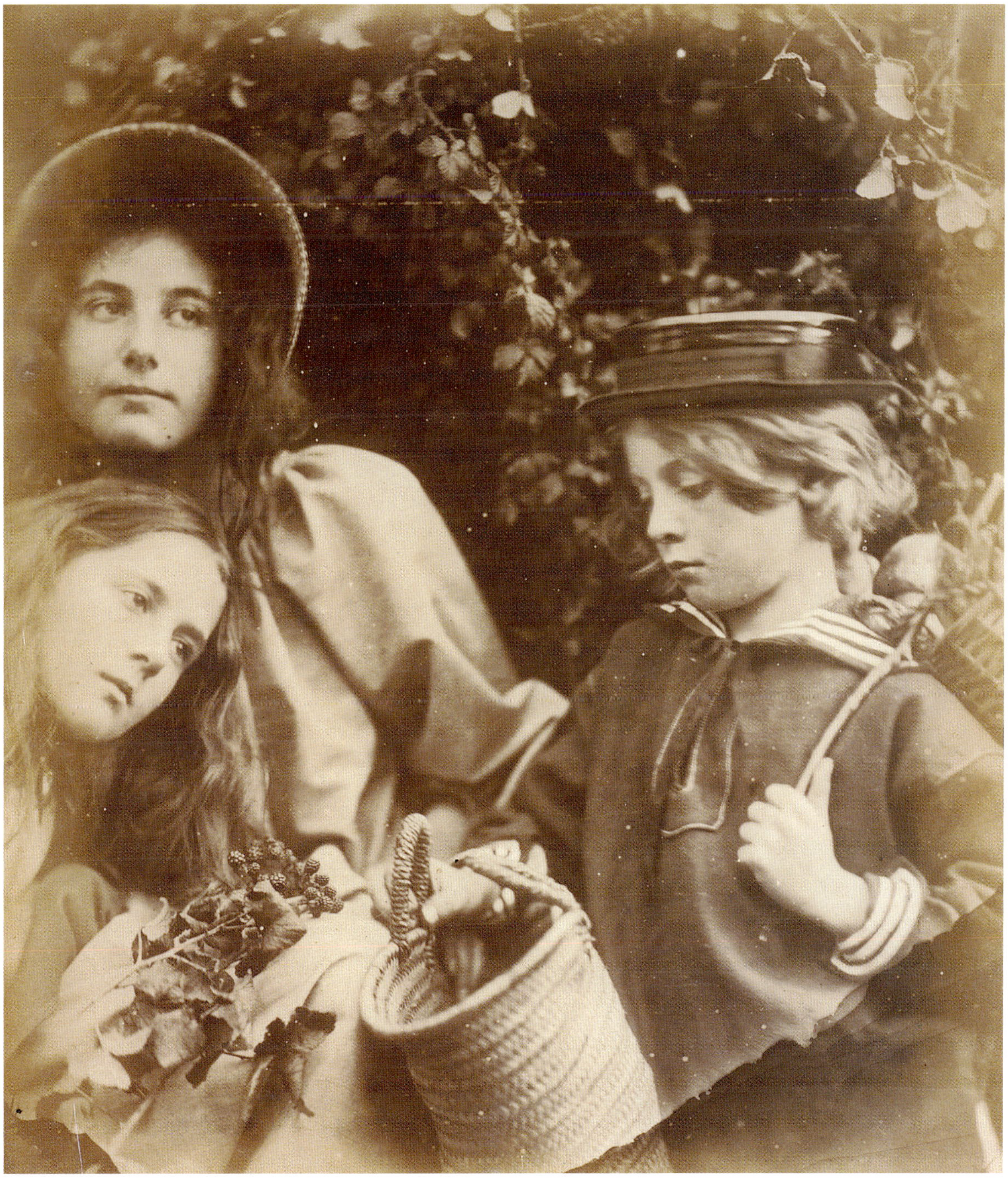

Blackberry Gathering, 1868–70
Elizabeth Keown, Kate Keown and Freddy Gould
Albumen print, 335 x 285mm (13¼ x 11¼")
Royal Photographic Society

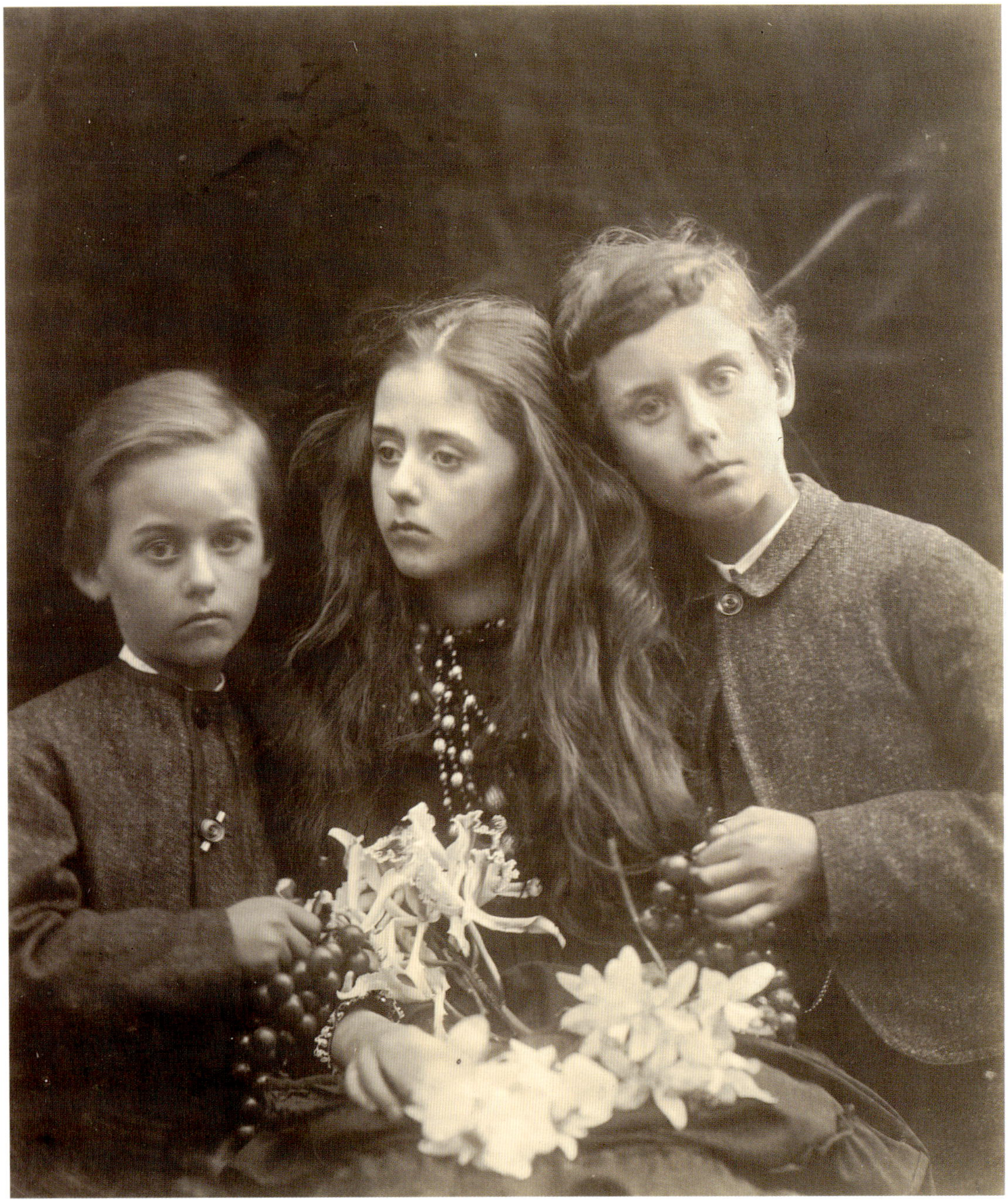

Days at Freshwater, August 1870
Claud Anson, Florence Anson and unknown boy
Albumen print, 340 x 284mm (13⅜ x 11⅛")
The Marjorie and Leonard Vernon Collection

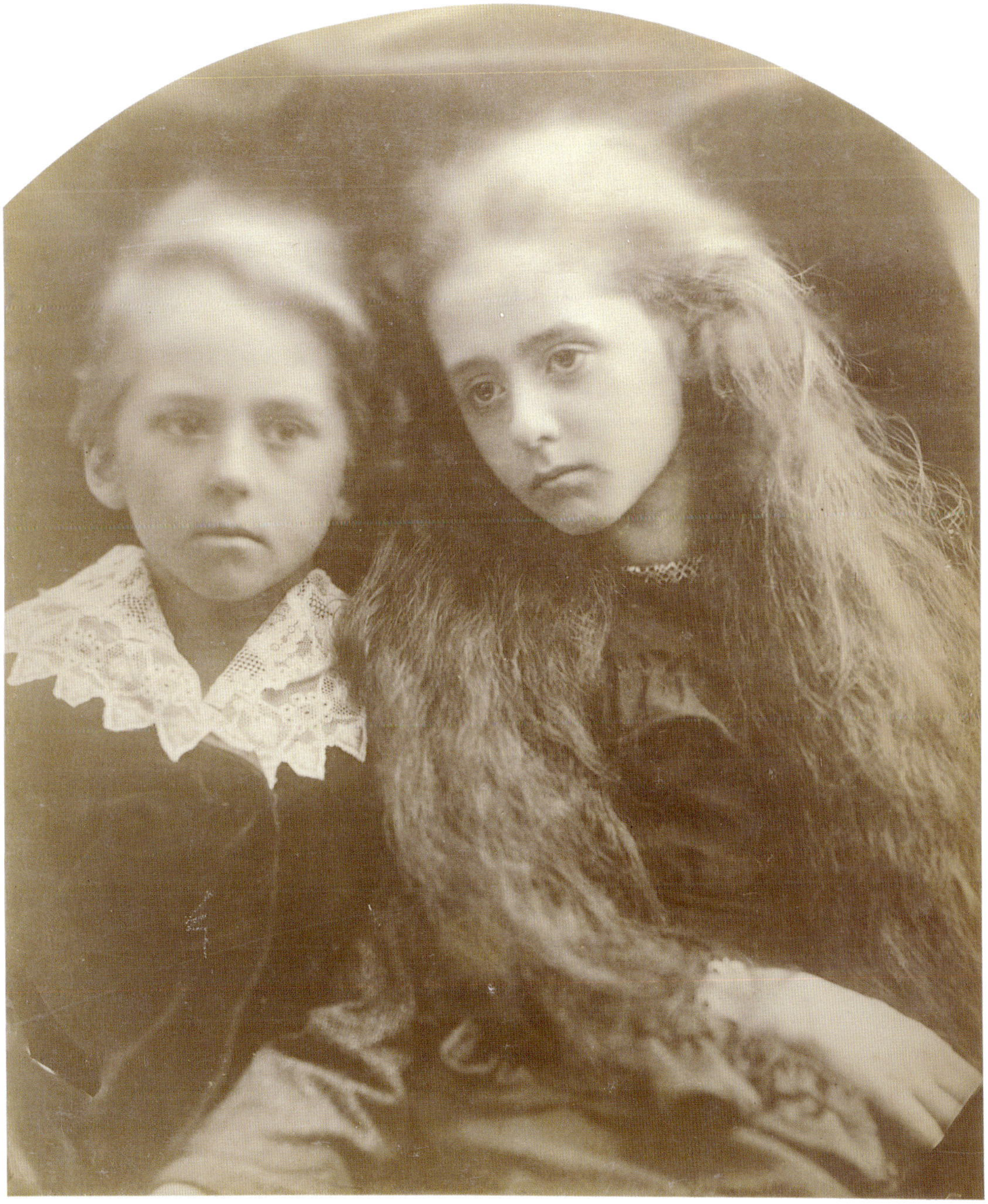

Claud & Lady Florence Anson, August 1870
Albumen print, 342 x 281mm (13½ x 11⅛")
Royal Photographic Society

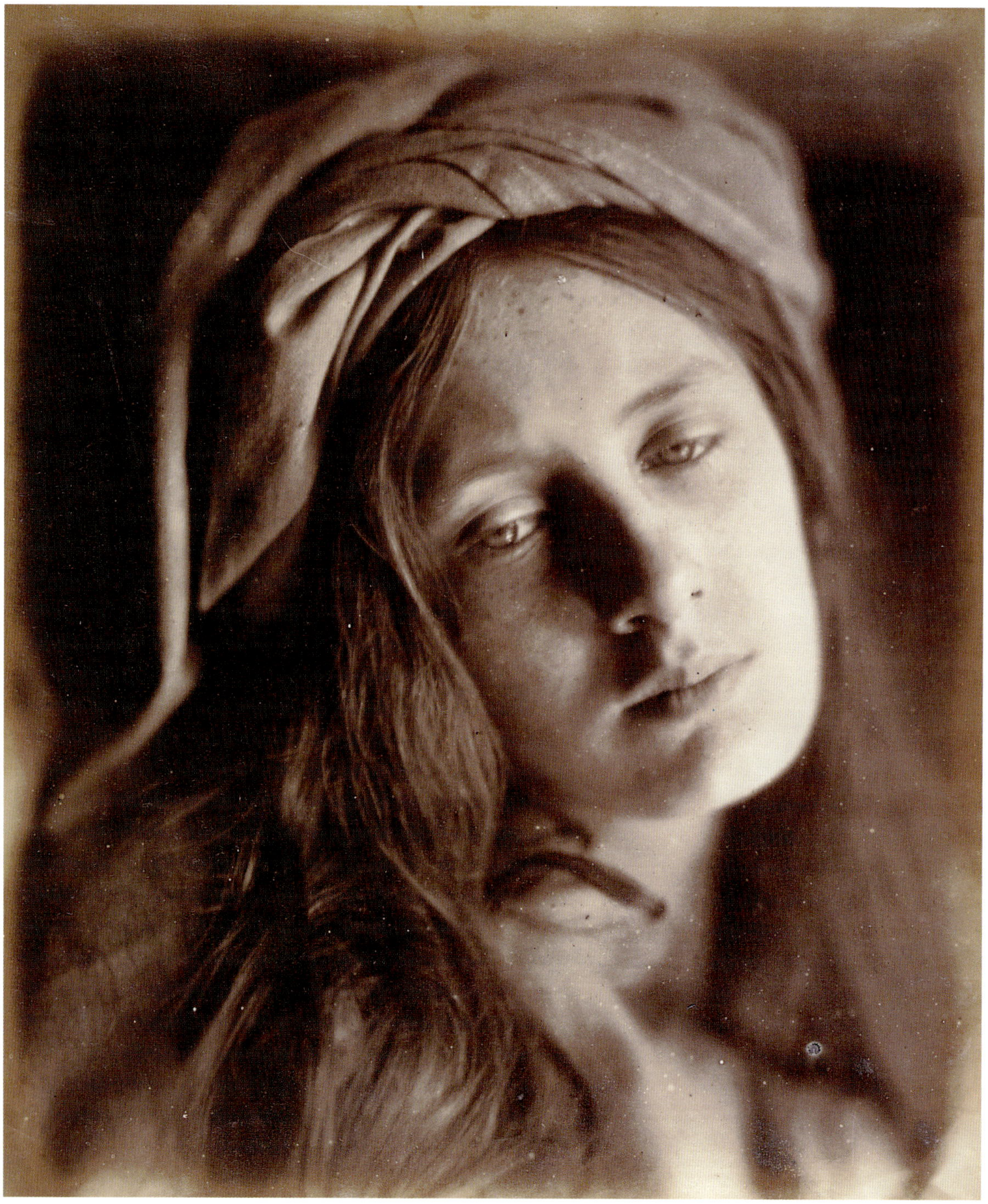

Study of Beatrice Cenci, 1866
May Prinsep
Albumen print, 335 x 267mm (13¼ x 10½")
National Museum of Photography, Film & Television, Bradford

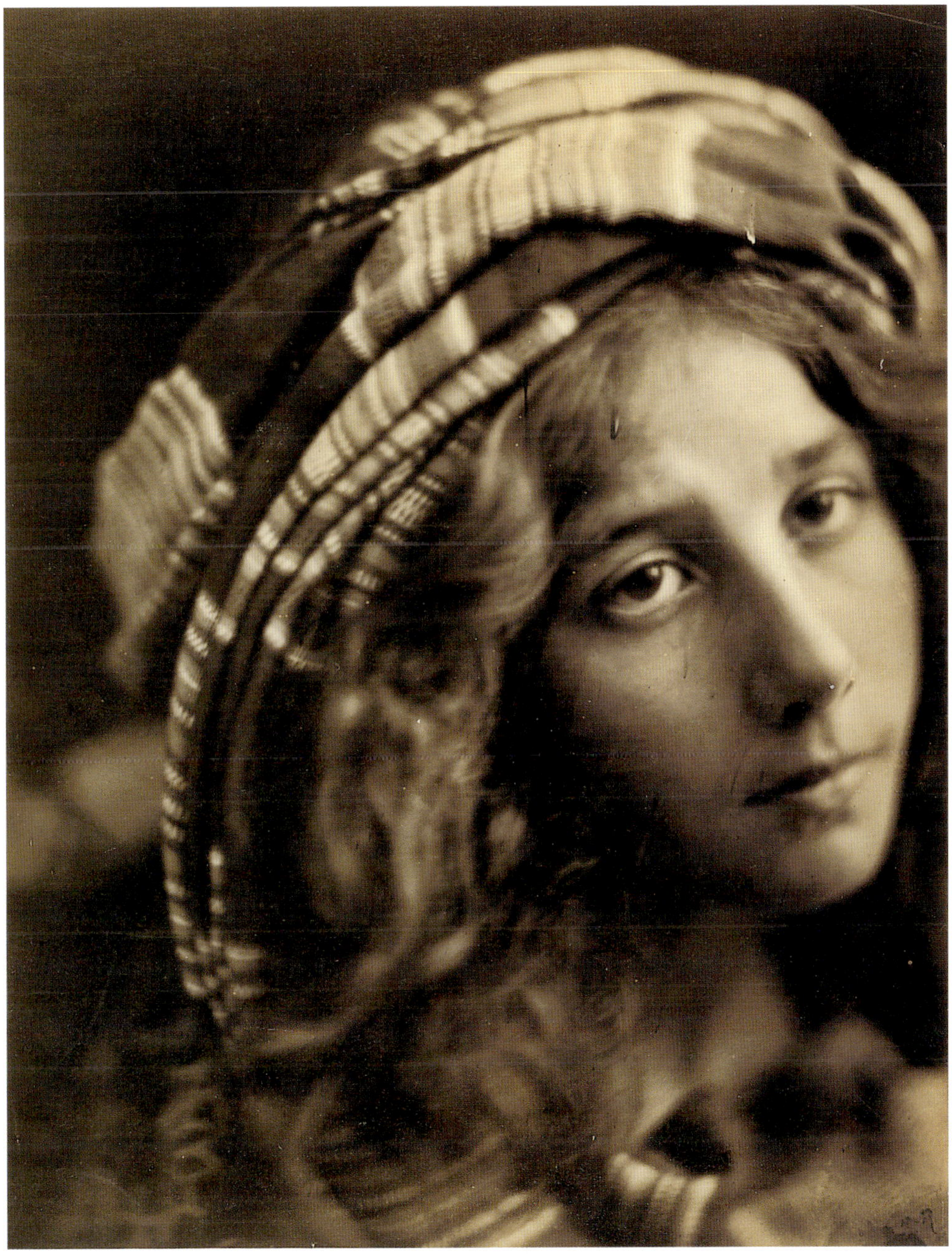

Beatrice Cenci, May 1868
Kate Keown
Albumen print, 327 x 246mm (12⅞ x 9⅝")
The J. Paul Getty Museum, Los Angeles

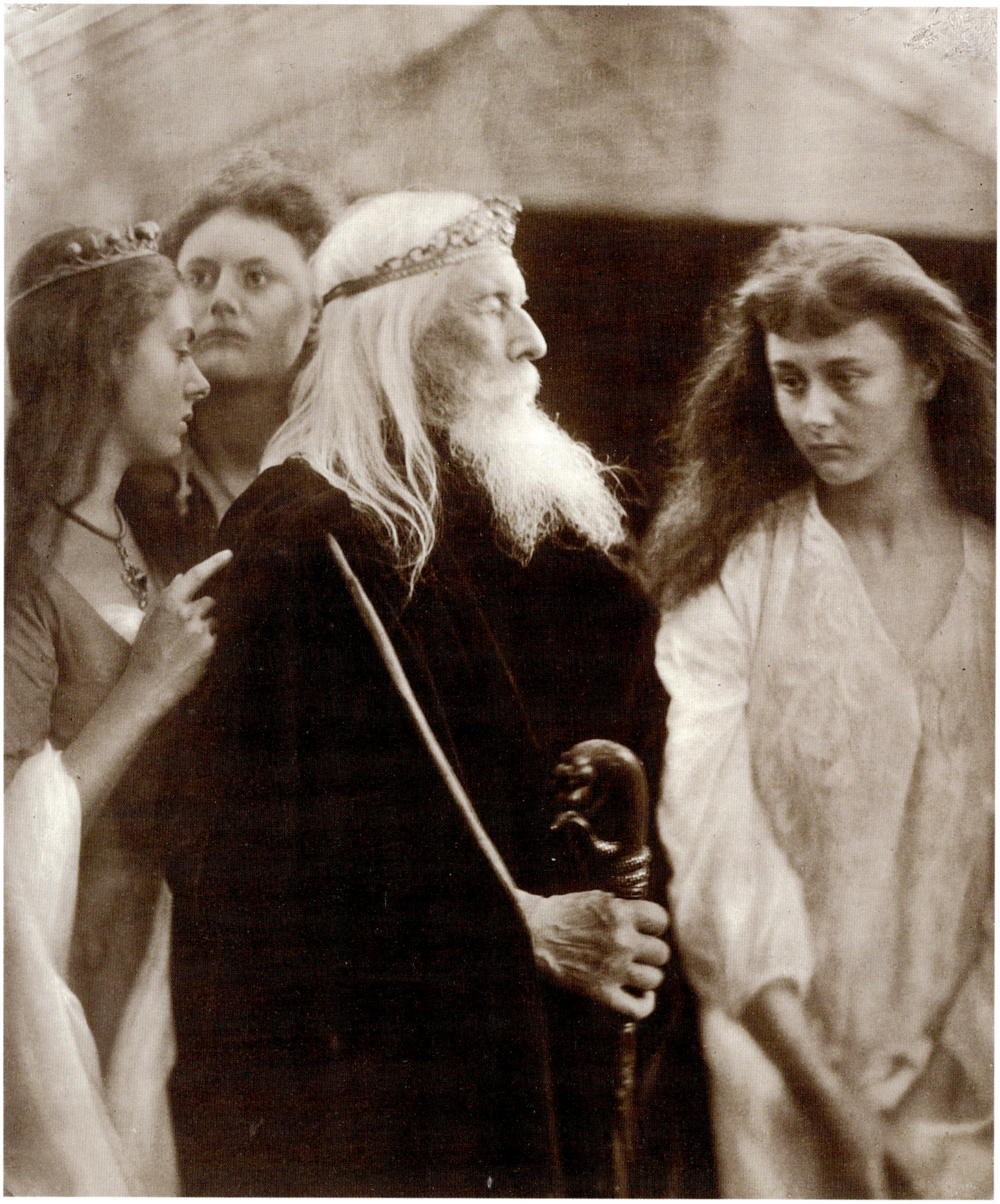

King Lear allotting his Kingdom to his three daughters, 1872
Marina Liddell, Edith Liddell, Charles Hay Cameron and Alice Liddell
Carbon print, 345 x 285mm (13⅝ x 11¼")
Royal Photographic Society

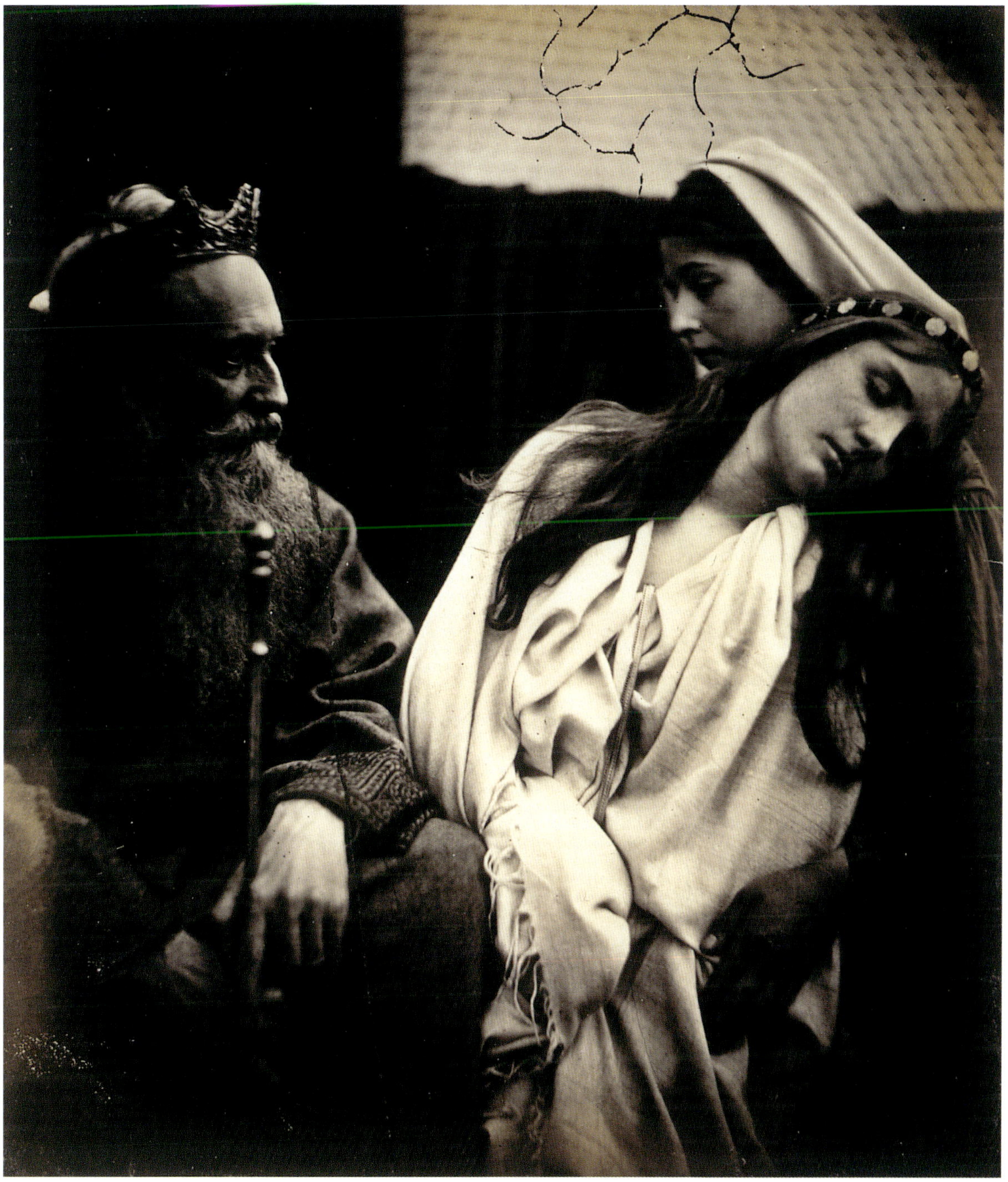

King Ahasuerus & Queen Esther in Apocrypha, 1865
Sir Henry Taylor, Mary Ryan and Mary Kellaway
Albumen print, 317 x 271mm (12½ x 10⅝")
National Museum of Photography, Film & Television, Bradford

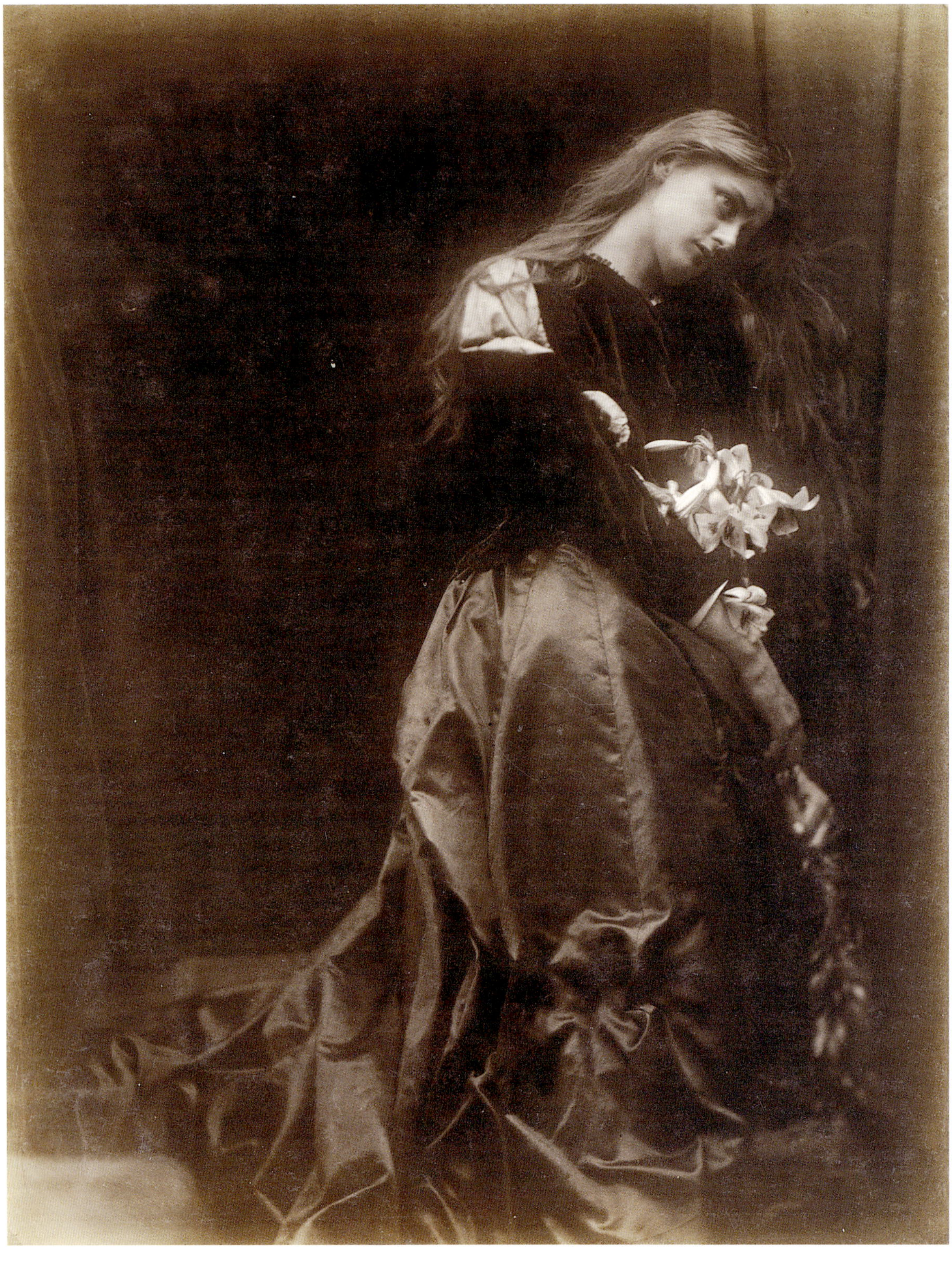

Gretchen, 1870–4
Unknown woman
Albumen print, 349 x 262mm (13¾ x 10⅜")
Royal Photographic Society

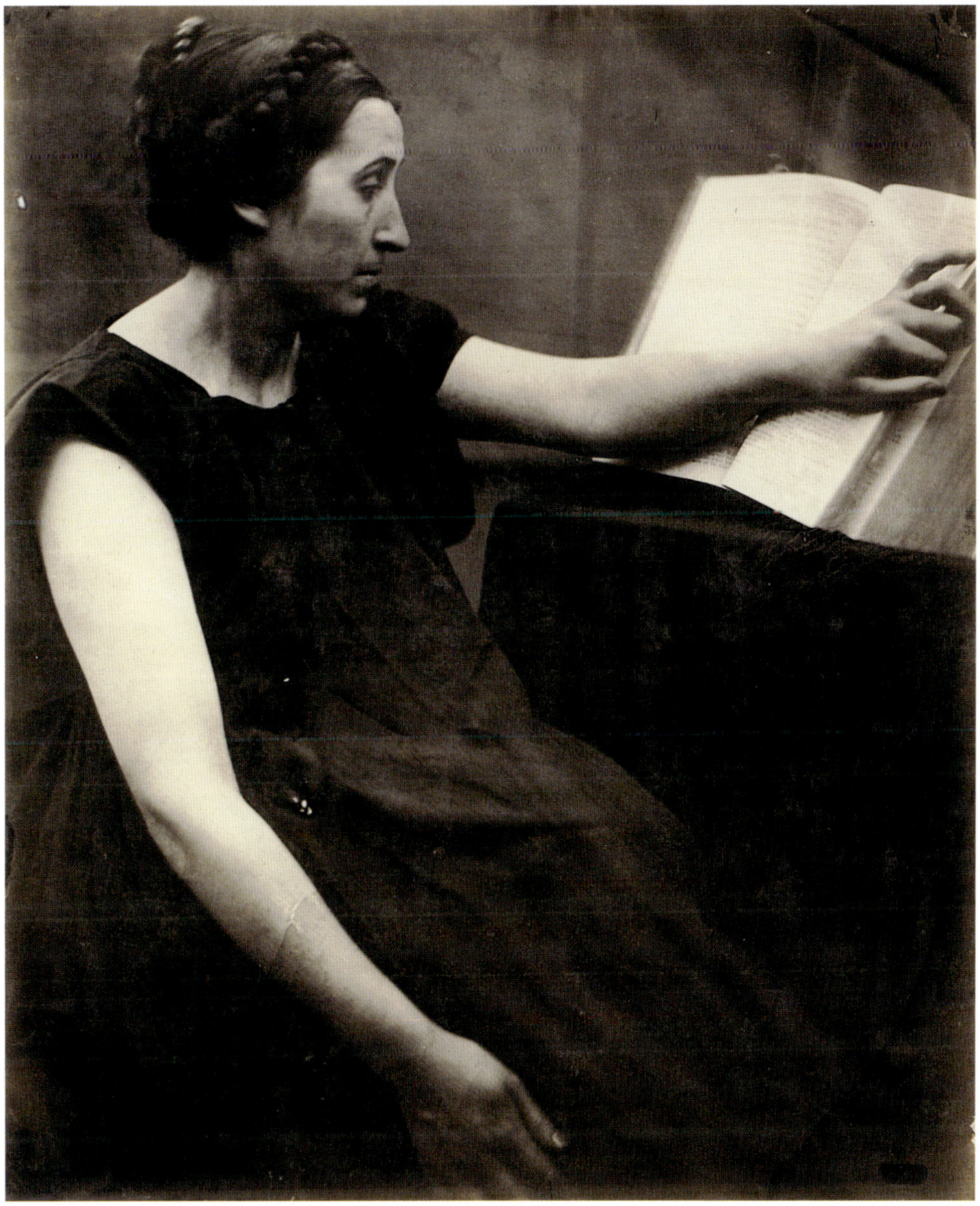

A Sibyl, 1870
Unknown woman
Albumen print, 268 x 216mm (10½ x 8½")
Royal Photographic Society

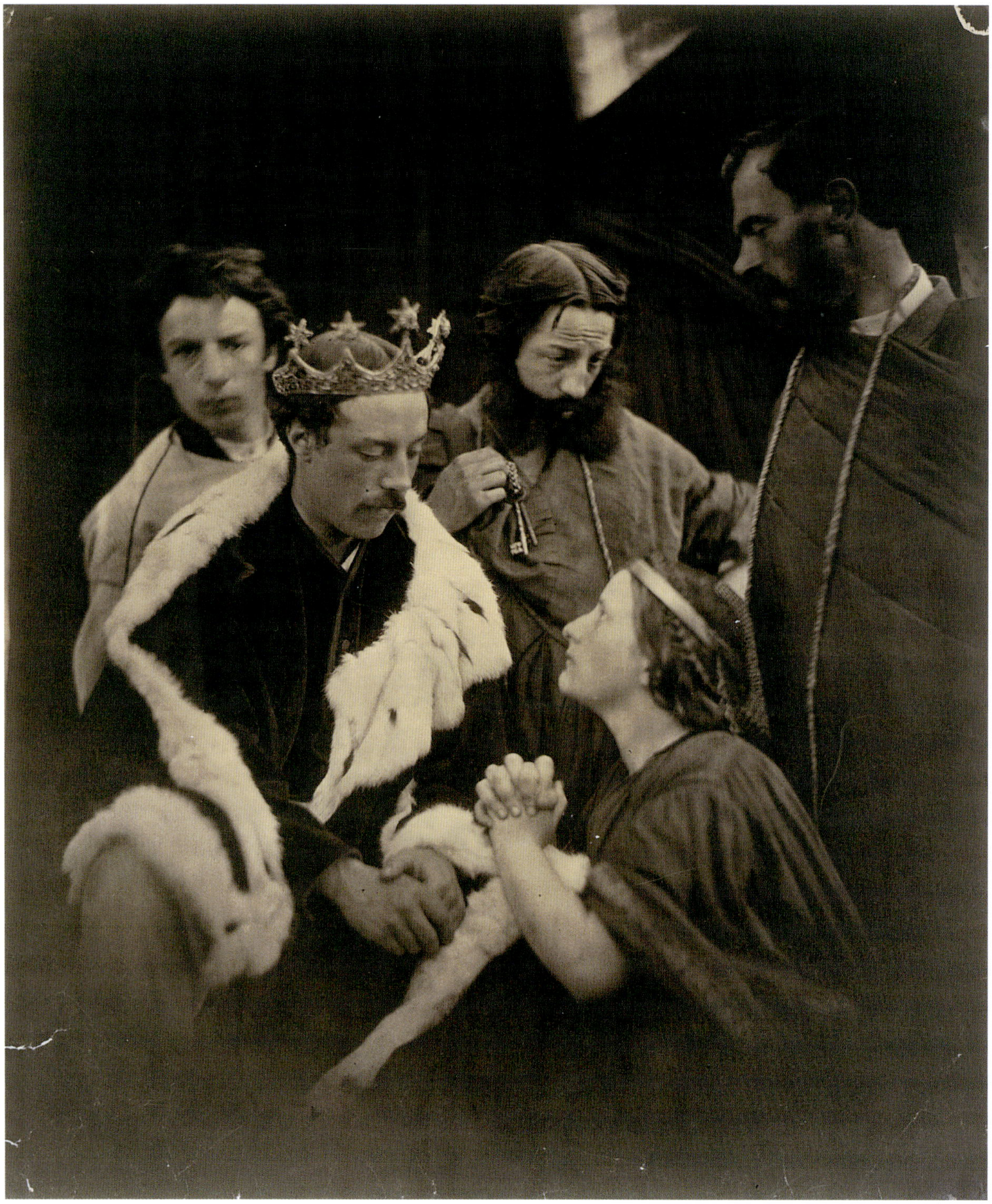

Queen Philippa interceding for the Burghers of Calais, 1872–4
Henry Herschel Hay Cameron, Ewen Cameron, two unknown men and Louise Trench
Albumen print, 355 x 291mm (14 x 11½")
Royal Photographic Society

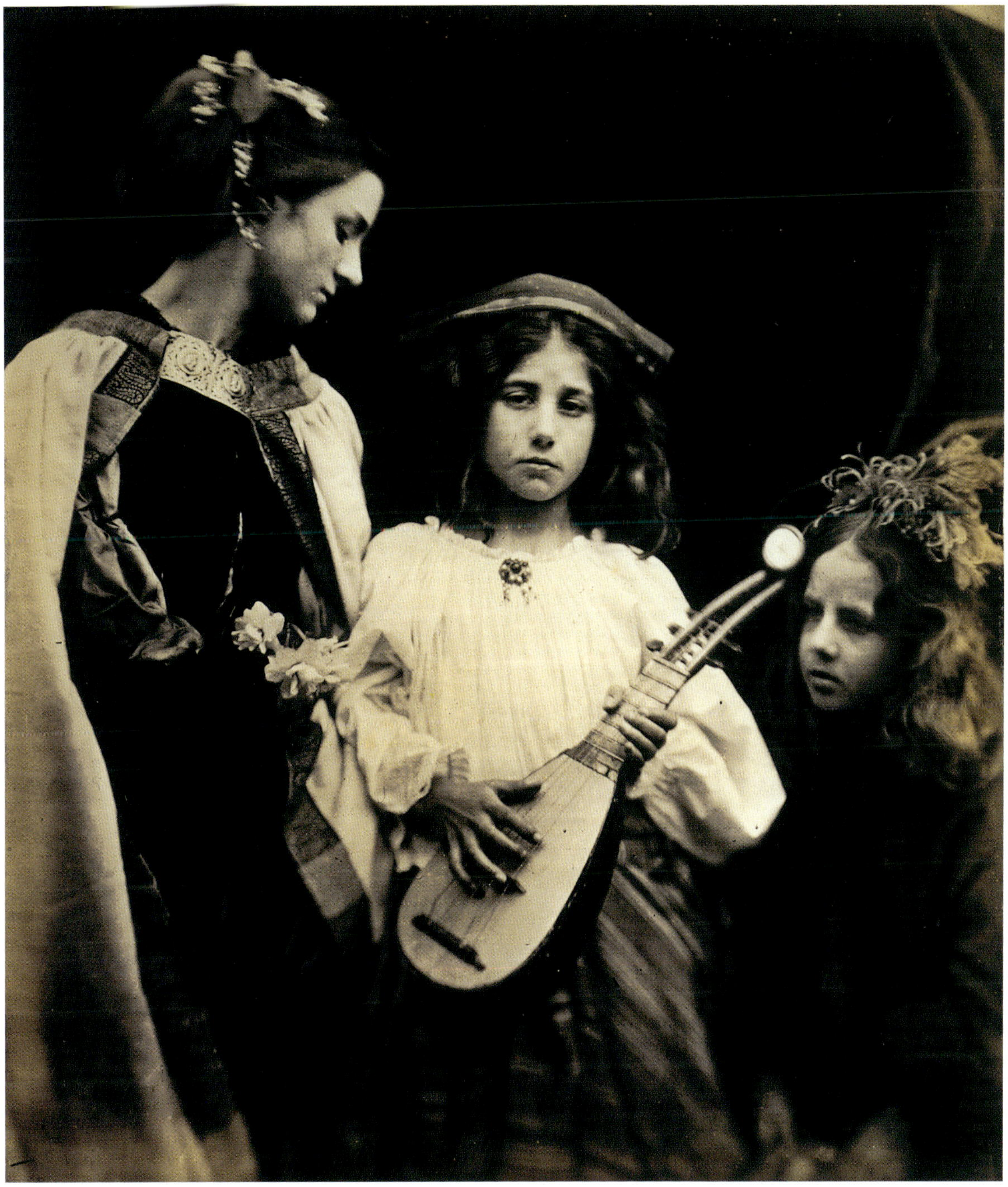

The Minstrel Group We sing a slow contented song and knock at Paradise, 1867
Mary Ryan, Elizabeth and Kate Keown
Albumen print, 325 x 277mm (12¾ x 10⅞")
National Museum of Photography, Film & Television, Bradford

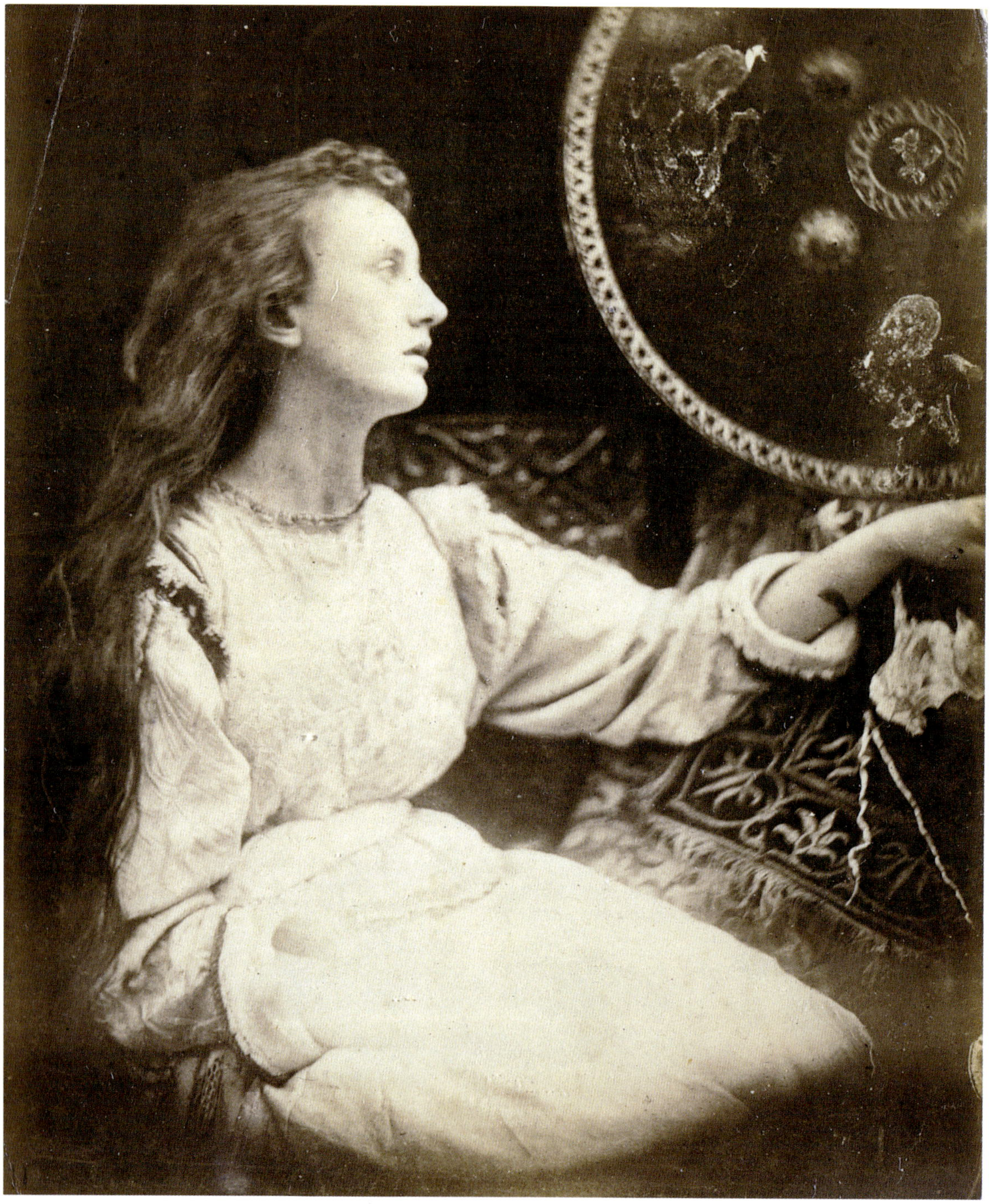

Elaine, 1874 (Illustration to Tennyson's *Idylls of the King and Other Poems*)
May Prinsep
Albumen print, 122 x 99mm (4¾ x 3⅞")
Royal Photographic Society

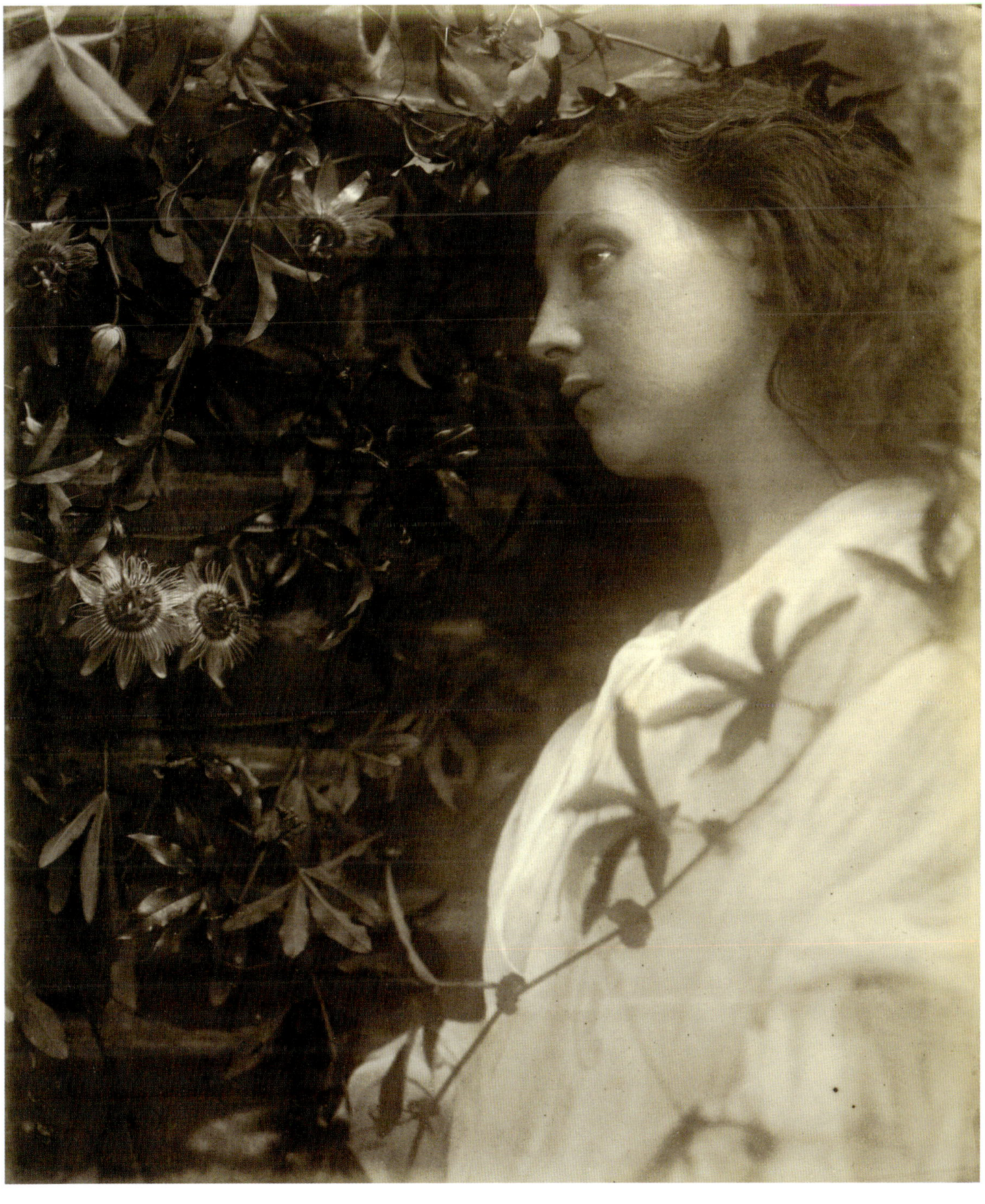

Maud, 1875 (Illustration to Tennyson's *Idylls of the King and Other Poems*)
Mary Ann Hillier
Albumen print, 329 x 271mm (13 x 10⅝")
The J. Paul Getty Museum, Los Angeles

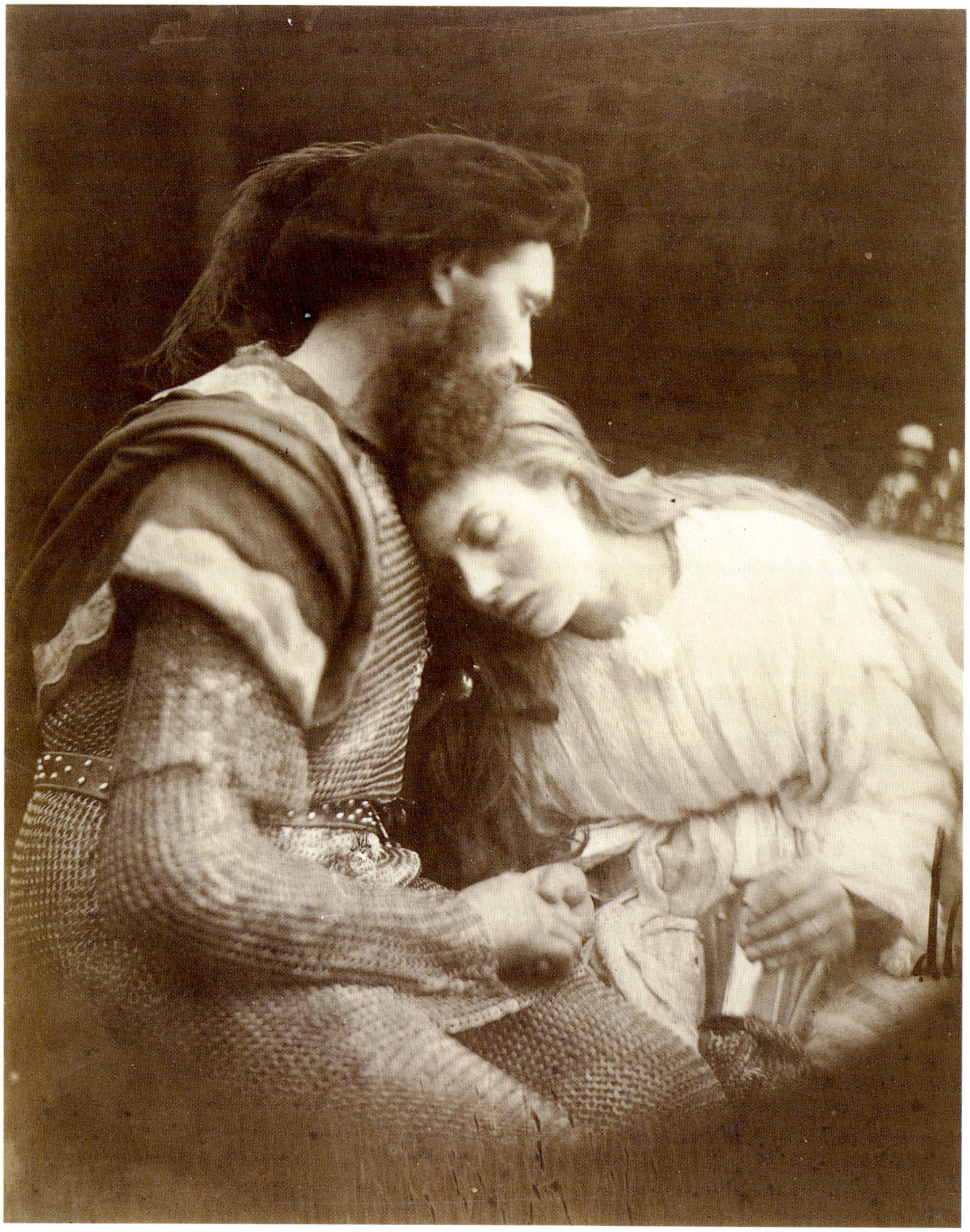

The Parting of Sir Lancelot and Queen Guinevere, 1874 (Illustration to Tennyson's *Idylls of the King and Other Poems*)
Andrew Hichens and May Prinsep
Albumen print, 342 x 266mm (13½ x 10½")
Royal Photographic Society

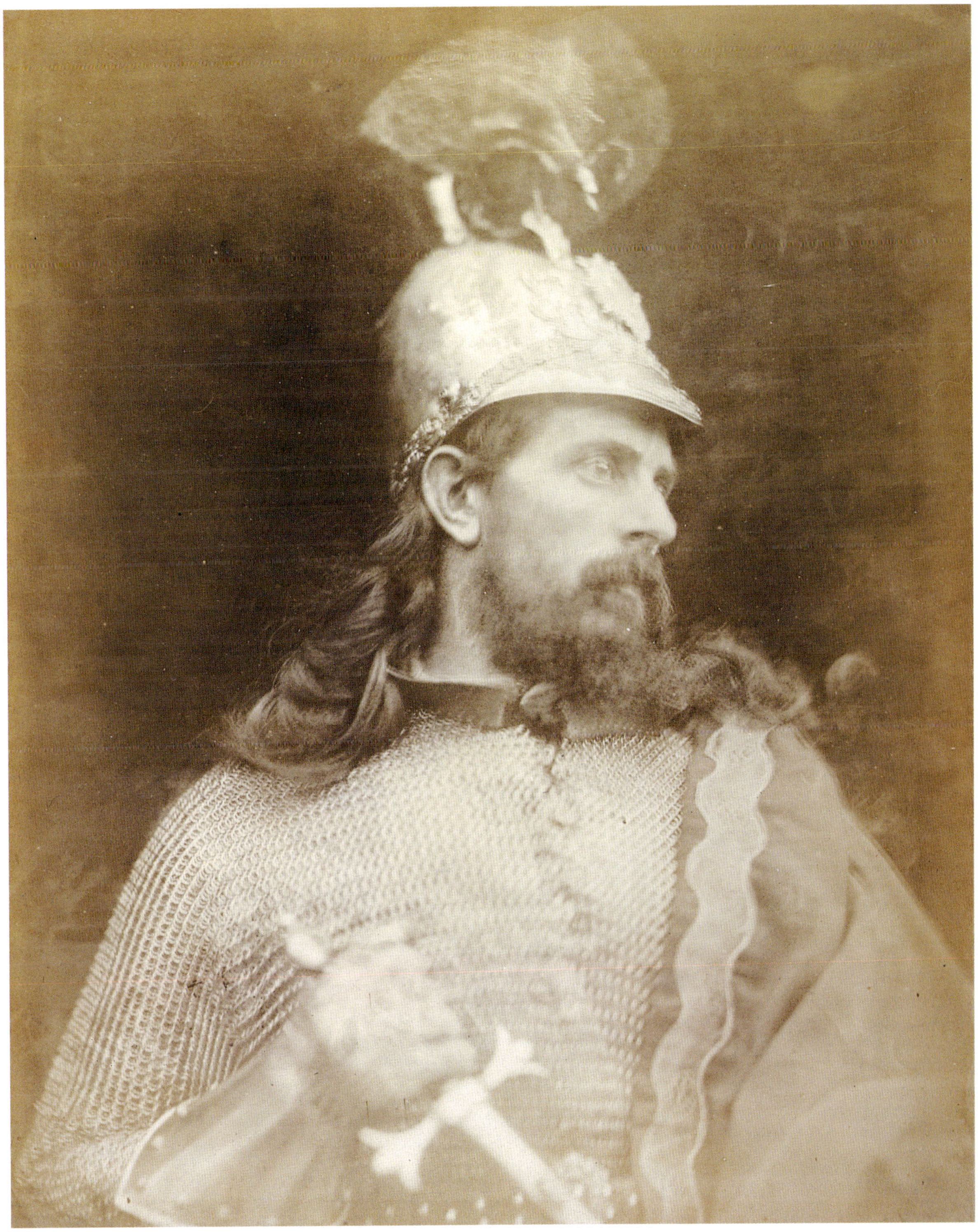

King Arthur, 1874 (Illustration to Tennyson's *Idylls of the King and Other Poems*)
William Warder
Albumen print, 358 x 280mm (14⅛ x 11")
Royal Photographic Society

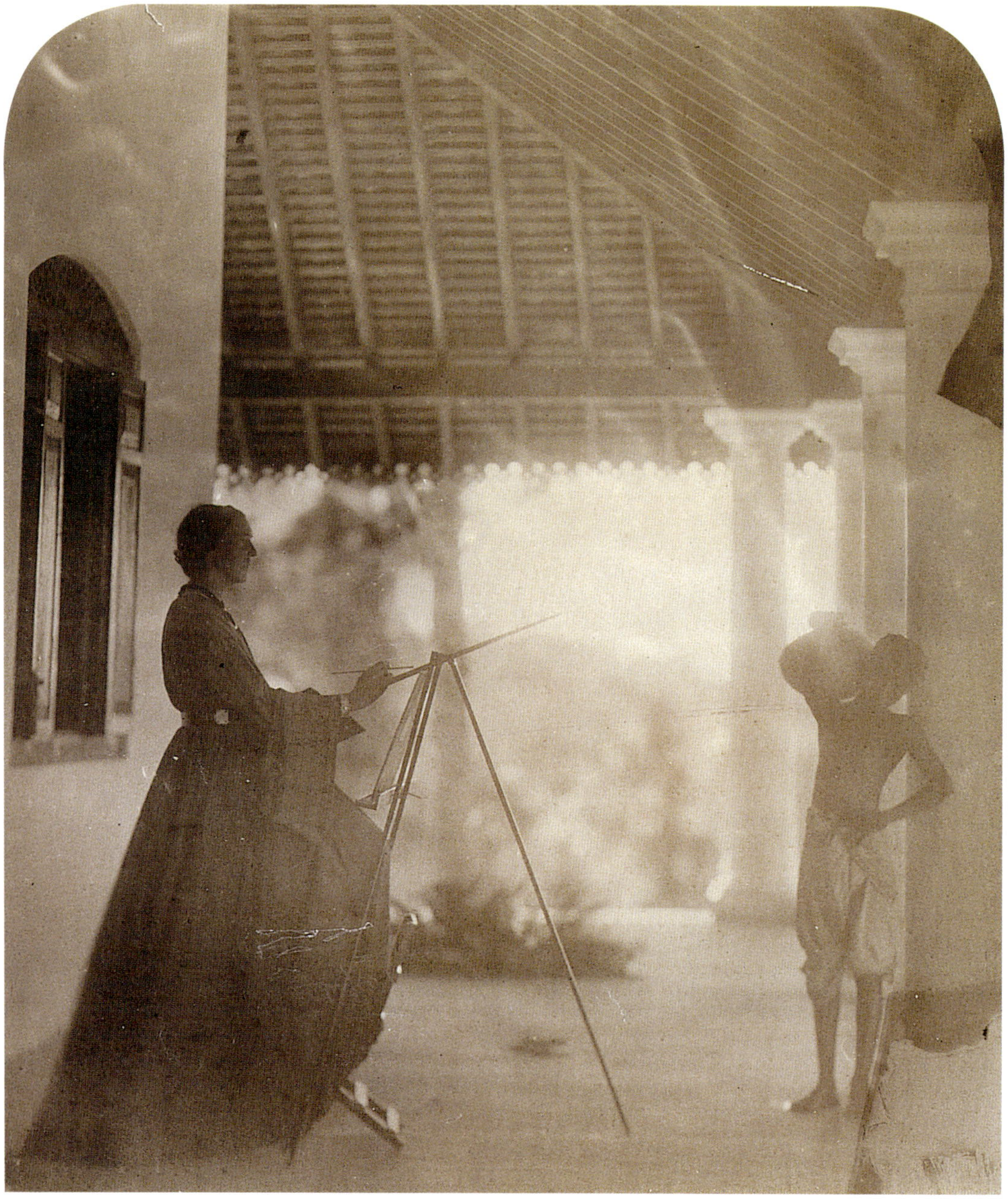

Marianne North in Mrs Cameron's house in Ceylon, January 1877
Albumen print, 277 x 236mm (10⅞ x 9¼")
Private Collection

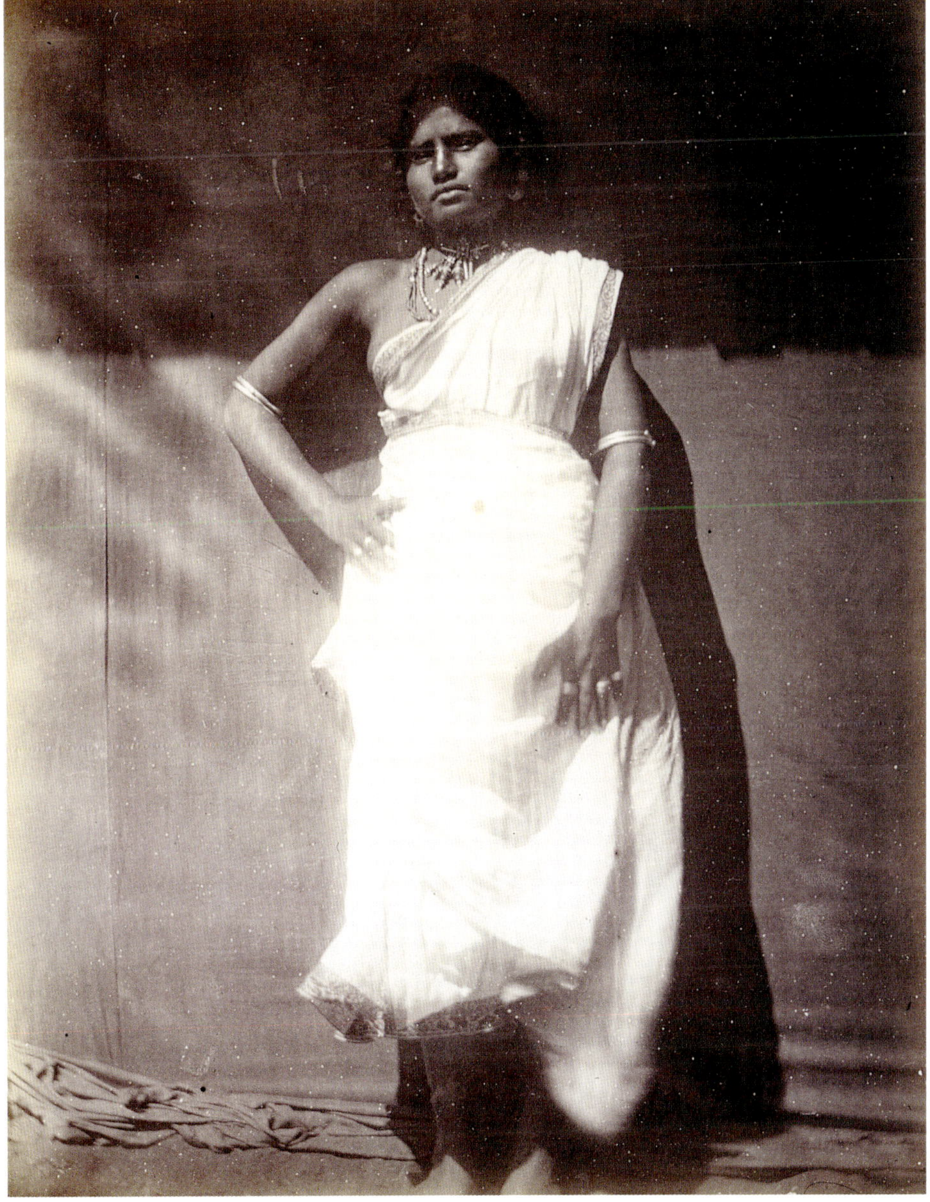

Untitled (Ceylon), 1875–9
Albumen print, 270 x 202mm (10⅝ x 8")
Royal Photographic Society

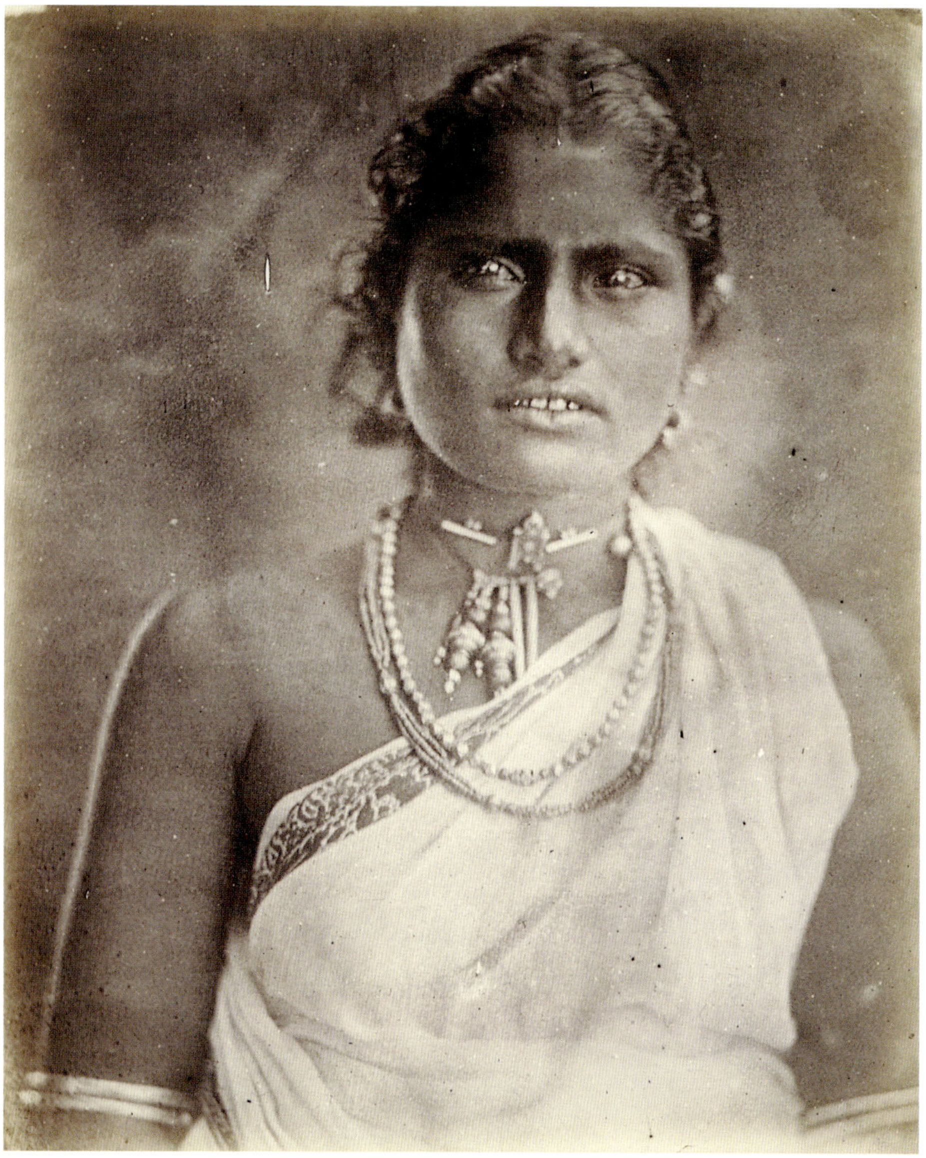

Untitled (Ceylon), 1875–9
Albumen print from wet collodion negative, 222 x 177mm (8¾ x 7")
Harriott A. Fox Endowment, 1970.840. The Art Institute of Chicago

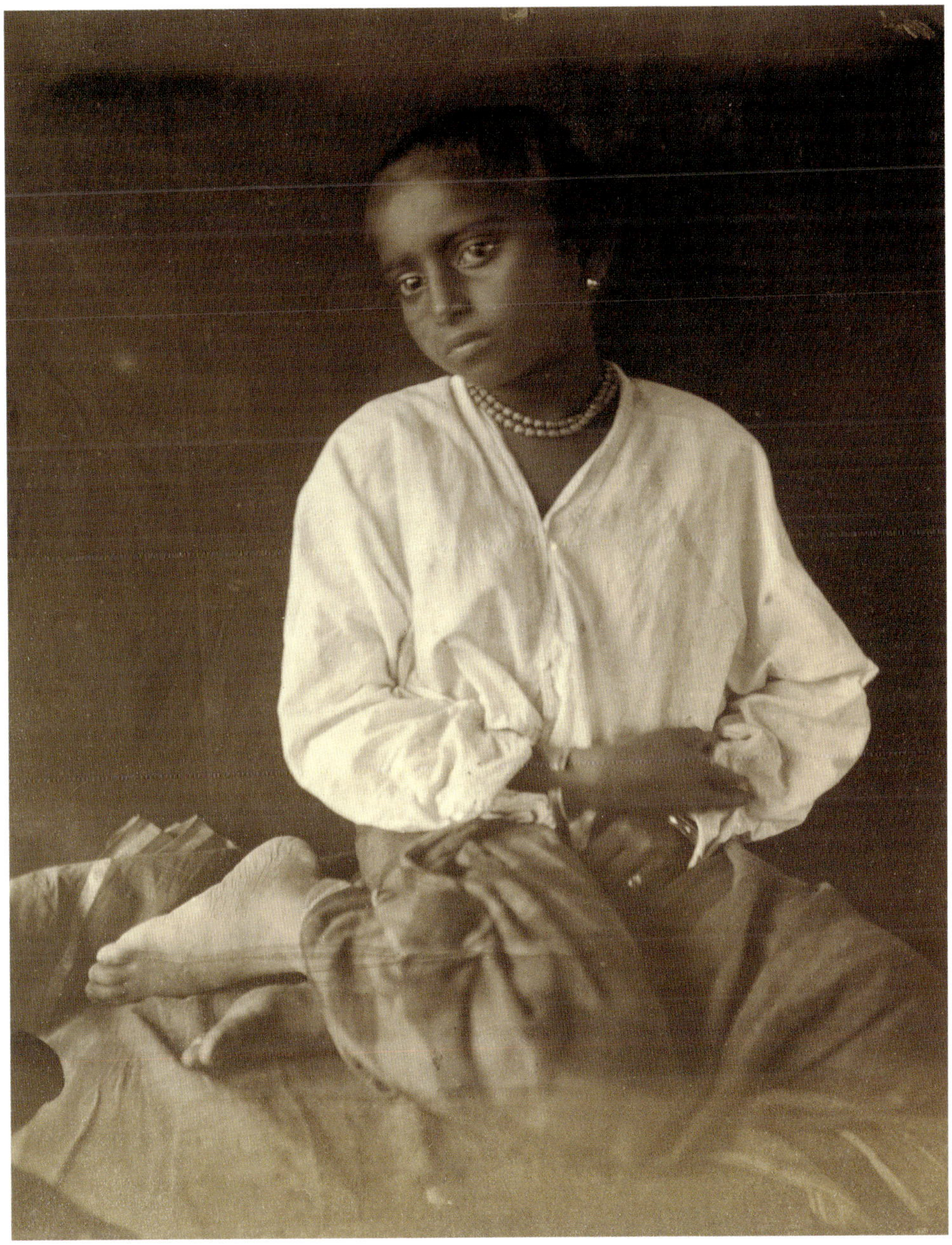

Untitled (Ceylon), 1875–9
Albumen print, 229 x 179mm (9⅞ x 7⅜")
The J. Paul Getty Museum, Los Angeles

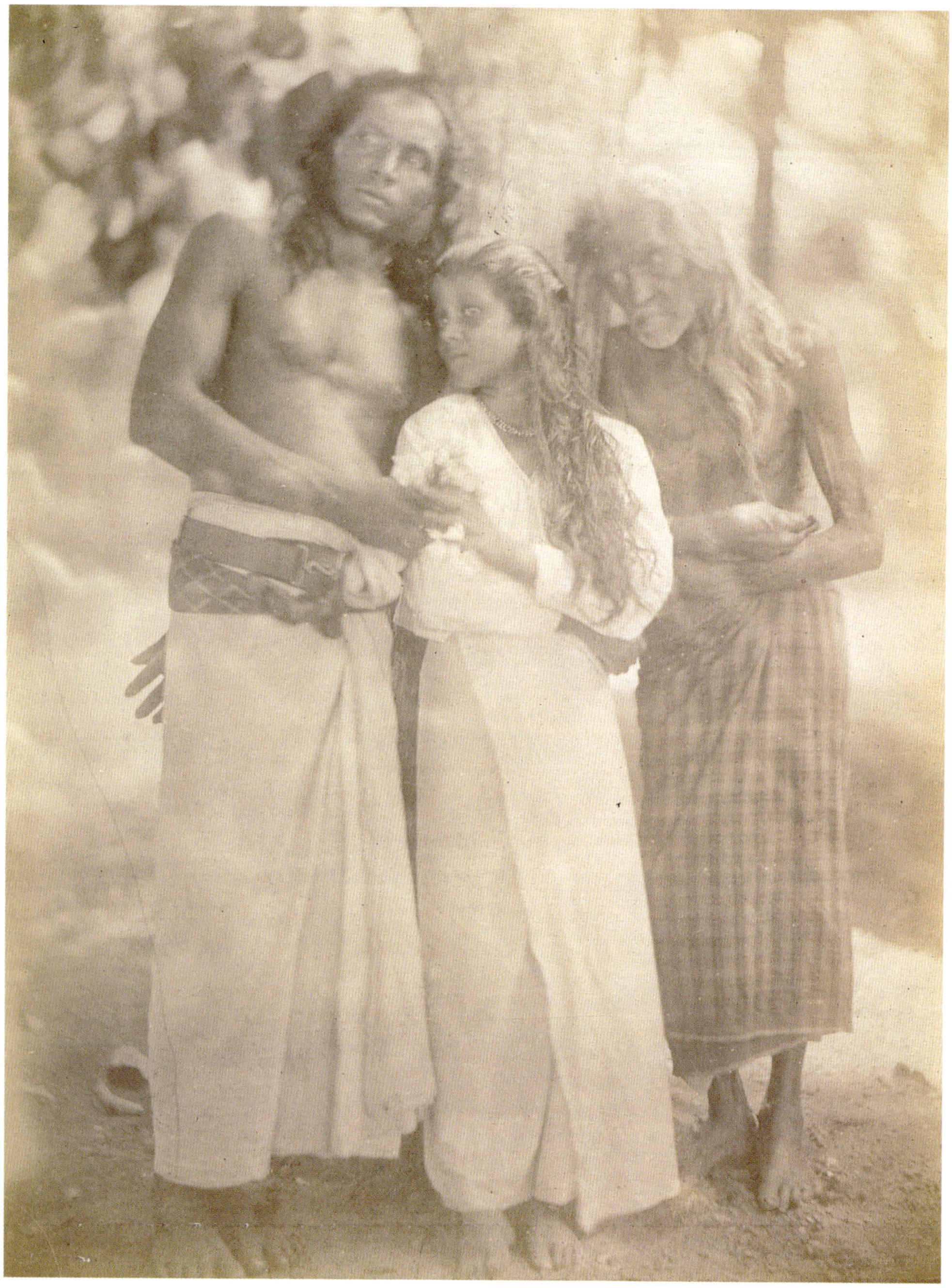

A Group of Kalutara Peasants, 1875–9
Albumen print, 270 x 199mm (10⅝ x 7⅞")
The Metropolitan Museum of Art, The Elisha Whittelsey Collection, The Elisha Whittelsey Fund, 1972 (1972.692)

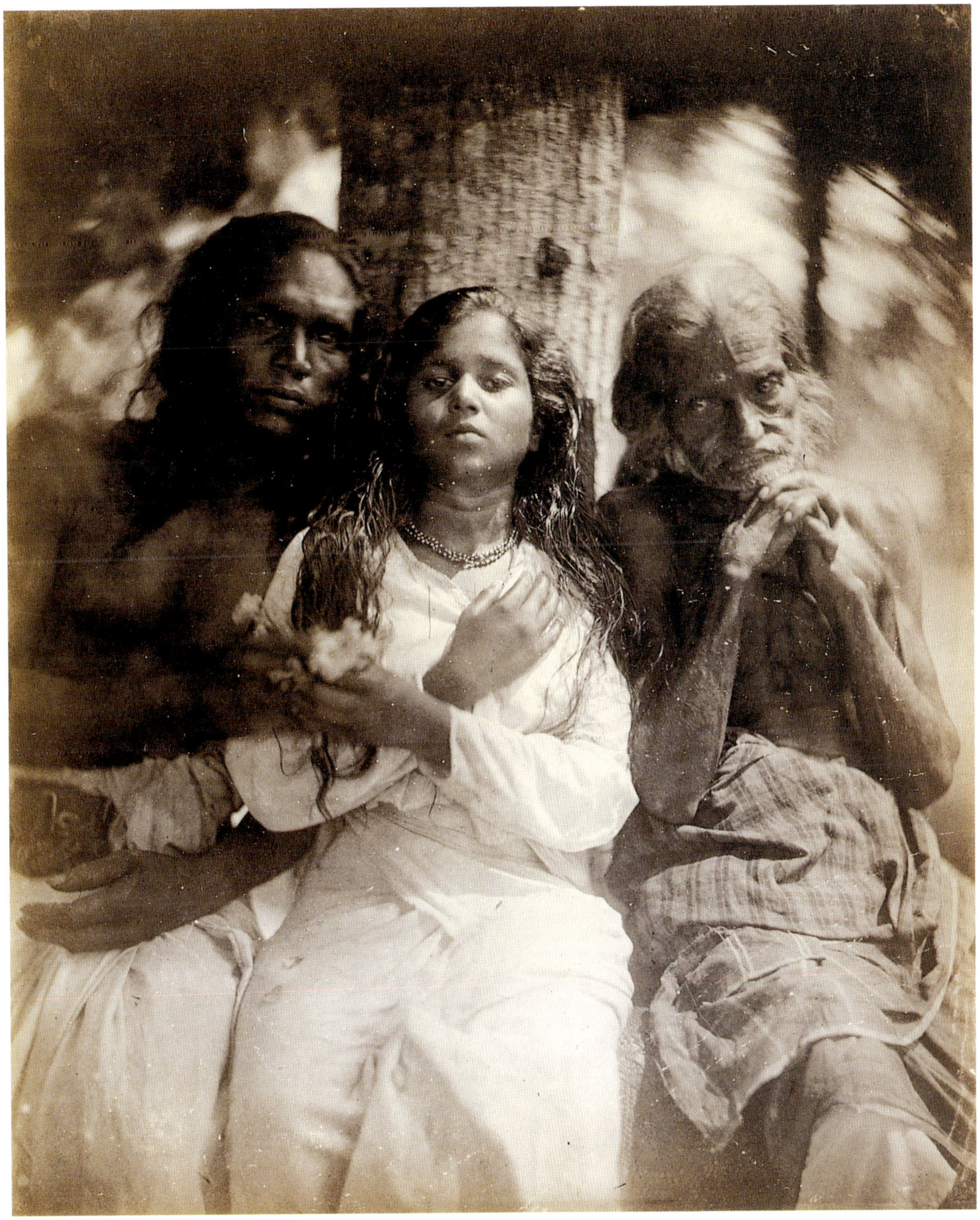

A Group of Kalutara Peasants, 1878
Albumen print, 342 x 271mm (13½ x 10⅝")
Royal Photographic Society

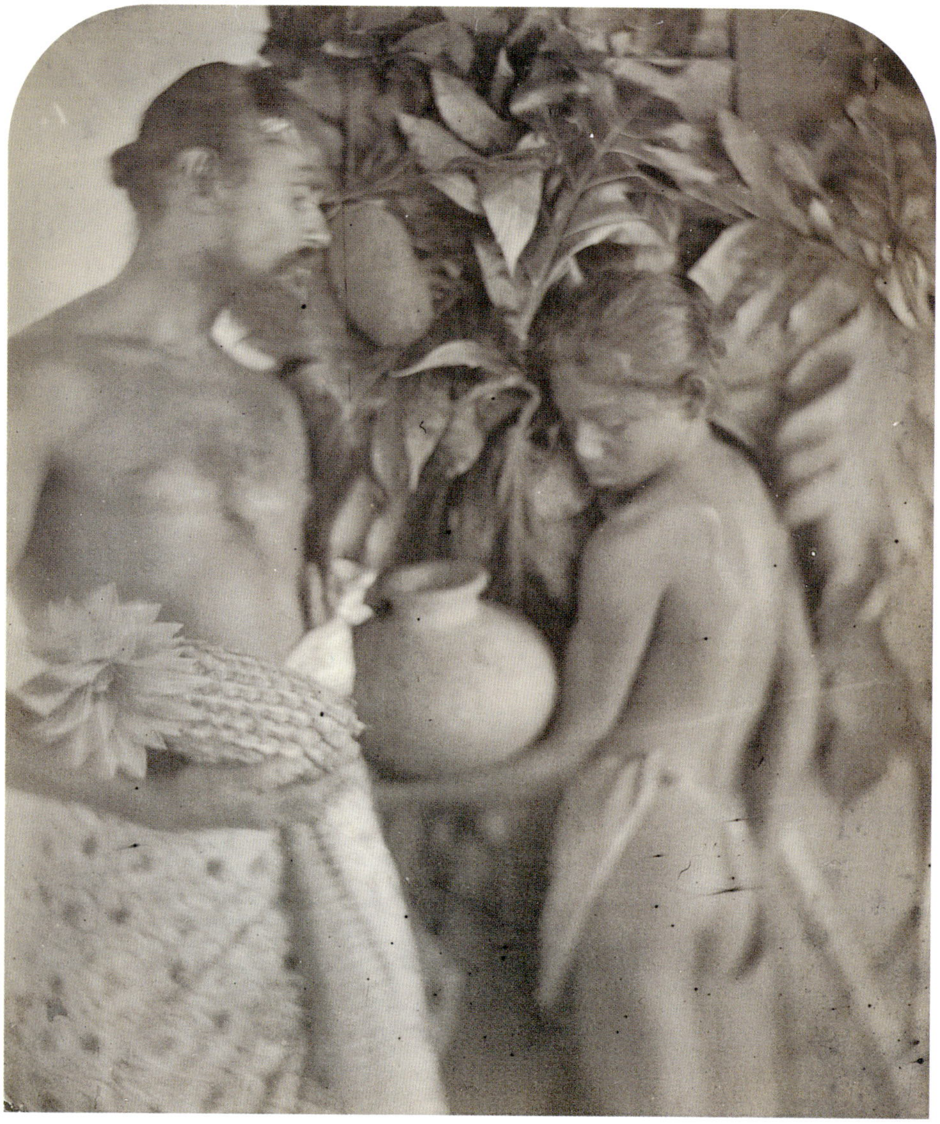

Kalutara Peasant Man and Woman, 1875–9
Albumen print, 276 x 229mm (10⅞ x 9")
Gernsheim Collection, Harry Ransom Humanities Research Center, The University of Texas at Austin

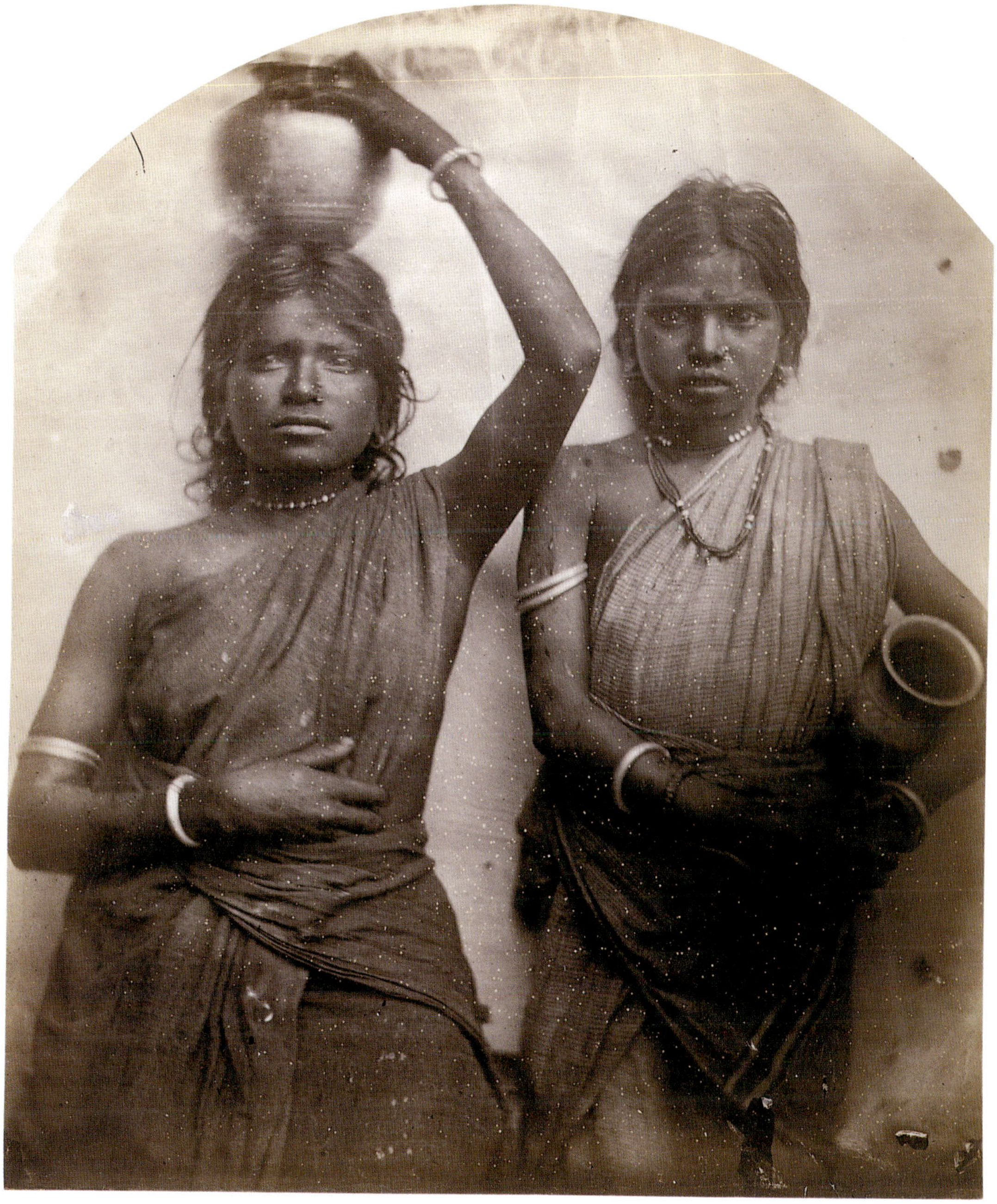

Untitiled (Ceylon), 1875–9
Albumen print, 280 x 228mm (11 x 9")
Royal Photographic Society

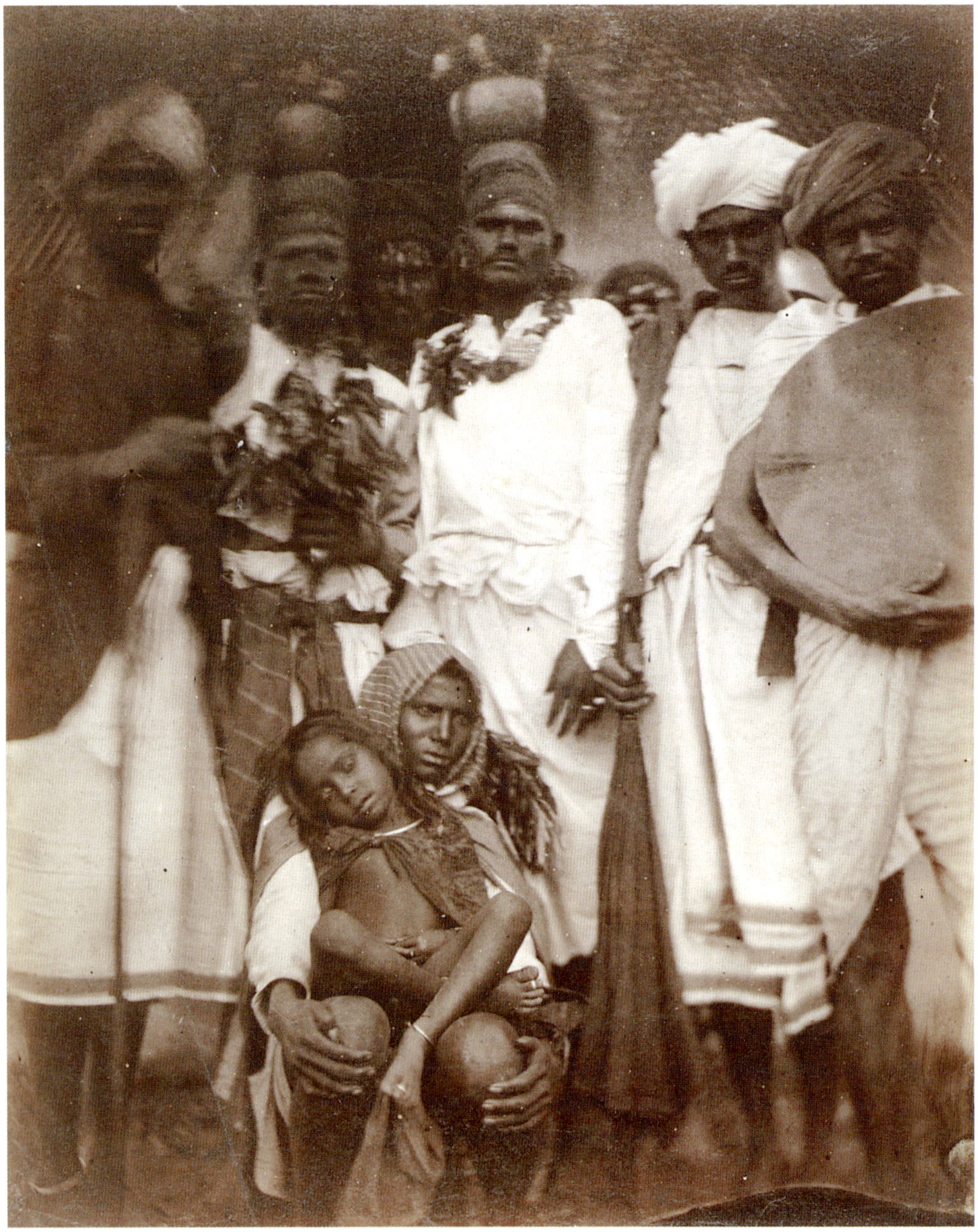

Untitled (Ceylon), 1875–9
Albumen print, 287 x 225mm (11¼ x 8⅞")
National Museum of Photography, Film & Television, Bradford

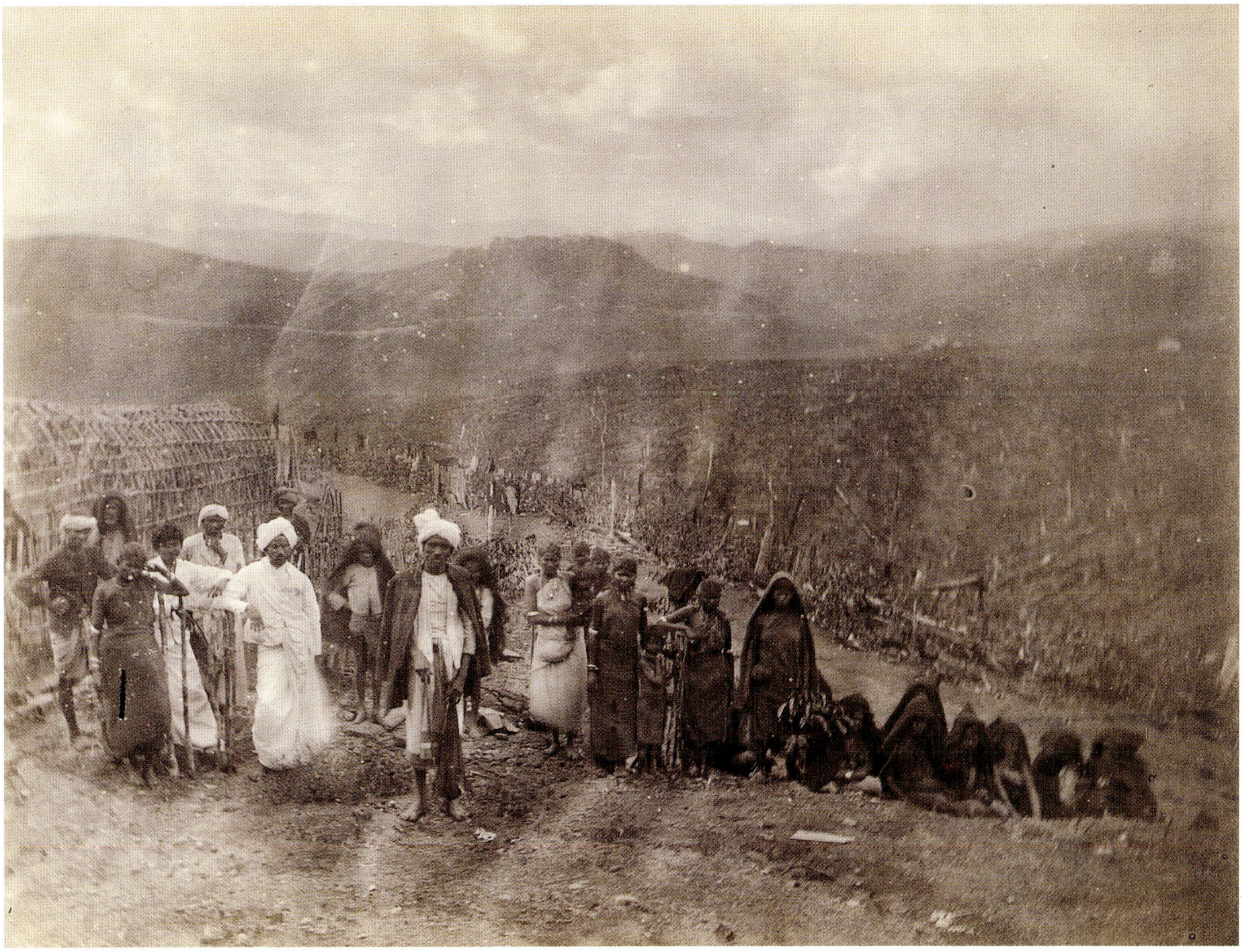

Estate workers (Ceylon), 1875–9
Albumen print, 186 x 249mm (7¼ x 9½")
National Museum of Photography, Film & Television, Bradford

BIBLIOGRAPHY

H. Allingham and D. Radford (eds.), *William Allingham: A Diary* (Macmillan & Co., London, 1907; second edition, with introduction by John Julius Norwich, Penguin Books, London, 1985)

Nina Auerbach, *Ellen Terry: Player in Her Times* (J.M. Dent & Sons Ltd, London, 1987)

Michael Bartram, *The Pre-Raphaelite Camera: Aspects of Victorian Photography* (Weidenfeld & Nicolson, London, 1985)

Quentin Bell, *Virginia Woolf* (The Hogarth Press, London, 1972)

Wilfrid Blunt, *England's Michelangelo* (Hamish Hamilton, London, 1975)

Ronald Chapman, *The Laurel and the Thorn: A Study of G.F. Watts* (Faber & Faber, London, 1945)

John Charlton, *Osborne House* (Her Majesty's Stationery Office, London, 1972)

G.K. Chesterton, *G.F. Watts* (Duckworth, London, 1904; reprinted 1975)

Morton Cohen, *Lewis Carroll: A Biography* (Macmillan & Co., London, 1995)

Morton Cohen (ed.), *The Letters of Lewis Carroll*, I (Macmillan & Co., London, 1979)

Christina Colvin, *Maria Edgeworth: Letters from England 1813–1844* (Oxford University Press, Oxford, 1971)

Sir Henry Cotton, *Indian and Home Memories* (T. Fisher Unwin, London, 1911)

Julian Cox, *In Focus: Julia Margaret Cameron* (The J. Paul Getty Museum, Los Angeles, 1996)

Julian Cox and Colin Ford, *Julia Margaret Cameron: The Collected Photographs* (The J. Paul Getty Museum, Los Angeles, 2003)

Edith Craig and Christopher St John, *Ellen Terry's Memoirs* (Victor Gollancz, London, 1933)

Caroline Dakers, *The Holland Park Circle: Artists and Victorian Society* (Yale University Press, New Haven and London, 1999)

William Dalrymple, *From the Holy Mountain: A Journey in the Shadow of Byzantium* (Flamingo, London, 1998)

Virginia Dodier, *Lady Hawarden: Studies from Life 1857–1864* (Aperture, New York, 1999)

Edith Nicholl Ellison, *A Child's Recollections of Tennyson* (J. M. Dent & Co., London, 1907)

David S. Evans and others, *Herschel at the Cape* (University of Texas Press, Austin, 1969)

Kathleen Fitzpatrick, *Lady Henry Somerset* (Jonathan Cape, London, 1923)

Colin Ford, *The Cameron Collection* (Van Nostrand Reinhold, in association with the National Portrait Gallery, London, 1975)

——, *The Herschel Album* (National Portrait Gallery, London, 1975)

Colin Ford and Roy Strong, *An Early Victorian Album* (Alfred A. Knopf, New York, 1976)

Roger Fry and Virginia Woolf, *Victorian Photographs of Famous Men & Fair Women by Julia Margaret Cameron* (The Hogarth Press, London, 1926; second edition with additional photographs and preface by Tristram Powell, 1973)

Hester Thackeray Fuller, *Three Freshwater Friends: Tennyson, Watts and Mrs Cameron* (Isle of Wight County Press, Newport, second reprint, 1955)

Hester Thackeray Fuller and Violet Hammersley (eds.), *Thackeray's Daughter: Some Recollections of Anne Thackeray Ritchie* (Euphorion Books, Dublin, 1951)

Winifred Gérin, *Anne Thackeray Ritchie: A Biography* (Oxford University Press, Oxford, 1981)

Helmut Gernsheim, *Julia Margaret Cameron: Her Life and Photographic Work* (The Fountain Press, London, 1948; second edition, Gordon Fraser, London, 1975)

Juliet Hacking, *Princes of Victorian Bohemia* (Prestel, Munich, London, and New York, and the National Portrait Gallery, London, 2000)

Violet Hamilton, *Annals of My Glass House: Photographs by Julia Margaret Cameron* (Scripps College and University of Washington Press, Seattle and London, 1996)

Edna Healey, *Emma Darwin: The Inspirational Wife of a Genius* (Headline Book Publishing, London, 2001)

Brian Hill, *Julia Margaret Cameron: A Victorian Family Portrait* (Peter Owen, London, 1973)

Tim Hilton, *Ruskin: The Later Years* (Yale University Press, New Haven and London, 2000)

James O. Hoge, *The Letters of Emily Lady Tennyson* (Pennsylvania State University, Philadelphia, 1974)

James O. Hoge (ed.), *Lady Tennyson's Journal* (University Press of Virginia, Charlottesville, 1981)

Amanda Hopkinson, *Julia Margaret Cameron* (Virago Press, London, 1986)

E.O. Hoppé, *Hundred Thousand Exposures: The Success of a Photographer* (Focal Press, London, 1945)

Jeremy Howard, *Whisper of the Muse: The World of Julia Margaret Cameron* (P. & D. Colnaghi, London, 1990)

William Holman Hunt, *Pre-Raphaelitism and the Pre-Raphaelite Brotherhood*, 2 volumes (Macmillan & Co., London, 1905)

Derek Hudson, *Lewis Carroll* (Constable & Co., London, 1995)

Russell Jackson, *Victorian Theatre* (A. & C. Black, London, 1989)

Eugenia Parry Janis and others, *For my best beloved Sister Mia: An Album of Photographs by Julia Margaret Cameron* (exh. cat., University of New Mexico Art Museum, Albuquerque, New Mexico, 1994)

M.M. Kaye (ed.), *The Golden Calm: An English Lady's Life in Moghul Delhi* (Webb & Bower, Exeter, 1980)

Charles Kingsley, *Charles Kingsley, His Letters and Memories of His Life*, edited by his wife, 2 volumes (Henry S. King & Co., London, 1877)

A.G.C. Liddell, *Notes from the Life of an Ordinary Mortal* (John Murray, London, 1911)

Joanne Lukitsh, *Cameron: Her Work and Career* (International Museum of Photography at George Eastman House, Rochester, New York, 1986)

Jeremy Maas, *Gambart: Prince of the Victorian Art World* (Barrie & Jenkins, London, 1975)

——, *The Victorian Art World in Photographs* (Barrie & Jenkins, London, 1984)

Robert B. Martin, *Tennyson, The Unquiet Heart* (Oxford University Press, Oxford, and Faber & Faber, London, 1980)

Michael Mason, *The Making of Victorian Sexual Attitudes* (Oxford University Press, Oxford, 1994)

Anita Ventura Mozley, *Mrs Cameron's Photographs from the Life* (Stanford University Museum of Art, Stanford, 1974)

David Newsome, *Victorian World Picture* (John Murray, London, 1997)

Marianne North, *Recollections of a Happy Life*, edited by Mrs. J. A. Symonds, 2 volumes (Macmillan & Co., London, 1892)

Graham Ovenden (ed.), *A Victorian Album: Julia Margaret Cameron and Her Circle* (Secker & Warburg, London, 1975)

Frederick Page (ed.), *The Poems of Coventry Patmore* (Oxford University Press, London, 1949)

John Pemble (ed.), *Miss Fane in India* (Alan Sutton, Gloucester, 1985)

F.B. Pinion, *A Tennyson Chronology* (Macmillan & Co., London, 1990)

F.B. and M. Pinion, *The Collected Sonnets of Charles Tennyson Turner* (Macmillan & Co., London, 1988)

David Piper, *The English Face* (Thames & Hudson, London, 1957; second edition National Portrait Gallery, London, 1978)

Gordon N. Ray (ed.), *The Letters and Private Papers of William Makepeace Thackeray*, 4 volumes (Oxford University Press, London, 1945–6)

Anne Thackeray Ritchie, *Old Kensington* (Smith, Elder & Co., London, 1873; reprinted Thoemmes Press, Bristol, 1995)

——, *Toilers and Spinsters and Other Essays* (Smith, Elder & Co., London, 1874)

——, *From an Island* (Bernhard Tauchnitz, Leipzig, 1877; reprinted Hunnyhill Publications, Newport, Isle of Wight, 1996)

——, *Records of Tennyson, Ruskin and Browning* (Macmillan & Co., London, 1892)

Anne Thackeray Ritchie and Henry H.H. Cameron, *Alfred, Lord Tennyson and His Friends* (T. Fisher Unwin, London, 1893)

P.G. Scott, *Tennyson's Enoch Arden: A Victorian Bestseller* (Tennyson Society, Lincoln, 1970)

Joseph Slater, *The Correspondence of Emerson and Carlyle* (Columbia University Press, New York, 1964)

Sara Stevenson, *The Personal Art of David Octavius Hill* (Yale University Press, New Haven and London, 2002)

Virginia Surtees (ed.), *The Diaries of George Price Boyce* (Real World, Norwich, 1980)

Henry Taylor, *Notes from Life in Six Essays* (John Murray, London, 1847)

——, *Autobiography of Henry Taylor*, 2 volumes (Longmans, London, 1885)

Roger Taylor and Edward Wakeling, *Lewis Carroll: Photographer* (Princeton University Press and Princeton University Library, Princeton and Oxford, 2002)

Tom Taylor (ed.), *The Life of Benjamin Robert Haydon*, 2 volumes (Longmans, London, 1853)

Una Taylor, *Guests and Memories: Annals of a Seaside Villa* (Humphrey Milford, London, 1924)

Hallam, Lord Tennyson, *Alfred, Lord Tennyson: A Memoir by His Son*, I and II (Macmillan & Co., London, 1898)

Michael Thorn, *Tennyson* (Little, Brown & Co., London, 1992)

Ann Thwaite, *Emily Tennyson: The Poet's Wife* (Faber & Faber, London, 1996)

Laura, Lady Troubridge, *Memories and Reflections* (London, William Heinemann, 1925)

Edward Wakeling (ed.), *Lewis Carroll's Diaries: The Private Journals of Charles Lutwidge Dodgson*, 5 volumes (Lewis Carroll Society, Luton, 1993–9)

Mary Seton Watts, *George Frederic Watts, The Annals of an Artist's Life*, 3 volumes (Macmillan & Co., London, 1912)

Mike Weaver, *Julia Margaret Cameron 1815–1879* (John Hansard Gallery, Southampton, 1984)

——, Mike Weaver, *Whisper of the Muse: The Overstone Album & Other Photographs by Julia Margaret Cameron* (The J. Paul Getty Museum, Malibu, 1986)

——, *British Photography in the Nineteenth Century: The Fine Art Tradition* (Cambridge University Press, Cambridge, 1989)

Agnes Grace Weld, *Glimpses of Tennyson and of some of his Relations and Friends* (Williams & Norgate, London, 1902)

Sylvia Wolf, *Julia Margaret Cameron's Women* (Yale University Press, New Haven and London, 1998)

Virginia Woolf, *To the Lighthouse* (Hogarth Press, London,1927; reprint 1932)

W. Aldis Wright, *Letters and Literary Remains of Edward Fitzgerald*, 3 volumes (Macmillan & Co., London, 1889)

Macaulay, Thomas Babington 17, 19
Mackenzie, Adeline Maria (*née* Pattle) 16, 17, 61
Mackenzie, Colin 17, 61
Maclear, Captain John 79
Maclear, Julia (*née* Herschel) 17, 79
Maclise, Daniel 73
The Passing of Arthur 73
Macmillan's Magazine 77
Macready, William 74
MacTier, Adeline 36, 39
Madonna Riposata Resting in hope, La *154*
Mangles, James 32
Mariana 69
Mario, Giovanni *74* (Caldesi & Co.)
Marx, Karl 47
Mary Mother *152*
Maud 68, *71*, 72, *191*
Maull & Polyblank: *Mrs Beeton* 50, 53–4, *54*
Maurice, Frederick Denison 48–9
May Day *150*
May Queen 72
Mayall, J.J.E. 45
Prince Albert 45, *46*
Tennyson 48
Mayne, Roger: *Keith Johnstone* 46, *46*
Michelangelo Buonarroti *44*, 50, 55, *97*
Mildmay, Lady 88
Mill, John Stuart 19
Millais, Sir John Everett 49, 71, 87
Mariana 69
Ophelia 73
Minstrel Group..., The *189*
Morris, Jane 55
Mountain Nymph Sweet Liberty, The *117*
My Grandchild aged 2 years & 3 months *168*

Napier, General Robert 66
National Portrait Gallery 45–6, 48, 49, 50, 53, 84–5
Nicholl, Edith 71
Niepce, Joseph Nicéphore 19
Norman, Adeline *158*
Norman, Charles 35, 79, *158*
Norman, Julia (*née* Cameron) 15, 17, 20, 35, 49, 79
Norman, Margaret *158*
North, Marianne 53, 78–9, *194*
Bombay Pedlars on Mrs Cameron's Verandah, Kalutara *78*

'On a Portrait' 88
Ottington, Ellen 78
'Our Royal Cousin' *175*

Palmerston, Henry Temple, 3rd Viscount 45
Parting of Sir Lancelot and Queen Guinevere, The *192*
Passing of Arthur, The 73
Patmore, Coventry 54
The Angel in the House 54
Patti, Adelina 26, *74* (Caldesi & Co.)
Pattle, Adéline (*née* de l'Etang) 16, 20
Pattle, Adeline Maria *see* Mackenzie, Adeline Maria
Pattle, James 16, 20
Pattle, Sara *see* Prinsep, Sara
Pattle, Sophia *see* Dalrymple, Sophia, Lady
Pattle, Virginia *see* Somers, Virginia, Countess
Paul and Virginia *164*
Peacock, Emily 54, *122*, *123*
Peacock, Mary *123*
Perugino, Pietro 55, 70, *124*
Philpot, Annie W. 36, 39, 40, *40*, 62, *92*
Philpot, Revd William B. 39–40
Photographic Journal 83, 87
Photographic News 45, 47, 53
Photographic Society of London (*later* Royal Photographic Society) 38, 84
exhibitions 36, 65, 83, 84, 86, 87
Pickersgill, Henry W.: *Sir John Herschel* *17*
'Pictet', Baby (Georgina Pictet) 62, *63*, *95*
Pinturicchio (Bernardino di Betto) 70
Pre-Raphaelite Brotherhood 20, 38, 54, 55, 57, 69, 72
Pre-Raphaelite Study, A 69
Priestley, J.B. 58
Prince, Rose (?) *153*
Princess, The 72
Prinsep, Annie 71
Prinsep, (Henry) Thoby 16, 20, 22, 38, 54
Prinsep, Henry (son) 17
Prinsep, James: *Julia Margaret Cameron* *16*
Prinsep, Lucy 71
Prinsep, May 54, 55, 56, 57, *71* (engraving), 74, *130*, *131*, *151*, *182*, *190*, *192*
Prinsep, Sara (*née* Pattle) 16, 17, 20, 22, 25, 26, 28, 36, 54
Prinsep, Val 22, *175*

Quarterly Review 35
Queen Philippa interceding for the Burghers of Calais *188*

Raphael 55, 70, 83
Red and White Roses, The *178*
Rejlander, Oscar G. 30, 36, 84, 87
The Tennysons *30*
Rembrandt van Rijn 70, 85, 87
Reni, Guido 70
Return after 3 days, The *155*
Ritchie, Anne (*née* Thackeray) 20, 25–6, 31, 56–7
From an Island 31, 54
Old Kensington 26, 31
Robertson, Walford Graham 55
Robinson, Henry Peach 72–3, 83
Rose bud garden of girls, The *148*
Rossetti, Christina 28, 53
Rossetti, Dante Gabriel 55, 70
Beata Beatrix 55
Rossetti, William M. 36, 61
Royal Photographic Society *see* Photographic Society of London
Ruskin, John 32, 49–50, 70
Ryan, Sir Edward 72
Ryan, Mary (*later* Cotton) 31, 54, 55, 56, 61, *124*, *125*, *127*, *150*, *151*, *155*, *185*, *189*

Sadness *139*
Sassoferrato (Giovanni Battista Salvi): *The Virgin in Prayer* 70
Scharf, Sir George 45
Senior, Jane 41
Shaw, George Bernard 65
Shelley, Percy Bysshe: *The Cenci* 73–4

Sibyl, A 187
Siddal, Elizabeth 55
Sidgwick, Henry 32
Silvy, Camille: *Duchess of Cambridge 56*
Simeon, Sir John *110*
Sisters 54, *123*
Smith, M.H. Stephen 36, 38
Somers, 3rd Earl 22, 38
Somers, Virginia, Countess (*née* Pattle) 20, 22, 25, 26, 36, 38, 39, 70
Southey, Reginald 38–9
Charles and Harry (Henry) Cameron 38
Hallam and Lionel Tennyson 38
Spartali, Marie 53, 55, *137*
Spedding, James 26, 42, 49
Speedy, Captain Tristram 66, *177*
Spencer-Stanhope, John R. 25
Stanfield, Clarkson 85
Stephen, Julia, Lady *see* Duckworth, Julia
Stephen, Sir Leslie 54, 80
Stieglitz, Alfred 84, 87
Stillman, W.J. 53
Study after the manner of Francia, A 55, *125*
Study of King David 109
Summer Days 151
Sun Artists (journal) 83–4
Suspense 57, *140*
Sutcliffe, Frank M. 72

Talbot, William Henry Fox 15, 19, 38, 84, 85
Taylor, Lady Alice 20
Taylor, Sir Henry 20, *21*, 22, 28, 31, 42, 49, 55, 70, 74, 80, 83, *106*, *107*, *109*, *185*
Philip van Artevelde 74
Taylor, Tom 25, 26, 28
Tennyson, Alfred, Lord 20, 26, 28, *29*, 30, *30* (Rejlander), 31, 32, 38, 46, 47–8, 49, 50, 56, 62, 65, 70–1, 72, 73, 74, 83, *102*, *104*
Becket 74
The Cup 74
Enoch Arden *71*, 73, 74
Idylls of the King 58, *71*, 71–2, *72*, 77, *191–3*
In Memoriam 49, 62, 71
Maud 30, 49, *71*, 72
May Queen 55, 72
The Princess 72
Queen Mary 74
Tennyson, Emily, Lady 20, 28, 30, *30* (Rejlander), 38, 57, 69, 70
Tennyson, Hallam 30, *30* (Rejlander), 32, 38, *38* (Southey), 48, 71
Tennyson, Horatio 38
Tennyson, Lionel 30, *30* (Rejlander), 38, *38* (Southey), 48, 70, 71, *172*, *173*, *174*
Terry, Ellen 28, 31, 49, 58, 61, 74, 84, *139*
Terry, Kate 28
Thackeray, William Makepeace 15, 20, 22, 26, 31
Thatched House Theatre 70, *70*, 71, 74
Theodore II, Emperor of Ethiopia 66
Thorn, Michael 38
Times, The: obituaries 80
Trench, Louise *188*
Trollope, Anthony 31, 49
Turner, Charles Tennyson 47, 77
Twilight hour, The 145
Two Little Girls Wearing Hats 171

Unknown Man 113 (1868–74), *159* (1868–72)
Unknown Woman 136
Untitled (Ceylon) 76, *195*, *196*, *197*, *201*, *202*

Vaughan, Henry H. 31
Vectis 141
Vere de Vere, Lady Clara 118
Victoria, Queen 15, 28, 30, 31, 47, 66
Victoria Adelaide Mary Louise, Princess 58

Ward, Wilfrid 32, 55, 74
Warder, William *72* (engraving), *193*
Watts, George Frederic 22, *24*, 25, 26, *27*, 31, 35, 36, 38, 42, 48, 49, 50, 55, 57, 70, *101*, *103*, *108*
Britomart and her Nurse 36
Choosing 28
Fair Daffodil 55
Wedderburn, May 71
Whisper of the Muse, The 70, *108*
Wild Flower, The 144
Wilson, Cyllena 61, *141*
Wilson, Melita 61
Wilson, Revd Samuel Sheridan 61
Wilson, Sheridan 61
Wolf, Sylvia 53
Woolf, Virginia (*née* Stephen) 26, 54, 74, 80
Freshwater 31, 80
The Searchlight 77, 80
To the Lighthouse 54
Wynfield, David W. 36, 38, 46, 86, 87, 88
self-portrait *37*

Young Astyanax 163
Young Endymion, The 16

Picture credits

pp.14, 17 (top), 37, 46 (top), 54, 56, 82, 84, 98, 100, 121: © National Portrait Gallery, London; p.16: © Collection Sven Gahlin, London; p.17 (bottom), 31, 40, 46 (bottom), 47: © Private Collections; pp.18, 21, 44, 52, 64, 68, 76, 97, 105, 107, 108, 126, 135, 137, 153, 158, 166–7, 183, 191, 197: © The J. Paul Getty Museum, Los Angeles; pp.24, 27, 29, 34, 60, 63, 78, 92–6, 101–4, 106, 109, 112, 114, 116, 119, 120, 124–5, 127, 130–1, 140, 143, 154–5, 163–5, 170, 173, 182, 185, 189, 202: © The National Museum of Photography, Film & Television, Bradford/Science and Society Picture Library; p.26: © The Royal Borough of Kensington & Chelsea Libraries and Arts Service; p.30: Copyright Reading Museum Service (Reading Borough Council). All rights reserved; p.38: Cotsen Children's Library at Princeton University Library; p.41: Patrons' Permanent Fund, Photograph © 2002 Board of Trustees, National Gallery of Art, Washington; pp.70, 123, 136, 156–7, 162: Wilson Centre for Photography; pp.71, 72: © Julia Margaret Cameron Trust, Isle of Wight; p.73: © Reserved; pp.74, 122, 128, 134, 150: © V&A Picture Library; p.78: Reproduced with the kind permission of the Trustees of the Royal Botanic Gardens, Kew; pp.99, 110–11, 113, 117–18, 129, 132–3, 138–9, 141–2, 144–9, 152, 159, 161, 168–9, 175, 181, 184, 186–8, 190, 192–3, 195, 199, 201, 203: Royal Photographic Society Collection/National Museum of Photography, Film & Television; p.115: Courtesy George Eastman House; pp.151, 171–2, 174: Tennyson Research Centre, Lincoln; p.160: Liverpool Libraries and Information Services; p.176: Collection of JGS, Inc., New York; p.177: © National Gallery of Canada; p.180: The Marjorie and Leonard Vernon Collection; p.194: © Private Collection; p.196: Harriott A. Fox Endowment, 1970.840, image © The Art Institute of Chicago; p.198: Photograph © 2002 The Metropolitan Museum of Art; p.200: Gernsheim Collection, Harry Ransom Humanities Research Center, The University of Texas at Austin.